AS / Year 1
Chemistry

Exam Board: OCR A

Revising for Chemistry exams is stressful, that's for sure — even just getting your notes sorted out can leave you needing a lie down. But help is at hand...

This brilliant CGP book explains **everything you'll need to learn** (and nothing you won't), all in a straightforward style that's easy to get your head around. We've also included **exam questions** to test how ready you are for the real thing.

There's even a free Online Edition you can read on your computer or tablet!

How to get your free Online Edition

Go to **cgpbooks.co.uk/extras** and enter this code...

3918 9140 2150 3880

This code only works for one person. If somebody else has used this book before you, they might have already claimed the Online Edition.

A-Level revision? It has to be CGP!

Contents

Module 4: Section 2 — Alcohols, Haloalkanes & Analysis

Published by CGP

Editors:
Katie Braid, Gordon Henderson, Emily Howe, Sarah Pattison and Sophie Scott

Contributors:
Antonio Angelosanto, Vikki Cunningham, Ian H. Davis, John Duffy, Max Fishel, Emma Grimwood, Lucy Muncaster, Derek Swain, Paul Warren and Chris Workman.

ISBN: 978 1 78294290 0

With thanks to Rachel Kordan and Jamie Sinclair for the proofreading.
With thanks to Jan Greenway for the copyright research.

With thanks to NASA / Goddard Space Flight Center / Science Photo Library for permission to reproduce the photograph used on page 106.

Graph to show trend in atmospheric CO_2 Concentration and global temperature on page 108 based on data by EPICA Community Members 2004 and Siegenthaler et al 2005.

Cover Photo **Laguna Design**/Science Photo Library.

Clipart from Corel®
Printed by Elanders Ltd, Newcastle upon Tyne.

Based on the classic CGP style created by Richard Parsons.

The Scientific Process

'How Science Works' is all about the scientific process — how we develop and test scientific ideas.
It's what scientists do all day, every day (well except at coffee time — never come between scientists and their coffee).

Scientists Come Up with *Theories* — Then *Test Them...*

Science tries to explain **how** and **why** things happen. It's all about seeking and gaining **knowledge** about the world around us. Scientists do this by **asking** questions and **suggesting** answers and then **testing** them, to see if they're correct — this is the **scientific process**.

1) **Ask** a question — make an **observation** and ask **why or how** whatever you've observed happens.
   E.g. Why does sodium chloride dissolve in water?

2) **Suggest** an answer, or part of an answer, by forming a **theory** or a **model**
   (a possible **explanation** of the observations or a description of
   what you think is happening actually happening).
   E.g. Sodium chloride is made up of charged particles
   which are pulled apart by the polar water molecules.

   > A theory is only scientific
   > if it can be tested.

3) Make a **prediction** or hypothesis — a **specific testable statement**,
   based on the theory, about what will happen in a test situation.
   E.g. A solution of sodium chloride will conduct electricity much better than water does.

4) Carry out **tests** — to provide **evidence** that will support the prediction or refute it.
   E.g. Measure the conductivity of water and of sodium chloride solution.

...Then They *Tell* Everyone About Their *Results...*

The results are **published** — scientists need to let others know about their work. Scientists publish their results in **scientific journals**. These are just like normal magazines, only they contain **scientific reports** (called papers) instead of the latest celebrity gossip.

1) Scientific reports are similar to the **lab write-ups** you do in school. And just as a lab write-up is **reviewed** (marked) by your teacher, reports in scientific journals undergo **peer review** before they're published.

   Scientists use standard terminology when writing their reports. This way they know that other scientists will understand them. For instance, there are internationally agreed rules for naming organic compounds, so that scientists across the world will know exactly what substance is being referred to. See page 85.

2) The report is sent out to **peers** — other scientists who are experts in the **same area**. They go through it bit by bit, examining the methods and data, and checking it's all clear and logical. When the report is approved, it's **published**. This makes sure that work published in scientific journals is of a **good standard**.

3) But peer review **can't guarantee** the science is **correct** — other scientists still need to **reproduce** it.

4) Sometimes **mistakes** are made and bad work is published. Peer review **isn't perfect** but it's probably the best way for scientists to self-regulate their work and to publish **quality reports**.

...Then *Other Scientists* Will *Test* the Theory Too

1) Other scientists read the published theories and results, and try to **test the theory** themselves. This involves:
   • Repeating the **exact same experiments**.
   • Using the theory to make **new predictions** and then testing them with **new experiments**.

2) If all the experiments in the world provide evidence to back it up, the theory is thought of as **scientific 'fact'**.

3) If **new evidence** comes to light that **conflicts** with the current evidence the theory is questioned all over again. More rounds of **testing** will be carried out to try to find out where the theory **falls down**.

> This is how the scientific process works — evidence supports a theory, loads of other scientists read it and test it for themselves, eventually all the scientists in the world agree with it and then bingo, you get to learn it.

This is how scientists arrived at the structure of the atom (see p.16-17) — and how they came to the conclusion that electrons are arranged in shells and orbitals. As is often the case, it took years and years for these models to be developed and accepted.

The Scientific Process

If the **Evidence** Supports a Theory, It's **Accepted** — for Now

Our currently accepted theories have survived this '**trial by evidence**'. They've been tested **over and over again** and each time the results have backed them up. **BUT**, and this is a big but (teehee), they never become totally indisputable fact. Scientific **breakthroughs** or **advances** could provide new ways to question and test the theory, which could lead to **changes and challenges** to it. Then the testing starts all over again...

And this, my friend, is the **tentative nature of scientific knowledge** — it's always **changing** and **evolving**.

For example, when CFCs were first used in fridges in the 1930s, scientists thought they were problem-free — there was no evidence to say otherwise. It was decades before anyone found out that CFCs were actually making a massive hole in the ozone layer. See p 106.

Evidence Comes From **Lab Experiments...**

1) Results from **controlled experiments** in **laboratories** are **great**.

2) A lab is the easiest place to **control variables** so that they're all **kept constant** (except for the one you're investigating).

3) This means you can draw meaningful **conclusions**.

> For example, if you're investigating how temperature affects the rate of a reaction, you need to keep everything but the temperature constant, e.g. the pH of the solution, the concentration of the solution, etc.

...But You **Can't** Always do a Lab Experiment

There are things you **can't** study in a lab. And outside the lab controlling the variables is tricky, if not impossible.

- *Are increasing CO_2 emissions causing climate change?*
  There are other variables which may have an effect, such as changes in solar activity. You can't easily rule out every possibility. Also, climate change is a very **gradual process**. Scientists won't be able to tell if their predictions are correct for donkey's years.

- *Does drinking chlorinated tap water increase the risk of developing certain cancers?*
  There are always differences between groups of people. The best you can do is to have a **well-designed study** using **matched groups** — **choose two groups** of people (those who drink tap water and those who don't) which are **as similar as possible** (same mix of ages, same mix of diets etc). But you still can't rule out every possibility. Taking new-born identical twins and treating them identically, except for making one drink gallons of tap water and the other only pure water, might be a fairer test, but it would present huge **ethical problems**.

Samantha thought her study was very well designed — especially the fitted bookshelf.

Science Helps to Inform **Decision-Making**

Lots of scientific work eventually leads to **important discoveries** that **could** benefit humankind — but there are often **risks** attached (and almost always **financial costs**). **Society** (that's you, me and everyone else) must weigh up the information in order to **make decisions** — about the way we live, what we eat, what we drive, and so on. Information can also be used by **politicians** to devise policies and laws.

- **Chlorine** is added to water in **small quantities** to disinfect it. Some studies link drinking chlorinated water with certain types of cancer (see page 65). But the risks from drinking water contaminated by nasty bacteria are far, far greater. There are other ways to get rid of bacteria in water, but they're heaps **more expensive**.

- Scientific advances mean that **non-polluting hydrogen-fuelled cars** can be made. They're better for the environment, but are really expensive. And it'd cost a lot to adapt filling stations to store hydrogen.

- Pharmaceutical drugs are really expensive to develop, and drug companies want to make money. So they put most of their efforts into developing drugs that they can sell for a good price. Society has to consider the **cost** of buying new drugs — the **NHS** can't afford the most expensive drugs without **sacrificing** something else.

So there you have it — how science works...

Hopefully these pages have given you a nice intro to how science works. You need to understand it for the exam, and for life. Once you've got it sussed it's time to move on to the really good stuff — the chemistry. Bet you can't wait...

Planning Experiments

As well as doing practical work in class, you can get asked about it in your exams too. Harsh I know, but that's how it goes. You need to be able to plan the perfect experiment and make improvements to ones other people have planned.

Make Sure You **Plan** Your **Experiment Carefully**

It's really important to plan an experiment well if you want to get accurate and precise results. Here's how to go about it...

Have a peek at page 12 to find out more about accurate and precise results.

1) Work out the **aim** of the experiment — what are you trying to find out?
2) Identify the **independent**, **dependent** and other **variables** (see below).
3) Decide what **data** to collect.
4) Select **appropriate equipment** which will give you accurate results.
5) Make a **risk assessment** and plan any safety precautions.
6) Write out a **detailed method**.
7) Carry out **tests** — to gather **evidence** to address the aim of your experiment.

Make it a **Fair Test** — Control your **Variables**

You probably know this all off by heart but it's easy to get mixed up sometimes. So here's a quick recap:

Variable — A variable is a **quantity** that has the **potential to change**, e.g. mass. There are two types of variable commonly referred to in experiments:

* **Independent variable** — the thing that you **change** in an experiment.
* **Dependent variable** — the thing that you **measure** in an experiment.

As well as the independent and dependent variables, you need to think of all the other variables in your experiment and plan ways to keep each of those the same.

For example, if you're investigating the effect of **temperature** on rate of reaction using the apparatus on the right, the variables will be:

Independent variable	Temperature
Dependent variable	Volume of gas produced — you can measure this by collecting it in a gas syringe.
Other variables	E.g. concentration and volume of solutions, mass of solids, pressure, the presence of a catalyst and the surface area of any solid reactants.

You MUST control your other variables so they're always the same.

Collect the Appropriate **Data**

Experiments always involve collecting **data** and you need to decide what data to collect.

1) There are different types of data, so it helps to know what they are:

* **Discrete** — you get discrete data by **counting**. E.g. the number of bubbles produced in a reaction.
* **Continuous** — a continuous variable can have **any value** on a scale. For example, the volume of gas produced. You can never measure the exact value of a continuous variable.
* **Categoric** — a categoric variable has values that can be sorted into **categories**. For example, the colours of solutions might be blue, red and green.

2) You need to make sure the data you collect is appropriate for your experiment.

Example: A student suggests measuring the rate of the following reaction by observing how conductivity changes over the course of the reaction:
$$NaOH_{(aq)} + CH_3CH_2Br_{(l)} \rightarrow CH_3CH_2OH_{(l)} + NaBr_{(aq)}$$
Suggest what is wrong with the student's method, and how it could be improved.

You couldn't collect data about how the **conductivity changes** over the course of the reaction, because there are **salts** in both the reactants and the products.

Instead you could use a **pH meter** to measure how the **pH changes** from basic (due to sodium hydroxide) to neutral.

Planning Experiments

Choose *Appropriate* Equipment — Think about *Size* and *Sensitivity*

Selecting the right apparatus may sound easy but it's something you need to think carefully about.

1) The equipment has to be **appropriate** for the specific experiment.

> For example, if you want to measure the volume of gas produced in a reaction, you need to make sure you use apparatus which will collect the gas, without letting any escape.

2) The equipment needs to be the right **size**.

> For example, if you're using a gas syringe to collect a gas, it needs to be big enough to collect **all** the gas produced during the experiment, or the plunger will just fall out the end. You might need to do some **calculations** to work out what size of syringe to use.

3) The equipment needs to be the right level of **sensitivity**.

> If you want to measure 10 cm³ of a liquid, it will be more accurate to use a measuring cylinder that is graduated to the nearest 0.5 cm³ than to the nearest 1 cm³. A burette would be most accurate though (they can measure to the nearest 0.1 cm³).

Risk Assessments Help You to Work Safely

1) When you're planning an experiment, you need to carry out a **risk assessment**. To do this, you need to identify:
   - All the **dangers** in the experiment, e.g. any hazardous compounds or naked flames.
   - **Who** is at **risk** from these dangers.
   - What can be done to **reduce the risk**, such as wearing goggles or working in a fume cupboard.
2) You need to make sure you're working **ethically** too. This is most important if there are other people or animals involved. You have to put their welfare first.

Methods Must be Clear and Detailed

When **writing** or **evaluating** a method, you need to think about all of the things on these two pages. The method must be **clear** and **detailed** enough for anyone to follow — it's important that **other people** can recreate your experiment and get the **same** results. Make sure your method includes:

1) All **substances** and **quantities** to be used.
2) How to **control** variables.
3) The exact **apparatus** needed (a diagram is usually helpful to show the set up).
4) Any **safety precautions** that should be taken.
5) What **data** to collect and **how** to collect it.

Practice Questions

Q1 Briefly outline the steps involved in planning an experiment.

Q2 What three things should you consider when choosing the best apparatus for your experiment?

Exam Question

> Q1 A student carries out an experiment to investigate how the rate of the following reaction changes with the concentration of hydrochloric acid: $Mg_{(s)} + 2HCl_{(aq)} \rightarrow MgCl_{2\,(aq)} + H_{2\,(g)}$
>
> The student decides to measure how the pH changes over time using litmus paper.
> Explain why this method of measuring pH is unsuitable, and suggest an alternative method. [2 marks]

Revision time — independent variable. Exam mark — dependent variable...

I wouldn't advise you to investigate the effect of revision on exam marks. Just trust me — more revision = better marks. But if you were to investigate it, there are all manner of variables that you'd need to control. The amount of sleep you had the night before, how much coffee you drank in the morning, your level of panic on entering the exam hall...

Practical Techniques

The way you carry out your experiment is important, so here's a nice round up of some of the techniques chemists use all the time. You've probably met some of them before, which should hopefully make it all a bit easier. Hopefully... :-)

Results Should be **Precise**

1) **Precise** results are **repeatable** and **reproducible**. **Repeatable** means that if the **same** person does the experiment again using the same methods and equipment, they'll get the same results. **Reproducible** means that if someone **else** does the experiment, or a different **method** or piece of **equipment** is used, the results will still be the same.

2) To make sure your results are precise, you need to **minimise** any **errors** that might sneak into your data. This includes: ⟹
   - using **apparatus** and **techniques** correctly,
   - taking **measurements** correctly,
   - **repeating** your experiments and calculating a **mean**.

Make Sure You **Measure** Substances **Correctly**

The **state** (solid, liquid or gas) that your substance is in will determine **how** you decide to measure it.

1) You weigh **solids** using a **balance**. Here are a couple of things to look out for:
   - Put the container you are weighing your substance into on the balance, and make sure the balance is set to exactly zero before you start weighing out your substance.
   - If you need to **transfer** the solid into another container, make sure that it's **all** transferred. For example, if you're making up a standard solution you could wash any remaining solid into the new container using the solvent. Or, you could **reweigh** the weighing container after you've transferred the solid so you can work out **exactly** how much you added to your experiment.

2) There are a few methods you might use to measure the volume of a liquid. Whichever method you use, always read the volume from the **bottom** of the **meniscus** (the curved upper surface of the liquid) when it's at **eye level**.

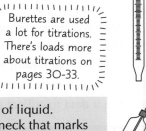

Read volume from here — the bottom of the meniscus.

> **Pipettes** are long, narrow tubes that are used to **suck up** an **accurate volume** of liquid and transfer it to another container. They are often **calibrated** to allow for the fact that the last drop of liquid stays in the pipette when the liquid is ejected. This reduces transfer errors.

> **Burettes** measure from **top** to **bottom** (so when they are **full**, the scale reads **zero**). They have a **tap** at the bottom which you can use to release the liquid into another container (you can even release it drop by drop). To use a burette, take an **initial reading**, and once you've released as much liquid as you want, take a **final reading**. The **difference** between the readings tells you how much liquid you used.

Burettes are used a lot for titrations. There's loads more about titrations on pages 30-33.

> **Volumetric flasks** allow you to **accurately** measure a very **specific** volume of liquid. They come in various **sizes** (e.g. 100 ml, 250 ml) and there's a **line** on the neck that marks the volume that they measure. They're used to make **accurate dilutions** and **standard solutions**. To use them, first measure out and add the liquid or solid that is being diluted or dissolved. Rinse out the measuring vessel into the volumetric flask with a little solvent to make sure everything's been transferred. Then fill the flask with solvent to the **bottom** of the neck. Fill the neck **drop by drop** until the bottom of the meniscus is **level** with the line.

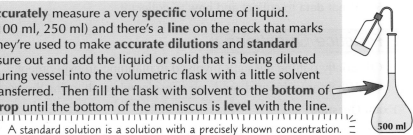

A standard solution is a solution with a precisely known concentration. You can find out how they're made and used on page 31.

3) Gases can be measured with a **gas syringe**. They should be measured at **room temperature** and **pressure** as the **volume** of a gas **changes** with temperature and pressure. Before you use the syringe, you should make sure it's completely **sealed** and that the **plunger** moves **smoothly**.

> Once you've measured a quantity of a substance you need to be careful you don't **lose** any. In particular, think about how to minimise losses as you transfer it from the measuring equipment to the reaction container.

Practical Techniques

Measure **Temperature** Accurately

I'm sure you've heard this before, so I'll be quick... You can use a **thermometer** or a **temperature probe** to measure the temperature of a substance (a temperature probe is like a thermometer but it will always have a **digital display**).

- Make sure the **bulb** of your thermometer or temperature probe is **completely submerged** in any mixture you're measuring.
- Wait for the temperature to **stabilise** before you take an initial reading
- If you're using a thermometer with a scale, read off your measurement at **eye level** to make sure it's accurate.

Qualitative Tests Can be Harder to **Reproduce**

Qualitative tests measure **physical qualities** (e.g. colour) while **quantitative** tests measure numerical data, (e.g. mass).

So if you carried out a reaction and noticed that heat was produced, this would be a **qualitative** observation. If you **measured** the temperature change with a thermometer, this would be **quantitative**.

Qualitative tests can be harder to **reproduce** because they're often **subjective** (based on **opinion**), such as describing the **colour** or **cloudiness** of a solution. There are ways to **reduce** the subjectivity of qualitative results though. For example:

> - If you're looking for a **colour change**, put a **white background** behind your reaction container.
> - If you're looking for a **precipitate** to form, mark an **X** on a piece of paper and place it under the reaction container. Your solution is 'cloudy' when you can **no longer see** the X.

There are Specific Techniques for Synthesising **Organic Compounds**

Synthesis is used to **make** one **organic compound** from another. There are a number of techniques that chemists use to help them make and purify their products:

These techniques are covered in more detail on pages 112-113.

1) **Reflux** — heating a reaction mixture in a flask fitted with a **condenser** so that any materials that **evaporate**, condense and drip back into the mixture.
2) **Distillation** — gently heating a mixture so that the compounds evaporate off in order of **increasing boiling point** and can be collected separately. This can be done **during** a reaction to collect a product as it forms, or **after** the reaction is **finished** to purify the mixture.
3) **Removing water soluble impurities** — adding **water** to an organic mixture in a separating funnel. Any **water soluble impurities** move out of the organic layer and dissolve in the aqueous layer. The layers have different **densities** so are easy to separate.

Practice Questions

Q1 Give three ways that you could improve the precision of an experiment.

Q2 How would you measure out a desired quantity of a solid? And a gas?

Q3 How could you make the results of an experiment measuring time taken for a precipitate to form less subjective?

Exam Question

Q1 A student dilutes a 1 mol dm^{-3} solution of sodium chloride to 0.1 mol dm^{-3} as follows:

He measures 10 cm^3 of 1 mol dm^{-3} sodium chloride solution in a pipette and puts this into a 100 cm^3 volumetric flask. He then tops up the volumetric flask with distilled water until the top of the meniscus is at 100 cm^3.

a) What has the student done incorrectly? What should he have done instead? [1 mark]

b) Which of the arrows in the diagram on the right indicates the level to which you should fill a volumetric flask? [1 mark]

Reflux, take it easy...

It might seem like there's a lot to do to make sure your results are accurate, but you should get lots of practice in practicals. Before long you'll be measuring temperatures and volumes with your eyes shut (metaphorically speaking).

Presenting Results

Once you've collected the data from your experiment, it's not time to stop, put your feet up and have a cup of tea — you've got some presenting to do. Results tables need converting into graphs and other pretty pictures.

Organise Your Results in a **Table**

It's a good idea to set up a table to **record** the **results** of your experiment in. When you draw a table, make sure you **include** enough **rows** and **columns** to **record all of the data** you need. You might also need to include a column for **processing** your data (e.g. working out an average).

Make sure each **column** has a **heading** so you know what's going to be recorded where.

The **units** should be in the **column heading**, not the table itself.

Temperature (°C)	Time (s)	Volume of gas evolved (cm³)			Average volume of gas evolved (cm³)
		Run 1	**Run 2**	**Run 3**	
20	**10**	8.1	7.6	8.5	(8.1 + 7.6 + 8.5) ÷ 3 = 8.1
	20	17.7	19.0	20.1	(17.7 + 19.0 + 20.1) ÷ 3 = 18.9
	30	28.5	29.9	30.0	(28.5 + 29.9 + 30.0) ÷ 3 = 29.5

You'll need to repeat each test **at least three** times to check your results are **precise**.

You can find the **mean result** by **adding up** the data from each repeat and **dividing** by the number of repeats.

Graphs: **Line, Bar or Scatter** — Use the **Best Type**

You'll often need to make a **graph** of your results.
Graphs make your data **easier to understand** — so long as you choose the right type.

When drawing graphs, the dependent variable should go on the y-axis, the independent on the x-axis.

Line graphs are best when you have **two sets of continuous data**. For example:

Graph to Show Volume of Oxygen Evolved Against Time in Decomposition of H_2O_2

Volume of oxygen evolved (cm³) — Time (s)

Use simple scales — this'll make it easier to plot points.

Scatter plots are great for showing how two sets of data are related (or **correlated**).

Don't try to join all the points — draw a **line of best fit** to show the **trend**.

Scatter Graph to Show Relationship Between Relative Molecular Masses and Melting Points of Straight-Chain Alcohols

Melting point (K) — Relative Molecular Mass

You should use a **bar chart** when one of your data sets is **categoric**. For example:

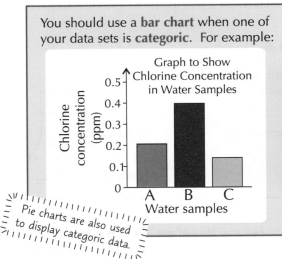

Graph to Show Chlorine Concentration in Water Samples

Chlorine concentration (ppm) — Water samples A B C

Pie charts are also used to display categoric data.

Apple and blackberry was number one on Jane's pie chart

Whatever type of graph you make, you'll ONLY get full marks if you:

- Choose a sensible **scale** — don't do a tiny graph in the corner of the paper, or massive axes where the data only takes up a tiny part of the graph.
- **Label** both **axes** — including units.
- Plot your points accurately — use a **sharp pencil**.

Sometimes you might need to work out the gradient of a graph, e.g. to work out the rate of a reaction. There are details of how to do this on pages 78 and 79.

Presenting Results

Don't Forget About Units

Units are really important — 10 g is a bit different from 10 kg, so make sure you don't forget to add them to your **tables** and **graphs**. It's often a good idea to write down the units on each line of any **calculations** you do — it makes things less confusing, particularly if you need to convert between two different units.

Here are some useful examples:

Concentration can be measured in **mol dm⁻³ (M)** and **mol cm⁻³**.

$$mol\ dm^{-3} \xrightarrow[\times 1000]{\div 1000} mol\ cm^{-3}$$

Example: Write 2 mol dm⁻³ in mol cm⁻³.

To convert 0.2 mol dm⁻³ into mol cm⁻³ you divide by 1000.

$0.2\ mol\ dm^{-3} \div 1000 = 2 \times 10^{-4}\ mol\ cm^{-3}$

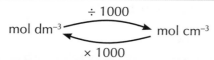 Standard form is useful for writing very big or very small numbers.

Volume can be measured in **m³, dm³ and cm³**.

$$m^3 \xrightleftharpoons[\div 1000]{\times 1000} dm^3 \xrightleftharpoons[\div 1000]{\times 1000} cm^3$$

Example: Write 6 dm³ in m³ and cm³.

To convert 6 dm³ into m³ you divide by 1000.
$6\ dm^3 \div 1000 = 0.006\ m^3 = 6 \times 10^{-3}\ m^3$
To convert 6 dm³ into cm³ you multiply by 1000.
$6\ dm^3 \times 1000 = 6000\ cm^3 = 6 \times 10^3\ m^3$

Round to the Lowest Number of Significant Figures

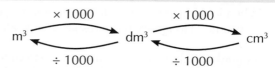 The first significant figure of a number is the first digit that isn't a zero. The second, third and fourth significant figures follow on immediately after the first (even if they're zeros).

You always need to be aware of **significant figures** when working with data.

1) The rule is the same for when doing calculations with the results from your experiment, or when doing calculations in the exam — you have to round your answer to the **lowest number of significant figures** (s.f.) given in the question.

2) It always helps to write down the number of significant figures you've rounded to after your answer — it shows you really know what you're talking about.

3) If you're converting between **standard** and **ordinary form**, you have to keep the **same number** of significant figures. For example, 0.0060 mol dm⁻³ is the same as 6.0 × 10⁻³ mol dm⁻³ — they're both given to 2 s.f..

Example: 13.5 cm³ of a 0.51 mol dm⁻³ solution of sodium hydroxide reacts with 1.5 mol dm⁻³ hydrochloric acid. Calculate the volume of hydrochloric acid required to neutralise the sodium hydroxide

3 s.f. ← 2 s.f. ← You don't need to round intermediate answers. Rounding too early will make your final answer less accurate.

No. of moles of NaOH: $(13.5\ cm^3 \times 0.51\ mol\ dm^{-3}) \div 1000 = 6.885 \times 10^{-3}\ mol$
Volume of HCl: $(6.885 \times 10^{-3})\ mol \times 1000 \div 1.5\ mol\ dm^{-3} = 4.59\ cm^3 = \mathbf{4.6\ cm^3\ (2\ s.f.)}$
Final answer should be rounded to 2 s.f. ↗

Make sure all your units match when you're doing calculations.

Practice Questions

Q1 Why is it always a good idea to repeat your experiments?
Q2 How would you convert an answer from m³ to dm³?
Q3 How do you decide how many significant figures you should round your answer to?

Exam Question

Q1 10 cm³ sodium hydroxide solution is titrated with 0.50 mol dm⁻³ hydrochloric acid to find its concentration. The titration is repeated three times and the volumes of hydrochloric acid used are: 7.30 cm³, 7.25 cm³, 7.25 cm³.

a) What is the mean volume of hydrochloric acid recorded in dm³? [1 mark]

b) What is the concentration of hydrochloric acid in mol cm⁻³? [1 mark]

Significant figures — a result of far too many cream cakes...

When you draw graphs, always be careful to get your axes round the right way. The thing you've been changing (the independent variable) goes on the x-axis, and the thing you've been measuring (the dependent variable) is on the y-axis.

Analysing Results

You're not quite finished yet... there's still time to look at your results and try and make sense of them. Graphs can help you to see patterns but don't try and read too much in to them — they won't tell you what grade you're going to get.

Watch Out For **Anomalous** Results

1) Anomalous results are ones that **don't fit** in with the other values and are likely to be wrong.
2) They're often due to **random errors**, e.g. if a drop in a titration is too big and shoots past the end point, or if a syringe plunger gets stuck whilst collecting gas produced in a reaction.

There's more about random errors on pages 12 and 13.

3) When looking at results in tables or graphs, you always need to look to see if there are any anomalies — you need to **ignore** these results when calculating means or drawing lines of best fit.

Example: Calculate the mean volume from the results in the table below.

Titration Number	1	2	3	4
Titre Volume (cm³)	15.20	15.30	15.25	15.50

Titre **4** isn't **concordant** (doesn't match) the other results so you need to ignore it and just use the other three:

$$\frac{15.20 + 15.30 + 15.25}{3} = 15.25 \text{ cm}^3$$

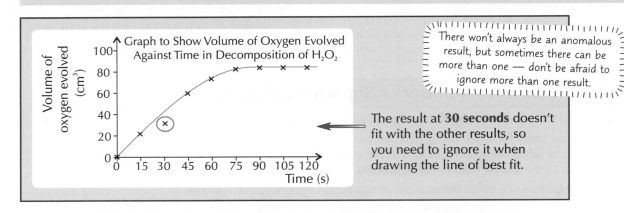

Graph to Show Volume of Oxygen Evolved Against Time in Decomposition of H_2O_2

There won't always be an anomalous result, but sometimes there can be more than one — don't be afraid to ignore more than one result.

The result at **30 seconds** doesn't fit with the other results, so you need to ignore it when drawing the line of best fit.

Scatter Graphs Show The **Relationship** Between Variables

Correlation describes the **relationship** between two variables — the independent one and the dependent one. Data can show:

(1) **Positive correlation**
As one variable **increases** the other **increases**.

Positive

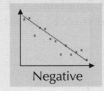

(2) **Negative correlation**
As one variable **increases** the other **decreases**.

Negative

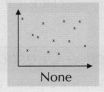

(3) **No correlation**
There is **no relationship** between the two variables.

None

Correlation **Doesn't** Mean **Cause** — Don't Jump to Conclusions

1) Ideally, only **two** quantities would **ever** change in any experiment — everything else would remain **constant**.

2) But in experiments or studies outside the lab, you **can't** usually control all the variables. So even if two variables are correlated, the change in one may **not** be causing the change in the other. Both changes might be caused by a **third variable**.

Example:
Some studies have found a correlation between **drinking chlorinated tap water** and the risk of developing certain cancers. So some people argue that water shouldn't have chlorine added.

BUT it's hard to control all the **variables** between people who drink tap water and people who don't. It could be due to other lifestyle factors.

Or, the cancer risk could be affected by something else in tap water — or by whatever the non-tap water drinkers drink instead...

Analysing Results

Don't Get **Carried Away** When Drawing Conclusions

The **data** should always **support** the conclusion. This may sound obvious but it's easy to **jump** to conclusions. Conclusions have to be **specific** — not make sweeping generalisations.

Example:

1) The rate of an enzyme-controlled reaction was measured at **10 °C, 20 °C, 30 °C, 40 °C, 50 °C** and **60 °C**. All other variables were kept constant, and the results are shown in the graph below.

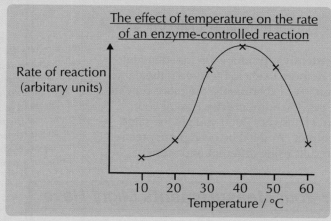

The effect of temperature on the rate of an enzyme-controlled reaction

Rate of reaction (arbitary units) vs Temperature / °C

2) A science magazine **concluded** from this data that enzyme X works best at **40 °C**.

3) The data **doesn't** support this. The enzyme **could** work best at 42 °C or 47 °C but you can't tell from the data because **increases** of **10 °C** at a time were used. The rate of reaction at in-between temperatures **wasn't** measured.

4) All you know is that it's faster at **40 °C** than at any of the other temperatures tested.

5) The experiment **ONLY** gives information about this particular enzyme-controlled reaction. You can't conclude that **all** enzyme-controlled reactions happen faster at a particular temperature — only this one. And you can't say for sure that doing the experiment at, say, a different constant pressure, wouldn't give a different optimum temperature.

Practice Questions

Q1 How do you treat anomalous results when calculating averages? And when drawing lines of best fit?

Q2 What is negative correlation?

Exam Question

Q1 A student carried out an investigation to study how the rate of a reaction changed with temperature. He plotted his results on the graph shown on the right.

a) Give the temperatures at which any anomalous results occurred. [1 mark]

b) What type of correlation is there between temperature and rate of reaction? [1 mark]

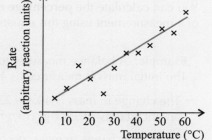

Rate (arbitrary reaction units) vs Temperature (°C)

c) Which of the following statements are appropriate conclusions to draw from this experiment?

1 The rate of the reaction is highest at 60 °C.
2 Increasing the temperature causes the rate of the reaction to increase.
3 Between 5 °C and 60 °C, the rate of the reaction increased as temperature increased.

A Statements 1, 2 and 3.   B Statements 2 and 3 only.

C Statement 3 only.   D Statement 2 only. [1 mark]

Correlation Street — my favourite programme...

Watch out for bias when you're reading about the results of scientific studies. People often tell you what they want you to know. So a bottled water company might say that studies have shown that chlorinated tap water can cause cancer, without mentioning any of the doubts in the results. After all, they want to persuade you to buy their drinks.

Evaluating Experiments

So you've planned an experiment, collected your data (no less than three times, mind you) and put it all onto a lovely graph. Now it's time to sit back, relax and... work out everything you did wrong. That's science, I'm afraid.

You Need to Look **Critically** at Your Experiment

There are a few terms that'll come in handy when you're evaluating how convincing your results are...

1) **Valid results** — Valid results answer the **original question**. For example, if you haven't **controlled all the variables** your results won't be valid, because you won't be testing just the thing you wanted to.

2) **Accurate results** — Accurate results are those that are **really close** to the **true** answer.

3) **Precise results** — Precise results can be **consistently reproduced** in independent experiments. If results are reproducible they're more likely to be **true**. If the data isn't precise you **can't draw** a valid **conclusion**. For experiments, the **more repeats** you do, and the closer together the data you get, the **more precise** it is. If you get the **same result** twice, it could be the correct answer. But if you get the same result **20 times**, it's much more likely to be correct. And it'd be even more precise if everyone in the class gets about the same results using **different apparatus**.

Precise results are sometimes called reliable results. So, just like precise results, reliable results are repeatable and reproducible, and you can improve the reliability of an experiment by taking repeat readings and calculating a mean.

Uncertainty is the Amount of **Error** Your **Measurements** Might Have

1) Any measurements you make will have **uncertainty** in them due to the limits to the **sensitivity** of the equipment you used.

2) If you use a weighing scale that measures to the nearest 0.1 g, then the **true** weight of any substance you weigh could be up to 0.05 g **more than** or **less than** your reading. Your measurement has an **uncertainty** (or error) of ±0.05 g in either direction.

3) The **±** sign tells you the **range** in which the true value could lie. The range can also be called the **margin of error**.

4) For any piece of equipment you use, the uncertainty will be **half** the **smallest increment** the equipment can measure, in either direction.

5) If you're **combining measurements**, you'll need to combine their **uncertainties**. For example, if you're calculating a temperature change by measuring an initial and a final temperature, the **total** uncertainty for the temperature change will be the uncertainties for both measurements added together.

The **Percentage Error** in a Result Should be Calculated

You can calculate the **percentage error** of a measurement using this equation:

$$\text{percentage error} = \frac{\text{uncertainty}}{\text{reading}} \times 100$$

Percentage error is sometimes called percentage uncertainty.

Example: A balance measures to the nearest 0.2 g, and is used to measure the **change in mass** of a substance. The initial mass is measured as 40.4 g. The final mass is measured as 22.0 g. Calculate the percentage error.

The change in mass is 40.4 − 22.0 = 18.4 g. The balance measures to the nearest 0.2 g, so **each reading** has an uncertainty of ±0.1 g. **Two** readings have been combined, so the **total uncertainty** is 0.1 × 2 = 0.2 g.

So for the **change in mass**, percentage error = $\frac{0.2}{18.4} \times 100 = 1.1\%$

The percentage error for each reading is just 0.1 ÷ reading × 100. E.g. for the initial mass it's 0.1 ÷ 40.4 × 100 = 0.2%

You Can **Minimise** the Percentage Error

1) One obvious way to **reduce errors** in your measurements is to use the most **sensitive equipment** available to you.

2) A bit of clever **planning** can also improve your results. If you measure out **5 cm³** of liquid in a measuring cylinder that has increments of 0.1 cm³ then the percentage error is (0.05 ÷ 5) × 100 = **1%**. But if you measure **10 cm³** of liquid in the same measuring cylinder the percentage error is (0.05 ÷ 10) × 100 = **0.5%**. Hey presto — you've just halved the percentage error. So the percentage error can be reduced by planning an experiment so you use a **larger volume** of liquid.

3) The general principle is that the **smaller** the measurement, the **larger** the percentage error.

Evaluating Experiments

Errors Can Be Systematic or Random

1) **Systematic errors** are the same every time you repeat the experiment. They may be caused by the **set-up** or **equipment** you used. For example, if the 10.00 cm³ pipette you used to measure out a sample for titration actually only measured 9.95 cm³, your sample would have been about 0.05 cm³ too small **every time** you repeated the experiment.

2) **Random errors** vary — they're what make the results a bit **different** each time you repeat an experiment. The errors when you make a reading from a burette are random. You have to estimate or round the level when it's between two marks — so sometimes your figure will be **above** the real one, and sometimes it will be **below**.

3) **Repeating an experiment** and finding the mean of your results helps to deal with **random errors**. The results that are a bit high will be **cancelled out** by the ones that are a bit low. So your results will be more **precise** (reliable). But repeating your results won't get rid of any **systematic errors**, so your results won't get more **accurate**.

This should be a photo of a scientist. I don't know what happened — it's a random error...

Think About How the Experiment Could Be Improved

In your evaluation you need to think about anything that you could have done differently to improve your results. Here are some things to think about...

1) **Whether your method gives you valid results.**
   - Will the data you collected answer the question your experiment aimed to answer?
   - Did you control all your variables?

2) **How you could improve the accuracy of your results.**
   - Was the apparatus you used on an appropriate scale for your measurements?
   - Could you use more sensitive equipment to reduce the random errors and uncertainty of your results?

3) **Whether your results are precise.**
   - Did you repeat the experiment, and were the results you got similar?

Practice Questions

Q1 What's the difference between the accuracy and precision of results?

Q2 What's the uncertainty of a balance that reads to the nearest 0.1 g?

Q3 How do you calculate percentage error?

Q4 Give two ways of reducing percentage error.

Q5 How can you reduce the random errors in your experiments?

Exam Question

Q1 A student carried out an experiment to determine the temperature change in the reaction between citric acid and sodium bicarbonate using the following method:

1. Measure out 25.0 cm³ of 1.00 mol dm⁻³ citric acid solution in a measuring cylinder and put it in a polystyrene cup.
2. Weigh out 2.10 g sodium bicarbonate and add it to the citric acid solution.
3. Place a thermometer in the solution and measure the temperature change over one minute.

a) The measuring cylinder the student uses measures to the nearest 0.5 cm³.
   What is the percentage error of the student's measurement?
   [1 mark]

b) The student's result is different to the documented value. How could you change the method to give a more accurate measurement for the change in temperature of the complete reaction?
   [2 marks]

___

Repeat your results: Your results, your results, your results, your results...

So there you have it, folks. All you need to know about planning, carrying out and analysing experiments. Always look out for where errors could be creeping in to your experimental methods. And make sure you're confident at working out uncertainties and percentage errors. Have another read of that bit if you're feeling a bit... well... uncertain.

The Atom

This stuff about atoms and elements should be ingrained in your brain from GCSE. You do need to know it perfectly though if you are to negotiate your way through the field of man-eating tigers which is Chemistry.

Atoms are made up of **Protons**, **Neutrons** and **Electrons**

Atoms are the stuff **all** elements and compounds are made of.
They're made up of 3 types of **subatomic** particle — **protons**, **neutrons** and **electrons**.

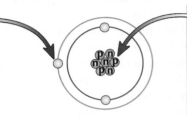

Electrons

1) Electrons have **−1** charge.

2) They whizz around the nucleus in **orbitals**. The orbitals take up most of the **volume** of the atom.

Nucleus

1) Most of the **mass** of the atom is concentrated in the nucleus.

2) The **diameter** of the nucleus is rather titchy compared to the whole atom.

3) The nucleus is where you find the **protons** and **neutrons**.

The mass and charge of these subatomic particles are **tiny**, so **relative mass** and **relative charge** are used instead.

Subatomic particle	Relative mass	Relative charge
Proton	1	+1
Neutron	1	0
Electron, e⁻	$\frac{1}{2000}$	−1

The mass of an electron is negligible compared to a proton or a neutron — this means you can usually ignore it.

Nuclear Symbols Show Numbers of **Subatomic Particles**

You can figure out the **number** of protons, neutrons and electrons from the **nuclear symbol**.

Mass (nucleon) number
This tells you the **total** number of **protons** and **neutrons** in the nucleus.

$$_{Z}^{A}X$$

Element symbol

Sometimes the atomic number is left out of the nuclear symbol, e.g. ⁷Li. You don't really need it because the element's symbol tells you its value.

Atomic (proton) number

1) This is the number of **protons** in the nucleus — it identifies the element.

2) **All** atoms of the same element have the **same** number of protons.

1) For **neutral** atoms, which have no overall charge, the number of electrons is **the same as** the number of protons.

2) The number of neutrons is just **mass number minus atomic number**, i.e. 'top minus bottom' in the nuclear symbol.

Nuclear Symbol	Atomic Number	Mass Number	Protons	Electrons	Neutrons
$_{3}^{7}Li$	3	7	3	3	7 − 3 = 4
$_{9}^{19}F$	9	19	9	9	19 − 9 = 10
$_{12}^{24}Mg$	12	24	12	12	24 − 12 = 12

"Hello, I'm Newt Ron..."

Ions have **Different** Numbers of **Protons** and **Electrons**

Negative ions have **more electrons** than protons...   ...and **positive** ions have **fewer electrons** than protons.

F⁻

The negative charge means that there's 1 more electron than there are protons. F has 9 protons (see table above), so F⁻ must have 10 electrons. The overall charge = +9 − 10 = −1.

Mg²⁺

The 2+ charge means that there are 2 fewer electrons than there are protons. Mg has 12 protons (see table above), so Mg²⁺ must have 10 electrons. The overall charge = +12 − 10 = +2.

The Atom

Isotopes are Atoms of the Same Element with Different Numbers of Neutrons

Make sure you **learn** this definition and totally **understand** what it means —

> **Isotopes of an element are atoms with the same number of protons but different numbers of neutrons.**
>
> 35 – 17 = 18 neutrons ⟵ **Different** mass numbers mean different ⟶ 37 – 17 = 20 neutrons
> masses and different numbers of neutrons.
>
> $^{35}_{17}\text{Cl}$ The **atomic numbers** are the same. $^{37}_{17}\text{Cl}$
> **Both** isotopes have 17 protons and 17 electrons.
>
> Chlorine-35 and chlorine-37 are examples of isotopes.

1) It's the **number** and **arrangement** of electrons that decides the **chemical properties** of an element. Isotopes have the **same configuration of electrons**, so they've got the **same** chemical properties.

2) Isotopes of an element do have slightly different **physical properties** though, such as different densities, rates of diffusion, etc. This is because **physical properties** tend to depend more on the **mass** of the atom.

Here's another example — naturally occurring **magnesium** consists of 3 isotopes.

^{24}Mg (79%)	^{25}Mg (10%)	^{26}Mg (11%)
12 protons	12 protons	12 protons
12 neutrons	**13** neutrons	**14** neutrons
12 electrons	12 electrons	12 electrons

The periodic table gives the atomic number for each element. The other number isn't the mass number — it's the relative atomic mass (see page 18). They're a bit different, but you can often assume they're equal — it doesn't matter unless you're doing really accurate work.

Practice Questions

Q1 Draw a diagram showing the structure of an atom, labelling each part.
Q2 Where is the mass concentrated in an atom, and what makes up most of the volume of an atom?
Q3 Draw a table showing the relative charge and relative mass of the three subatomic particles found in atoms.
Q4 Using an example, explain the terms 'atomic number' and 'mass number'.
Q5 Define the term 'isotopes' and give examples.

Exam Questions

Q1 Hydrogen, deuterium and tritium are all isotopes of each other.

a) Identify one similarity and one difference between these isotopes. [2 marks]

b) Deuterium can be written as ^{2}H. Determine the number of protons, neutrons and electrons in a neutral deuterium atom. [1 mark]

c) Write a nuclear symbol for tritium, given that it has 2 neutrons. [1 mark]

Q2 This question relates to the atoms or ions A to D: A. $^{32}_{16}\text{S}^{2-}$, B. $^{40}_{18}\text{Ar}$, C. $^{30}_{16}\text{S}$, D. $^{42}_{20}\text{Ca}$.

a) Identify the similarity for each of the following pairs.

i) A and B. [1 mark]
ii) A and C. [1 mark]
iii) B and D. [1 mark]

b) Which two of the atoms or ions are isotopes of each other? Explain your reasoning. [2 marks]

Got it learned yet? — Isotope so...

This is a nice straightforward page just to ease you in to things. Remember that positive ions have fewer electrons than protons, and negative ions have more electrons than protons. Get that straightened out or you'll end up in a right mess. There's nowt too hard about isotopes neither. They're just the same element with different numbers of neutrons.

Atomic Models

Things ain't how they used to be, you know. Take atomic structure, for starters.

The **Accepted Model** of the **Atom** Has **Changed** Throughout History

The model of the atom you're expected to know (the one on page 14) is the currently **accepted model**. It fits all the observations and evidence we have so far, so we **assume it's true** until someone shows that it's **incomplete or wrong**. In the past, completely different models were accepted, because they fitted the evidence available at the time:

1) Some **ancient Greeks** thought that all matter was made from **indivisible particles**.

2) At the start of the 19th century John Dalton described atoms as **solid spheres**, and said that different types of sphere made up the different elements.

The Greek word atomos means 'uncuttable'.

3) But as scientists did more experiments, our currently accepted models began to emerge, with modifications or refinements being made to take account of new evidence.

Experimental Evidence Showed that Atoms Weren't Solid Spheres

In 1897 J J Thomson did a whole series of experiments and concluded that atoms **weren't** solid and indivisible.

1) His measurements of **charge** and **mass** showed that an atom must contain even smaller, negatively charged particles. He called these particles 'corpuscles' — we call them **electrons**.

2) The 'solid sphere' idea of atomic structure had to be changed. The new model was known as the '**plum pudding model**' — a positively charged sphere with negative electrons embedded in it.

positively charged 'pudding'

delicious pudding

Rutherford Showed that the Plum Pudding Model Was Wrong

1) In 1909 Ernest Rutherford and his students Hans Geiger and Ernest Marsden conducted the famous **gold foil experiment**. They fired **alpha particles** (which are positively charged) at an extremely thin sheet of gold.

2) From the plum pudding model, they were expecting **most** of the alpha particles to be deflected **very slightly** by the positive 'pudding' that made up most of an atom.

3) In fact, most of the alpha particles passed **straight through** the gold atoms, and a very small number were deflected **backwards** (through more than 90°). This showed that the plum pudding model **couldn't be right**.

4) So Rutherford came up with a model that **could** explain this new evidence — the **nuclear model** of the atom:

A few alpha particles are deflected very strongly by the nucleus.

Most of the alpha particles pass through empty space.

1) There is a **tiny, positively charged nucleus** at the centre of the atom, where most of the atom's mass is concentrated.

2) The nucleus is surrounded by a '**cloud**' of **negative electrons**.

3) Most of the atom is **empty space**.

Rutherford's **Nuclear Model** Was **Modified** Several Times

Rutherford's model seemed pretty convincing, but (there's always a but)... the scientists of the day didn't just say, "Well done Ernest old chap, you've got it", then all move to Patagonia to farm goats. No, they stuck at their experiments, wanting to be sure of the truth. (And it's just conceivable they wanted some fame and fortune too.)

1) Henry Moseley discovered that the charge of the nucleus **increased** from one element to another in units of one.

2) This led Rutherford to investigate the nucleus further. He finally discovered that it contained **positively charged** particles that he called **protons**. The charges of the nuclei of different atoms could then be explained — the atoms of **different elements** have a **different number of protons** in their nucleus.

3) There was still one problem with the model — the nuclei of atoms were **heavier** than they would be if they just contained protons. Rutherford predicted that there were other particles in the nucleus, that had **mass but no charge** — and the **neutron** was eventually discovered by James Chadwick.

This is nearly always the way scientific knowledge develops — **new evidence** prompts people to come up with **new, improved ideas**. Then other people go through each new, improved idea with a fine-tooth comb as well — modern '**peer review**' (see p.2) is part of this process.

Atomic Models

The **Bohr Model** Was a Further Improvement

1) Scientists realised that electrons in a 'cloud' around the nucleus of an atom would **spiral down** into the nucleus, causing the atom to **collapse**. Niels Bohr proposed a new model of the atom with four basic principles:

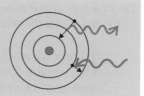

- Electrons can only exist in **fixed orbits**, or **shells**, and not anywhere in between.
- Each shell has a **fixed energy**.
- When an electron moves between shells **electromagnetic radiation** is **emitted** or **absorbed**.
- Because the energy of shells is fixed, the radiation will have a **fixed frequency**.

2) The frequencies of radiation emitted and absorbed by atoms were already known from experiments. The Bohr model fitted these observations — it looked good.

3) The Bohr model also explained why some elements (the noble gases) are **inert**. He said that the shells of an atom can only hold **fixed numbers of electrons**, and that an element's reactivity is due to its electrons. Atoms will react in order to gain full shells of electrons. When an atom has **full shells** of electrons it is **stable** and does not react.

There's **More Than One** Model of Atomic Structure in Use Today

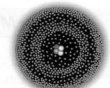

1) We now know that the Bohr model is **not perfect** — but it's still widely used to describe atoms because it's simple and explains many **observations** from experiments, like bonding and ionisation energy trends.

2) The most accurate model we have today involves complicated quantum mechanics. Basically, you can never **know** where an electron is or which direction it's going in at any moment, but you can say **how likely** it is to be at any particular point in the atom. Oh, and electrons can act as **waves** as well as particles (but you don't need to worry about the details).

The quantum model of an atom with two shells of electrons. The denser the dots, the more likely an electron is to be there.

3) This model might be **more accurate**, but it's a lot harder to get your head round and visualise. It **does** explain some observations that can't be accounted for by the Bohr model though. So scientists use whichever model is most relevant to whatever they're investigating.

Practice Questions

Q1 What particle did J J Thomson discover?

Q2 Describe the model of the atom that was adopted because of Thomson's work.

Q3 Who developed the 'nuclear' model of the atom? What evidence did they have for it?

Exam Question

Q1 Scientific theories are constantly being revised in the light of new evidence. New theories are accepted if they have been successfully tested by experiments or because they help to explain certain observations.

a) Niels Bohr thought that the model of the atom proposed by Ernest Rutherford did not describe the electrons in an atom correctly. Why did he think this and how was his model of the atom different from Rutherford's?　　　　　　[2 marks]

b) According to the Bohr model, what happens when electrons in an atom move from one shell to another?　[1 mark]

c) How did Bohr explain the lack of reactivity of the noble gases?　　　　　　[2 marks]

These models are tiny — even smaller than size zero, I reckon...

The process of developing a model to fit the evidence available, looking for more evidence to show if it's correct or not, then revising the model if necessary is really important. It happens with all new scientific ideas. Remember, scientific 'facts' are only accepted as true because no one's proved yet that they aren't. It might all be bunkum.

Relative Mass

Relative mass... What? Eh?... Read on...

Relative Masses are Masses of Atoms Compared to Carbon-12

The actual mass of an atom is **very**, **very tiny**.
Don't worry about exactly how tiny for now, but it's far **too small** to weigh. So, the mass of one atom is compared to the mass of a different atom. This is its **relative mass**. Here are some **definitions** for you to learn:

The **relative atomic mass**, A_r, is the weighted **mean mass** of an atom of an element, compared to $1/12^{th}$ of the mass of an atom of **carbon-12**.

Relative isotopic mass is the mass of an atom of an **isotope**, compared with $1/12^{th}$ of the mass of an atom of **carbon-12**.

1) Relative atomic mass is an **average**, so it's not usually a whole number.
2) Relative isotopic mass is usually a **whole number**.

E.g. a natural sample of chlorine contains a mixture of ^{35}Cl (75%) and ^{37}Cl (25%), so the relative isotopic masses are **35** and **37**. But its relative atomic mass is **35.5**.

Jason's shirt was isotropical...

Relative Molecular Masses are Masses of Molecules

The **relative molecular mass** (or **relative formula mass**), M_r, is the average mass of a molecule or formula unit, compared to $1/12^{th}$ of the mass of an atom of **carbon-12**.

Don't worry, this is one definition that you **don't** need to know for the exam.
But... you **do** need to know how to **work out** the **relative molecular mass**, and the **relative formula mass**, so it's probably best if you **learn** what they mean anyway.

1) **Relative molecular mass** is used when referring to **simple molecules**.
2) To find the relative molecular mass, just **add up** the **relative atomic mass values** of all the atoms in the molecule.

$$E.g.\ M_r(C_2H_6O) = (2 \times 12) + (6 \times 1) + 16 = 46$$

1) **Relative formula mass** is used for compounds that are **ionic** (or **giant covalent**, such as SiO_2).
2) To find the relative formula mass, **add up** the **relative atomic masses** (A_r) of all the ions in the formula unit. (A_r of ion = A_r of atom. The electrons make no difference to the mass.)

$$E.g.\ M_r(CaF_2) = 40 + (2 \times 19) = 78$$

A_r Can Be Worked Out from Isotopic Abundances

You need to know how to calculate the **relative atomic mass** (A_r) of an element from its **isotopic abundances**.
1) Different isotopes of an element occur in different quantities, or isotopic abundances.
2) To work out the relative atomic mass of an element, you need to work out the **average** mass of all its atoms.
3) If you're given the isotopic abundances in **percentages**, all you need to do is follow these two easy steps:

Step 1: Multiply each **relative isotopic mass** by its % **relative isotopic abundance**, and **add up** the results.
Step 2: Divide by **100**.

Example: Find the relative atomic mass of boron given that 20.0 % of the boron atoms found on Earth have a relative isotopic mass of 10.0, while 80.0 % have a relative isotopic mass of 11.0.

Step 1: $(20 \times 10) + (80 \times 11) = 1080$
Step 2: $1080 \div 100 = \textbf{10.8}$

Relative Mass

Mass Spectrometry Can Tell Us About Isotopes

Mass spectra are produced by mass spectrometers — devices which are used to find out what samples are made up of by measuring the masses of their components. Mass spectra can tell us dead useful things, e.g. the **relative isotopic masses and abundances** of different elements.

This is the mass spectra for chlorine.

The **y-axis** gives the **abundance of ions**, often as a percentage. For an element, the **height** of each peak gives the **relative isotopic abundance**.

The **x-axis** units are given as a 'mass/charge' ratio (you may sometimes see it written as **m:z**). Since the charge on the ions is mostly **+1**, you can often assume the x-axis is simply the **relative isotopic mass**.

This spectra shows that chlorine exists as 2 isotopes. 75.5% of chlorine is ^{35}Cl, and 24.5% is ^{37}Cl.

Mass spectra can be used to work out the relative atomic masses of different elements.

The method for working out the relative atomic mass from a graph is a bit different to working it out from percentages, but it starts off in the same way.

Step 1: Multiply each **relative isotopic mass** by its **relative isotopic abundance**, and **add up** the results.

Step 2: Divide by the **sum** of the isotopic abundances.

Example: Use the data from this mass spectrum to work out the relative atomic mass of neon. Give your answer to 1 decimal place.

Step 1: $(20 \times 114.0) + (21 \times 0.2) + (22 \times 11.2) = 2530.6$

Step 2: $(114.0 + 0.2 + 11.2 = 125.4)$
$2530.6 \div 125.4 = \textbf{20.2}$

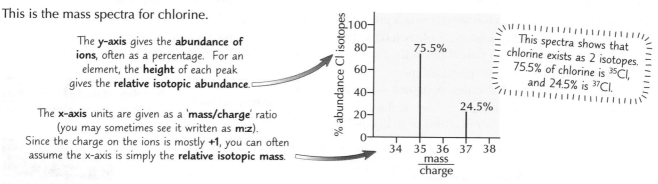

Practice Questions

Q1 Explain what relative atomic mass (A_r) and relative isotopic mass mean.

Q2 Explain the difference between relative molecular mass and relative formula mass.

Q3 Explain what relative isotopic abundance means.

Exam Questions

Q1 Copper exists in two main isotopic forms, ^{63}Cu and ^{65}Cu.

a) Calculate the relative atomic mass of copper using the information from the mass spectrum. [2 marks]

b) Explain why the relative atomic mass of copper is not a whole number. [2 marks]

Q2 The percentage make-up of naturally occurring potassium is: 93.1% ^{39}K, 0.120% ^{40}K and 6.77% ^{41}K. Use the information to determine the relative atomic mass of potassium. [2 marks]

You can't pick your relatives, you just have to learn them...

Isotopic masses are a bit frustrating. Why can't all atoms of an element just be the same? But the fact is they're not, so you're going to have to learn how to use those spectra to work out the relative atomic masses of different elements. The actual maths is pretty simple. A pinch of multiplying, a dash of addition, some division to flavour and you're away.

The Mole

It'd be handy to be able to count out atoms — but they're way too tiny. You can't even see them, never mind get hold of them with tweezers. But not to worry — using the idea of relative mass, you can figure out how many atoms you've got.

A Mole is Just a (Very Large) Number of Particles

Chemists often talk about 'amount of substance'. Basically, all they mean is 'number of particles'.

1) Amount of substance is measured using a unit called the **mole** (or **mol**). The number of moles is given the symbol **n**.

2) The number of **particles** in one mole is 6.02×10^{23}. This number is **the Avogadro constant, N_A**.
   It's given to you on your data sheet in the exam, so don't worry about learning its value, just what it means.

3) It **doesn't matter** what the particles are.
   They can be atoms, molecules, penguins — **anything**.

4) Here's a nice simple formula for finding the number of moles from the number of atoms or molecules:

$$\text{Number of moles} = \frac{\text{Number of particles you have}}{\text{Number of particles in a mole}}$$

> **Example:** I have 1.50×10^{24} carbon atoms. How many moles of carbon is this?
>
> $$\text{Number of moles} = \frac{1.50 \times 10^{24}}{6.02 \times 10^{23}} \approx \textbf{2.49 moles}$$

Molar Mass is the Mass of One Mole

Molar mass, M, is the mass of **one mole** of something. Just remember:

Molar mass is just the same as the relative molecular mass, M_r.

That's why the mole is such a ridiculous number of particles (6.02×10^{23}) — it's the number of particles for which the weight in g is the same as the relative molecular mass.

The only difference is it has units of 'grams per mole', so you stick a 'g mol^{-1}' on the end...

> **Example:** Find the molar mass of $CaCO_3$.
>
> Relative formula mass, M_r, of $CaCO_3 = 40.1 + 12.0 + (3 \times 16.0) = 100.1$
> So the molar mass, M, is **100.1 g mol^{-1}** — i.e. 1 mole of $CaCO_3$ weighs 100.1 g.

Here's another formula.
This one's really important — you need it **all the time**:

$$\text{Number of moles} = \frac{\text{mass of substance}}{\text{molar mass}}$$

> **Example:** How many moles of aluminium oxide are present in 5.1 g of Al_2O_3?
>
> Molar mass, M, of $Al_2O_3 = (2 \times 27.0) + (3 \times 16.0) = 102.0$ g mol^{-1}
>
> Number of moles of $Al_2O_3 = \frac{5.1}{102.0} = \textbf{0.05 moles}$

You can re-arrange this equation using this formula triangle:

mass / moles | molar mass

> **Example:** How many moles of chlorine molecules are present in 71.0 g of chlorine gas?
>
> We're talking chlorine **molecules** (not chlorine atoms), so it's Cl_2 we're interested in.
> Molar mass, M, of $Cl_2 = (2 \times 35.5) = 71.0$ g mol^{-1}
>
> Number of moles of $Cl_2 = \frac{71.0}{71.0} = \textbf{1 mole}$

But note that it would be 2 moles of chlorine atoms, since chlorine atoms have a molar mass of 35.5 g mol^{-1}.

You Need to be able to work out the Number of Atoms in Something

> **Example:** How many atoms are in 8.5 g of H_2S?
>
> Molar mass, M, of $H_2S = 1.0 + 1.0 + 32.1 = 34.1$ g mol^{-1}
> Number of moles of $H_2S = \frac{8.5}{34.1} = 0.249$ moles
> Number of molecules of $H_2S = 0.249 \times 6.02 \times 10^{23} = 1.50 \times 10^{23}$
> There are 3 atoms in 1 molecule of H_2S so, total no. atoms $= 1.50 \times 10^{23} \times 3 = \textbf{4.5} \times \textbf{10}^{23}$ (2 s.f)

Multiplying moles by Avogadro's constant gives you the number of molecules/particles.

The Mole

All Gases Take Up the **Same Volume** under the Same Conditions

The space that one mole of a gas occupies at a certain temperature and pressure
is known as the **molar gas volume**. It has units of **dm³ mol⁻¹**.
If temperature and pressure stay the same, **one mole** of **any** gas always has the **same volume**.
At **room temperature and pressure** (r.t.p.), this happens to be **24 dm³ mol⁻¹** (r.t.p is 298 K (25 °C) and 101.3 kPa).
Here's the formula for working out the number of moles in a volume of gas.

$$\text{Number of moles} = \frac{\text{Volume in dm}^3}{\text{Molar gas volume}}$$

At r.t.p, just substitute 24 dm³ mol⁻¹ into
this equation as the molar gas volume.

Example: How many moles are there in 6.0 dm³ of oxygen gas at r.t.p.?

$$\text{Number of moles} = \frac{6.0}{24} = \textbf{0.25 moles of oxygen molecules}$$

This is oxygen <u>molecules</u>, not
atoms, as gaseous oxygen exists
as O_2, not lone O atoms.

Ideal Gas equation — $pV = nRT$

In the real world, it's not always room temperature and pressure.
The **ideal gas equation** lets you find the **number of moles** in a certain volume at **any temperature and pressure**.

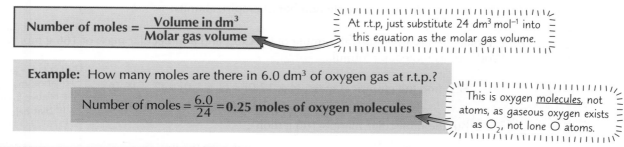

$pV = nRT$ Where: p = pressure (Pa)

1 cm³ = 1 × 10⁻⁶ m³
1 dm³ = 1 × 10⁻³ m³

V = volume (m³)

n = number of moles

R is the gas constant. Don't worry
about what it means. Just learn it.

R = 8.314 J K⁻¹ mol⁻¹

T = temperature (K)

K = °C + 273

Example: At a temperature of 60.0 °C and a pressure of 250 kPa, a gas occupied a
volume of 1100 cm³ and had a mass of 1.60 g. Find its relative molecular mass.

1 kPa = 1000 Pa

$$n = \frac{pV}{RT} = \frac{(250 \times 10^3) \times (1.1 \times 10^{-3})}{8.314 \times 333} = 0.0993 \text{ moles}$$

1100 cm³ = 1.1 × 10⁻³ m³

If 0.0993 moles is 1.60 g, then 1 mole = $\frac{1.60}{0.0993}$ = 16.1 g. So the relative molecular mass (M_r) is **16.1**.

Practice Questions

Q1 How many molecules are there in one mole of ethane molecules?

Q2 What is the equation for working out the number of moles of something from a given mass?

Q3 What volume does 1 mole of gas occupy at r.t.p.?

Exam Questions

Q1	How many atoms are in 7.3 g of HCl?	[2 marks]
Q2	Calculate the mass of 0.360 moles of ethanoic acid, CH_3COOH.	[2 marks]
Q3	At what temperature will 1.28 g of chlorine gas occupy 98.6 dm³, at a pressure of 175 Pa?	[2 marks]
Q4	What volume will be occupied by 88 g of propane gas (C_3H_8) at r.t.p.?	[2 marks]

Put your back teeth on the scale and find out your molar mass...

*You need this stuff for loads of calculation questions. You'll almost definitely need to use all the formulae to find out
things like the volume of a gas or the number of moles in a volume of gas. Before tackling a question, sit down and see
what information you have, what equations you can use and how you can rearrange them to get the answer.*

Empirical and Molecular Formulae

Here's another page piled high with numbers — it's all just glorified maths really.

Empirical and Molecular Formulae are Ratios

You have to know what's what with empirical and molecular formulae, so here goes...

1) The **empirical formula** gives the smallest whole number ratio of atoms of each element in a compound.

2) The **molecular formula** gives the **actual** numbers of atoms of each type of element in a molecule.

3) The molecular formula is made up of a **whole number** of empirical units.

Example: A molecule has an empirical formula of $C_4H_3O_2$, and a molecular mass of 166 g mol^{-1}. Work out its molecular formula.

First find the **empirical mass**: $(4 \times 12.0) + (3 \times 1.0) + (2 \times 16.0)$
$$= 48.0 + 3.0 + 32.0 = 83.0 \text{ g mol}^{-1}$$

Empirical mass is just like the relative formula mass... (if that helps at all...).

Compare the empirical and molecular masses.

But the **molecular mass** is 166 g mol^{-1},

so there are $\frac{166}{83.0} = 2$ empirical units in the molecule.

The molecular formula must be the **empirical formula × 2**,

so the molecular formula = $C_8H_6O_4$. So there you go.

Empirical Formulae are Calculated from Experiments

You need to be able to work out empirical formulae from **experimental results** too.

Example: When a hydrocarbon is burnt in excess oxygen, 4.4 g of carbon dioxide and 1.8 g of water are made. What is the empirical formula of the hydrocarbon?

First work out how many moles of the products you have.

$$\text{No. of moles of } CO_2 = \frac{\text{mass}}{M} = \frac{4.4}{12.0 + (2 \times 16.0)} = \frac{4.4}{44.0} = 0.10 \text{ moles}$$

1 mole of CO_2 contains 1 mole of carbon atoms, so you must have started with **0.10 moles of carbon atoms**.

$$\text{No. of moles of } H_2O = \frac{1.8}{(2 \times 1.0) + 16.0} = \frac{1.8}{18.0} = 0.10 \text{ moles}$$

1 mole of H_2O contains 2 moles of hydrogen atoms (H), so you must have started with **0.20 moles of hydrogen atoms**.

Ratio $C:H = 0.10:0.20$. Now you divide both numbers by the **smallest** — here it's 0.10.

So, the ratio $C:H = 1:2$. So the empirical formula must be CH_2.

This works because the only place the carbon in the carbon dioxide and the hydrogen in the water could have come from is the hydrocarbon.

As if that's not enough, you also need to know how to work out empirical formulae from the **percentages** of the different elements.

Example: A compound is found to have percentage composition 56.5% potassium, 8.70% carbon and 34.8% oxygen by mass. Calculate its empirical formula.

These answers are given to 3 significant figures.

In **100 g** of compound there are:

Use $n = \frac{\text{mass}}{M}$

$\frac{56.5}{39.1} = 1.45 \text{ moles of K}$ $\frac{8.70}{12.0} = 0.725 \text{ moles of C}$ $\frac{34.8}{16.0} = 2.18 \text{ moles of O}$

Divide each number of moles by the **smallest number** — in this case it's 0.725.

K: $\frac{1.45}{0.725} = 2.00$ C: $\frac{0.725}{0.725} = 1.00$ O: $\frac{2.18}{0.725} = 3.01$

The ratio of $K:C:O \approx 2:1:3$. So you know the empirical formula's got to be K_2CO_3.

Empirical and Molecular Formulae

Molecular Formulae are Calculated from Experimental Data Too

Once you know the empirical formula, you just need a bit more info and you can work out the **molecular formula** too.

Example:

When 4.6 g of an alcohol, with molar mass 46 g mol^{-1}, is burnt in excess oxygen, it produces 8.8 g of carbon dioxide and 5.4 g of water.
Calculate the empirical formula for the alcohol and then its molecular formula.

Alcohols contain C, H and O.

The carbon in the CO_2 and the hydrogen in the H_2O must have come from the alcohol — work out the number of moles of each of these.

No. of moles of $CO_2 = \frac{mass}{M} = \frac{8.8}{44} = 0.2$ moles

1 mole of CO_2 contains 1 mole of C. So, 0.2 moles of CO_2 contains **0.2 moles of C**.

No. of moles $H_2O = \frac{mass}{M} = \frac{5.4}{18} = 0.3$ moles

1 mole of H_2O contains 2 moles of H. So, 0.3 moles of H_2O contains **0.6 moles of H**.

Mass of C = no. of moles $\times$ M = $0.2 \times 12.0 = 2.4$ g

Mass of H = no. of moles $\times$ M = $0.6 \times 1.0 = 0.6$ g

Mass of O = $4.6 - (2.4 + 0.6) = 1.6$ g

Number of moles O = $\frac{mass}{M} = \frac{1.6}{16.0} = 0.1$ moles

Now work out the mass of carbon and hydrogen in the alcohol. The rest of the mass of the alcohol must be oxygen — so work out that too. Once you know the mass of O, you can work out how many moles there are of it.

Molar Ratio = C : H : O = $0.2 : 0.6 : 0.1 = 2 : 6 : 1$

Empirical formula = C_2H_6O

Mass of empirical formula = $(2 \times 12.0) + (6 \times 1.0) + 16.0 = 46.0$ g

In this example, the mass of the empirical formula equals the molecular mass, so the empirical and molecular formulae are the same.

Molecular formula = C_2H_6O

When you know the number of moles of each element, you've got the molar ratio. Divide each number by the smallest.

Compare the empirical and molecular masses.

Practice Questions

Q1 Define 'empirical formula'.

Q2 What is the difference between a molecular formula and an empirical formula?

Exam Questions

Q1 Hydrocarbon X has a molecular mass of 78 g. It is found to have 92.3% carbon and 7.7% hydrogen by mass. Calculate the empirical and molecular formulae of X. [3 marks]

Q2 When 1.2 g of magnesium ribbon is heated in air, it burns to form a white powder, which has a mass of 2 g. What is the empirical formula of the powder? [2 marks]

Q3 When 19.8 g of an organic acid, A, is burnt in excess oxygen, 33.0 g of carbon dioxide and 10.8 g of water are produced. Calculate the empirical formula for A and hence its molecular formula, if $M_r(A) = 132$.

Hint: organic acids contain C, H and O.

[4 marks]

The Empirical Strikes Back...

With this stuff, it's not enough to learn a few facts parrot-fashion, to regurgitate in the exam — you've gotta know how to use them. The only way to do that is to practise. Go through all the examples on these two pages again, this time working the answers out for yourself. Then test yourself on the exam questions. It'll help you sleep at night — honest.

Equations and Calculations

Balancing equations'll cause you a few palpitations — as soon as you make one bit right, the rest goes pear-shaped.

Balanced Equations have **Equal Numbers** of each Atom on **Both Sides**

1) Balanced equations have the **same number** of each atom on **both** sides. They're... well... you know... balanced.

2) You can only add more atoms by adding **whole reactants** or **products**. You do this by putting a number **in front** of a substance or changing one that's already there. You **can't** mess with formulae — ever.

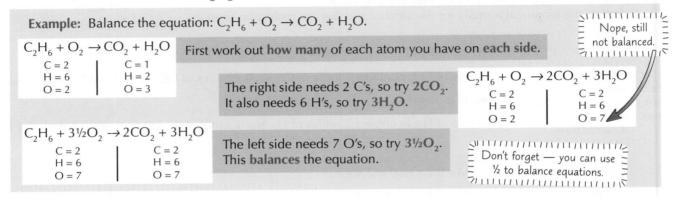

Example: Balance the equation: $C_2H_6 + O_2 \rightarrow CO_2 + H_2O$.

$C_2H_6 + O_2 \rightarrow CO_2 + H_2O$ First work out **how many** of each atom you have on **each side**.

C = 2	C = 1
H = 6	H = 2
O = 2	O = 3

The right side needs 2 C's, so try **$2CO_2$**. It also needs 6 H's, so try **$3H_2O$**.

Nope, still not balanced.

$C_2H_6 + O_2 \rightarrow 2CO_2 + 3H_2O$

C = 2	C = 2
H = 6	H = 6
O = 2	O = 7

$C_2H_6 + 3\frac{1}{2}O_2 \rightarrow 2CO_2 + 3H_2O$

C = 2	C = 2
H = 6	H = 6
O = 7	O = 7

The left side needs 7 O's, so try **$3\frac{1}{2}O_2$**. This **balances** the equation.

Don't forget — you can use ½ to balance equations.

Ionic Equations Only Show the **Reacting Particles**

1) You can also write an **ionic equation** for any reaction involving **ions** that happens **in solution**.

2) In an ionic equation, only the **reacting particles** (and the **products** they form) are included.

Example: Here is the **full balanced equation** for the reaction of **nitric acid** with **sodium hydroxide**:

$$HNO_3 + NaOH \rightarrow NaNO_3 + H_2O$$

The **ionic** substances in this equation will **dissolve**, breaking up into ions in solution. You can rewrite the equation to show all the **ions** that are in the reaction mixture:

$$H^+ + NO_3^- + Na^+ + OH^- \rightarrow Na^+ + NO_3^- + H_2O$$

Leave anything that isn't an ion in solution (like the H_2O) as it is.

To get from this to the ionic equation, just cross out any ions that appear on **both sides** of the equation — in this case, that's the sodium ions (Na^+) and the nitrate ions (NO_3^-). So the **ionic equation** for this reaction is:

$$H^+ + OH^- \rightarrow H_2O$$

An ion that's present in the reaction mixture, but doesn't get involved in the reaction is called a <u>spectator ion</u>.

3) When you've written an ionic equation, check that the **charges** are **balanced**, as well as the atoms — if the charges don't balance, the equation isn't right.

In the example above, the **net charge** on the left hand side is +1 + –1 = 0 and the net charge on the right hand side is **0** — so the charges balance.

Balanced Equations can be used to Work out **Masses**

Balanced equations show the **reaction stoichiometry** (see page 32). The reaction stoichiometry tells you the ratios of reactants to products, i.e. how many moles of product are formed from a certain number of moles of reactants.

Example: Calculate the mass of iron oxide produced if 28 g of iron is burnt in air. $2Fe + \frac{3}{2}O_2 \rightarrow Fe_2O_3$

The molar mass, M, of Fe = 55.8 g mol⁻¹, so the number of moles in 28 g of Fe = $\frac{mass}{M} = \frac{28}{55.8} = 0.50$ moles.

From the equation: 2 moles of Fe produces 1 mole of Fe_2O_3, so 0.50 moles of Fe produces 0.25 moles of Fe_2O_3.

Once you know the number of moles and the molar mass (M) of Fe_2O_3, it's easy to work out the mass.

M of Fe_2O_3 = (2 × 55.8) + (3 × 16) = 159.6 g mol⁻¹

Mass of Fe_2O_3 = no. of moles × M = 0.25 × 159.6 = **40 g (2 s.f)**

Equations and Calculations

That's not all... Balanced Equations can be used to Work Out Gas Volumes

It's pretty handy to be able to work out **how much gas** a reaction will produce, so that you can use **large enough apparatus**. Or else there might be a rather large bang.

Example: How much gas is produced when 15 g of sodium is reacted with excess water at r.t.p.?

$$2Na_{(s)} + 2H_2O_{(l)} \rightarrow 2NaOH_{(aq)} + H_{2\,(g)}$$

M of Na = 23,0 g mol^{-1}, so number of moles in 15 g of Na = $\frac{15}{23.0}$ = 0.65 moles

Excess water means you know all the sodium will react.

From the equation, 2 moles Na produces 1 mole H$_2$,

so you know 0.65 moles Na produces $\frac{0.65}{2}$ = 0.325 moles H$_2$.

So the volume of H$_2$ = 0.325 × 24 = **7.8 dm^3**

The reaction happens at room temperature and pressure, so you know 1 mole takes up 24 dm^3 (p. 21).

State Symbols Give a bit More Information about the Substances

State symbols are put after each reactant and product in an equation. They tell you what **state of matter** things are in.

| s = solid | l = liquid | g = gas | aq = aqueous (solution in water) |

To show you what I mean, here's an example —

$$CaCO_{3\,(s)} + 2HCl_{(aq)} \rightarrow CaCl_{2\,(aq)} + H_2O_{(l)} + CO_{2\,(g)}$$

solid   solution   solution   liquid   gas

Practice Questions

Q1 What is the difference between a molecular equation and an ionic equation?
Q2 What is the state symbol for a solution of hydrochloric acid?

Exam Questions

Q1 Balance the following equation.

$$KI_{(aq)} + Pb(NO_3)_{2\,(aq)} \rightarrow PbI_{2\,(s)} + KNO_{3\,(aq)}$$

[1 mark]

Q2 Use the equation given to calculate the mass of ethene required to produce 258 g of chloroethane, C_2H_5Cl.

$$C_2H_4 + HCl \rightarrow C_2H_5Cl$$

[2 marks]

Q3 What volume of oxygen is required, at room temperature and pressure for the complete combustion of 3.50×10^{-2} mol of butane (C_4H_{10})?

[2 marks]

Q4 15.0 g of calcium carbonate is heated strongly so that it fully decomposes. $CaCO_{3\,(s)} \rightarrow CaO_{(s)} + CO_{2\,(g)}$

a) Calculate the mass of calcium oxide produced. [2 marks]

b) Calculate the volume of gas produced. [1 mark]

Don't get in a state about equations...

You're probably completely fed up with all these equations, calculations, moles and whatnot... well hang in there — there are just a few more pages coming up. I've said it once, and I'll say it again — practise, practise, practise... it's the only road to salvation (by the way, where is salvation anyway?). Keep going... you're nearly there.

Formulae of Ionic Compounds

Ahh — ions. My favourite topic. In fact, the only things better than ions are probably ionic compounds, and here's a page all about them. It's like Christmas has come early...

Ions are made when Electrons are Transferred

1) Ions are formed when electrons are **transferred** from one atom to another.

2) The simplest ions are single atoms which have either lost or gained electrons so as to have a **full outer shell**.

A sodium atom (Na) **loses** 1 electron to form a sodium ion (Na^+)

A magnesium atom (Mg) **loses** 2 electrons to form a magnesium ion (Mg^{2+})

A chlorine atom (Cl) **gains** 1 electron to form a chloride ion (Cl^-)

An oxygen atom (O) **gains** 2 electrons to form an oxide ion (O^{2-})

$$Na \rightarrow Na^+ + e^-$$
$$Mg \rightarrow Mg^{2+} + 2e^-$$
$$Cl + e^- \rightarrow Cl^-$$
$$O + 2e^- \rightarrow O^{2-}$$

3) You **don't** have to remember what ion **each element** forms — nope, you just look at the Periodic Table.

4) Elements in the same **group** all have the same number of **outer electrons**. So they have to **lose or gain** the same number to get the full outer shell that they're aiming for. And this means that they form ions with the **same charges**.

Group 1 = 1^+ ions

Group 2 = 2^+ ions

Group 6 = 2^- ions

Group 7 = 1^- ions

Not all Ions are Made from Single Atoms

There are lots of ions that are made up of a group of atoms with an overall charge. These are called **molecular ions**.
You need to remember the formulae and the names of these ions:

Name	Formula
Nitrate	NO_3^-
Carbonate	CO_3^{2-}
Sulfate	SO_4^{2-}
Hydroxide	OH^-
Ammonium	NH_4^+
Zinc Ion	Zn^{2+}
Silver Ion	Ag^+

Amanda had a large overall charge.

Don't forget to learn the charge on each ion too.

Charges in Ionic Compounds Always Balance

1) **Ionic compounds** are made when positive and negative ions **bond** together. They do this through **ionic bonding**, but that's another story (see pages 42-43).

2) The charges on an **ionic compound** must always balance out to zero. For example...

- In **NaCl**, the +1 charge on the Na^+ ion balances the –1 charge on the Cl^- ion.
- In **$MgCl_2$**, the +2 charge on the Mg^{2+} ion balances the two –1 charges on the two Cl^- ions.

Example: What is the formula of potassium sulfate?

Potassium is in Group 1 of the periodic table, so will therefore form ions with a +1 charge: K^+.
The formula for the sulfate ion is SO_4^{2-}.
For every **one** sulfate ion, you will need **two** potassium ions to balance the charge: $(+1 \times 2) + (-2) = 0$.
So the formula is **K_2SO_4**.

Formulae of Ionic Compounds

Salts are Ionic Compounds

1) When **acids** and **bases** react, they form **water** and a **salt** (p. 28-29).

2) **Salts** are **ionic compounds**. All solid salts consist of a **lattice** of positive and negative ions. In some salts, **water molecules** are incorporated in the lattice too.

3) The water in a lattice is called **water of crystallisation**. A solid salt containing water of crystallisation is **hydrated**. A salt is **anhydrous** if it doesn't contain water of crystallisation.

4) **One mole** of a particular hydrated salt always has the **same number of moles** of water of crystallisation — its **formula** shows **how many** (it's always a whole number).

5) For example, **hydrated copper sulfate** has **five** moles of water for every mole of the salt. So its formula is $CuSO_4.5H_2O$. ← Notice that there's a dot between $CuSO_4$ and $5H_2O$.

6) Many hydrated salts **lose** their water of crystallisation **when heated**, to become **anhydrous**. If you know the mass of the salt when hydrated and anhydrous, you can work its formula out like this:

> Here's a tiny part of the lattice in a hydrated salt.
>
> Water molecules are **polar** (see p. 48). They're held in place in the lattice because they're attracted to the ions.

Example: Heating 3.210 g of hydrated magnesium sulfate, $MgSO_4.XH_2O$, forms 1.567 g of anhydrous magnesium sulfate. Find the value of **X** and write the formula of the hydrated salt.

First you find the number of moles of water lost.

| Mass of water lost: | $3.210 - 1.567 = 1.643$ g |
| Number of moles of water lost: | mass ÷ molar mass = 1.643 g ÷ 18 g mol^{-1} = **0.09127 moles** |

Then you find the number of moles of anhydrous salt.

| Molar mass of $MgSO_4$: | $24.3 + 32.1 + (4 \times 16.0) = 120.4$ g mol^{-1} |
| Number of moles (in 1.567 g): | mass ÷ molar mass = 1.567 g ÷ 120.4 g mol^{-1} = **0.01301 moles** |

Now you work out the ratio of moles of anhydrous salt to moles of water in the form 1:n.

| From the experiment, | **0.01301 moles of salt : 0.09127 moles of water,** |
| So, | 1 mole of salt : $\frac{0.09127}{0.01301} = 7.015$ moles of water. |

> You might be given the percentage of the mass that is water — use the method on page 22.

X must be a whole number, and some errors are to be expected in any experiment, so you can safely round off your result — so the formula of the hydrated salt is $MgSO_4.7H_2O$.

Practice Questions

Q1 What charge do the ions formed by Group 7 elements have?

Q2 What is the formula for the hydroxide ion?

Q3 Why can water molecules become fixed in an ionic lattice?

Exam Questions

Q1 What is the formula of scandium sulfate, given that the scandium ion has a charge of +3? [1 mark]

Q2 Use the periodic table to work out the formula of sodium oxide. [1 mark]

Q3 A sample of hydrated calcium sulfate, $CaSO_4.XH_2O$, was prepared by reacting calcium hydroxide with sulfuric acid. 1.883 g of hydrated salt was produced. This was then heated until all the water of crystallisation was driven off and the product was then reweighed. Its mass was 1.133 g.

a) How many moles of anhydrous calcium sulfate were produced? [2 marks]

b) Calculate the value of X in the formula $CaSO_4.XH_2O$. (X is a whole number.) [3 marks]

Ioning — every scientist's favourite household chore...

I prefer dusting personally. But even if you're a fan of vacuuming or sweeping, make sure you take the time to learn the rules for working out the charges on different ions. The periodic table is great for working out the charges of the ions of elements in groups 1, 2, 6 and 7, but the best way to remember the charges on molecular ions is to just learn them.

MODULE 2 : SECTION 1 — ATOMS AND REACTIONS

Acids and Bases

Acid's a word that's thrown around willy-nilly — but now for the truth...

Acids are all about Hydrated Protons

1) Acids are **proton donors**. When mixed with **water**, all acids **release hydrogen ions** — H^+ (these are just **protons**, but you never get them by themselves in water — they're always combined with H_2O to form hydroxonium ions, H_3O^+).

2) **Bases** do the opposite — they're proton acceptors and want to **grab H^+ ions**.

3) Bases that are soluble in water are known as **alkalis**. They release OH^- ions in solution.

> **Acids** produce $H^+_{(aq)}$ ions in an aqueous solution.
> **Alkalis** produce $OH^-_{(aq)}$ ions in an aqueous solution.

You'll need to learn the formulae and names of these acids and bases.

4) Some common acids are: **HCl** (hydrochloric acid), **H_2SO_4** (sulfuric acid), **HNO_3** (nitric acid) and **CH_3COOH** (ethanoic acid).

5) And some common bases are: **NaOH** (sodium hydroxide), **KOH** (potassium hydroxide) and **NH_3** (ammonia).

Acids and Bases Can Be Strong or Weak

1) The reaction between acids and water, and bases and water is **reversible**, so at any one point in time, both the forwards and backwards reactions will be happening.

> Acids: $HA + H_2O \rightleftharpoons H_3O^+ + A^-$

> Bases: $B + H_2O \rightleftharpoons BH^+ + OH^-$

These are really reversible reactions, but the equilibrium lies extremely far to the right.

2) For **strong acids**, e.g. HCl, very little of the reverse reaction happens, so nearly all the acid will dissociate (or ionise) in water, and **nearly all** the H^+ ions are released.

$$HCl_{(aq)} \rightarrow H^+_{(aq)} + Cl^-_{(aq)}$$

3) The same thing applies with **strong bases**, e.g. NaOH. Again, the forwards reaction is favoured, so nearly all the base dissociate in water and **lots** of OH^- ions are released.

$$NaOH_{(aq)} \rightarrow Na^+_{(aq)} + OH^-_{(aq)}$$

4) For **weak acids**, e.g. CH_3COOH, the backwards reaction is favoured, so only a small amount of the acid will dissociate in water and **only a few** H^+ ions are released.

$$CH_3COOH_{(aq)} \rightleftharpoons CH_3COO^-_{(aq)} + H^+_{(aq)}$$

5) Again, **weak bases**, such as NH_3, ionise only slightly in water. The backwards reaction is favoured so only a small amount of the base dissociates and **only a few** OH^- ions are released.

$$NH_{3(aq)} + H_2O_{(l)} \rightleftharpoons NH_4^+_{(aq)} + OH^-_{(aq)}$$

Acids React to Form Neutral Salts

Acids and **bases neutralise** each other. In the **neutralisation** reaction between acids and alkalis, a **salt** and **water** are produced.

1) It's the hydrogen ions released by the acid and the hydroxide ions released by the alkali that combine to form water.

$$H^+_{(aq)} + OH^-_{(aq)} \rightleftharpoons H_2O_{(l)}$$

2) You get a **salt** when the hydrogen ions in the acid are replaced by **metal ions** or **ammonium (NH_4^+) ions** from the alkali.

$$E.g. \ HCl_{(aq)} + KOH_{(aq)} \rightarrow KCl_{(aq)} + H_2O_{(l)}$$

3) Different acids produce **different salts** — sulfuric acid (H_2SO_4) produces salts called **sulfates**, hydrochloric acid (HCl) produces **chlorides**, and nitric acid (HNO_3) produces **nitrates**.

Ammonia is a bit of an exception as it doesn't directly produce hydroxide ions, but **aqueous ammonia** is still an **alkali**. This is because the reaction between ammonia and water produces hydroxide ions. Ammonia accepts a hydrogen ion from water molecules, forming an ammonium ion and a hydroxide ion. In this way, ammonia can **neutralise acids**.

$$NH_{3(aq)} + H_2O_{(l)} \rightleftharpoons NH_4^+_{(aq)} + OH^-_{(aq)}$$

Acids and Bases

Acids React with **Metals** and **Metal Compounds**

1) As you've seen, when **acids** react with **bases**, they **neutralise** each other and produce a **salt**.

2) **Metal oxides**, **metal hydroxides** and **metal carbonates** are all common bases that'll react with acids. **Metals** will also react with acids.

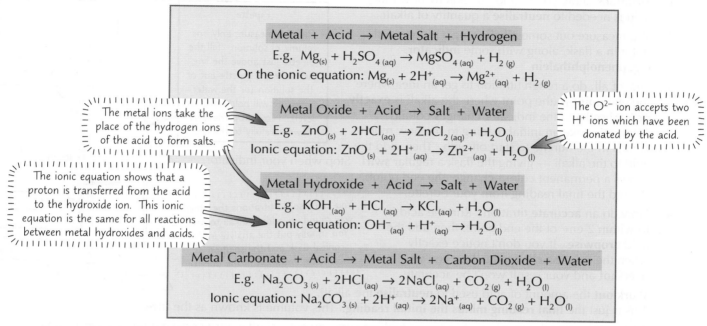

The metal ions take the place of the hydrogen ions of the acid to form salts.

The ionic equation shows that a proton is transferred from the acid to the hydroxide ion. This ionic equation is the same for all reactions between metal hydroxides and acids.

The O^{2-} ion accepts two H^+ ions which have been donated by the acid.

Metal + Acid → Metal Salt + Hydrogen
E.g. $Mg_{(s)} + H_2SO_{4 (aq)} \rightarrow MgSO_{4 (aq)} + H_{2 (g)}$
Or the ionic equation: $Mg_{(s)} + 2H^+_{(aq)} \rightarrow Mg^{2+}_{(aq)} + H_{2 (g)}$

Metal Oxide + Acid → Salt + Water
E.g. $ZnO_{(s)} + 2HCl_{(aq)} \rightarrow ZnCl_{2 (aq)} + H_2O_{(l)}$
Ionic equation: $ZnO_{(s)} + 2H^+_{(aq)} \rightarrow Zn^{2+}_{(aq)} + H_2O_{(l)}$

Metal Hydroxide + Acid → Salt + Water
E.g. $KOH_{(aq)} + HCl_{(aq)} \rightarrow KCl_{(aq)} + H_2O_{(l)}$
Ionic equation: $OH^-_{(aq)} + H^+_{(aq)} \rightarrow H_2O_{(l)}$

Metal Carbonate + Acid → Metal Salt + Carbon Dioxide + Water
E.g. $Na_2CO_{3 (s)} + 2HCl_{(aq)} \rightarrow 2NaCl_{(aq)} + CO_{2 (g)} + H_2O_{(l)}$
Ionic equation: $Na_2CO_{3 (s)} + 2H^+_{(aq)} \rightarrow 2Na^+_{(aq)} + CO_{2 (g)} + H_2O_{(l)}$

Ammonia reacts with **Acids** to make **Ammonia Salts**

The reaction of ammonia with nitric acid produces ammonium nitrate. Ammonium sulfate is made if ammonia reacts with sulfuric acid.

Ammonia + Acid → Ammonium salt
E.g. $NH_{3 (aq)} + HNO_{3 (aq)} \rightarrow NH_4NO_{3 (aq)}$
Ionic equation: $NH_{3 (aq)} + H^+_{(aq)} \rightarrow NH_4^+_{(aq)}$

This reaction is actually:
$NH_4^+ + OH^- + HNO_3 \rightarrow NH_4NO_3 + H_2O$
as the reactant is aqueous ammonia.

Practice Questions

Q1 Define an acid, a base and an alkali.
Q2 Name three common acids.
Q3 What products are formed when an acid and an alkali react?

Exam Questions

Q1 A solution of magnesium chloride can be made in the laboratory using dilute hydrochloric acid.

    a) Name a compound that could be used, with hydrochloric acid, to make magnesium chloride. [1 mark]

    b) Write a balanced equation for this reaction. [1 mark]

Q2 Sodium hydroxide reacts with nitric acid at room temperature to produce water and a soluble salt.

    a) Write a balanced equation, including state symbols for this reaction. [1 mark]

    b) What is the name given to this type of reaction? [1 mark]

It's a stick-up — your protons or your life...

All acids have protons to give away and bases just love to take them. It's what makes them acids and bases. It's like how bus drivers drive buses... it's what makes them bus drivers. Learn the formulae for the common acids — hydrochloric, sulfuric, nitric and ethanoic, and the common alkalis — sodium hydroxide, potassium hydroxide and aqueous ammonia.

Titrations

Titrations are used to find out the concentrations of acid or alkali solutions. They're a bit fiddly to set up, but all titrations are kind of similar, so once you can do one, you can pretty much do them all.

Titrations Let You Work Out **Neutralisation Quantities**

1) **Titrations** allow you to find out **exactly** how much acid is needed to **neutralise** a quantity of alkali.

2) You measure out some **alkali** using a pipette and put it in a flask, along with some **indicator**, e.g. **phenolphthalein**.

3) First of all, do a rough titration to get an idea where the **end point** is (the point where the alkali is **exactly neutralised** and the indicator changes colour). To do this, take an initial reading to see how much acid is in the burette to start off with. Then, add the **acid** to the alkali — giving the flask a regular **swirl**. Stop when your indicator shows a permanent colour change (the end point). Record the final reading from your burette.

4) Now do an **accurate** titration. Run the acid in to within 2 cm³ of the end point, then add the acid **dropwise**. If you don't notice exactly when the solution changed colour you've **overshot** and your result won't be accurate

5) **Work out** the amount of acid used to **neutralise** the alkali. This is just the **final reading minus the initial reading**. This volume is known as the **titre**.

6) It's best to **repeat** the titration a few times, making sure you get a similar answer each time — your readings should be within 0.1 cm³ of each other. Then calculate a **mean**, ignoring any anomalous results. Remember to wash out the conical flask between each titration to remove any acid or alkali left in it.

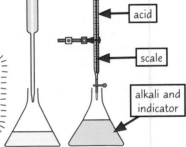

Pipette
Pipettes measure only one volume of solution. Fill the pipette just above the line, then take the pipette out of the solution (or the water pressure will hold up the level). Now drop the level down carefully to the line.

Burette
Burettes measure different volumes and let you add the solution drop by drop.

acid

scale

alkali and indicator

You can also do titrations the other way round — adding alkali to acid. You usually put the analyte in the conical flask and the solution of known concentration in the burette.

Titrations need to be done **Accurately**

1) When doing a titration, it's really important that you take your readings accurately.

2) When taking a reading from a burette, you should read from the bottom of the **meniscus**.

3) You don't have to read to the smallest graduation, e.g. 0.1 cm³. You can make your readings **more accurate** by taking readings to the nearest 0.05 cm³.

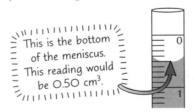

This is the bottom of the meniscus. This reading would be 0.50 cm³.

This reading is half way between two graduation marks. This reading would be 0.65 cm³.

Indicators Show you when the Reaction's **Just Finished**

Indicators change **colour**, as if by magic. In titrations, indicators that change colour quickly over a **very small pH range** are used so you know **exactly** when the reaction has ended.

The main two indicators for **acid/alkali reactions** are —

> **methyl orange** — turns **yellow** to **red** when adding acid to alkali.
> **phenolphthalein** — turns **pink** to **colourless** when adding acid to alkali.

When you're doing a titration where the end point is marked by a colour change, it's a good idea to carry out your titration on a white tile, or a sheet of white paper. That way, it's much easier to see exactly when the end point is.

Universal indicator is no good here — its colour change is too gradual.

Choppy seas made it difficult for Captain Blackbird to read the burette accurately.

Titrations

Titrations are done with Standard Solutions

1) In a titration, you have **one unknown concentration** to work out. To work out the concentration of the unknown solution, known as the **analyte**, you have to know the concentration of the solution you're titrating it against.

2) A solution that has a precisely known concentration is called a **standard solution**. Standard solutions are made by dissolving a **known amount** of **solid** in a known amount of **water** to create a known concentration.

3) To make up a standard solution, follow these steps:

> 1) Using a **precise** balance, carefully weigh out the required mass of solid onto a watch glass.
>
> 2) Transfer this solid to a beaker. Use some water to **wash** any bits of solid from the watch glass into the beaker.
>
> 3) Add water to the beaker to **completely dissolve** the solid. Use a glass rod to **stir** the solution to help the solid dissolve.
>
> *When making up standard solutions, you should use distilled water. This is just pure water with nothing else in it.*
>
> 4) Once the solid has dissolved, transfer the solution into a **volumetric flask**. You'll need to use a volumetric flask that's the same size as the volume of solution you want to make up. **Rinse** the beaker and glass rod with water, transferring this water into the volumetric flask.
>
> 5) Use water to fill the volumetric flask up to the **graduation line**. Use a **pipette** to add the final few drops to make sure you don't add too much water and overshoot the graduation line.
>
> 6) Put the lid on the flask and turn the flask over a few times to thoroughly **mix** the solution.

In a Solution the Concentration is Measured in mol dm⁻³

1) The **concentration** of a solution is how many **moles** are dissolved per **1 dm³** of solution. Units are **mol dm⁻³**.

2) Here's the formula to find the **number of moles**, (**n**).

$$\text{Number of moles} = \frac{\text{Concentration} \times \text{volume (in cm}^3)}{1000}$$ or $$\text{Number of moles} = \text{Concentration} \times \text{Volume (in dm}^3)$$

1 dm³ = 1000 cm³ = 1 litre

3) To make a standard solution, you often have to calculate the mass of solid you'll need from a given volume and concentration.

> **Example:** What mass of solid sodium carbonate, Na_2CO_3, is needed to make 250 cm³ of 0.300 mol dm⁻³ sodium carbonate solution?
>
> Start by working out how many **moles** of Na_2CO_3 are needed using the equation:
>
> moles = concentration × volume $\implies$ $n = 0.300 \times \left(\frac{250}{1000}\right) = 0.0750$ moles
>
> Use mass = moles × M to work out the mass of Na_2CO_3 required.
>
> mass = $0.0750 \times [(2 \times 23.0) + 12.0 + (3 \times 16.0)] = 0.0750 \times 106 = $ **7.95 g**

Make sure all your values are in the correct units — here, the concentration is given in mol dm⁻³ so you need to convert the volume to dm³.

Practice Questions

Q1 Describe the procedure for doing a titration.

Q2 What colour change would you expect to see if you added an excess of hydrochloric acid to a conical flask containing sodium hydroxide and methyl orange?

Exam Questions

Q1 What mass of solid sodium hydrogen sulfate ($NaHSO_4$) would be required to make up 250 cm³ of a standard solution of sodium hydrogen sulfate of concentration 0.600 mol dm⁻³? [2 marks]

Q2* Describe how indicators are used and explain the importance of selecting an appropriate indicator when carrying out a titration. Include examples of indicators that would and would not be suitable for use in titrations. [6 marks]

Burettes and pipettes — big glass things, just waiting to be dropped...

Titrations are all about being accurate and precise. Make sure you're really careful when measuring out solutions, and reading values off your burette. An error in your experiment means you'll have errors all through your calculations.

* The quality of your extended response will be assessed for this question.

Titration Calculations

There's far more to a titration than just simply doing it.
Once you've got all those readings, there's a whole load of calculations to carry out. You've been warned...

You can Calculate **Concentrations** from Titrations

Example: 25.0 cm³ of 0.500 mol dm⁻³ HCl was used to neutralise 35.0 cm³ of NaOH solution. Calculate the concentration of the sodium hydroxide solution in mol dm⁻³.

First write a **balanced equation** and decide **what you know** and what you **need to know**:

$$HCl \quad + \quad NaOH \rightarrow NaCl + H_2O$$
$$25.0 \text{ cm}^3 \qquad 35.0 \text{ cm}^3$$
$$0.500 \text{ mol dm}^{-3} \qquad ?$$

Now work out how many **moles of HCl** you have. You'll need to use the equation linking no. moles, concentration and volume — have a look back at the last page if you can't remember it.

No. of moles of HCl $= \dfrac{\text{concentration} \times \text{volume (cm}^3)}{1000} = \dfrac{0.500 \times 25.0}{1000} = 0.0125$ moles

You need to be able to work out concentration in g dm⁻³ too. To do this, just convert moles into mass and use:
$$Conc = \dfrac{\text{mass (g)} \times 1000}{\text{volume (cm}^3)}$$

From the equation, you know 1 mole of HCl neutralises 1 mole of NaOH.
So 0.0125 moles of HCl must neutralise **0.0125** moles of NaOH.
Now it's a doddle to work out the **concentration of NaOH**.

Concentration of NaOH $= \dfrac{\text{moles of NaOH} \times 1000}{\text{volume (cm}^3)} = \dfrac{0.0125 \times 1000}{35.0} = \textbf{0.36 mol dm}^{-3}$

You have to account for **Reaction Stoichiometry**

1) A balanced equation will tell you the **reaction stoichiometry** — this is how many moles of one reactant react with how many moles of another reactant.

2) In titration calculations, you have to use the **balanced equation** when working out **concentrations**, as the stoichiometry of a reaction affects the ratios between each of the reactants and products in your reaction.

I'll show them who's unbalanced...

Example: This equation shows the reaction between sodium hydroxide and sulfuric acid:
$$2NaOH + H_2SO_4 \rightarrow Na_2SO_4 + 2H_2O$$
Given that it takes 19.1 cm³ of 0.200 mol dm⁻³ NaOH to completely neutralise 25.0 cm³ of the acid, calculate the concentration of the sulfuric acid.

First, work out the number of moles of NaOH in 19.1 cm³ of 0.200 mol dm⁻³ NaOH solution.

$$\text{moles} = \text{concentration} \times \text{volume (dm}^3)$$

$$n = 0.200 \times (19.1 \div 1000) = 0.00382 \text{ moles}$$

This reaction doesn't happen as a 1:1 molar reaction, but happens in a **2:1 ratio** of NaOH:H₂SO₄. For every 2 moles of NaOH, you only require 1 mole of H₂SO₄ for the reaction to happen. So, you have half the number of moles of H₂SO₄ as you have NaOH.

$$\text{moles } H_2SO_4 = \text{moles of NaOH} \div 2$$

$$= 0.00382 \div 2 = 0.00191 \text{ moles}$$

So, concentration of H₂SO₄ $= \dfrac{\text{moles of } H_2SO_4 \times 1000}{\text{volume (cm}^3)} = \dfrac{0.00191 \times 1000}{25.0} = \textbf{0.0764 mol dm}^{-3}$

Titration Calculations

Polyprotic Acids donate More than One Proton

You may have to do calculations that involve acids that donate **more** than **one proton**. These are known as **polyprotic acids**.

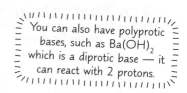

You can also have polyprotic bases, such as $Ba(OH)_2$, which is a diprotic base — it can react with 2 protons.

- Diprotic acids donate two protons, e.g. sulfuric acid (H_2SO_4), carbonic acid (H_2CO_3) and hydrogen sulfide (H_2S).
- Triprotic acids donate three protons, e.g. phosphoric acid (H_3PO_4).

Compared to a monoprotic acid, you'll need **double** the number of moles of base to neutralise a **diprotic acid**. You'll need to **triple** the number of moles of base to neutralise a **triprotic acid** compared to a monoprotic acid. So, remember to take this into account when you're working out these sorts of titration calculations.

You can Calculate Volumes for Reactions from Moles and Concentrations

Example: 20.4 cm^3 of a 0.500 mol dm^{-3} solution of sodium carbonate reacts with 1.50 mol dm^{-3} nitric acid. Calculate the volume of nitric acid required to neutralise the sodium carbonate.

First write a **balanced equation** for the reaction and decide **what you know** and what you **want to know**:

$$Na_2CO_3 \quad + \quad 2HNO_3 \rightarrow 2NaNO_3 + H_2O + CO_2$$
$$20.4 \ cm^3 \qquad\qquad ?$$
$$0.500 \ mol \ dm^{-3} \quad 1.50 \ mol \ dm^{-3}$$

Calculating volumes for reactions is useful when you're planning quantities to use in titration experiments.

Now work out how many **moles** of Na_2CO_3 you've got:

$$\text{No. of moles of } Na_2CO_3 = \frac{\text{concentration} \times \text{volume } (cm^3)}{1000} = \frac{0.500 \times 20.4}{1000} = 0.0102 \text{ moles}$$

The reaction happens in a 1:2 molar ratio of $Na_2CO_3 : HNO_3$.
1 mole of Na_2CO_3 neutralises 2 moles of HNO_3, so 0.0102 moles of Na_2CO_3 neutralises **0.0204 moles of HNO_3**.
Now you know the number of moles of HNO_3 and the concentration, you can work out the **volume**:

$$\text{Volume of } HNO_3 \ (cm^3) = \frac{\text{number of moles} \times 1000}{\text{concentration}} = \frac{0.0204 \times 1000}{1.50} = \textbf{13.6 } cm^3$$

Practice Questions

Q1 What equation links the number of moles, concentration and volume (in cm^3)?

Exam Questions

Q1 Calculate the concentration (in mol dm^{-3}) of a solution of ethanoic acid, CH_3COOH, if 25.4 cm^3 of it is neutralised by 14.6 cm^3 of 0.500 mol dm^{-3} sodium hydroxide solution.

$CH_3COOH + NaOH \rightarrow CH_3COONa + H_2O$ [3 marks]

Q2 You are supplied with 0.750 g of calcium carbonate and a solution of 0.250 mol dm^{-3} sulfuric acid. What volume of acid will be needed to neutralise the calcium carbonate?

$CaCO_3 + H_2SO_4 \rightarrow CaSO_4 + H_2O + CO_2$ [3 marks]

Q3 In a titration, 17.1 cm^3 of 0.250 mol dm^{-3} hydrochloric acid neutralises 25.0 cm^3 calcium hydroxide solution.

a) Write out a balanced equation for this reaction. [1 mark]

b) Work out the concentration of the calcium hydroxide solution. [3 marks]

DJs can't do titrations — they just keep on dropping the base...

This looks like a horrible load of calculations, but it's really not that bad. Just remember the equation linking concentration, volume (in cm^3 and dm^3) and moles and you'll be able to work out pretty much everything.

Atom Economy and Percentage Yield

How to make a subject like chemistry even more exciting — introduce the word 'economy'...

The **Theoretical Yield** of a Product is the **Maximum** you could get

1) The **theoretical yield** is the **mass of product** that **should** be made in a reaction if **no** chemicals are 'lost' in the process. You can use the **masses of reactants** and a **balanced equation** to calculate the theoretical yield for a reaction.

2) The **actual** mass of product (the **actual yield**) is always **less** than the theoretical yield. Some chemicals are always 'lost', e.g. some solution gets left on filter paper, or is lost during transfers between containers.

3) The **percentage yield** is the **actual** amount of product you collect, written as a percentage of the theoretical yield. You can work out the percentage yield with this formula:

$$\text{percentage yield} = \frac{\text{actual yield}}{\text{theoretical yield}} \times 100\%$$

Example: Ethanol can be oxidised to form ethanal: $C_2H_5OH + [O] \rightarrow CH_3CHO + H_2O$
9.2 g of ethanol was reacted with an oxidising agent in excess and 2.1 g of ethanal was produced. Calculate the theoretical yield and the percentage yield.

[O] is just the symbol for any oxidising agent.

Number of moles = mass of substance ÷ molar mass

Moles of C_2H_5OH = $9.2 \div [(2 \times 12.0) + (5 \times 1.0) + 16.0 + 1.0] = 9.2 \div 46.0 = 0.2$ moles

1 mole of C_2H_5OH produces 1 mole of CH_3CHO, so 0.2 moles of C_2H_5OH will produce 0.2 moles of CH_3CHO.

M of CH_3CHO = $(2 \times 12.0) + (4 \times 1.0) + 16.0 = 44.0$ g mol^{-1}

Theoretical yield (mass of CH_3CHO) = number of moles × M = $0.2 \times 44.0 = \textbf{8.8 g}$

So, if the actual yield was 2.1 g, the percentage yield = $\frac{\text{actual yield}}{\text{theoretical yield}} \times 100\% = \frac{2.1}{8.8} \times 100\% \approx \textbf{24\%}$

Atom Economy is a Measure of the **Efficiency** of a Reaction

1) The **percentage yield** tells you how wasteful the **process** is — it's based on how much of the product is lost because of things like reactions not completing or losses during collection and purification.

2) But percentage yield doesn't measure how wasteful the **reaction** itself is. A reaction that has a 100% yield could still be very wasteful if a lot of the atoms from the **reactants** wind up in **by-products** rather than the **desired product**.

3) **Atom economy** is a measure of the proportion of reactant **atoms** that become part of the desired product (rather than by-products) in the **balanced** chemical equation. It's calculated using this formula:

$$\% \text{ atom economy} = \frac{\text{molecular mass of desired product}}{\text{sum of molecular masses of all products}} \times 100\%$$

4) In an **addition reaction**, the reactants **combine** to form a **single product**. The atom economy for addition reactions is **always 100%** since no atoms are wasted.

E.g. ethene (C_2H_4) and hydrogen react to form ethane (C_2H_6) in an addition reaction: $C_2H_4 + H_2 \rightarrow C_2H_6$
The **only product** is ethane (the desired product). No reactant atoms are wasted so the atom economy is **100%**.

5) A **substitution reaction** is one where some atoms from one reactant are **swapped** with atoms from another reactant. This type of reaction **always** results in **at least two products** — the desired product and at least one by-product.

An example is the reaction of bromomethane (CH_3Br) with sodium hydroxide (NaOH) to make methanol (CH_3OH): $CH_3Br + NaOH \rightarrow CH_3OH + NaBr$
This is **more wasteful** than an addition reaction because the Na and Br atoms aren't part of the desired product.

Always make sure you're using a balanced equation.

$$\% \text{ atom economy} = \frac{\text{molecular mass of desired product}}{\text{sum of molecular masses of all products}} \times 100\%$$

$$= \frac{M_r(CH_3OH)}{M_r(CH_3OH) + M_r(NaBr)} \times 100\%$$

$$= \frac{(12.0 + (3 \times 1.0) + 16.0 + 1.0)}{(12.0 + (3 \times 1.0) + 16.0 + 1.0) + (23.0 + 79.9)} \times 100\% = \frac{32.0}{32.0 + 102.9} \times 100\% = \textbf{23.7\%}$$

Atom Economy and Percentage Yield

Reactions can Have High Percentage Yields and Low Atom Economies

Example: 0.475 g of CH_3Br reacts with an excess of NaOH in this reaction: $CH_3Br + NaOH \rightarrow CH_3OH + NaBr$
0.153 g of CH_3OH is produced. What is the percentage yield?

Number of moles = mass of substance ÷ molar mass

Moles of CH_3Br = 0.475 ÷ (12 + (3 × 1) + 79.9) = 0.475 ÷ 94.9 = **0.00501 moles**

The reactant:product ratio is 1:1, so the maximum number of moles of CH_3OH is **0.00501**.

Theoretical yield = 0.00501 × $M(CH_3OH)$ = 0.00501 × (12.0 + (3 × 1.0) + 16.0 + 1.0) = 0.00501 × 32 = **0.160 g**

$$\text{percentage yield} = \frac{\text{actual yield}}{\text{theoretical yield}} \times 100\% = \frac{0.153}{0.160} \times 100\% = \mathbf{95.6\%}$$

So this reaction has a very high percentage yield but, as you saw on the previous page, the atom economy is low.

It's Important to Develop Reactions that are Sustainable

1) Companies in the chemical industry will often choose to use reactions with high atom economies. High atom economy has **environmental** and **economic benefits**.

2) A **low atom economy** means there's lots of **waste** produced. It costs money to **separate** the desired product from the waste products and more money to dispose of the waste products **safely** so they don't harm the environment.

3) **Reactant chemicals** are usually costly. It's a **waste of money** if a high proportion of them end up as useless products.

4) Reactions with low atom economies are **less sustainable**. Many raw materials are in **limited supply**, so it makes sense to use them efficiently so they last as long as possible. Also, waste has to go somewhere — it's better for the environment if less is produced.

5) Reactions conditions with **high energy demands**, e.g. **high temperatures** and **high pressures**, cost a lot to maintain. **Lower temperatures** and **pressures** are cheaper to run and better for the environment.

6) Raw materials that come from **renewable sources**, e.g. plants, enzymes, are better for the environment than materials from **non-renewable sources**, e.g. crude oil, coal.

Fermentation is an example of a sustainable reaction.

Practice Questions

Q1 How many products are there in an addition reaction?

Q2 Why do reactions with high atom economy save chemical companies money and cause less environmental impact?

Exam Questions

Q1 Reactions 1 and 2 below show two possible ways of preparing the compound chloroethane (C_2H_5Cl):

1    $C_2H_5OH + PCl_5 \rightarrow C_2H_5Cl + POCl_3 + HCl$
2    $C_2H_4 + HCl \rightarrow C_2H_5Cl$

a) Which of these is an addition reaction? [1 mark]

b) Calculate the atom economy for reaction 1. [2 marks]

c) Reaction 2 has an atom economy of 100%. Explain why this is, in terms of the products of the reaction. [1 mark]

Q2 Phosphorus trichloride (PCl_3) reacts with chlorine to give phosphorus pentachloride (PCl_5):

$PCl_3 + Cl_2 \rightarrow PCl_5$

a) 0.275 g of PCl_3 reacts with an excess of chlorine. What is the theoretical yield of PCl_5? [2 marks]

b) When this reaction is performed 0.198 g of PCl_5 is collected. Calculate the percentage yield. [1 mark]

c) Changing conditions such as temperature and pressure will alter the percentage yield of this reaction. Will changing these conditions affect the atom economy? Explain your answer. [2 marks]

I knew a Tommy Conomy once... strange bloke...

These pages shouldn't be too much trouble — you've survived worse already. Make sure that you get plenty of practice using the percentage yield and atom economy formulae. And whatever you do, don't get mixed up between percentage yield (which is to do with the process) and atom economy (which is to do with the reaction).

Oxidation Numbers

This double page has more occurrences of "oxidation" than the Beatles' "All You Need is Love" features the word "love".

Oxidation Numbers *Tell you how Many* **Electrons Atoms** *have*

When atoms **react** or **bond** to other atoms, they can **lose** or **gain** electrons. The **oxidation number** tells you how many electrons an atom has donated or accepted to form an **ion**, or to form part of a **compound**. There are certain rules you need to remember to help you assign oxidation numbers. Here they are...

1) All uncombined elements have an oxidation number of **0**. This means they haven't accepted or donated any electrons. Elements that are bonded to identical atoms will also have an oxidation number of **0**.

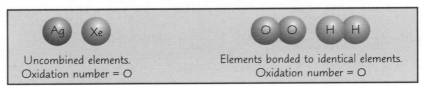

Uncombined elements. Oxidation number = O

Elements bonded to identical elements. Oxidation number = O

2) The oxidation number of a simple, monatomic ion (that's an ion consisting of just one atom) is the same as its **charge**.

Oxidation number = +1   Oxidation number = +2

3) For **molecular ions** (see page 26), the sum of the oxidation numbers is the same as the overall charge of the ion. Each of the constituent atoms will have an oxidation number of its own, and the **sum** of their oxidation numbers equals the **overall oxidation number**.

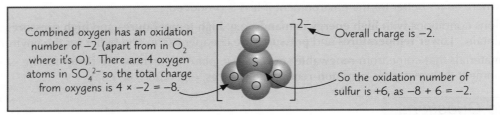

Combined oxygen has an oxidation number of –2 (apart from in O_2 where it's O). There are 4 oxygen atoms in SO_4^{2-} so the total charge from oxygens is $4 \times -2 = -8$.

Overall charge is –2.

So the oxidation number of sulfur is +6, as $-8 + 6 = -2$.

4) For a neutral compound, the overall oxidation number is **0**. If the compound is made up of more than one element, each element will have its own oxidation number.

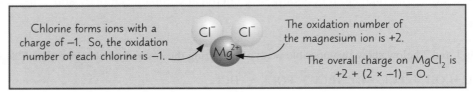

Chlorine forms ions with a charge of –1. So, the oxidation number of each chlorine is –1.

The oxidation number of the magnesium ion is +2.

The overall charge on $MgCl_2$ is $+2 + (2 \times -1) = O$.

5) You'll need to **learn** these oxidation numbers.

- **Oxygen** nearly always has an oxidation number of **–2**, except in **peroxides** (O_2^{2-}) where it's **–1**, and **molecular oxygen** (O_2) where it's **0**.
- **Hydrogen** always has an oxidation number of **+1**, except in **metal hydrides** (MH_x, where M = metal) where it's **–1** and in **molecular hydrogen** (H_2) where it's **0**.

Roman Numerals *tell you the* **Oxidation Number**

If an element can have **multiple** oxidation numbers, or **isn't** in its 'normal' oxidation state, its oxidation number can be shown by using **Roman numerals**, e.g. (I) = +1, (II) = +2, (III) = +3 and so on. The Roman numerals are written after the name of the element they correspond to.

E.g.   In iron(II) sulfate, iron has an oxidation number of +2. Formula = $FeSO_4$

In iron(III) sulfate, iron has an oxidation number of +3. Formula = $Fe_2(SO_4)_3$

Hands up if you like Roman numerals...

Oxidation Numbers

-ate Compounds Contain Oxygen and Another Element

1) Ions with names ending in -ate (e.g. sulfate, nitrate, chlorate, carbonate) contain **oxygen** and another element. For example, sulfates contain sulfur and oxygen, nitrates contain nitrogen and oxygen... and so on.

2) Sometimes the 'other' element in the ion can exist with different oxidation numbers, and so form different '-ate ions'. In these cases, the oxidation number is attached as a Roman numeral **after** the name of the -ate compound.
   The roman numerals correspond to the **non-oxygen** element in the -ate compound.

   E.g. In sulfate(VI) ions, the **sulfur** has oxidation number **+6** — this is the SO_4^{2-} ion.
   In sulfate(IV) ions, the **sulfur** has oxidation number **+4** — this is the SO_3^{2-} ion.
   In nitrate(III), **nitrogen** has an oxidation number of **+3** — this is the NO_2^- ion.

If there are no oxidation numbers shown, assume nitrate = NO_3^- and sulfate = SO_4^{2-}.

You Can Work Out Oxidation Numbers from Formulae or Systematic Names

You might need to **work out** the oxidation numbers of different elements in a compound from its **formula** or **systematic name**. You'll also need to be able to work out the formulae of compounds from their systematic names and visa versa.

Example: What is the formula of iron(III) sulfate?

From the systematic name, you can tell iron has an **oxidation number** of +3.
The formula of the sulfate ion is SO_4^{2-} and it has an **overall charge** of –2.
The overall charge of the compound is 0, so you need to find a ratio of $Fe^{3+} : SO_4^{2-}$ that will make the overall charge 0.

$$(+3 \times 2) + (-2 \times 3) = 6 + -6 = 0$$ The ratio of $Fe : SO_4$ is **2 : 3**.
So the formula is **$Fe_2(SO_4)_3$**.

Example: What is the systematic name for ClO_2^-?

This formula contains **chlorine** and **oxygen**, so it's a **chlorate**.
Oxygen usually exists with an oxidation number of **–2**.
There are 2 oxygens, so this will make the total charge from oxygens $-2 \times 2 = -4$.
The overall charge on the molecule is –1, so chlorine must have an oxidation number of **+3**, since $-4 + 3 = -1$. So, the systematic name is **chlorate(III)**.

Practice Questions

Q1 What is the oxidation number of H in H_2?
Q2 What is the usual oxidation number for oxygen when it's combined with another element?
Q3 What is the oxidation number of sulfur in a sulfate(IV) ion?

Exam Questions

Q1 What is the systematic name of $Cr_2(SO_4)_3$? [1 mark]

Q2 What is the formula of iron(II) nitrate? [1 mark]

Q3 Lead sulfate can be formed by reacting lead oxide (PbO) with warm sulfuric acid in a ratio of 1:1.

   a) What is the formula of lead sulfate? [1 mark]

   b) Calculate the oxidation number of lead in:
      i) lead oxide   ii) lead sulfate   [2 marks]

Sockidation number — a measure of how many odd socks are in my drawers...

There isn't any tricky maths involved with oxidation numbers, just a bit of adding, some subtracting... maybe a bit of multiplying if you're unlucky. The real trick is to learn the rules about predicting oxidation numbers for those elements and molecular ions that come up all the time, especially the ones for those pesky metal hydrides and peroxides.

Redox Reactions

Redox reactions can be tricky to get your head around at first. It will help you loads if you're confident about all the oxidation number stuff on the last two pages before you start tackling this.

If Electrons are Transferred, it's a **Redox Reaction**

1) A **loss** of electrons is called **oxidation**. A **gain** in electrons is called **reduction**.

2) Reduction and oxidation happen **simultaneously**
   — hence the term "**redox**" reaction.

3) An **oxidising agent accepts** electrons and gets reduced.

4) A **reducing agent donates** electrons and gets oxidised.

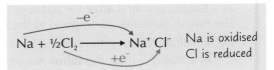

$$Na + \tfrac{1}{2}Cl_2 \xrightarrow{\;-e^-\;} Na^+ Cl^- \qquad +e^-$$

Na is oxidised
Cl is reduced

Oxidation Numbers go *Up* or *Down* as Electrons are *Lost* or *Gained*

1) The oxidation number for an atom will **increase by 1** for each **electron lost**.

2) The oxidation number will **decrease by 1** for each **electron gained**.

3) To work out whether something has been **oxidised** or **reduced**, you need to assign each element an oxidation number **before** the reaction, and **after** the reaction.

4) If the oxidation number has increased, then the element has **lost** electrons and been **oxidised**.

5) If the oxidation number has decreased, then the element has **gained** electrons and been **reduced**.

> Check back at the rules for assigning oxidation numbers on page 36 if you're unsure about this.

Example: Identify the oxidising and reducing agents in this reaction: $4Fe + 3O_2 \rightarrow 2Fe_2O_3$

Iron has gone from having an oxidation number of 0, to an oxidation number of +3.
It's **lost electrons** and has been **oxidised**. This makes it the **reducing agent** in this reaction.

Oxygen has gone from having an oxidation number of 0, to an oxidation number of –2.
It's **gained electrons** and has been **reduced**. This means it's the **oxidising agent** in this reaction.

Example: Identify the oxidising and reducing agents in this reaction: $2Na + Cl_2 \rightarrow 2NaCl$

Sodium has gone from having an oxidation number of 0, to an oxidation number of +1.
It's **lost an electron** and has been **oxidised**, so it's a **reducing agent**.

Chlorine has gone from having an oxidation number of 0, to an
oxidation number of –1. It's **gained an electron** and has been **reduced**,
so it's an **oxidising agent**.

6) When **metals** form compounds, they generally **donate** electrons to form **positive ions** — meaning they usually have **positive oxidation numbers**.

7) When **non-metals** form compounds, they generally **gain** electrons — meaning they usually have **negative oxidation numbers**.

It can be quite difficult remembering all these rules.
So here's a helpful memory aid to make these oxidation and
reduction rules a little bit easier. Just remember **OIL RIG**.

Oxidation
Is
Loss

Reduction
Is
Gain

PC Honey was a
reducing agent where
crime was concerned.

Redox Reactions

Metals are Oxidised when they react with Acids

1) On page 29 you saw how metals react with acids to produce a salt and hydrogen gas. Well this is a redox reaction:

- The metal atoms are **oxidised**, losing electrons to form **positive metal ions** (in **salts**).
- The hydrogen ions in solution are **reduced**, gaining electrons and forming hydrogen molecules.

2) For example, magnesium reacts with dilute hydrochloric acid like this:

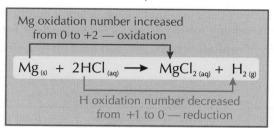

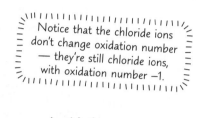

Notice that the chloride ions don't change oxidation number — they're still chloride ions, with oxidation number –1.

3) If you use **sulfuric acid** instead of hydrochloric acid, exactly the same processes of **oxidation** and **reduction** take place. For example, potassium is oxidised to K⁺ ions:

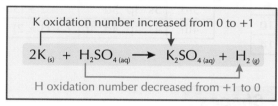

Practice Questions

Q1 Is an oxidising agent reduced or oxidised in a redox reaction?

Q2 Would the oxidation number of an element that is reduced get bigger, smaller, or stay the same?

Q3 What generally happens to the number of electrons a metal has when it forms a compound?

Q4 Describe what happens, in terms of oxidation and reduction, when metals react with acids.

Exam Questions

Q1 Nitric acid reacts with solid iron. What sort of a reaction is this? [1 mark]

Q2 Which of these equations shows a redox reaction?

A $HCl + NaOH \rightarrow NaCl + H_2O$ **B** $NaCl + AgNO_3 \rightarrow AgCl + NaNO_3$

C $BaBr_2 + H_2S \rightarrow BaS + 2HBr$ **D** $N_2 + O_2 \rightarrow 2NO$ [1 mark]

Q3 Concentrated sulfuric acid reacts with iron to produce iron(II) sulfate and one other product.

a) Write a balanced chemical equation for this reaction. [1 mark]

b) Use your answer to part a) to identify the oxidising agent and the reducing agent. [1 mark]

Q4 This equation shows the reaction of aluminium and iodine:

$2Al_{(s)} + 3I_{2\,(g)} \rightarrow 2AlI_{3\,(s)}$

Use oxidation numbers to show that aluminium has been oxidised. [1 mark]

Redox — relax in a lovely warm bubble bath...

*The thing here is to take your time. Questions on redox reactions aren't usually that hard, but they are easy to get wrong. So don't panic, take it easy, and get all the marks. Remember your nifty friend the **oil rig**. Oxidation Is Loss, Reduction Is Gain. Oxidation Is Loss, Reduction Is Gain. Oxidation Is Loss, Reduction Is Gain... Have you got it yet?*

Electronic Structure

Those little electrons prancing about like mini bunnies decide what'll react with what — it's what chemistry's all about.

Electron Shells are Made Up of Sub-Shells and Orbitals

1) In the currently accepted model of the atom, electrons have fixed energies.

2) They move around the nucleus in **shells** (sometimes called **energy levels**). These shells are all given numbers known as **principal quantum numbers**.

3) Shells **further** from the nucleus have a higher **energy** (and a larger principal quantum number) than shells closer to the nucleus.

> You don't need to worry too much about the f-sub-shell, but it's good to know it's there.

4) Shells are divided up into **sub-shells**. Different electron shells have different numbers of sub-shells, each of which has a different energy. Sub-shells are called **s-, p-, d-** or **f-sub-shells**.

5) These sub-shells have different numbers of **orbitals**, which can each hold up to **2 electrons**.

This table shows the number of electrons that fit in each type of sub-shell.

Sub-shell	Number of orbitals	Maximum electrons
s	1	$1 \times 2 = 2$
p	3	$3 \times 2 = 6$
d	5	$5 \times 2 = 10$
f	7	$7 \times 2 = 14$

And this one shows the sub-shells and electrons in the first four energy levels.

Shell	Sub-shells	Total number of electrons	
1st	1s	2	$= 2$
2nd	2s 2p	$2 + (3 \times 2)$	$= 8$
3rd	3s 3p 3d	$2 + (3 \times 2) + (5 \times 2)$	$= 18$
4th	4s 4p 4d 4f	$2 + (3 \times 2) + (5 \times 2) + (7 \times 2)$	$= 32$

Orbitals Have Characteristic Shapes

There are a few things you need to know about orbitals... like what they are...

1) An orbital is the **bit of space** that an electron moves in. Orbitals within the same sub-shell have the **same energy**.

2) If there are two electrons in an orbital, they have to 'spin' in **opposite** directions — this is called **spin-pairing**.

3) s orbitals are **spherical** — p orbitals have **dumbbell shapes**. There are three p orbitals and they're at right angles to one another.

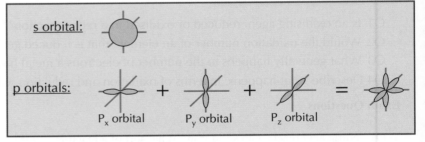

s orbital:

p orbitals: P_x orbital $+$ P_y orbital $+$ P_z orbital $=$

You Can Show Electron Configuration in Different Ways

The **number** of electrons that an atom or ion has, and how they are **arranged**, is called its **electron configuration**. Electron configurations can be shown in different ways. E.g. an atom of neon has 10 electrons — two in the 1s sub-shell, two in the 2s sub-shell and six in the 2p sub-shell. You can show this using...

Sub-shell notation: $1s^2\ 2s^2\ 2p^6$

Energy shell / level (principal quantum number)   Sub-shell   Number of electrons

Electrons in boxes:

1) Each **box** represents one **orbital** and each **arrow** represents one **electron**.

2) The up and down arrows represent electrons **spinning** in opposite directions. Two electrons can only occupy the same orbital if they have **opposite** spin.

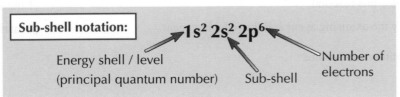

1s   2s   2p

Electronic Structure

Work Out **Electron Configurations** by Filling the **Lowest** Energy Levels First

You can figure out most electron configurations pretty easily, so long as you know a few simple rules —

1) Electrons fill up the **lowest** energy sub-shells first.

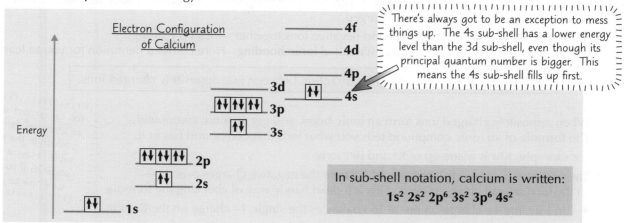

There's always got to be an exception to mess things up. The 4s sub-shell has a lower energy level than the 3d sub-shell, even though its principal quantum number is bigger. This means the 4s sub-shell fills up first.

In sub-shell notation, calcium is written:
$1s^2\ 2s^2\ 2p^6\ 3s^2\ 3p^6\ 4s^2$

2) Electrons fill orbitals with the same energy **singly** before they start sharing.

Nitrogen: Oxygen:

3) For the configuration of **ions** from the **s** and **p** blocks of the periodic table, just **remove or add** the electrons to or from the highest-energy occupied sub-shell. E.g. $Mg^{2+} = 1s^2\ 2s^2\ 2p^6$, $Cl^- = 1s^2\ 2s^2\ 2p^6\ 3s^2\ 3p^6$.

Watch out — **noble gas symbols**, like that of argon (Ar), are sometimes used in electron configurations. For example, calcium ($1s^2\ 2s^2\ 2p^6\ 3s^2\ 3p^6\ 4s^2$) can be written as $[Ar]4s^2$, where $[Ar] = 1s^2\ 2s^2\ 2p^6\ 3s^2\ 3p^6$.

Practice Questions

Q1 How many electrons do full s, p and d sub-shells contain?

Q2 What is an atomic orbital?

Q3 Draw diagrams to show the shapes of an s and a p orbital.

Q4 Write down the sub-shells in order of increasing energy up to 4p.

Exam Questions

Q1 Potassium reacts with oxygen to form potassium oxide, K_2O.

   a) Give the electron configurations of the K atom and K^+ ion using sub-shell notation.   [2 marks]

   b) Give the electron configuration of the oxide ion using 'electrons in boxes' notation.   [1 mark]

Q2 This question concerns electron configurations in atoms and ions.

   a) Identify the element with the 4th shell configuration of $4s^2\ 4p^2$.   [1 mark]

   b) Suggest the identity of an atom, a positive ion and a negative ion with the configuration $1s^2\ 2s^2\ 2p^6\ 3s^2\ 3p^6$.   [3 marks]

   c) Give the electron configuration of the Al^{3+} ion using sub-shell notation.   [1 mark]

Q3 a) Write the electron configuration of a silicon atom using sub-shell notation.   [1 mark]

   b) How many orbitals contain an unpaired electron in a silicon atom?   [1 mark]

She shells sub-sells on the shesore...

Electrons fill up the orbitals kind of like how strangers fill up seats on a bus. Everyone tends to sit in their own seat till they're forced to share. Except for the huge, scary man who comes and sits next to you. Make sure you learn the order that the sub-shells are filled up, so you can write electron configurations for any atom or ion they throw at you.

Ionic Bonding

There are two main types of bonding — ionic and covalent. You need to get them both totally sussed.

Ionic Bonding is when Ions are Stuck Together by Electrostatic Attraction

1) Ions are formed when electrons are **transferred** from one atom to another so as to have **full outer shells**. They may be positively or negatively charged.

2) **Electrostatic attraction** holds positive and negative ions together — it's **very** strong. When atoms are held together like this, it's called **ionic bonding**. Here comes a definition for you to learn...

> An **ionic bond** is an **electrostatic attraction** between two **oppositely charged** ions.

When oppositely charged ions form an **ionic bond**, you get an **ionic compound**. The **formula** of an ionic compound tells you what **ions** that compound has in it.

For example, KBr is made up of K^+ and Br^- ions.

The positive charges in the compound **balance** the negative charges exactly — so the total overall charge is **zero**. This is a dead handy way of checking the formula.

- In **KBr**, the 1+ charge on the K^+ ion balances the single 1– charge on the Br^- ion.
- In **MgBr$_2$** the 2+ charge on the Mg^{2+} ion balances the two 1– charges on the two Br^- ions.

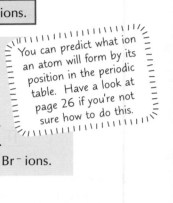
You can predict what ion an atom will form by its position in the periodic table. Have a look at page 26 if you're not sure how to do this.

Dot-and-Cross Diagrams Show Where the Electrons in a Bond Come From

Dot-and-cross diagrams show the **arrangement** of electrons in an atom or ion. Each electron is represented by a dot or a cross. They can also show which **atom** the electrons in a **bond** originally came from.

For example, **sodium chloride** is an ionic compound:

1) The formula of sodium chloride is **NaCl**. It tells you that sodium chloride is made up of **Na^+** and **Cl^- ions** in a 1:1 ratio.

2) A dot-and-cross diagram shows how ionic bonding works in sodium chloride —

Don't forget to include the charges of the ions on dot-and-cross diagrams.

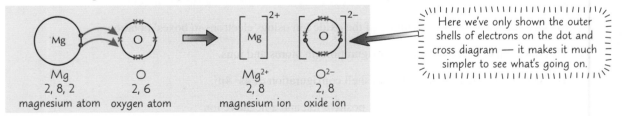

Here, the dots represent the Na electrons and the crosses represent the Cl electrons (all electrons are really identical, but this is a good way of following their movement).

Na	Cl	Na⁺	Cl⁻
2, 8, 1	2, 8, 7	2, 8	2, 8, 8
sodium atom	chlorine atom	sodium ion	chloride ion

3) **Magnesium oxide**, MgO, is another good example:

Here we've only shown the outer shells of electrons on the dot and cross diagram — it makes it much simpler to see what's going on.

Mg	O	Mg²⁺	O²⁻
2, 8, 2	2, 6	2, 8	2, 8
magnesium atom	oxygen atom	magnesium ion	oxide ion

4) When there's a 1:2 ratio of ions, such as in **magnesium chloride**, MgCl$_2$, you draw dot-and-cross diagrams like this:

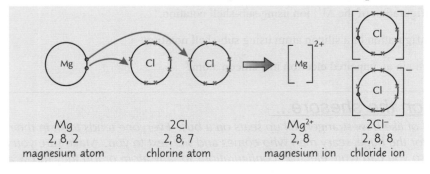

Mg	2Cl	Mg²⁺	2Cl⁻
2, 8, 2	2, 8, 7	2, 8	2, 8, 8
magnesium atom	chlorine atom	magnesium ion	chloride ion

Dot
(cross)

Ionic Bonding

Sodium Chloride has a *Giant Ionic Lattice* Structure

1) In **sodium chloride**, the Na^+ and Cl^- ions are packed together alternately in a regular structure called a **lattice**.

2) The structure's called '**giant**' because it's made up of the same basic unit repeated over and over again.

3) It forms because each ion is electrostatically attracted in **all directions** to ions of the **opposite** charge.

4) The sodium chloride lattice is **cube** shaped — different ionic compounds have different shaped structures, but they're all still giant lattices.

5) Sodium chloride's got very strong **ionic bonds**, so it takes loads of **energy** to break up the lattice. This gives it a high melting point (801°C).

The Na^+ and Cl^- ions alternate.

The lines show the ionic bonds between the ions.

But it's not just melting points — the structure decides other **physical properties** too...

Ionic Structure Explains the *Behaviour* of Ionic Compounds

1) **Ionic compounds conduct electricity when they're molten or dissolved — but not when they're solid.**
   The ions in a liquid are mobile (and they carry a charge).
   In a solid they're fixed in position by the strong ionic bonds.

2) **Ionic compounds have high melting and boiling points.**
   The giant ionic lattices are held together by strong electrostatic forces. It takes loads of energy to overcome these forces, so their melting and boiling points are very high.

3) **Ionic compounds tend to dissolve in water.**
   Water molecules are polar — part of the molecule has a small negative charge, and the other bits have small positive charges (see p.48). The water molecules are attracted to the charged ions. They pull the ions away from the lattice and cause it to dissolve.

Practice Questions

Q1 How do ions form?

Q2 What is an ionic bond?

Q3 Draw a dot-and-cross diagram showing the bonding between magnesium and oxygen.

Q4 Why do many ionic compounds dissolve in water?

Exam Questions

Q1 a) What type of structure does sodium chloride have? [1 mark]

    b) Would you expect sodium chloride to have a high or a low melting point?
Explain your answer. [2 marks]

Q2 Calcium oxide is an ionic compound with ionic formula CaO.

    a) Draw a dot-and-cross diagram to show the bonding in calcium oxide. Show the outer electrons only. [2 marks]

    b) Solid calcium oxide does not conduct electricity, but molten calcium oxide does.
Explain this with reference to ionic bonding. [3 marks]

The name's Bond... Ionic Bond... Electrons taken, not shared...

It's all very well learning the properties of ionic compounds, but make sure you can also explain why they do what they do. Remember — atoms are lazy. It's easier to lose two electrons to get a full shell than it is to gain six, so that's what an atom will do. And practise drawing dot-and-cross diagrams to show ionic bonding— they're easy marks in exams.

Covalent Bonding

And now for covalent bonding — this is when atoms share electrons with one another so they've all got full outer shells.

Molecules are Groups of Atoms Bonded Together

Molecules form when **two or more** atoms bond together — it doesn't matter if the atoms are the **same** or **different**. Chlorine gas (Cl_2), carbon monoxide (CO), water (H_2O) and ethanol (C_2H_5OH) are all molecules.

Molecules are held together by **covalent bonds**. In covalent bonding, two atoms **share** electrons, so they've **both** got full outer shells of electrons.

E.g. two hydrogen atoms bond covalently to form a molecule of hydrogen.

Covalent bonding happens between nonmetals. Ionic bonding is between a metal and a nonmetal.

Here's the definition you need to know:

> A **covalent bond** is the strong **electrostatic attraction** between a **shared pair of electrons** and the **nuclei** of the bonded atoms.

Make sure you can Draw the Bonding in these Molecules

1) Dot-and-cross diagrams can be used to show how electrons behave in **covalent bonds**.

2) The bonded molecules are drawn with their outer atomic orbitals **overlapping**. The shared electrons that make up the covalent bond are drawn **within** the overlapping area.

3) To simplify the diagrams, not all the electrons in the molecules are shown — just the ones in the **outer shells**:

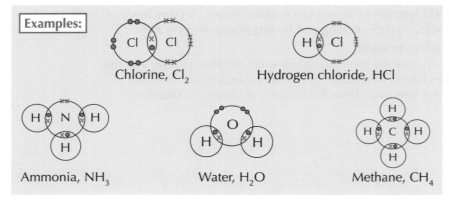

Examples:
Chlorine, Cl_2 Hydrogen chloride, HCl
Ammonia, NH_3 Water, H_2O Methane, CH_4

4) Most of the time the central atom ends up with **eight electrons** in its **outer shell**. This is good for the atom — it's a very **stable** arrangement.

The outer electrons in hydrogen are in the first electron shell, which only needs two electrons to be filled.

Some Covalent Compounds Are Special Cases

There are always a few pesky exceptions to make life that bit trickier...

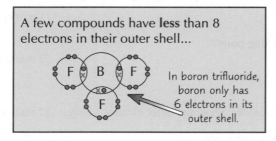

A few compounds have **less** than 8 electrons in their outer shell...

In boron trifluoride, boron only has 6 electrons in its outer shell.

...and a few compounds can use d orbitals to 'expand the octet'. This means they have **more** than 8 electrons in their outer shell.

In sulfur hexafluoride, sulfur has 12 electrons in its outer shell.

The Strength of a Covalent Bond is Shown by its Average Bond Enthalpy

1) Average bond enthalpy measures the **energy** required to **break** a covalent bond.

2) The **stronger** a bond is, the more energy is required to break it, and so the **greater** the value of the average bond enthalpy.

There's loads more about enthalpy changes on pages 68-73.

Covalent Bonding

Some Atoms Share **More Than One Pair** of Electrons

1) Atoms don't just form single bonds — some can form **double** or even **triple covalent bonds**.

2) These multiple bonds contain **more than one** shared pairs of electrons between two atoms.

3) An example of a molecule that has a double bond is **oxygen**, O_2:

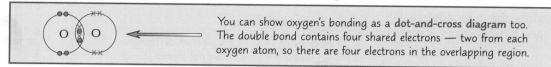

You can show oxygen's bonding as a **dot-and-cross diagram** too. The double bond contains four shared electrons — two from each oxygen atom, so there are four electrons in the overlapping region.

4) Nitrogen can triple bond, and carbon dioxide has two double bonds:

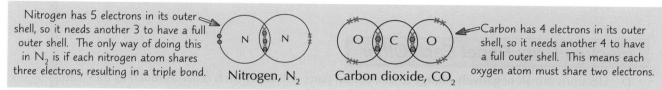

Nitrogen has 5 electrons in its outer shell, so it needs another 3 to have a full outer shell. The only way of doing this in N_2 is if each nitrogen atom shares three electrons, resulting in a triple bond.

Nitrogen, N_2

Carbon dioxide, CO_2

Carbon has 4 electrons in its outer shell, so it needs another 4 to have a full outer shell. This means each oxygen atom must share two electrons.

Dative Covalent Bonding is where **Both Electrons** come from **One Atom**

The **ammonium ion** (NH_4^+) is formed by dative covalent (or coordinate) bonding.
It forms when the nitrogen atom in an ammonia molecule **donates a pair of electrons** to a proton (H^+):

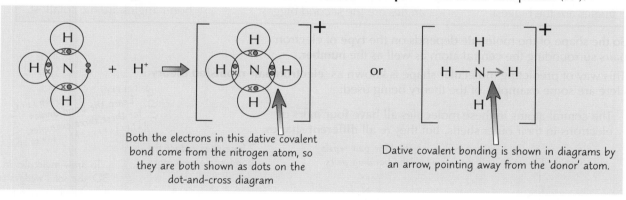

Both the electrons in this dative covalent bond come from the nitrogen atom, so they are both shown as dots on the dot-and-cross diagram

Dative covalent bonding is shown in diagrams by an arrow, pointing away from the 'donor' atom.

Practice Questions

Q1 Draw a dot-and-cross diagram to show the arrangement of the outer electrons in a molecule of hydrogen chloride.

Q2 How does the value of average bond enthalpy change as bond strength increases?

Q3 Name a molecule with a double covalent bond. Draw a diagram showing the outer electrons in this molecule.

Exam Questions

Q1 Carbon tetrachloride, CCl_4, is a covalently bonded molecule.

a) What is a covalent bond?

[1 mark]

b) Draw a dot-and-cross diagram to show the electron arrangement in a molecule of carbon tetrachloride (CCl_4).

[2 marks]

Q2 a) What type of bonding is present in the ammonium ion (NH_4^+)?

[1 mark]

b) Explain how this type of bonding occurs.

[1 mark]

Interesting fact #795 — $TiCl_4$ is known as 'tickle' in the chemical industry...

More pretty diagrams to learn here — practise till you get every single dot and cross in the right place. It's amazing to think of these titchy little atoms sorting themselves out so they've got full outer shells of electrons. Remember — covalent bonding happens between two nonmetals, whereas ionic bonding happens between a metal and a nonmetal.

Shapes of Molecules

Chemistry would be heaps more simple if all molecules were flat. But they're not.

Molecular Shape depends on Electron Pairs around the Central Atom

Molecules and molecular ions come in loads of **different shapes**.
The shape depends on the **number** of pairs of electrons in the outer shell of the central atom.

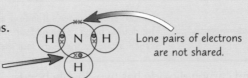

In ammonia, the outermost shell
of nitrogen has four pairs of electrons.

Bonding pairs of electrons are shared
with another atom in a covalent bond.

Lone pairs of electrons
are not shared.

A lone pear.

Electron Pairs Repel Each Other

1) Electrons are all **negatively charged**, so electron pairs will **repel** each other as much as they can.

2) This sounds straightforward, but the **type** of the electron pair affects **how much** it repels other electron pairs. Lone pairs repel **more** than bonding pairs.

3) This means the **greatest** angles are between **lone pairs** of electrons, and bond angles between bonding pairs are often **reduced** because they are pushed together by lone pair repulsion.

Lone pair/lone pair angles are the biggest.	Lone pair/bonding pair angles are the second biggest.	Bonding pair/bonding pair bond angles are the smallest.

4) So the shape of the molecule depends on the **type** of electron pairs surrounding the central atom as well as the **number.**

5) This way of predicting molecular shape is known as '**electron pair repulsion theory**'. Here are some examples of the theory being used:

Learn the bond angles for these three examples.

The central atoms in these molecules all have **four pairs** of electrons in their outer shells, but they're all **different shapes**.

The lone pair repels
the bonding pairs

2 lone pairs reduce the
bond angle even more

Methane — no lone pairs.
All the bond angles are 109.5°.

Ammonia — 1 lone pair.
All three bond angles are 107°.

Water — 2 lone pairs.
The bond angle is 104.5°.

To draw molecules in
3D, use solid wedges to
show bonds pointing out
of the page towards you,
and broken lines to show
bonds pointing into the
page away from you.

You Can Use Electron Pairs to Predict the Shapes of Molecules

To predict the shape of a molecule, you first have to know how many bonding and non-bonding electron pairs are on the central atom. Here's how:

1) Find the **central atom** (the one all the other atoms are bonded to).

2) Work out the number of **electrons** in the **outer shell** of the central atom. Use the periodic table to do this.

3) The **molecular formula** tells you how many atoms the central atom is **bonded** to. From this you can work out how many electrons are **shared with** the central atom.

4) **Add up** the electrons and **divide by 2** to find the **number of electron pairs** on the central atom. If you have an ion remember to account for its **charge**.

If there's a double bond, count it as two bonds.

5) **Compare** the number of **electron pairs** with the number of **bonds** to find the number of **lone pairs**.

6) You can then use the **number of electron pairs** and the number of **lone pairs** and **bonding centres** around the central atom to work out the **shape** of the molecule (see next page).

Bonding centres are the atoms bonded to the central atom.

Shapes of Molecules

Practise **Drawing** these Molecules

Once you know how many electron pairs are on the central atom, you can use **electron pair repulsion theory** to work out the **shape** of the molecule.

These are the common shapes that you need to be able to draw:

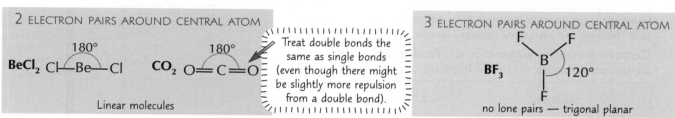

2 ELECTRON PAIRS AROUND CENTRAL ATOM

BeCl₂ Cl—Be—Cl 180°

CO₂ O=C=O 180°

Linear molecules

Treat double bonds the same as single bonds (even though there might be slightly more repulsion from a double bond).

3 ELECTRON PAIRS AROUND CENTRAL ATOM

BF₃ F F F B 120°

no lone pairs — trigonal planar

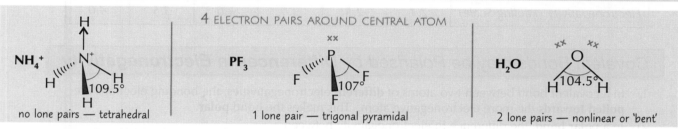

4 ELECTRON PAIRS AROUND CENTRAL ATOM

NH₄⁺ H H N⁺ H H 109.5°

no lone pairs — tetrahedral

PF₃ F P F F 107°

1 lone pair — trigonal pyramidal

H₂O O H 104.5° H

2 lone pairs — nonlinear or 'bent'

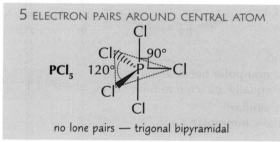

5 ELECTRON PAIRS AROUND CENTRAL ATOM

PCl₅ Cl Cl 90° P Cl 120° Cl Cl

no lone pairs — trigonal bipyramidal

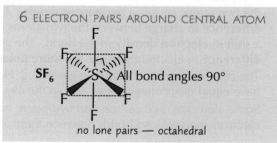

6 ELECTRON PAIRS AROUND CENTRAL ATOM

SF₆ F F F S F All bond angles 90° F F

no lone pairs — octahedral

Practice Questions

Q1 What is a lone pair of electrons?

Q2 Write down the order of the strength of repulsion between different kinds of electron pair.

Q3 Explain why a water molecule is not linear.

Q4 Draw a tetrahedral molecule.

Exam Questions

Q1 a) Draw the shapes of the following molecules, showing the approximate values of the bond angles on the diagrams and naming each shape.

    i) NCl₃   [3 marks]

    ii) BCl₃   [3 marks]

  b) Explain why the shapes of NCl₃ and BCl₃ are different.   [3 marks]

Q2 The displayed formula of an organic compound is shown. Use electron pair repulsion theory to predict the shape and relevant bond angles of the bonds around atoms A, B and C.

     O=C—C—C—O—H with atom A, atom B, atom C labelled   [3 marks]

These molecules ain't square...

In the exam, those evil examiners might try to throw you by asking you for the shape of an unfamiliar molecule. Don't panic — you can use the steps on page 46 to work out the shape of any covalent molecule. So practise, practise practise until you can work out shapes and draw them while standing on your head. And don't forget the bond angles.

Polarity and Intermolecular Forces

This topic is a bit of a monster, I'm afraid, and it's full of some really important stuff that you need to get your head around. Don't worry though — we'll get through it together. First up, it's electronegativity and polar bonds.

Some Atoms **Attract** Bonding Electrons More than Other Atoms

> An atom's ability to attract the electron pair in a covalent bond is called **electronegativity.**

Fluorine is the most electronegative element. Oxygen, nitrogen and chlorine are also very strongly electronegative.

Electronegativity is measured on the **Pauling Scale**. The greater an element's Pauling value, the **higher** its electronegativity.

Electronegativity increases across periods and decreases down groups (ignoring the noble gases).

Element	H	C	N	Cl	O	F
Electronegativity (Pauling Scale)	2.1	2.5	3.0	3.0	3.5	4.0

Covalent Bonds may be Polarised by **Differences** in **Electronegativity**

1) In a covalent bond between two atoms of **different** electronegativities, the bonding electrons are **pulled towards** the more electronegative atom. This makes the bond **polar**.

2) In a **polar bond**, the difference in electronegativity between the two atoms causes a **permanent dipole**. A dipole is a **difference in charge** between the two atoms caused by a shift in **electron density** in the bond. The greater the **difference** in electronegativity, the **more polar** the bond.

$$\delta+ \quad \delta- \\ H \!-\! \overset{\circ}{\underset{\times}{C}} l$$

'δ' (delta) means 'slightly', so 'δ+' means 'slightly positive'.

3) The covalent bonds in diatomic gases (e.g. H_2, Cl_2) are **non-polar** because the atoms have **equal** electronegativities and so the electrons are equally attracted to both nuclei.

$$H \!-\! \overset{\circ}{\underset{\times}{} }\! H$$

4) Some elements, like carbon and hydrogen, have pretty **similar** electronegativities, so bonds between them are essentially **non-polar**.

In Polar **Molecules**, Charge is Arranged **Unevenly**

Polar bonds have **permanent dipoles**. The **arrangement** of polar bonds in a molecule determines whether or not the **molecule** will have an **overall dipole**.

1) If the polar bonds are arranged **symmetrically** so that the dipoles **cancel** each other out, then the molecule has no overall dipole and is **non-polar**. E.g. carbon dioxide contains two polar bonds but has no overall dipole moment.

2) But if the polar bonds are arranged so that they **don't cancel** each other out then charge is arranged **unevenly** across the whole molecule, and it will have an **overall dipole**. Molecules with an overall dipole are **polar**. E.g. water is polar because the negative charge is positioned more towards the **oxygen** atom.

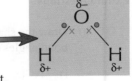

3) To work out whether a molecule has an overall dipole, first you need to draw it in **3D**. Then label the **partial charges** on each atom, and look to see if they cancel each other out.

There's a Gradual **Transition** from Ionic to Covalent Bonding

1) Only bonds between atoms of a **single** element, like diatomic gases such as hydrogen (H_2) or oxygen (O_2), can be **purely covalent**. This is because the **electronegativity difference** between the atoms is **zero** and so the bonding electrons are arranged completely **evenly** within the bond.

2) At the same time, very few compounds are completely ionic.

3) Really, most compounds come somewhere **in between** the two extremes — meaning they've often got ionic **and** covalent properties. E.g. covalent hydrogen chloride gas molecules dissolve to form hydrochloric acid, which is an ionic solution.

$$HCl_{(g)} \xrightarrow{H_2O} H^+_{(aq)} + Cl^-_{(aq)}$$

4) You can use electronegativity to **predict** what type of bonding will occur between two atoms. The higher the difference in electronegativity, the more ionic in character the bonding becomes.

Polarity and Intermolecular Forces

Intermolecular forces are the things that hold molecules together. They're weak, but important — without them we'd just be a cloud of gassy stuff. How polar a molecule is affects the type of intermolecular forces it will form. Onwards...

Intermolecular Forces are **Very Weak**

Intermolecular forces are forces between molecules. They're much **weaker** than covalent, ionic or metallic bonds. There are three types of intermolecular force you need to know about.

1) **Induced dipole-dipole** or **London (dispersion)** forces.
2) **Permanent dipole-dipole** interactions.
3) **Hydrogen bonding** (this is the strongest type).

Sometimes the term 'van der Waals forces' is used to refer to the first two types.

Induced Dipole-Dipole Forces are Found Between **All** Atoms and Molecules

Induced dipole-dipole forces cause **all** atoms and molecules to be **attracted** to each other. Even **noble gas atoms** are affected, despite not being at all interested in forming other types of bond. Here's why...

1) **Electrons** in charge clouds are always **moving** really quickly. At any particular moment, the electrons in an atom are likely to be more to one side than the other. At this moment, the atom would have a **temporary dipole**.

2) This dipole can cause **another** temporary (induced) dipole in the opposite direction on a neighbouring atom. The two dipoles are then **attracted** to each other.

3) The second dipole can cause yet another dipole in a **third atom**. It's kind of like a domino rally.

4) Because the electrons are constantly moving, the dipoles are being **created** and **destroyed** all the time. Even though the dipoles keep changing, the **overall effect** is for the atoms to be **attracted** to each other.

charge cloud ← → nucleus

Stronger **Induced Dipole-Dipole Forces** mean **Higher Boiling Points**

1) Not all induced dipole-dipole forces are the same strength — larger molecules have **larger electron clouds**, meaning **stronger** induced dipole-dipole forces. Molecules with greater **surface areas** also have stronger induced dipole-dipole forces because they have a **bigger exposed electron cloud**.

2) When you **boil** a liquid, you need to **overcome** the intermolecular forces, so that the particles can **escape** from the liquid surface. It stands to reason that you need **more energy** to overcome **stronger** intermolecular forces, so liquids with stronger induced dipole-dipole forces will have **higher boiling points**.

3) This graph of the boiling points of Group 4 hydrides shows the trend. As you go down the group, the induced dipole-dipole forces (and the boiling points) increase because the number of **shells** of electrons increases, and so atomic/molecular **size** increases.

Induced dipole-dipole forces affect other physical properties, such as melting point and viscosity, too.

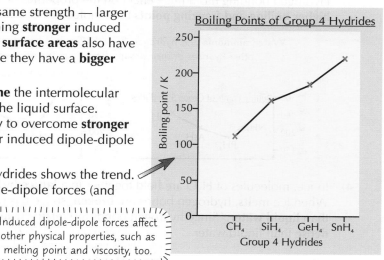

Boiling Points of Group 4 Hydrides

Boiling point / K

CH_4 SiH_4 GeH_4 SnH_4
Group 4 Hydrides

Induced Dipole-Dipole Forces Can Hold Molecules in a **Lattice**

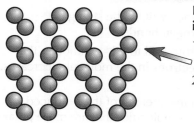

Induced dipole-dipole forces are responsible for holding **iodine** molecules together in a **lattice**.

1) Iodine atoms are held together in pairs by **strong** covalent bonds to form molecules of I_2.

2) But the molecules are then held together in a **molecular lattice** arrangement by **weak induced dipole-dipole** attractions.

MODULE 2: SECTION 2 — ELECTRONS, BONDING & STRUCTURE

Polarity and Intermolecular Forces

Two more types of intermolecular force for you to get under your belt. It must just be your lucky day.

Polar Molecules Form Permanent Dipole-Dipole Interactions

The δ+ and δ- charges on **polar molecules** cause **weak electrostatic forces** of attraction **between** molecules. These are called **permanent dipole-dipole interactions**.

E.g. hydrogen chloride gas has polar molecules.

$$\overset{\delta+}{H}\!-\!\overset{\delta-}{Cl}\cdots\overset{\delta+}{H}\!-\!\overset{\delta-}{Cl}\cdots\overset{\delta+}{H}\!-\!\overset{\delta-}{Cl}$$

Permanent dipole-dipole interactions happen **in addition to** (not instead of) induced dipole-dipole interactions.

Permanent polar bonding.

Hydrogen Bonding is the Strongest Intermolecular Force

1) Hydrogen bonding can **only** happen when **hydrogen** is covalently bonded to **fluorine**, **nitrogen** or **oxygen**. Hydrogen has a **high charge density** because it's so small, and fluorine, nitrogen and oxygen are very **electronegative**. The bond is so **polarised** that a weak bond forms between the hydrogen of one molecule and a lone pair of electrons on the fluorine, nitrogen or oxygen in **another molecule**.

2) Molecules which have hydrogen bonding usually contain **–OH** or **–NH** groups.

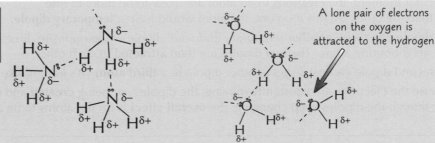

Water and ammonia both have hydrogen bonding.

A lone pair of electrons on the oxygen is attracted to the hydrogen

3) Hydrogen bonding has a huge effect on the properties of substances. They are **soluble** in water and have **higher boiling and freezing points** than molecules of a similar size that are **unable** to form hydrogen bonds.

Water, ammonia and hydrogen fluoride generally have the **highest boiling points** if you compare them with other hydrides in their groups, because of the **extra energy** needed to break the hydrogen bonds.

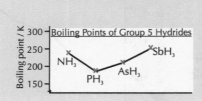

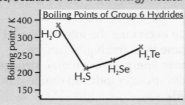

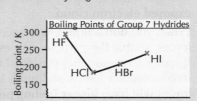

4) In ice, molecules of H_2O are held together in a **lattice** by hydrogen bonds. When ice **melts**, hydrogen bonds are **broken**, so ice has **more** hydrogen bonds than **liquid water**. Since hydrogen bonds are relatively **long**, this makes ice **less dense** than liquid water.

This is unusual... most substances get denser when they freeze.

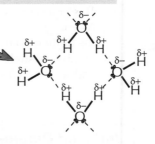

Intermolecular Forces Explain the Trends in Boiling Points

1) In general, the **main factor** that determines the boiling point of a substance will be the strength of the **induced dipole-dipole forces** (unless the molecule can form **hydrogen bonds**).

2) This explains why the boiling points of the Group 7 hydrides **increase** from HCl to HI — although the permanent dipole-dipole interactions are **decreasing**, the **number of electrons** in the molecule increases, so the **strength** of the induced dipole-dipole interactions also **increases**.

3) But if you have two molecules with a **similar number** of electrons, then the strength of their induced dipole-dipole interactions will be **similar**. So if one of the substances has molecules that are more **polar** than the other, it will have stronger **permanent dipole-dipole** interactions and so a higher boiling point.

Polarity and Intermolecular Forces

Intermolecular Forces Explain the **Behaviour** of Simple Covalent Compounds

Simple covalent compounds have low melting and boiling points.

The intermolecular forces that hold together the molecules in simple covalent compounds are **weak** so don't need much energy to **break**. So the melting and boiling points are normally **low** — they are often **liquids** or **gases** at room temperature. As intermolecular forces get **stronger**, melting and boiling points **increase**.

Polar molecules are soluble in water.

Water is a **polar** molecule, so only tends to dissolve other polar substances. Compounds with **hydrogen bonds**, such as ammonia or ethanoic acid, can form hydrogen bonds with water molecules, so will be **soluble**. Molecules that only have induced dipole-dipole forces, such as methane, will be **insoluble**.

Simple covalent compounds don't conduct electricity.

Even though some covalent molecules have permanent dipoles, overall covalent molecules are **uncharged**. This means they can't conduct electricity.

Covalent Bonds **Don't** Break during **Melting** and **Boiling***

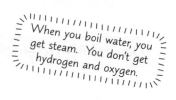
When you boil water, you get steam. You don't get hydrogen and oxygen.

This is something that confuses loads of people — get it sorted in **your** head now...

1) To **melt** or **boil** a simple covalent compound you only have to overcome the **intermolecular forces** that hold the molecules together.

2) You **don't** need to break the much stronger covalent bonds that hold the atoms together in the molecules. (That's why simple covalent compounds have relatively **low melting** and **boiling points**.)

> **Example**
> Chlorine, Cl_2, has **stronger** covalent bonds than bromine, Br_2. But under normal conditions, chlorine is a **gas** and bromine a **liquid**. Bromine has the higher boiling point because its molecules are **bigger**, giving stronger induced dipole-dipole forces.

*Except for giant molecular substances, like diamond.

Practice Questions

Q1 What is a dipole?

Q2 What is the only situation in which a bond is purely covalent?

Q3 Explain why induced dipole-dipole interactions are present even in inert atoms like argon.

Q4 How does the boiling point of a substance change if the strength of induced dipole-dipole interactions increases?

Q5 What atoms must be covalently bonded to hydrogen for hydrogen bonding to exist?

Q6 What types of forces must be overcome in order for a simple molecular substance to boil or melt?

Exam Questions

Q1 a) Define the term electronegativity. [1 mark]

   b) Draw the shapes of the following molecules, marking any bond polarities clearly on your diagram:
      i) Br_2 ii) H_2O iii) NH_3 [3 marks]

Q2 a) Name three types of intermolecular force. [3 marks]

   b) Water, H_2O, boils at 373 K.

      i) Explain why water's boiling point is higher than expected in comparison to other similar molecules. [2 marks]

      ii) Draw a labelled diagram showing the intermolecular bonding that takes place in water. [2 marks]

May the force be with you...

Phew! You made it. You definitely deserve a break. Remember — induced dipole-dipole interactions occur between all molecules. Permanent dipole-dipole interactions only form if a molecule has an overall dipole, and you only need to think about hydrogen bonding if the molecule contains oxygen, nitrogen or fluorine covalently bonded to hydrogen.

The Periodic Table

As far as Chemistry topics go, the periodic table is a bit of a biggie. So much so that you really should know the history of it. So make yourself comfortable and I'll tell you a story that began... oh, about 200 years ago...

In the **1800s**, Elements Could Only Be Grouped by **Atomic Mass**

1) In the early 1800s, there were only two ways to categorise elements — by their **physical and chemical properties** and by their **relative atomic mass**. (The modern periodic table is arranged by **proton number**, but back then, they knew nothing about protons or electrons. The only thing they could measure was relative atomic mass.)

2) In 1817, Johann Döbereiner attempted to group similar elements — these groups were called **Döbereiner's triads**. He saw that **chlorine**, **bromine** and **iodine** had similar characteristics. He also realised that other properties of bromine (e.g. atomic weight) fell **halfway** between those of chlorine and iodine. He found other such groups of three elements (e.g. lithium, sodium and potassium), and called them **triads**. It was a start.

3) An English chemist called **John Newlands** had the first good stab at making a table of the elements in 1863. He noticed that if he arranged the elements in order of **mass**, similar elements appeared at regular intervals — every **eighth element** was similar. He called this the **law of octaves**, and he listed some known elements in rows of seven so that the similar elements lined up in columns.

Li	Be	B	C	N	O	F
Na	Mg	Al	Si	P	S	Cl

4) But the pattern broke down on the third row, with many transition metals like Fe, Cu and Zn messing it all up.

Dmitri Mendeleev Created the **First Accepted Version**

1) In 1869, Russian chemist **Dmitri Mendeleev** produced a better table, which wasn't far off the one we have today.

2) He arranged all the known elements by atomic mass, but left **gaps** in the table where the next element didn't seem to fit. That way he could keep elements with similar chemical properties in the same group.

3) He also predicted the properties of **undiscovered elements** that would go in the gaps.

	Group 1	Group 2	Group 3	Group 4	Group 5	Group 6	Group 7
Period 1	H						
Period 2	Li	Be	B	C	N	O	F
Period 3	Na	Mg	Al	Si	P	S	Cl
Period 4	K Cu	Ca Zn	*	Ti *	V As	Cr Se	Mn Br
Period 5	Rb Ag	Sr Cd	Y In	Zr Sn	Nb Sb	Mo Te	* I

4) When elements were **later discovered** (e.g. germanium, scandium and gallium) with properties that matched Mendeleev's predictions, it showed that clever old Mendeleev had got it right.

The **Modern Periodic Table** Arranges Elements by **Proton Number**

The modern periodic table is pretty much the one produced by Henry Moseley in 1914. He arranged the elements by **increasing atomic (proton) number** rather than by mass.

f-block elements

1) The periodic table is arranged into **periods** (rows) and **groups** (columns).

2) All the elements **within a period** have the same number of **electron shells** (if you don't worry about the sub-shells). The elements of Period 1 (hydrogen and helium) both have 1 electron shell, the elements in Period 2 have 2 electron shells, and so on... This means there are **repeating trends** in the physical and chemical properties of the elements across each period (e.g. decreasing atomic radius). These trends are known as **periodicity**.

3) All the elements **within a group** have the same number of **electrons in their outer shell**. This means they have **similar chemical properties**. The group number tells you the number of electrons in the outer shell, e.g. Group 1 elements have 1 electron in their outer shell, Group 4 elements have 4 electrons, etc... (Except for Group 0 elements — they have 8 electrons in their outer shell.)

The Periodic Table

You Can Use the Periodic Table to Work Out *Electron Configurations*

The periodic table can be split into an
s-block, **d-block** and **p-block** like this:
Doing this shows you which sub-shells
all the electrons go into.

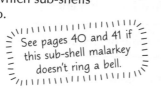

See pages 40 and 41 if
this sub-shell malarkey
doesn't ring a bell.

1) The **s-block** elements have an outer shell electron configuration of s¹ or s².

> **Example:** Lithium ($1s^2\ 2s^1$) and magnesium ($1s^2\ 2s^2\ 2p^6\ 3s^2$)

2) The **p-block** elements have an outer shell electron configuration of s²p¹ to s²p⁶.

> **Example:** Chlorine ($1s^2\ 2s^2\ 2p^6\ 3s^2\ 3p^5$)

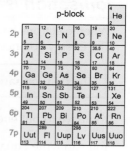

I named my tortoise Neon
— he's got a lovely, full shell.

3) The **d-block** elements have electron configurations in which d sub-shells are being filled.

> **Example:** Cobalt ($1s^2\ 2s^2\ 2p^6\ 3s^2\ 3p^6\ 3d^7\ 4s^2$)

Even though the 3d sub-shell fills last in
cobalt, it's not written at the end of the line.

When you've got the periodic table **labelled** with the
shells and **sub-shells** like the one up there, it's pretty
easy to read off the electron structure of any element.
Just start with the first period and work your way
across and down until you get to your element.

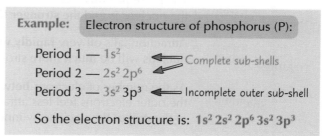

Example: Electron structure of phosphorus (P):

Period 1 — $1s^2$ ⟸ Complete sub-shells
Period 2 — $2s^2\ 2p^6$
Period 3 — $3s^2\ 3p^3$ ⟸ Incomplete outer sub-shell

So the electron structure is: $1s^2\ 2s^2\ 2p^6\ 3s^2\ 3p^3$

Practice Questions

Q1 In what order are the elements set out in the modern periodic table?
Q2 What is the name given to the rows in the periodic table?
Q3 What is the name given to the columns in the periodic table?

Exam Questions

Q1 Which of the following is the electronic configuration of sodium?

    A $1s^2\ 2s^2\ 2p^6\ 3p^1$ B $1s^2\ 2s^2\ 2p^6\ 3s^1$ C $1s^2\ 2p^6\ 3s^1$ D $1s^2\ 2s^2\ 2p^6\ 3s^2\ 3p^1$ [1 mark]

Q2 Which of the following is the electronic configuration of bromine?

    A $1s^2\ 2s^2\ 2p^6\ 3s^2\ 3p^6\ 3d^{10}\ 4s^2\ 4p^3$ B $1s^2\ 2s^2\ 2p^6\ 3s^2\ 3p^6\ 3d^5$

    C $1s^2\ 2s^2\ 2p^6\ 3s^2\ 3p^6\ 3d^{10}\ 4s^1$ D $1s^2\ 2s^2\ 2p^6\ 3s^2\ 3p^6\ 3d^{10}\ 4s^2\ 4p^5$ [1 mark]

Q3 State the block in the periodic table to which bromine belongs.   [1 mark]

Q4 Explain, in terms of protons, why aluminium is placed directly after magnesium in the Periodic Table.   [1 mark]

Periodic — probably the best table in the world...*

*Dropped History for Chemistry, did you? Ha, bet you're regretting that now... If so, you'll enjoy the free History lesson
that you get here with the periodic table. Make sure you learn all the key details and particularly how to read
electron configurations from the periodic table. That stuff is going to be popping up again later on...*

*Excluding the Dinner and the Round, of course.

Ionisation Energies

These pages get a trifle brain-boggling, so I hope you've got a few aspirin handy...

Ionisation is the Removal of One or More Electrons

When electrons have been removed from an atom or molecule, it's been **ionised**.
The energy you need to remove the first electron is called the **first ionisation energy**:

> The **first ionisation energy** is the energy needed to remove **1 mole** of **electrons** from **1 mole** of **gaseous** atoms.

You have to put energy **in** to ionise an atom or molecule, so it's an **endothermic process**.

You can write **equations** for this process — here's the equation for the **first ionisation of oxygen**:

You can read all about endothermic reactions on p.68.

$$O_{(g)} \rightarrow O^+_{(g)} + e^- \qquad \text{1st ionisation energy} = +1314 \text{ kJ mol}^{-1}$$

Here are a few rather important points about ionisation energies:
1) You **must** use the gas state symbol, **(g)**, because ionisation energies are measured for gaseous atoms.
2) Always refer to **1 mole** of atoms, as stated in the definition, rather than to a single atom.
3) The **lower** the ionisation energy, the **easier** it is to form an ion.

The Factors Affecting Ionisation Energy are...

Nuclear charge
The **more protons** there are in the nucleus, the more positively charged the nucleus is and the **stronger the attraction** for the electrons.

Atomic radius
Attraction falls off very **rapidly with distance**. An electron **close** to the nucleus will be **much more** strongly attracted than one further away.

Shielding
As the number of electrons **between** the outer electrons and the nucleus **increases**, the outer electrons feel less attraction towards the nuclear charge. This lessening of the pull of the nucleus by inner shells of electrons is called **shielding**.

> A **high ionisation energy** means there's a **strong attraction** between the **electron** and the **nucleus**, so **more energy** is needed to overcome the attraction and remove the electron.

Ionisation Energy Decreases Down a Group

1) As you **go down** a group in the periodic table, ionisation energies generally **fall**, i.e. it gets **easier** to remove outer electrons.

2) It happens because:
   - Elements further down a group have **extra electron shells** compared to ones above. The extra shells mean that the atomic radius is larger, so the outer electrons are **further away** from the nucleus, which greatly reduces their attraction to the nucleus.
   - The extra inner shells **shield** the outer electrons from the attraction of the nucleus.

The positive charge of the nucleus does increase as you go down a group (due to the extra protons), but this effect is overridden by the effect of the extra shells.

First ionisation energies of the first five elements of Group 1.

[Bar chart: First ionisation energies (kJ mol⁻¹) on y-axis from 0 to 600, elements Li, Na, K, Rb, Cs on x-axis. Li ≈ 520, Na ≈ 490, K ≈ 425, Rb ≈ 400, Cs ≈ 370.]

3) This provides **evidence** that electron shells **really exist** — a decrease in ionisation energy going down a group supports the Bohr model of the atom (see page 17).

Ionisation Energies

Ionisation Energy **Increases** Across a Period

The graph below shows the first ionisation energies of the elements in **Periods 2** and **3**.

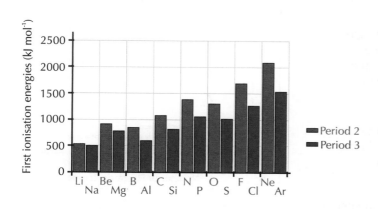

1) As you **move across** a period, the **general trend** is for the ionisation energies to **increase** — i.e. it gets harder to remove the outer electrons.

2) This is because the number of protons is increasing. As the **positive charge** of the nucleus increases, the electrons are **pulled closer** to the nucleus, making the atomic radius smaller.

3) The extra electrons that the elements gain across a period are added to the **outer energy level** so they don't really provide any extra shielding effect (shielding works with inner shells mainly).

There are **two exceptions** to the trend — the first ionisation energy **decreases** between Groups 2 and 3, and between Groups 5 and 6. On the graph, you can see this as **small drops** between those groups. Here's why...

The Drop Between Groups 2 and 3 is Due to **Sub-Shell Structure**

1) The outer electron in Group 3 elements is in a **p orbital** rather than an s orbital.

2) A p orbital has a **slightly higher** energy than an s orbital in the same shell, so the electron is, on average, to be found **further** from the nucleus.

3) The p orbital also has additional shielding provided by the **s electrons**.

4) These factors **override** the effect of the increased nuclear charge, resulting in the ionisation energy **dropping** slightly.

E.g.

	Electron structure	1st ionisation energy
Be	$1s^2\ 2s^2$	900 kJ mol^{-1}
B	$1s^2\ 2s^2\ 2p^1$	801 kJ mol^{-1}

The Drop Between Groups 5 and 6 is Due to **p Orbital Repulsion**

1) In the Group 5 elements, the electron is being removed from a **singly-occupied** orbital (see page 41 for more on sub-shell filling).

2) In the Group 6 elements, the electron is being removed from an orbital containing **two electrons**.

3) The **repulsion** between two electrons in an orbital means that electrons are **easier to remove** from shared orbitals.

E.g.

	Electron structure	1st ionisation energy
N	$1s^2\ 2s^2\ 2p^3$	1402 kJ mol^{-1}
O	$1s^2\ 2s^2\ 2p^4$	1314 kJ mol^{-1}

Successive Ionisation Energies Involve Removing **Additional** Electrons

You can remove **all** the electrons from an atom, leaving only the nucleus.
Each time you remove an electron, there's a **successive ionisation energy**.

Example: The equation for the **second ionisation of oxygen** is:

$$O^+_{(g)} \rightarrow O^{2+}_{(g)} + e^-$$ 2nd ionisation energy = **+3388 kJ mol^{-1}**

Ionisation Energies

Successive Ionisation Energies Show **Shell Structure**

A **graph** of successive ionisation energies (like this one for sodium) provides evidence for the **shell structure** of atoms.

1) **Within each shell**, successive ionisation energies **increase**. This is because electrons are being removed from an **increasingly positive ion**, and there's also **less repulsion** amongst the remaining electrons. So the electrons are **held more strongly** by the nucleus.

2) The **big jumps** in ionisation energy happen when a new shell is broken into — an electron is being removed from a shell **closer** to the nucleus.

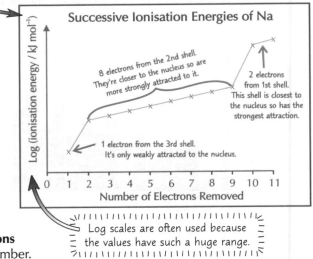

Successive Ionisation Energies of Na

8 electrons from the 2nd shell. They're closer to the nucleus so are more strongly attracted to it.

2 electrons from 1st shell. This shell is closest to the nucleus so has the strongest attraction.

1 electron from the 3rd shell. It's only weakly attracted to the nucleus.

1) Graphs like this can tell you which **group** of the periodic table an element belongs to. Just count **how many electrons are removed** before the first big jump to find the group number.

Log scales are often used because the values have such a huge range.

> E.g. In the graph for sodium, **one electron** is removed before the first big jump — sodium is in **group 1**.

2) The graphs can also be used to predict the **electronic structure** of an element. Working from **right to left**, count how many points there are before each big jump to find how many electrons are in each shell, starting with the first.

> E.g. The graph has **2 points** on the right-hand side, then a jump, then **8 points**, a jump, and **1 final point**. Sodium has **2 electrons** in the first shell, 8 in the second and 1 in the third.

Practice Questions

Q1 Write the definition of the first ionisation energy.

Q2 Name three factors which affect the size of an ionisation energy.

Q3 How does the first ionisation energy change as you go down a group?

Exam Questions

Q1 This graph shows the successive ionisation energies of a certain element.

a) To which group of the periodic table does this element belong? [1 mark]

b) Explain why it takes more energy to remove each successive electron. [2 marks]

c) What causes the sudden increases in ionisation energy? [1 mark]

d) What is the total number of shells of electrons in this element? [1 mark]

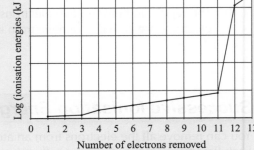

Q2* State and explain the trend in the first ionisation energy across Period 3. [6 marks]

Shirt crumpled? Ionise it.

When you're talking about ionisation energies in exams, always use the three main factors — shielding, nuclear charge and atomic radius. Make sure you're comfortable interpreting the jumps in those graphs without getting stressed. And recite the definition of the first ionisation energy to yourself until you're muttering it in your sleep.

* The quality of your extended response will be assessed for this question.

Structure, Bonding and Properties

Atoms can form giant structures as well as piddling little molecules — well... 'giant' in molecular terms anyway.
Compared to structures like the Eiffel Tower or even your granny's carriage clock, they're still unbelievably tiny.

Diamond, Graphite and Graphene are Giant Covalent Lattices

1) **Giant covalent lattices** are huge networks of **covalently** bonded atoms. (They're sometimes called **macromolecular structures** too.)

2) **Carbon** atoms can form this type of structure because they can each form four strong, covalent bonds.

3) Different forms of the **same element** in the **same state** are called **allotropes**. Carbon has several allotropes, but luckily you only need to know about three of them — **diamond**, **graphite** and **graphene**.

Diamond — not to be confused with a giant lettuce.

Diamond is the Hardest known Substance

In diamond, each carbon atom is **covalently bonded** to **four** other carbon atoms. The atoms arrange themselves in a **tetrahedral** shape — its crystal lattice structure.

Because it has **lots** of **strong covalent** bonds:

1) Diamond has a **very high melting point** — it actually sublimes at over 3800 K.

2) Diamond is extremely **hard** — it's used in diamond-tipped drills and saws.

3) **Vibrations** travel easily through the stiff lattice, so it's a **good thermal conductor**.

4) It **can't conduct** electricity — all the outer electrons are held in localised bonds.

5) It won't dissolve in **any** solvent.

You can 'cut' diamond to form gemstones. Its structure makes it refract light a lot, which is why it sparkles.

'Sublimes' means it changes straight from a solid to a gas, skipping out the liquid stage.

Silicon (which is in the same periodic group as carbon) also forms a **crystal lattice** structure with **similar properties** to carbon. Each silicon atom is able to form **four** strong, covalent bonds.

Graphite Has Loads of Layers

Graphite's **structure** means it has some **different properties** from diamond.

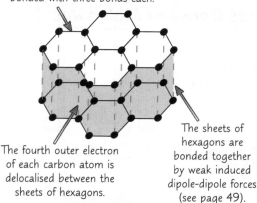

The carbon atoms are arranged in sheets of flat hexagons covalently bonded with three bonds each.

The fourth outer electron of each carbon atom is delocalised between the sheets of hexagons.

The sheets of hexagons are bonded together by weak induced dipole-dipole forces (see page 49).

1) The weak forces **between** the layers in graphite are easily broken, so the sheets can slide over each other — graphite feels **slippery** and is used as a **dry lubricant** and in **pencils**.

2) The 'delocalised' electrons in graphite aren't attached to any particular carbon atom and are **free to move** along the sheets, so an **electric current** can flow.

3) The layers are quite **far apart** compared to the length of the covalent bonds, so graphite is **less dense** than diamond and is used to make **strong**, **lightweight** sports equipment.

4) Because of the **strong covalent bonds** in the hexagon sheets, graphite also has a **very high melting point** (it sublimes at over 3900 K).

5) Like diamond, graphite is **insoluble** in any solvent. The covalent bonds in the sheets are **too strong** to break.

58

Structure, Bonding and Properties

Graphene *is* One Layer *of Graphite*

Graphene is a **sheet** of carbon atoms joined together in **hexagons**.
The sheet is just **one atom** thick, making it a
two-dimensional compound.

Graphene's **structure** gives it some pretty **useful properties**.

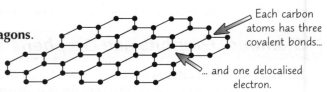

Each carbon atoms has three covalent bonds...

... and one delocalised electron.

1) Like in graphite, the **delocalised electrons** in graphene are **free to move** along the sheet. Without layers, they can move **quickly** above and below the sheet, making graphene the **best known** electrical conductor.

2) The **delocalised electrons** also strengthen the covalent bonds between the carbon atoms. This makes graphene extremely **strong**.

3) A single layer of graphene is **transparent** and incredibly **light**.

Due to its high strength, low mass, and good electrical conductivity, graphene has potential applications in **high-speed electronics** and **aircraft technology**. Its flexibility and transparency also make it a potentially useful material for **touchscreens** on smartphones and other electronic devices.

Like diamond and graphite, graphene has high melting and boiling points and it's insoluble due to its strong covalent bonds.

Metals *have Giant Structures Too*

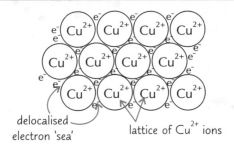

delocalised electron 'sea'

lattice of Cu^{2+} ions

Metal elements exist as **giant metallic lattice structures**.

1) The electrons in the outermost shell of a metal atom are **delocalised** — the electrons are free to move about the metal. This leaves a positively charged **metal cation**, e.g. Na^+, Mg^{2+}, Al^{3+}.

2) The metal cations are **electrostatically attracted** to the delocalised negative electrons. They form a lattice of closely packed cations in a **sea** of delocalised electrons — this is **metallic bonding**.

Metallic bonding explains the properties of metals —

1) The **number of delocalised electrons per atom** affects the melting point. The **more** there are, the **stronger** the bonding will be and the **higher** the melting point. Mg^{2+} has **two** delocalised electrons per atom, so it's got a **higher melting point** than Na^+, which only has **one**. The **size** of the metal ion and the **lattice structure** also affect the melting point. A smaller ionic radius will hold the delocalised electrons closer to the nuclei.

2) As there are **no bonds** holding specific ions together, the metal ions can slide past each other when the structure is pulled, so metals are **malleable** (can be hammered into sheets) and **ductile** (can be drawn into a wire).

3) The delocalised electrons can pass **kinetic energy** to each other, making metals **good thermal conductors**.

4) Metals are **good electrical conductors** because the **delocalised electrons** can move and carry a **current**.

5) Metals are **insoluble**, except in **liquid metals**, because of the **strength** of the metallic bonds.

Simple Molecular Structures *Have* Weak *Bonds* Between Molecules

1) Simple molecular structures contain only a **few** atoms — e.g. oxygen (O_2), chlorine (Cl_2) and phosphorous (P_4).

2) The covalent bonds **between** the atoms in the molecule are very strong, but the **melting** and **boiling points** of simple molecular substances depend upon the strength of the **induced dipole-dipole forces** (see p.49-51) **between** their molecules. These intermolecular forces are weak and easily overcome, so these elements have **low** melting and boiling points.

3) More atoms in a molecule mean stronger induced dipole-dipole forces. For example, in Period 3 sulfur is the **biggest molecule** (S_8), so it's got **higher** melting and boiling points than phosphorus or chlorine.

4) The noble gases have **very low** melting and boiling points because they exist as **individual atoms** (they're monatomic), resulting in **very weak** induced dipole-dipole forces.

Structure, Bonding and Properties

Bond Strength Affects Melting and Boiling Points Across a Period

As you go across a period, the **type** of bond formed between the atoms of an element **changes**. This affects the **melting** and **boiling points** of the element. The graph on the right shows the trend in boiling points across **Periods 2 and 3**.

1) For the **metals** (Li, Be, Na, Mg and Al), melting and boiling points **increase** across the period because the **metallic bonds** get stronger as the **ionic radius** decreases and the number of **delocalised electrons** increases.

2) The elements with **giant covalent lattice** structures (C and Si) have **strong covalent bonds** linking all their atoms together. **A lot** of energy is needed to break these bonds.

3) The elements that form **simple molecular structures** have only **weak intermolecular forces** to overcome between their molecules, so they have **low** melting and boiling points.

4) The noble gases (neon and argon) have the **lowest** melting and boiling points in their periods because they are held together by the **weakest** forces.

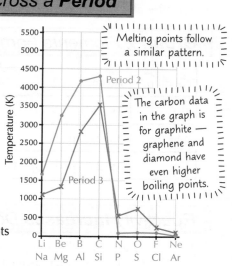

Melting points follow a similar pattern.

The carbon data in the graph is for graphite — graphene and diamond have even higher boiling points.

Bonding and Properties — A Quick Summary

Bonding	Examples	Melting and boiling points	Typical state at STP	Does solid conduct electricity?	Does liquid conduct electricity?	Is it soluble in water?
Ionic	NaCl MgCl$_2$	High	Solid	No (ions are held firmly in place)	Yes (ions are free to move)	Yes
Simple molecular (covalent)	CO$_2$ I$_2$ H$_2$O	Low (have to overcome induced dipole-dipole forces or hydrogen bonds, not covalent bonds)	Sometimes solid, usually liquid or gas (water is liquid because it has hydrogen bonds)	No	No	Depends on how polarised the molecule is
Giant covalent lattice	Diamond Graphite Graphene	High	Solid	No (except graphite and graphene)	— (will generally sublime)	No
Metallic	Fe Mg Al	High	Solid	Yes (delocalised electrons)	Yes (delocalised electrons)	No

Practice Questions

Q1 Diamond has a giant covalent lattice structure. Give two properties that it has as a result of this.

Q2 What forces exist between the carbon sheets in graphite?

Q3 Which element in Period 3 has the highest melting point? Which has the highest boiling point?

Exam Questions

Q1 Explain why the melting point of magnesium is higher than that of sodium. [3 marks]

Q2 This table shows the melting points for the Period 3 elements.

Element	Na	Mg	Al	Si	P	S	Cl	Ar
Melting point / K	371	923	933	1687	317	392	172	84

In terms of structure and bonding explain why:

a) silicon has a high melting point. [2 marks]

b) the melting point of sulfur is higher than that of phosphorus. [2 marks]

Q3* Compare and explain the electrical conductivities of diamond, graphite and graphene in terms of their structure and bonding. [6 marks]

Carbon is a girl's best friend...

Examiners love giving you questions on carbon structures. Close the book and do a quick sketch of each allotrope, together with a list of their properties — then look back at the page and see what you missed. And while you're at it, have a go at remembering all the stuff from that table up there — I can almost guarantee you'll need it at some point.

* The quality of your extended response will be assessed for this question.

Group 2 — The Alkaline Earth Metals

It would be easy for Group 2 elements to feel slightly inferior to those in Group 1. They're only in the second group, after all. That's why you should try to get to know and like them. They'd really appreciate it, I'm sure.

Group 2 Elements Form 2+ Ions

Element	Atom	Ion
Be	$1s^2\,2s^2$	$1s^2$
Mg	$1s^2\,2s^2\,2p^6\,3s^2$	$1s^2\,2s^2\,2p^6$
Ca	$1s^2\,2s^2\,2p^6\,3s^2\,3p^6\,4s^2$	$1s^2\,2s^2\,2p^6\,3s^2\,3p^6$

Group 2 elements all have two electrons in their outer shell (s^2).

They lose their two outer electrons to form **2+ ions**. Their ions then have every atom's dream electronic structure — that of a **noble gas**.

Reactivity **Increases** Down Group 2

1) As you go down the group, the **ionisation energies** decrease. This is due to the **increasing atomic radius** and **shielding effect** (see p.54).

2) When Group 2 elements react they **lose electrons**, forming positive ions (**cations**). The easier it is to lose electrons (i.e. the lower the first and second ionisation energies), the more reactive the element, so **reactivity increases** down the group.

Mr Kelly has one final attempt at explaining electron shielding to his students...

Group 2 Elements React with **Water** and **Oxygen**

When Group 2 elements react, they are **oxidised** from a state of **0** to **+2**, forming M^{2+} ions.

M just represents any Group 2 metal.

$$M \rightarrow M^{2+} + 2e^-$$
Oxidation number: 0   +2

Example: $Ca \rightarrow Ca^{2+} + 2e^-$
  0   +2

There are a few reactions of Group 2 elements that you need to know...

These are all redox reactions — see p.38 and 39 for more info.

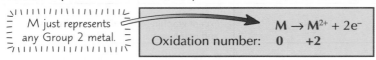

1 They react with WATER to produce HYDROXIDES.

The Group 2 metals react with water to give a **metal hydroxide** and **hydrogen**.

$$M_{(s)} + 2H_2O_{(l)} \rightarrow M(OH)_{2(aq)} + H_{2(g)}$$
Oxidation number: 0   +2

E.g. $Ca_{(s)} + 2H_2O_{(l)} \rightarrow Ca(OH)_{2(aq)} + H_{2(g)}$

Be	doesn't react
Mg	VERY slowly
Ca	steadily
Sr	fairly quickly
Ba	rapidly

2 They burn in OXYGEN to form OXIDES.

When Group 2 metals burn in oxygen, you get solid white **oxides**.

$$2M_{(s)} + O_{2(g)} \rightarrow 2MO_{(s)}$$
Oxidation number of metal: 0   +2
Oxidation number of oxygen: 0   −2

E.g. $2Ca_{(s)} + O_{2(g)} \rightarrow 2CaO_{(s)}$
  0   +2
   0   −2

3 They react with DILUTE ACID to produce a SALT and HYDROGEN.

When Group 2 metals react with dilute hydrochloric acid, you get a **metal chloride** and **hydrogen**.

$$M_{(s)} + 2HCl_{(aq)} \rightarrow MCl_{2(aq)} + H_{2(g)}$$
Oxidation number: 0   +2

E.g. $Ca_{(s)} + 2HCl_{(aq)} \rightarrow CaCl_{2(aq)} + H_{2(g)}$

Like with water, the reactions of Group 2 metals with dilute acid get more vigorous as you go down the group.

Different acids will produce different salts. E.g. if you use dilute sulfuric acid, you'll get a metal sulfate.

Group 2 — The Alkaline Earth Metals

Group 2 Oxides and Hydroxides are **Bases**

The **oxides** and **hydroxides** of Group 2 metals are **bases**. Most of them are **soluble** in water, so are also **alkalis**.

1) The **oxides** of the Group 2 metals react readily with **water** to form **metal hydroxides**, which dissolve. The **hydroxide ions, OH⁻**, make these solutions **strongly alkaline** (e.g. pH 12 – 13).

2) Magnesium oxide is an exception — it only reacts slowly and the hydroxide isn't very soluble.

3) The oxides form **more strongly alkaline** solutions as you go down the group, because the hydroxides get more soluble.

$$CaO_{(s)} + H_2O_{(l)} \rightarrow Ca^{2+}_{(aq)} + 2OH^-_{(aq)}$$

An alkali is a base that's soluble in water.

Group 2 Compounds are used to **Neutralise Acidity**

Group 2 elements are known as the **alkaline earth metals**, and many of their common compounds are used for neutralising acids. Here are a couple of common examples:

1) Calcium hydroxide (slaked lime, $Ca(OH)_2$) is used in **agriculture** to neutralise acidic soils.

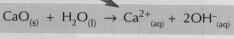

2) Magnesium hydroxide $(Mg(OH)_2)$ and calcium carbonate $(CaCO_3)$ are used in some indigestion tablets as **antacids**.

In both cases, the ionic equation for the neutralisation is $H^+_{(aq)} + OH^-_{(aq)} \rightarrow H_2O_{(l)}$

Example: $Mg(OH)_{2(s)} + 2HCl_{(aq)} \rightarrow 2H_2O_{(l)} + MgCl_{2(aq)}$

Daisy the cow*

Practice Questions

Q1 Which of the following increases in size down Group 2? A — atomic radius B — first ionisation energy

Q2 Which of these Group 2 metals is the least reactive? A — Mg B — Be C — Sr

Q3 Why does reactivity with water increase down Group 2?

Q4 Give a use of magnesium hydroxide.

Exam Questions

Q1 Calcium carbonate reacts with hydrochloric acid to produce a salt, carbon dioxide and water. Write an equation for this reaction. [1 mark]

Q2 Barium (Ba) can be burned in oxygen.

a) Write an equation for the reaction. [1 mark]

b) Show the change in oxidation state of barium. [1 mark]

c) Describe the pH of the solution formed when the product is added to water. [1 mark]

Q3 The table shows the atomic radii of three elements from Group 2.

Element	Atomic radius (nm)
X	0.105
Y	0.150
Z	0.215

a) Predict which element would react most rapidly with water. [1 mark]

b) Explain your answer. [2 marks]

I'm not gonna make it. You've gotta get me out of here, Doc...

We're deep in the dense jungle of Inorganic Chemistry now. Those carefree days of Module Two are well behind us. It's now an endurance test and you've just got to keep going. By now, all the facts are probably blurring into one. It's tough, but you've got to stay awake, stay focused and keep learning. That's all you can do.

*She wanted to be in the book. I said OK.

Group 7 — The Halogens

Now you can wave goodbye to those pesky s-block elements. Here come the halogens.

Halogens are the **Highly Reactive Non-Metals** of Group 7

The table below gives some of the main properties of the first 4 halogens.

halogen	formula	colour	physical state (at 20°C)	electronic structure
fluorine	F_2	pale yellow	gas	$1s^2\ 2s^2\ 2p^5$
chlorine	Cl_2	green	gas	$1s^2\ 2s^2\ 2p^6\ 3s^2\ 3p^5$
bromine	Br_2	red-brown	liquid	$1s^2\ 2s^2\ 2p^6\ 3s^2\ 3p^6\ 3d^{10}\ 4s^2\ 4p^5$
iodine	I_2	grey	solid	$1s^2\ 2s^2\ 2p^6\ 3s^2\ 3p^6\ 3d^{10}\ 4s^2\ 4p^6\ 4d^{10}\ 5s^2\ 5p^5$

The halogens exist as **diatomic** molecules (two atoms joined by a single covalent bond).

Their boiling and melting points **increase** down the group. This is due to the **increasing strength** of the **London** (induced dipole-dipole) **forces** as the size and relative mass of the atoms increases (see p.49-51 for more on intermolecular forces).

This trend is shown in the changes of **physical state** from chlorine (gas) to iodine (solid) — volatility **decreases** down the group. (A substance is said to be **volatile** if it has a low boiling point.)

> The word <u>halogen</u> should be used when describing the atom (X) or molecule (X_2), but the word <u>halide</u> is used to describe the negative ion (X⁻).

Halogens get **Less Reactive** Down the Group

1) Halogen atoms react by **gaining an electron** in their outer shell to form **1–** ions. This means they're **reduced**. As they're reduced, they **oxidise** another substance (it's a redox reaction) — so they're **oxidising agents**.

$$X + e^- \rightarrow X^-$$
ox. number: 0   –1

2) As you go down the group, the atomic radii **increase** so the outer electrons are **further** from the nucleus. The outer electrons are also **shielded** more from the attraction of the positive nucleus, because there are more inner electrons. This makes it **harder** for larger atoms to attract the electron needed to form an ion (despite the increased charge on the nucleus), so larger atoms are less reactive.

3) Another way of saying that the halogens get **less reactive** down the group is to say that they become **less oxidising**.

Halogens **Displace** Less Reactive Halide Ions from Solution

1) The halogens' **relative oxidising strengths** can be seen in their **displacement reactions** with halide ions.

For example, if you mix bromine water, $Br_{2(aq)}$, with potassium iodide solution ($KI_{(aq)}$), the bromine **displaces** the iodide ions (it oxidises them), giving iodine (I_2) and potassium bromide solution, $KBr_{(aq)}$.

Full equation: $Br_{2(aq)} + 2KI_{(aq)} \rightarrow 2KBr_{(aq)} + I_{2(aq)}$
Ionic equation: $Br_{2(aq)} + 2I^-_{(aq)} \rightarrow 2Br^-_{(aq)} + I_{2(aq)}$

Oxidation number of Br: 0 → –1
Oxidation number of I: –1 →   0

2) When these displacement reactions happen, there are **colour changes**.
3) You can make the changes easier to see by shaking the reaction mixture with an **organic solvent** like hexane. The halogen that's present will dissolve readily in the organic solvent, which settles out as a distinct layer above the aqueous solution.

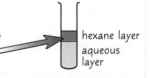
hexane layer
aqueous layer

4) This table summarises the colour changes you'll see:

	$KCl_{(aq)}$ — colourless		$KBr_{(aq)}$ — colourless		$KI_{(aq)}$ — colourless	
	In aqueous solution	In organic solution	In aqueous solution	In organic solution	In aqueous solution	In organic solution
Chlorine water $Cl_{2(aq)}$ — colourless	no reaction	no reaction	yellow (Br_2)	orange (Br_2)	orange/brown (I_2)	purple (I_2)
Bromine water $Br_{2(aq)}$ — yellow	no reaction	no reaction	no reaction	no reaction	orange/brown (I_2)	purple (I_2)
Iodine Solution $I_{2(aq)}$ — orange/brown	no reaction	no reaction	no reaction	no reaction	no reaction	no reaction

Group 7 — The Halogens

Displacement Reactions Can Help to Identify Solutions

These displacement reactions can be used to help **identify** which halogen (or halide) is present in a solution.

A **halogen** will **displace a halide** from solution if the halide is **below it** in the Periodic Table, e.g.

You can also say a halogen will oxidise a halide if the halide is below it in the Periodic Table.

Periodic table	Displacement reaction	Ionic equation
Cl	chlorine (Cl_2) will displace bromide (Br^-) and iodide (I^-)	$Cl_{2(aq)} + 2Br^-_{(aq)} \rightarrow 2Cl^-_{(aq)} + Br_{2(aq)}$ $Cl_{2(aq)} + 2I^-_{(aq)} \rightarrow 2Cl^-_{(aq)} + I_{2(aq)}$
Br	bromine (Br_2) will displace iodide (I^-)	$Br_{2(aq)} + 2I^-_{(aq)} \rightarrow 2Br^-_{(aq)} + I_{2(aq)}$
I	no reaction with F^-, Cl^-, Br^-	

Silver Nitrate Solution is used to Test for Halides

The test for halides is dead easy. First you add **dilute nitric acid** to remove ions that might interfere with the test. Then you just add **silver nitrate solution** ($AgNO_{3(aq)}$). A **precipitate** is formed (of the silver halide).

$$Ag^+_{(aq)} + X^-_{(aq)} \rightarrow AgX_{(s)} \text{ ...where X is Cl, Br or I}$$

1) The **colour** of the precipitate identifies the halide.
2) Then to be extra sure, you can test your results by adding **ammonia solution**. (Each silver halide has a different solubility in ammonia — the larger the ion is, the more difficult it is to dissolve.)

Silver nitrate test for halide ions...

Chloride Cl^-: **white** precipitate, dissolves in dilute $NH_{3(aq)}$
Bromide Br^-: **cream** precipitate, dissolves in conc. $NH_{3(aq)}$
Iodide I^-: **yellow** precipitate, insoluble in conc. $NH_{3(aq)}$

Practice Questions

Q1 Describe the trend in boiling points as you go down Group 7.
Q2 Going down the group, the halogens become less reactive. Explain why.
Q3 What do you see when potassium iodide is added to bromine water?
Q4 Write the ionic equation for the reaction that happens when chlorine is added to a solution of iodide ions.

Exam Questions

Q1 a) Write an ionic equation for the reaction between iodine solution and sodium astatide (NaAt). [1 mark]

b) For the equation in a), deduce which substance is oxidised. [1 mark]

Q2 Dilute nitric acid and silver nitrate solution are added to a solution containing halide ions. A yellow precipitate is formed that is insoluble in concentrated NH_3. What is the formula of this precipitate?

A AgI   B Ag_2O C AgCl   D AgBr [1 mark]

Q3 Which two solutions would react to give a product that is purple when dissolved in an organic solvent?

A Iodine water and potassium chloride solution   B Chlorine water and potassium bromide solution

C Bromine water and potassium iodide solution   D Bromine water and potassium chloride solution [1 mark]

If you're not part of the solution, you're part of the precipitate...

This looks like a lot of tricky stuff, but really it all boils down to who's the best at nabbing that extra electron — the smaller the atom, the better it is. Make sure you remember all those pretty colour changes too — they're important.

Disproportionation and Water Treatment

Here comes another page jam-packed with golden nuggets of halogen fun. Oh yes, I kid you not.
This page is the Alton Towers of Chemistry... white-knuckle excitement all the way...

Halogens Undergo **Disproportionation** with Alkalis

The halogens will react with cold dilute alkali solutions.
In these reactions, the halogen is simultaneously oxidised and reduced (called **disproportionation**)...

$$X_2 + 2NaOH \rightarrow NaXO + NaX + H_2O$$

Ionic equation: $\quad X_2 + 2OH^- \rightarrow XO^- + X^- + H_2O$

Oxidation number of X: $\quad 0 \qquad\qquad +1 \quad -1$

The halogens (except fluorine) can exist in a wide range of oxidation states.
E.g. chlorine can exist as:

−1	0	+1
Cl^-	Cl_2	ClO^-
chloride	chlorine	chlorate(I)

Chlorine and *Sodium Hydroxide* make Bleach

If you mix chlorine gas with cold, dilute aqueous sodium hydroxide, the above reaction takes place and you get **sodium chlorate(I) solution**, $NaClO_{(aq)}$, which just happens to be common household **bleach**.

$$2NaOH_{(aq)} + Cl_{2(g)} \rightarrow NaClO_{(aq)} + NaCl_{(aq)} + H_2O_{(l)}$$

Oxidation number of Cl: $\qquad\qquad 0 \qquad\quad +1 \qquad -1$

The oxidation number of Cl goes up <u>and</u> down so, you guessed it, it's <u>disproportionation</u>. Hurray.

The sodium chlorate(I) solution (bleach) has loads of uses — it's used in **water treatment**, to bleach **paper** and **textiles**... and it's good for **cleaning toilets**, too. Handy...

Chlorine is used to Kill Bacteria in Water

When you mix chlorine with water, it undergoes disproportionation.
You end up with a mixture of hydrochloric acid and **chloric(I) acid** (also called hypochlorous acid).

$$Cl_{2(g)} + H_2O_{(l)} \rightleftharpoons HCl_{(aq)} + HClO_{(aq)}$$

Oxidation number of Cl: $\quad 0 \qquad\qquad -1 \qquad\quad +1$

hydrochloric acid $\qquad$ chloric(I) acid

<u>Bromine</u> and <u>iodine</u> also undergo disproportionation when mixed with water.

Aqueous chloric(I) acid **ionises** to make **chlorate(I) ions** (also called hypochlorite ions).

$$HClO_{(aq)} + H_2O_{(l)} \rightleftharpoons ClO^-_{(aq)} + H_3O^+_{(aq)}$$

Chlorate(I) ions **kill bacteria**.

So, **adding chlorine** (or a compound containing chlorate(I) ions) to water can make it safe to **drink** or **swim** in.

Crystal and Shane were thrilled to hear that the water was safe to swim in.

Disproportionation and Water Treatment

Chlorine in Water — There are Benefits, Risks and Ethical Implications

1) Clean drinking water is amazingly important — around the world around **3.4 million people die** every year from waterborne diseases like cholera, typhoid and dysentery because they have to drink dirty water.

2) In the UK now we're lucky, because our drinking water is **treated** to make it safe.
   Chlorine is an important part of water treatment:

   - It **kills disease-causing microorganisms** (see previous page).
   - Some chlorine remains in the water and **prevents reinfection** further down the supply.
   - It prevents the growth of **algae**, eliminating **bad tastes** and **smells**, and **removes discolouration** caused by organic compounds.

3) However, there are risks from using chlorine to treat water:

   Chlorine gas is **very harmful** if it's breathed in — it irritates the **respiratory system**. **Liquid chlorine** on the skin or eyes causes severe **chemical burns**. Accidents involving chlorine could be really serious, or fatal.

   Water contains a variety of organic compounds, e.g. from the decomposition of plants. Chlorine reacts with these compounds to form **chlorinated hydrocarbons**, e.g. chloromethane (CH_3Cl) — and many of these chlorinated hydrocarbons are carcinogenic (cancer-causing). However, this increased cancer risk is small compared to the risks from untreated water — a cholera epidemic, say, could kill thousands of people.

4) There are ethical considerations too. We don't get a **choice** about having our water chlorinated — some people object to this as forced 'mass medication'.

5) **Alternatives** to chlorine include:

   Ozone (O_3) — a strong **oxidising** agent, which makes it great at **killing microorganisms**. However, it's **expensive** to produce and its **short half-life** in water means that treatment isn't permanent.

   Ultraviolet light — it kills microorganisms by **damaging** their DNA, but it is **ineffective in cloudy water** and, like O_3, it won't stop the water being contaminated further down the line.

Practice Questions

Q1 How is common household bleach formed?

Q2 Write the equation for the reaction of chlorine with water. State underneath the oxidation numbers of the chlorine.

Q3 What are the benefits of adding chlorine to drinking water?

Exam Questions

Q1 If liquid bromine is mixed with cold, dilute potassium hydroxide, potassium bromate(I) is formed.

   a) Give the ionic equation for the reaction.   [1 mark]

   b) What type of reaction is this?   [1 mark]

Q2 Iodide ions react with chlorate(I) ions and water to form iodine, chloride ions and hydroxide ions.

   a) Write a balanced equation for this reaction.   [1 mark]

   b) Show by use of oxidation states which substance has been oxidised and which has been reduced.   [1 mark]

Remain seated until the page comes to a halt. Please exit to the right...

Oooh, what a lovely page, if I do say so myself. I bet the question of how bleach is made and how chlorine reacts with sodium hydroxide has plagued your mind since childhood. Well now you know. And remember... anything that chlorine can do, bromine and iodine can generally do as well. Eeee... it's just fun, fun, fun all the way.

Tests for Ions

If someone hands you a test tube and asks you what's in it, the last thing you should do is stick your finger in and taste the stuff. In fact, don't do that at all. Try these tests instead...

Hydrochloric Acid Can Help Detect Carbonates

To **test for carbonates** (CO_3^{2-}), add a **dilute acid** (e.g. dilute hydrochloric acid) to your mystery sample. If **carbonates** are present then **carbon dioxide** will be released.

The equation for the reaction is: $\boxed{CO_3^{2-}{}_{(s)} + 2H^+{}_{(aq)} \rightarrow CO_{2(g)} + H_2O_{(l)}}$

carbonate + acid → carbon dioxide + water

Example: $CaCO_{3(s)} + HCl_{(aq)} \rightarrow CO_{2(g)} + H_2O_{(l)} + CaCl_{2(aq)}$

You can **test** for carbon dioxide using **limewater**. Carbon dioxide turns limewater **cloudy** — just bubble the gas through a test tube of limewater and watch what happens.

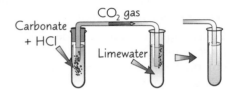

Test for Sulfates with HCl and Barium Chloride

Most sulfates are soluble in water, but **barium sulfate** is **insoluble**. So, to test for a **sulfate** ion (SO_4^{2-}), add dilute HCl, followed by **barium chloride solution**, $BaCl_2$.

If you get a **white precipitate** it'll be **barium sulfate**, which tells you your mystery substance is a sulfate.

The equation for the reaction is: $\boxed{Ba^{2+}{}_{(aq)} + SO_4^{2-}{}_{(aq)} \rightarrow BaSO_{4(s)}}$

Example: $Na_2SO_{4(aq)} + BaCl_{2(aq)} \rightarrow BaSO_{4(s)} + 2NaCl_{(aq)}$

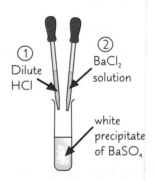

Test for Halides with Silver Nitrate

As you may remember from page 63, to test for **halide ions** just add **nitric acid**, then **silver nitrate solution**. If **chloride, bromide** or **iodide** is present, a **precipitate** will form.
The colour of the precipitate depends on the halide present:

Silver fluoride is soluble, so it won't give any precipitate.

Silver **chloride** (AgCl) is a **white precipitate**.
Silver **bromide** (AgBr) is a **cream precipitate**.
Silver **iodide** (AgI) is a **yellow precipitate**.

Nigel's favourite thing to test was Jen's patience.

You can test the **solubility** of these precipitates in **ammonia** to help you tell them apart.

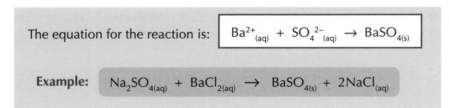

	Dissolves in dilute NH_3?	Dissolves in conc. NH_3?
AgCl	yes	yes
AgBr	no	yes
AgI	no	no

MODULE 3: SECTION 1 — THE PERIODIC TABLE

Tests for Ions

Use **NaOH** and **Litmus Paper** to Test for **Ammonium Compounds**

1) Ammonia gas (NH_3) is alkaline, so you can check for it using a damp piece of **red litmus paper**. If there's ammonia present, the paper will turn **blue**.

2) You can use this to **test** whether a substance contains **ammonium ions** (NH_4^+). Add some **sodium hydroxide** to your mystery substance in a test tube and **warm** the mixture. If there's ammonia given off this means there are ammonium ions in your mystery substance.

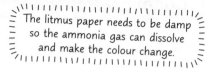
The litmus paper needs to be damp so the ammonia gas can dissolve and make the colour change.

$$NH_4^+{}_{(aq)} + OH^-{}_{(aq)} \rightarrow NH_{3(g)} + H_2O_{(l)}$$

Example: $NH_4Cl_{(aq)} + NaOH_{(aq)} \rightarrow NH_{3(g)} + H_2O_{(l)} + NaCl_{(aq)}$

HEAT

Watch Out for **False Positives**

1) As well as barium sulfate, barium carbonate and barium sulfite are also **insoluble**. So if you're testing for **sulfate ions**, you want to make sure that there are no **carbonate ions** or **sulfite ions** around first. (Otherwise your results won't mean much at all.)

2) Likewise, if you're testing for a **halide ion**, you want to rule out the presence of **sulfate ions** first. This is because sulfate ions will also produce a **precipitate** with silver nitrate.

3) A nifty way of getting round this is to first add a **dilute acid** to your test solutions. The acid will **get rid** of any lurking anions that you don't want.

The dilute acid mustn't interfere with the test you're doing — it's no good using HCl if you're testing for chloride ions.

4) You can also avoid mix-ups by doing your tests in this order:

(1) Test for carbonates →[no CO_2] (2) Test for sulfates →[no precipitate] (3) Test for halides

Practice Questions

Q1 Which halide ion will form a white precipitate when mixed with silver nitrate solution?
Q2 What colour will ammonia gas turn damp litmus paper?
Q3 Why should you add dilute HCl to a solution before carrying out the barium chloride test?

Exam Questions

Q1 Which of these would you expect to observe if you added dilute HCl to a solution containing carbonate ions?

A   A white precipitate will form.   B   Bubbles of gas will form.

C   A yellow precipitate will form.   D   No reaction will occur.   [1 mark]

Q2* You are given four test tubes, each containing one of the following solutions:

calcium carbonate   **sodium sulfate**   **ammonium carbonate**   **magnesium chloride**

Describe the tests that you would carry out to identify each solution with a positive test result. Include any observations that you would expect and the conclusions that you would draw from them.   [6 marks]

It's easy to detect negative ions — they're the gloomy ones...

So here's another couple of pages covered in reactions that you've just got to learn, I'm afraid. Try closing the book and scribbling down what reagent you would use to test for each ion, and what the positive result would look like in each case. Keep going until they're all sorted out in your head. Then chill with a well-earned cuppa — you've earned it.

* The quality of your extended response will be assessed for this question.

Enthalpy Changes

A whole new section to enjoy — but don't forget, Big Brother is watching...

Chemical Reactions Often Have Enthalpy Changes

When chemical reactions happen, some bonds are **broken** and some bonds are **made**. More often than not, this'll cause a **change in energy**. The souped-up chemistry term for this is **enthalpy change**.

> **Enthalpy change**, ΔH (delta H), is the heat energy transferred in a reaction at **constant pressure**. The units of ΔH are **kJ mol^{-1}**.

You write $\Delta H^\ominus$ to show that the measurements were made under **standard conditions** and that the elements were in their **standard states** (i.e. their physical states under standard conditions). Standard conditions are **100 kPa** (about 1 atm) **pressure** and a temperature of **298 K** (25 °C). The next page explains why this is necessary.

Reactions can be either Exothermic or Endothermic

> **Exothermic** reactions **give out** energy. ΔH is **negative**.

In exothermic reactions, the temperature often goes **up**.

> **Oxidation** is usually exothermic. Here are 2 examples:
> - The **combustion** of a fuel like methane:
>
> $$CH_{4(g)} + 2O_{2(g)} \rightarrow CO_{2(g)} + 2H_2O_{(l)} \qquad \Delta_r H^\ominus = -890 \text{ kJ mol}^{-1} \textbf{ exothermic}$$
> - The oxidation of **carbohydrates**, such as glucose, $C_6H_{12}O_6$, in respiration.

The symbols $\Delta_c H^\ominus$ and $\Delta_r H^\ominus$ (below) are explained on the next page.

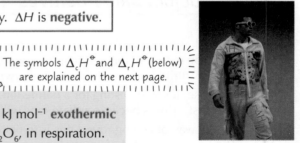

Fabio heard an exothermic onesie would increase his hotness.

> **Endothermic** reactions **absorb** energy. ΔH is **positive**.

In these reactions, the temperature often **falls**.

> - The **thermal decomposition** of calcium carbonate is endothermic:
>
> $$CaCO_{3(s)} \rightarrow CaO_{(s)} + CO_{2(g)} \qquad \Delta_r H^\ominus = +178 \text{ kJ mol}^{-1} \textbf{ endothermic}$$
> - The main reactions of **photosynthesis** are also endothermic — sunlight supplies the energy.

Enthalpy Profile Diagrams Show Energy Change in Reactions

1) **Enthalpy profile diagrams** show you how the enthalpy (energy) changes during reactions.

2) The **activation energy**, E_a, is the minimum amount of energy needed to begin breaking reactant bonds and start a chemical reaction. (There's more on activation energy on page 74.)

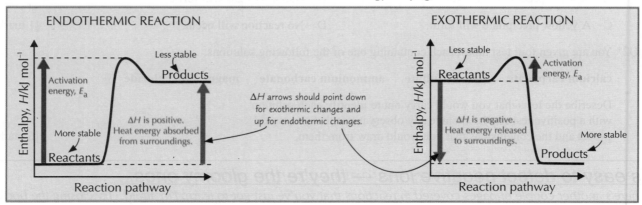

3) The **less enthalpy** a substance has, the **more stable** it is.

Enthalpy Changes

You Need to Specify the Conditions for Enthalpy Changes

1) You can't directly measure the **actual** enthalpy of a system. In practice, that doesn't matter, because it's only ever **enthalpy change** that matters. You can find enthalpy changes either by **experiment** or in **data books**.

2) Enthalpy changes you find in data books are usually **standard** enthalpy changes — enthalpy changes under **standard conditions** (**298 K** and **100 kPa**).

3) This is important because changes in enthalpy are affected by **temperature** and **pressure** — using standard conditions means that everyone can know **exactly** what the enthalpy change is describing.

There are Different Types of ΔH Depending On the Reaction

1) **Standard enthalpy change of reaction**, $\Delta_r H^{\ominus}$, is the enthalpy change when the reaction occurs in the **molar quantities** shown in the **chemical equation**, under standard conditions.

2) **Standard enthalpy change of formation**, $\Delta_f H^{\ominus}$, is the enthalpy change when **1 mole** of a **compound** is formed from its **elements** in their standard states, under standard conditions, e.g. $2C_{(s)} + 3H_{2(g)} + \frac{1}{2}O_{2(g)} \rightarrow C_2H_5OH_{(l)}$.

3) **Standard enthalpy change of combustion**, $\Delta_c H^{\ominus}$, is the enthalpy change when **1 mole** of a substance is completely **burned in oxygen**, under standard conditions.

4) **Standard enthalpy change of neutralisation**, $\Delta_{neut} H^{\ominus}$, is the enthalpy change when an **acid** and an **alkali** react together, under standard conditions, to form **1 mole of water**.

Practice Questions

Q1 Explain the terms exothermic and endothermic, giving an example reaction in each case.

Q2 Draw and label enthalpy profile diagrams for an exothermic and an endothermic reaction.

Q3 Define standard enthalpy of formation and standard enthalpy of combustion.

Exam Questions

Q1 Hydrogen peroxide, H_2O_2, can decompose into water and oxygen.

$$2H_2O_{2(l)} \rightarrow 2H_2O_{(l)} + O_{2(g)} \qquad \Delta H^{\ominus} = -98 \text{ kJ mol}^{-1}$$

Draw an enthalpy profile diagram for this reaction. Mark on the activation energy, E_a, and ΔH. [3 marks]

Q2 Methanol, $CH_3OH_{(l)}$, when blended with petrol, can be used as a fuel. $\Delta_c H^{\ominus}[CH_3OH] = -726 \text{ kJ mol}^{-1}$

a) Write an equation, including state symbols, for the standard enthalpy change of combustion of methanol. [1 mark]

b) Write an equation, including state symbols, for the standard enthalpy change of formation of methanol. [1 mark]

c) Petroleum gas is a fuel that contains propane, C_3H_8. Why does the following equation not represent a standard enthalpy change of combustion? [1 mark]

$$2C_3H_{8(g)} + 10O_{2(g)} \rightarrow 6CO_{2(g)} + 8H_2O_{(g)} \qquad \Delta_r H^{\ominus} = -4113 \text{ kJ mol}^{-1}$$

Q3 Coal is mainly carbon. It is burned as a fuel. $\Delta_c H^{\ominus} = -393.5 \text{ kJ mol}^{-1}$

a) Write an equation, including state symbols, for the standard enthalpy change of combustion of carbon. [1 mark]

b) Explain why the standard enthalpy change of formation of carbon dioxide will also be $-393.5 \text{ kJ mol}^{-1}$. [1 mark]

c) How much energy would be released when 1 tonne of carbon is burned? (1 tonne = 1000 kg) [2 marks]

Clap along if you feel like an enthalpy change without a roof...

Quite a few definitions here. And you need to know them all. If you're going to bother learning them, you might as well do it properly and learn all the pernickety details. They probably seem about as useful as a dead fly in your custard right now, but all will be revealed over the next few pages. Learn them now, so you've got a bit of a head start.

More on Enthalpy Changes

I bonded with my friend straight away. Now we're on the waiting list to be surgically separated.

Reactions are all about Breaking and Making Bonds

When reactions happen, **reactant bonds** are **broken** and **product bonds** are **formed**.

1) You **need** energy to break bonds, so bond breaking is **endothermic** (ΔH is **positive**).
2) Energy is **released** when bonds are formed, so this is **exothermic** (ΔH is **negative**).
3) The **enthalpy change** for a reaction is the **overall effect** of these two changes. If you need **more** energy to **break** bonds than is released when bonds are made, ΔH is **positive**. If you need **less**, ΔH is **negative**.

You need Energy to Break the Attraction between Atoms and Ions

1) In ionic bonding, **positive** and **negative ions** are attracted to each other. In covalent molecules, the **positive nuclei** are attracted to the **negative** charge of the shared electrons in a covalent bond.
2) You need energy to **break** this attraction — **stronger** bonds take more energy to break. The **amount of energy** you need per mole is called the **bond dissociation enthalpy**. (Of course it's got a fancy name — this is chemistry.)
3) Bond dissociation enthalpies always involve bond breaking in **gaseous compounds**. This makes comparisons fair.

Average Bond Enthalpies are not Exact

1) Water (H_2O) has **two O–H bonds**. You'd think it'd take the same amount of energy to break them both... but it **doesn't**.
2) The **data book** says the bond enthalpy for O–H is +463 kJ mol^{-1}. It's a bit different because it's the average for a **much bigger range** of molecules, not just water. For example, it includes the O–H bonds in alcohols and carboxylic acids too.

> The **first** bond, H–OH$_{(g)}$: $E(H–OH) = +492$ kJ mol^{-1}
> The **second** bond, H–O$_{(g)}$: $E(H–O) = +428$ kJ mol^{-1}
> (OH$^-$ is a bit easier to break apart because of the extra electron repulsion.)
> So, the **average** bond enthalpy is $(492 + 428) \div 2 = $ **+460 kJ mol^{-1}**.

3) So when you look up an **average bond enthalpy**, what you get is:

The energy needed to break **one mole** of bonds in the **gas phase**, averaged over **many different** compounds.

You can find out Enthalpy Changes in the Lab

1) To measure the **enthalpy change** for a reaction you only need to know **two things** —
   - the **number of moles** of the stuff that's reacting,
   - the change in **temperature**.
2) How you go about doing the experiment depends on what type of reaction it is.

- To find the enthalpy of **combustion** of a **flammable liquid**, you burn it — using apparatus like this...
- As the fuel burns, it heats the water. You can work out the **heat absorbed** by the water if you know the **mass of water**, the **temperature change of the water** (ΔT), and the **specific heat capacity of water** (= 4.18 J g^{-1} K^{-1}). See the next page for all the details.
- Ideally **all** the heat given out by the fuel as it burns would be **absorbed** by the water — allowing you to work out the enthalpy change of combustion (see the next page). In practice though, you **always** lose some heat (as you heat the apparatus and the surroundings).

> The specific heat capacity of a substance is the amount of heat energy it takes to raise the temperature of 1 g of that substance by 1 K.

Stirrer, Thermometer, Water, Combustion chamber, Air, Fuel (reactant)

3) Similar methods to this (all known as calorimetry) can also be used to calculate an enthalpy change for a reaction that happens **in solution**, such as **neutralisation** or **displacement**. For a neutralisation reaction, combine known quantities of acid and alkali in an insulated container, and measure the temperature change. The **heat given out** can be calculated using the formula on the next page.

More on Enthalpy Changes

Calculate **Enthalpy Changes** Using the **Equation q = mcΔT**

It seems there's a snazzy equation for everything these days, and enthalpy change is no exception:

$q = mc\Delta T$ where, q = heat lost or gained (in joules). This is the same as the enthalpy change if the pressure is constant.

m = mass of water in the calorimeter, or solution in the insulated container (in grams).

c = specific heat capacity of water (4.18 J g^{-1} K^{-1}).

ΔT = the change in temperature of the water or solution (in K). *This is the same as the change in °C.*

Example: In a laboratory experiment, 1.16 g of an organic liquid fuel was completely burned in oxygen. The heat formed during this combustion raised the temperature of 100 g of water from 295.3 K to 357.8 K. Calculate the standard enthalpy of combustion, $\Delta_c H^\ominus$, of the fuel. Its M_r is 58.0.

Remember — m is the mass of water, NOT the mass of fuel.

1 First off, you need to calculate the **amount of heat** given out by the fuel using $q = mc\Delta T$.

$q = mc\Delta T$

$q = 100 \times 4.18 \times (357.8 - 295.3) = 26\ 125$ J

$26\ 125 \div 1000 = 26.125$ kJ

If you're asked to calculate an enthalpy change, the answer should always be in kJ mol^{-1}. So change the amount of heat from J to kJ by dividing by 1000.

2 The standard enthalpy of combustion involves 1 mole of fuel. So next you need to find out **how many moles** of fuel produced this heat. It's back to the old n = mass ÷ M_r equation.

n = 1.16 ÷ 58.0 = 0.0200 mole of fuels

It's negative because combustion is an exothermic reaction.

3 So the heat produced by 1 mole of fuel = −26.125 ÷ 0.0200

$\approx$ **−1310 kJ mol^{-1}** (3 s.f.).

This is the standard enthalpy change of combustion.

The actual $\Delta_c H^\ominus$ of this compound is −1615 kJ mol^{-1} — lots of heat has been **lost** and not measured. For example, it's likely a bit would escape through the **calorimeter** and also the fuel might not **combust completely**.

Practice Questions

Q1 Briefly describe an experiment that could be carried out to find the enthalpy change of a reaction.

Q2 Why is the enthalpy change determined in a laboratory likely to be lower than the value shown in a data book?

Q3 What equation is used to calculate the heat change in a chemical reaction?

Exam Questions

Q1 A 50.0 cm^3 sample of 0.200 mol dm^{-3} copper(II) sulfate solution placed in a polystyrene beaker gave a temperature increase of 2.60 K when excess zinc powder was added and stirred. Calculate the enthalpy change when 1 mole of zinc reacts. Assume that the specific heat capacity for the solution is 4.18 J g^{-1} K^{-1}. Ignore the increase in volume due to the zinc.

The equation for the reaction is: $Zn_{(s)} + CuSO_{4(aq)} \rightarrow Cu_{(s)} + ZnSO_{4(aq)}$ [4 marks]

Q2 a) Explain why bond enthalpies determine whether a reaction is exothermic or endothermic. [2 marks]

b) Calculate the temperature change that should be produced when 1.000 kg of water is heated by burning 6.000 g of coal. Assume the coal is pure carbon.
[The specific heat capacity of water is 4.18 J g^{-1} K^{-1}. For carbon, $\Delta_c H^\ominus = -393.5$ kJ mol^{-1}] [3 marks]

Clap along if you feel like calorimetry is the truth...

Reactions are like pulling a model spaceship apart and building something new. Sometimes the bits get stuck together and you need to use loads of energy to pull 'em apart. Okay, so energy's not really released when you stick them together, but you can't have everything — and it wasn't that bad an analogy up till now.

Enthalpy Calculations

You can't always work out an enthalpy change by measuring a single temperature change. But there are other ways...

Hess's Law — the Total Enthalpy Change is **Independent** of the Route Taken

Hess's Law says that:

> The **total enthalpy change** of a reaction is always **the same**, no matter **which route** is taken.

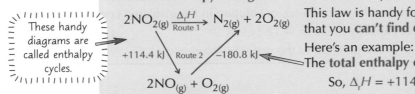

These handy diagrams are called enthalpy cycles.

$$2NO_{2(g)} \xrightarrow[\text{Route 1}]{\Delta_r H} N_{2(g)} + 2O_{2(g)}$$

+114.4 kJ ⟍ Route 2 ⟋ −180.8 kJ

$$2NO_{(g)} + O_{2(g)}$$

This law is handy for working out enthalpy changes that you **can't find directly** by doing an experiment.

Here's an example:
The **total enthalpy change** for route 1 is the **same as for route 2**.
So, $\Delta_r H = +114.4 + (−180.8) = $ **−66.4 kJ mol⁻¹**.

Enthalpy Changes Can be Worked Out From **Enthalpies of Formation**

Enthalpy changes of formation are useful for calculating enthalpy changes you can't find directly.
You need to know $\Delta_f H^{\ominus}$ for **all** the reactants and products that are **compounds** — $\Delta_f H^{\ominus}$ for elements is **zero**.

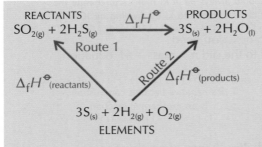

REACTANTS
$$SO_{2(g)} + 2H_2S_{(g)} \xrightarrow{\Delta_r H^{\ominus}} 3S_{(s)} + 2H_2O_{(l)}$$
PRODUCTS
Route 1

$\Delta_f H^{\ominus}$(reactants) Route 2 $\Delta_f H^{\ominus}$(products)

$$3S_{(s)} + 2H_{2(g)} + O_{2(g)}$$
ELEMENTS

$\Delta_f H^{\ominus}[SO_{2(g)}] = −297$ kJ mol⁻¹
$\Delta_f H^{\ominus}[H_2S_{(g)}] = −20.2$ kJ mol⁻¹
$\Delta_f H^{\ominus}[H_2O_{(l)}] = −286$ kJ mol⁻¹

Here's how to calculate $\Delta_r H^{\ominus}$ for the reaction:

$$SO_{2(g)} + 2H_2S_{(g)} \to 3S_{(s)} + 2H_2O_{(l)}$$

Using **Hess's Law**: Route 1 = Route 2
$\Delta_r H^{\ominus}$ + the sum of $\Delta_f H^{\ominus}$(reactants) = the sum of $\Delta_f H^{\ominus}$(products)
So, $\Delta_r H^{\ominus}$ = the sum of $\Delta_f H^{\ominus}$(products) – the sum of $\Delta_f H^{\ominus}$(reactants)

Just plug the numbers given on the left into the equation above:

$\Delta_r H^{\ominus} = [0 + (−286 \times 2)] − [−297 + (−20.2 \times 2)] = $ **−235 kJ mol⁻¹**

$\Delta_f H^{\ominus}$ of sulfur is zero — it's an element. | There are 2 moles of H_2O and 2 moles of H_2S.

It **always** works, no matter how complicated the reaction... e.g. $2NH_4NO_{3(s)} + C_{(s)} \to 2N_{2(g)} + CO_{2(g)} + 4H_2O_{(l)}$

Using Hess's Law: Route 1 = Route 2
$\Delta_f H^{\ominus}$(reactants) + $\Delta_r H^{\ominus}$ = $\Delta_f H^{\ominus}$(products)
$(2 \times −365) + 0 + \Delta_r H^{\ominus} = 0 + −394 + (4 \times −286)$
$\Delta_r H^{\ominus} = −394 + (−1144) − (−730)$
= **−808 kJ mol⁻¹**

Remember... $\Delta_f H$ for <u>any</u> element is zero.

REACTANTS
$$2NH_4NO_{3(s)} + C_{(s)} \xrightarrow{\Delta_r H^{\ominus}} 2N_{2(g)} + CO_{2(g)} + 4H_2O_{(l)}$$
PRODUCTS
Route 1
$\Delta_f H^{\ominus}$(reactants) Route 2 $\Delta_f H^{\ominus}$(products)
$$C_{(s)} + 2N_{2(g)} + 4H_{2(g)} + 3O_{2(g)}$$
ELEMENTS

$\Delta_f H^{\ominus}[NH_4NO_{3(s)}] = −365$ kJ mol⁻¹
$\Delta_f H^{\ominus}[CO_{2(g)}] = −394$ kJ mol⁻¹
$\Delta_f H^{\ominus}[H_2O_{(l)}] = −286$ kJ mol⁻¹

Enthalpy Changes Can be Worked Out From **Enthalpies of Combustion**

You can use a similar method to find an enthalpy change from **enthalpy changes of combustion**.

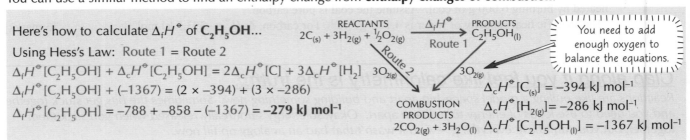

Here's how to calculate $\Delta_f H^{\ominus}$ of **C_2H_5OH**...

Using Hess's Law: Route 1 = Route 2
$\Delta_f H^{\ominus}[C_2H_5OH] + \Delta_c H^{\ominus}[C_2H_5OH] = 2\Delta_c H^{\ominus}[C] + 3\Delta_c H^{\ominus}[H_2]$
$\Delta_f H^{\ominus}[C_2H_5OH] + (−1367) = (2 \times −394) + (3 \times −286)$
$\Delta_f H^{\ominus}[C_2H_5OH] = −788 + −858 − (−1367) = $ **−279 kJ mol⁻¹**

REACTANTS
$$2C_{(s)} + 3H_{2(g)} + \tfrac{1}{2}O_{2(g)} \xrightarrow{\Delta_f H^{\ominus}} C_2H_5OH_{(l)}$$
PRODUCTS
Route 1
Route 2
$3O_{2(g)}$ ⟍ ⟋ $3O_{2(g)}$

COMBUSTION PRODUCTS
$2CO_{2(g)} + 3H_2O_{(l)}$

You need to add enough oxygen to balance the equations.

$\Delta_c H^{\ominus}[C_{(s)}] = −394$ kJ mol⁻¹
$\Delta_c H^{\ominus}[H_{2(g)}] = −286$ kJ mol⁻¹
$\Delta_c H^{\ominus}[C_2H_5OH_{(l)}] = −1367$ kJ mol⁻¹

Enthalpy Calculations

Enthalpy Changes Can Be Calculated using *Average Bond Enthalpies*

In any chemical reaction, energy is **absorbed** to **break bonds** and **given out** during **bond formation**. The difference between the energy absorbed and released is the overall **enthalpy change of reaction**:

Enthalpy Change of Reaction = Total Energy Absorbed − Total Energy Released

Example: Calculate the overall enthalpy change for this reaction: $N_{2(g)} + 3H_{2(g)} \rightarrow 2NH_{3(g)}$
Use the average bond enthalpy values in the table.

Bonds broken: 1 N≡N bond broken = 1×945 = 945 kJ mol^{-1}
3 H–H bonds broken = 3×436 = 1308 kJ mol^{-1}

Total Energy Absorbed = 945 + 1308 = **2253 kJ mol^{-1}**

Bonds formed: 6 N–H bonds formed = 6×391 = 2346 kJ mol^{-1}

Total Energy Released = **2346 kJ mol^{-1}**

Now you just subtract 'total energy released' from 'total energy absorbed':

Enthalpy Change of Reaction = 2253 − 2346 = **−93 kJ mol^{-1}**

Bond	Average Bond Enthalpy
N≡N	945 kJ mol^{-1}
H–H	436 kJ mol^{-1}
N–H	391 kJ mol^{-1}

Practice Questions

Q1 What is Hess's Law?

Q2 What is the standard enthalpy change of formation of any element?

Q3 Describe how you can make an enthalpy cycle to find the standard enthalpy change of a reaction using standard enthalpy changes of formation.

Exam Questions

Q1 Using the facts that the standard enthalpy change of formation of $Al_2O_{3(s)}$ is −1676 kJ mol^{-1} and the standard enthalpy change of formation of $MgO_{(s)}$ is −602 kJ mol^{-1}, calculate the enthalpy change of the following reaction.

$$Al_2O_{3(s)} + 3Mg_{(s)} \rightarrow 2Al_{(s)} + 3MgO_{(s)}$$

[2 marks]

Q2 Calculate the enthalpy change for the reaction below (the fermentation of glucose).

$$C_6H_{12}O_{6(s)} \rightarrow 2C_2H_5OH_{(l)} + 2CO_{2(g)}$$

Use the following standard enthalpies of combustion in your calculations:

$\Delta_c H^\ominus$(glucose) = −2820 kJ mol^{-1} $\Delta_c H^\ominus$(ethanol) = −1367 kJ mol^{-1} [2 marks]

Q3 Calculate the standard enthalpy of formation of propane from carbon and hydrogen. $3C_{(s)} + 4H_{2(g)} \rightarrow C_3H_{8(g)}$

Use the following data:

$\Delta_c H^\ominus$(propane) = −2220 kJ mol^{-1}, $\Delta_c H^\ominus$(carbon) = −394 kJ mol^{-1} , $\Delta_c H^\ominus$(hydrogen) = −286 kJ mol^{-1} [2 marks]

Q4 The table on the right shows some average bond enthalpy values.

Bond	C–H	C=O	O=O	O–H
Average Bond Enthalpy (kJ mol^{-1})	435	805	498	464

The complete combustion of methane can be represented by the following equation:

$$CH_{4(g)} + 2O_{2(g)} \rightarrow CO_{2(g)} + 2H_2O_{(l)}$$

Use the table of bond enthalpies above to calculate the enthalpy change for the reaction. [2 marks]

<u>Clap along if you know what Hess's Law is to you...</u>

To get your head around those enthalpy cycles, you're going to have to do more than skim them. It'll also help if you know the definitions for those standard enthalpy thingumabobs. I'd read those enthalpy cycle examples again and make sure you understand how the elements/compounds at each corner were chosen to be there.

Reaction Rates

The rate of a reaction is just how quickly it happens. Lots of things can make it go faster or slower.

Particles **Must** Collide to **React**

1) Particles in liquids and gases are **always moving** and **colliding** with **each other**. They **don't** react every time though — only when the **conditions** are right. A reaction **won't** take place between two particles **unless** —

> • They collide in the **right direction**. They need to be **facing** each other the right way.
> • They collide with at least a certain **minimum** amount of kinetic (movement) **energy**.

This stuff's called **Collision Theory**.

2) The **minimum amount of kinetic energy** particles need to react is called the **activation energy**. The particles need this much energy to **break the bonds** to start the reaction.

3) Reactions with **low activation energies** often happen **pretty easily**. But reactions with **high activation energies** don't. You need to give the particles extra energy by **heating** them.

To make this a bit clearer, here's an **energy profile diagram**.

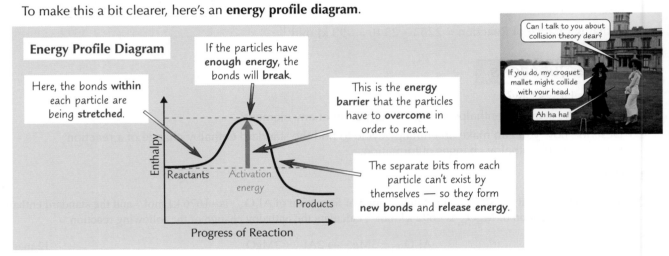

Energy Profile Diagram

Here, the bonds **within** each particle are being **stretched**.

If the particles have **enough energy**, the bonds will **break**.

This is the **energy barrier** that the particles have to **overcome** in order to react.

The separate bits from each particle can't exist by themselves — so they form **new bonds** and **release energy**.

Reactants — Activation energy — Products

Enthalpy / Progress of Reaction

Can I talk to you about collision theory dear?

If you do, my croquet mallet might collide with your head.

Ah ha ha!

Molecules **Don't** all have the **Same Amount of Energy**

Imagine looking down on Oxford Street when it's teeming with people. You'll see some people ambling along **slowly**, some hurrying **quickly**, but most of them will be walking with a **moderate speed**. It's the same with the **molecules** in a liquid or gas. Some **don't have much kinetic energy** and move **slowly**. Others have **loads** of **kinetic energy** and whizz along. But most molecules are somewhere **in between**.

If you plot a **graph** of the **numbers of molecules** in a substance with different **kinetic energies** you get a **Boltzmann distribution**. It looks like this —

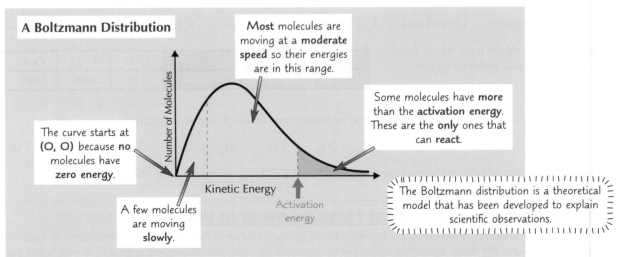

A Boltzmann Distribution

Most molecules are moving at a **moderate speed** so their energies are in this range.

Some molecules have **more** than the **activation energy**. These are the **only** ones that can **react**.

The curve starts at **(O, O)** because **no** molecules have **zero energy**.

A few molecules are moving **slowly**.

Number of Molecules / Kinetic Energy / Activation energy

The Boltzmann distribution is a theoretical model that has been developed to explain scientific observations.

Reaction Rates

Increasing the Temperature makes Reactions Faster

1) If you increase the **temperature**, the particles will, on average, have more **kinetic energy** and will move **faster**.

2) So, a **greater proportion** of molecules will have at least the **activation energy** and be able to **react**. This changes the **shape** of the **Boltzmann distribution curve** — it pushes it over to the **right**.

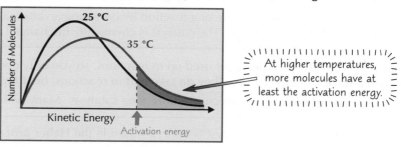

The total number of molecules is still the same, which means the area under each curve must be the same.

At higher temperatures, more molecules have at least the activation energy.

3) Because the molecules are flying about **faster**, they'll **collide more often**. This is **another reason** why increasing the temperature makes a reaction faster.

Concentration, Pressure and Catalysts also Affect the Reaction Rate

Increasing Concentration Speeds Up Reactions

If you increase the **concentration** of reactants in a **solution**, the particles will be **closer together**, on average. If they're closer, they'll **collide more frequently**. If there are **more collisions**, they'll have **more chances** to react.

Increasing Pressure Speeds Up Reactions

If any of your reactants are **gases**, increasing the **pressure** will increase the rate of reaction. It's pretty much the same as increasing the **concentration** of a solution — at higher pressures, the particles will be **closer together**, increasing the chance of **successful collisions**.

If one of the reactants is a solid, increasing its surface area makes the reaction faster too.

Catalysts Can Speed Up Reactions

Catalysts are really useful. They **lower the activation energy** by providing a **different way** for the bonds to be broken and remade. If the activation energy's **lower**, more particles will have **enough energy** to react. There's heaps of information about catalysts on the next two pages.

Practice Questions

Q1 Explain the term 'activation energy'.

Q2 Name four factors that affect the rate of a reaction.

Exam Questions

Q1 Nitrogen oxide (NO) and ozone (O_3) sometimes react to produce nitrogen dioxide (NO_2) and oxygen (O_2). How would increasing the pressure affect the rate of this reaction? Explain your answer. [2 marks]

Q2 On the right is a Boltzmann distribution curve for a sample of a gas at 25 °C.

a) Which of the curves, X or Y, shows the Boltzmann distribution curve for the same sample at 15 °C ? [1 mark]

b) Explain how this curve shows that the reaction rate will be lower at 15 °C than at 25 °C. [1 mark]

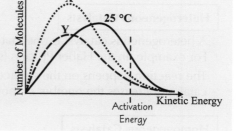

Clap along if you feel like reaction rates are what you wanna do...

This page isn't too hard to learn — no equations, no formulas... what more could you ask for. The only tricky thing might be the Boltzmann thingymajiggle. Remember, increasing concentration and pressure do exactly the same thing. The only difference is, you increase the concentration of a solution and the pressure of a gas.

Catalysts

Catalysts were tantalisingly mentioned on the last page — here's the full story...

Catalysts Increase the Rate of Reactions

You can use **catalysts** to make chemical reactions happen **faster**. Learn this definition:

> A **catalyst** increases the **rate** of a reaction by providing an **alternative reaction pathway** with a **lower activation energy**. The catalyst is **chemically unchanged** at the end of the reaction.

1) Catalysts are **great**. They **don't** get used up in reactions, so you only need a **tiny bit** of catalyst to catalyse a **huge** amount of stuff. They **do** take part in reactions, but they're **remade** at the end.

2) Catalysts are **very fussy** about which reactions they catalyse. Many will usually **only** work on a single reaction.

> An example of a catalyst is **iron**. It's used in the **Haber process** to make ammonia.
>
> $$N_{2(g)} + 3H_{2(g)} \underset{\overset{Fe_{(s)}}{\rightleftharpoons}}{} 2NH_{3(g)}$$

Enthalpy Profiles and Boltzmann Distributions Show Why Catalysts Work

If you look at an **enthalpy profile** together with a **Boltzmann Distribution**, you can see **why** catalysts work.

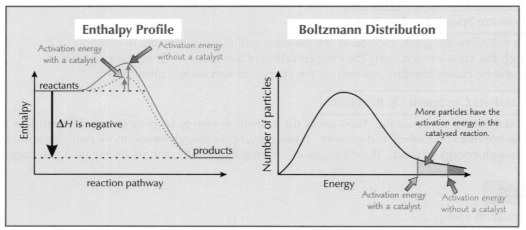

The 1985 Nobel Prize in Chemistry was awarded to Mr Tiddles for discovering catalysis.

The catalyst **lowers the activation energy**, meaning there are **more particles** with **enough energy** to react when they collide. So, in a certain amount of time, **more particles react**.

Catalysts can be Homogeneous or Heterogenous

Heterogeneous Catalysts

A heterogeneous catalyst is one that is in a **different phase** from the reactants — i.e. in a different **physical state**. For example, in the Haber Process (see above), **gases** are passed over a **solid iron catalyst**.

The **reaction** happens on the **surface** of the **heterogeneous catalyst**. So, **increasing** the **surface area** of the catalyst increases the number of molecules that can **react** at the same time, **increasing the rate** of the reaction.

Homogeneous Catalysts

Homogeneous catalysts are in the **same physical state** as the reactants.
Usually a **homogeneous** catalyst is an **aqueous catalyst** for a reaction between two **aqueous solutions**.

A homogeneous catalyst works by forming an **intermediate species**. The **reactants** combine with the **catalyst** to make an **intermediate species**, which then reacts to form the **products** and **reform the catalyst**.

Catalysts

Catalysts — Good for Industries...

Loads of industries rely on **catalysts**. They can dramatically lower production costs, give you more product in a shorter time and help make better products. Here are a few examples —

> Iron is used as a catalyst in **ammonia** production. If it wasn't for the catalyst, the **temperature** would have to be raised loads to make the reaction happen **quick enough**. Not only would this be bad for the fuel bills, it'd **reduce the amount of ammonia** produced.

Using a catalyst can change the properties of a product to make it more useful, e.g. **poly(ethene)**.

	Made without a catalyst	Made with a catalyst (a Ziegler-Natta catalyst, to be precise)
Properties of poly(ethene)	less dense, less rigid	more dense, more rigid, higher melting point

...and for Environmental Sustainability

1) Using catalysts means that lower temperatures and pressures can be used. So energy is saved, meaning **less CO_2** is released, and fossil fuel reserves are preserved. Catalysts can also **reduce waste** by allowing a different reaction to be used with a better **atom economy**. (See page 34 for more on atom economy.)

> For example, making the painkiller ibuprofen by the traditional method involves 6 steps and has an atom economy of 32%. Using catalysts, it can be made in **3 steps** with an **atom economy of 77%**.

2) **Catalytic converters** on cars are made from **alloys of platinum, palladium and rhodium**. They reduce the pollution released into the atmosphere by speeding up the reaction, $2CO + 2NO \rightarrow 2CO_2 + N_2$.

Practice Questions

Q1 Explain what a catalyst is.

Q2 Explain what the difference between a heterogeneous and a homogeneous catalyst is.

Q3 Describe three reasons why catalysts are useful for industry.

Exam Question

Q1 Sulfuric acid is manufactured by the contact process. In one of the stages, sulfur dioxide gas is mixed with oxygen gas and converted into sulfur trioxide gas. A solid vanadium(V) oxide (V_2O_5) catalyst is used. The enthalpy change for the uncatalysed reaction is -197 kJ mol^{-1}.

a) Write an equation for the catalysed reaction, including state symbols. [1 mark]

b) Which of the following enthalpy profile diagrams is correct for the catalysed reaction? [1 mark]

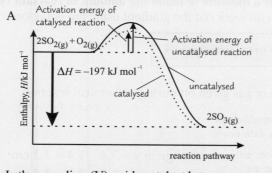
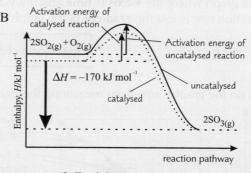

c) Is the vanadium(V) oxide catalyst heterogeneous or homogeneous? Explain your answer. [1 mark]

Catalysts and walking past bad buskers — increased speed but no change...

Whatever you do, don't confuse the Boltzmann diagram for catalysts with the one for a temperature change. Catalysts lower the activation energy without changing the shape of the curve. BUT, the shape of the curve does change with temperature. Get these mixed up and you'll be the laughing stock of the Examiners' tea room.

Calculating Reaction Rates

The rate of a reaction is just how quickly it happens. Seems simple enough, so let's crack on...

Reaction Rate is the Amount of Stuff Reacting Divided by Time

The **reaction rate** is the **rate** at which a **product is formed** or a **reactant is used up**. A simple equation for the rate of a chemical reaction is...

$$\text{rate of reaction} = \frac{\text{amount of reactant used or product formed}}{\text{time}}$$

There are Different ways to Investigate Reaction Rates

You can either measure how quickly the **reactants are used up** or how quickly the **products are formed** — it's usually **easier** to measure products forming. Here are a couple of ways to measure how quickly a product forms...

Change in mass

1) When the product is a **gas**, its formation can be measured using a **mass balance**.
2) The amount of product formed is the mass **disappearing** from the container.
3) When the reaction starts, you should start a **stop clock** or timer. Then take **mass measurements** at **regular time intervals**.
4) Make a **table** with a column for '**time**' and a column for '**mass**' and fill it in as the reaction goes on.
5) You'll know the reaction is **finished** when the reading on the mass balance **stops decreasing**.
6) This method is **very accurate** and easy to use but does **release gas** into the room, which could be **dangerous** if the gas is toxic or flammable.

Volume of gas given off

1) You can use a **gas syringe** to measure the **volume** of product formed.
2) The experiment is carried out the same way as above but you measure the **volume** of gas in the syringe rather than the mass from the balance.
3) This method is **accurate** but vigorous reactions can **blow the plunger** out of the syringe.

There are a few other ways to measure the amount of reactant used or product formed. For example, you can monitor **changes in pressure** (for gases), **changes in colour** (for solutions) or **changes in conductivity**. The best method **depends** on the **reaction** you're looking at.

You can Work out Reaction Rate from the Gradient of a Graph

If you have a graph where the **x-axis** is **time** and the **y-axis** is a measure of either the **amount of reactant** or **product**, then the reaction rate is just the **gradient** of the graph. You can work out the gradient using the equation...

$$\text{gradient} = \text{change in y} \div \text{change in x}$$

The data on the graph came from measuring the volume of gas given off during a chemical reaction.

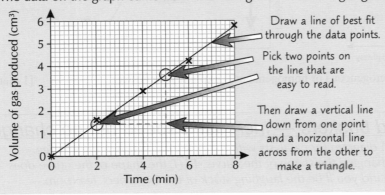

Draw a line of best fit through the data points.

Pick two points on the line that are easy to read.

Then draw a vertical line down from one point and a horizontal line across from the other to make a **triangle**.

change in y = 3.6 − 1.4 = 2.2 cm^3
change in x = 5.0 − 2.0 = 3.0 minutes
gradient = 2.2 ÷ 3.0 = 0.73 cm^3 min^{-1}

So the rate of reaction = **0.73 cm^3 min^{-1}**

MODULE 3 : SECTION 2 — PHYSICAL CHEMISTRY

Calculating Reaction Rates

You may need to **Work out** the **Gradient** from a **Curved Graph**

When the points on a graph lie in a **curve**, you can't draw a straight line of best fit through them. But you can still work out the gradient, and so the rate, at a **particular point** in the reaction by working out the **gradient of a tangent**.

Example: The graph below shows the mass of a reaction vessel measured at regular intervals during a chemical reaction. What is the rate of reaction at 3 mins?

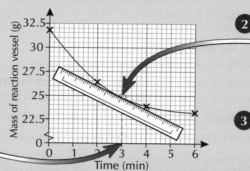

1 Find the point on the curve that you need to look at. The question asks about the rate of reaction at 3 mins, so find 3 on the x-axis and go up to the curve from there.

2 Place a ruler at that point so that it's just touching the curve. Position the ruler so that you can see the whole curve.

3 Adjust the ruler until the space between the ruler and the curve is equal on both sides of the point.

4 Draw a line along the ruler to make the tangent. Extend the line right across the graph — it'll help to make your gradient calculation easier as you'll have more points to choose from.

5 Calculate the gradient of the tangent to find the rate:
gradient = change in y ÷ change in x
= (27.50 − 22.00) ÷ (5.20 − 0.80)
= 5.50 cm³ ÷ 4.40 mins = 1.25 cm³ min⁻¹

So, the rate of reaction at 3 mins was **1.25 cm³ min⁻¹**.

Pick two points on the line that are easy to read.

Don't forget the units — you've divided cm³ by mins, so it's cm³ min⁻¹.

Practice Questions

Q1 Write the equation for reaction rate.

Q2 Describe how measuring a change in mass can help to work out the rate of a reaction.

Exam Question

Q1 Calcium and water react as in the equation below.

$$Ca_{(s)} + 2H_2O_{(l)} \rightarrow Ca(OH)_{2(aq)} + H_{2(g)}$$

a) From the graph on the right, work out the rate of reaction at 3 minutes. [3 marks]

b) Suggest how you would measure the volume of gas produced. [1 mark]

c) Explain why the method used here would be unsuitable for working out the rate of the reaction below. [1 mark]

$$6CO_{2(g)} + 6H_2O_{(l)} \rightarrow C_6H_{12}O_{6(aq)} + 6O_{2(g)}$$

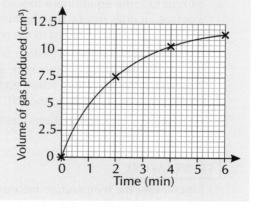

Calculate your reaction to this page. Boredom? How dare you...

Really, this stuff isn't too bad. Make sure you can write out the reaction rate equation in your sleep and that you understand what it means. It'll make handling the rest of the stuff on these pages easier. It might take a bit of practice to get the hang of these graphs but, as I'm sure you're tired of hearing, practice makes perfect. So get practising.

Dynamic Equilibrium

There's a lot of to-ing and fro-ing on this page. Mind your head doesn't start spinning.

Reversible Reactions Can Reach Dynamic Equilibrium

1) Lots of chemical reactions are **reversible** — they go **both ways**. To show a reaction's reversible, you stick in a $\rightleftharpoons$. Here's an example:

$$H_{2(g)} + I_{2(g)} \rightleftharpoons 2HI_{(g)}$$

This reaction can go in **either direction** —

forwards $H_{2(g)} + I_{2(g)} \rightleftharpoons 2HI_{(g)}$ ...or **backwards** $2HI_{(g)} \rightleftharpoons H_{2(g)} + I_{2(g)}$

2) As the **reactants** get used up, the **forward** reaction **slows down** — and as more **product** is formed, the **reverse** reaction **speeds up**.

3) After a while, the forward reaction will be going at exactly the **same rate** as the backward reaction, so the amounts of reactants and products **won't be changing** any more — it'll seem like **nothing's happening**.

4) This is called **dynamic equilibrium**. At equilibrium the **concentrations** of **reactants** and **products** stay **constant**.

5) A **dynamic equilibrium** can only happen in a **closed system**. This just means nothing can get in or out.

Le Chatelier's Principle Predicts what will Happen if Conditions are Changed

If you **change** the **concentration**, **pressure** or **temperature** of a reversible reaction, you tend to **alter** the **position of equilibrium**. This just means you'll end up with **different amounts** of reactants and products at equilibrium.

If the position of equilibrium moves to the **left**, you'll get more **reactants**.

$$H_{2(g)} + I_{2(g)} \rightleftharpoons 2HI_{(g)}$$

If the position of equilibrium moves to the **right**, you'll get more **products**.

$$H_{2(g)} + I_{2(g)} \rightleftharpoons 2HI_{(g)}$$

Le Chatelier's principle tells you how the **position of equilibrium** will change if a **condition changes**:

If there's a change in **concentration**, **pressure** or **temperature**, the equilibrium will move to help **counteract** the change.

So, basically, if you **raise the temperature**, the position of equilibrium will shift to try to **cool things down**. And, if you **raise the pressure or concentration**, the position of equilibrium will shift to try to **reduce it again**.

Here Are Some Handy Rules for Using Le Chatelier's Principle

CONCENTRATION $2SO_{2(g)} + O_{2(g)} \rightleftharpoons 2SO_{3(g)}$

1) If you **increase** the **concentration** of a **reactant** (SO_2 or O_2), the equilibrium tries to **get rid of** the extra reactant. It does this by making **more product** (SO_3). So the equilibrium's shifted to the **right**.

2) If you **increase** the **concentration** of the **product** (SO_3), the equilibrium tries to remove the extra product. This makes the **reverse reaction** go faster. So the equilibrium shifts to the **left**.

3) **Decreasing** the concentrations has the **opposite effect**.

PRESSURE (this only affects **gases**)

1) **Increasing** the pressure shifts the equilibrium to the side with **fewer** gas molecules. This **reduces** the pressure.

2) **Decreasing** the pressure shifts the equilibrium to the side with **more** gas molecules. This **raises** the pressure again.

There are 3 moles on the left, but only 2 on the right. So, increasing the pressure shifts the equilibrium to the right.

$$2SO_{2(g)} + O_{2(g)} \rightleftharpoons 2SO_{3(g)}$$

TEMPERATURE

1) **Increasing** the temperature means **adding heat**. The equilibrium shifts in the **endothermic** (positive ΔH) direction to absorb this heat.

2) **Decreasing** the temperature **removes heat**. The equilibrium shifts in the **exothermic** (negative ΔH) direction to try to **replace** the heat.

3) If the forward reaction's **endothermic**, the reverse reaction will be **exothermic**, and vice versa.

This reaction's exothermic in the forward direction ($\Delta H = -197$ kJ mol^{-1}). If you increase the temperature, the equilibrium shifts to the left to absorb the extra heat.

Exothermic $\Longrightarrow$
$$2SO_{2(g)} + O_{2(g)} \rightleftharpoons 2SO_{3(g)}$$
$\Longleftarrow$ Endothermic

Dynamic Equilibrium

Catalysts *Don't Affect* The Position of Equilibrium

Catalysts have **NO EFFECT** on the **position of equilibrium**. They **speed up** the **forward AND reverse** reactions by the **same amount**. They **can't** increase **yield** — but they **do** mean equilibrium is reached **faster**.

Ethanol can be formed from *Ethene* and *Steam*

1) The industrial production of **ethanol** is a good example of why Le Chatelier's principle is important in **real life**.

2) Ethanol is produced via a **reversible exothermic reaction** between **ethene** and **steam**:

3) The reaction is carried out at a pressure of **60-70 atmospheres** and a temperature of **300 °C**, with a **phosphoric(V) acid** catalyst.

$$C_2H_{4(g)} + H_2O_{(g)} \rightleftharpoons C_2H_5OH_{(g)} \qquad \Delta H = -46 \text{ kJ mol}^{-1}$$

The *Conditions* Chosen are a *Compromise*

1) Because it's an **exothermic reaction**, **lower** temperatures favour the forward reaction. This means **more** ethene and steam are converted to ethanol at lower temperatures — you get a better **yield**.

2) But **lower temperatures** mean a **slower rate of reaction**. You'd be **daft** to try to get a **really high yield** of ethanol if it's going to take you 10 years. So the 300 °C is a **compromise** between **maximum yield** and **a faster reaction**.

3) **Higher pressures** favour the **forward reaction,** so a pressure of **60-70 atmospheres** is used — **high pressure** moves the reaction to the side with **fewer molecules of gas**. **Increasing the pressure** also increases the **rate** of reaction.

4) Cranking up the pressure as high as you can sounds like a great idea so far. But **high pressures** are **expensive** to produce. You need **stronger pipes** and **containers** to withstand high pressure. In this process, increasing the pressure can also cause **side reactions** to occur.

5) So the **60-70 atmospheres** is a **compromise** between **maximum yield** and **expense**. In the end, it all comes down to **minimising costs**.

Mr and Mrs Le Chatelier celebrate another successful year in the principle business

Practice Questions

Q1 Using an example, explain the terms 'reversible reaction' and 'dynamic equilibrium'.

Q2 If the equilibrium moves to the right, do you get more products or reactants?

Q3 A reaction at equilibrium is endothermic in the forward direction. What happens to the position of equilibrium as the temperature is increased?

Exam Questions

Q1 Nitrogen and oxygen gases were reacted together in a closed flask and allowed to reach equilibrium, with nitrogen monoxide being formed. The forward reaction is endothermic.

$$N_{2(g)} + O_{2(g)} \rightleftharpoons 2NO_{(g)}$$

a) Explain how the following changes would affect the position of equilibrium of the above reaction:

   i) Pressure is increased.   [1 mark]

   ii) Temperature is reduced.   [1 mark]

   iii) Nitrogen monoxide is removed.   [1 mark]

b) What would be the effect of a catalyst on the composition of the equilibrium mixture?   [1 mark]

Q2 Explain why moderate reaction temperatures are a compromise for exothermic reactions.   [2 marks]

If it looks like I'm not doing anything, I'm just being dynamic... honest...

Equilibria never do what you want them to do. They always oppose you. Be sure you know what happens to an equilibrium if you change the conditions. About pressure — if there's the same number of gas moles on each side of the equation, you can raise the pressure as high as you like and it won't make a difference to the position of equilibrium.

The Equilibrium Constant

'Oh no, not another page on equilibria', I hear you cry... fair enough really.

K_c is the **Equilibrium Constant**

When you have a **homogeneous reaction** (where all the reactants and products are in the **same physical state**) that's reached **dynamic equilibrium**, you can work out the **equilibrium constant**, K_c, using the concentrations of the products and reactants at equilibrium. K_c gives you an idea of how far to the **left or right** the equilibrium is. Before you can calculate K_c, you have to write an **expression** for it. Here's how:

For the general reaction $\quad aA + bB \rightleftharpoons dD + eE, \quad K_c = \dfrac{[D]^d[E]^e}{[A]^a[B]^b}$

The products go on the top line.
The square brackets, [ ], mean concentration in mol dm^{-3}.

The lower-case letters a, b, d and e are the number of moles of each substance.

So for the reaction $\quad H_{2(g)} + I_{2(g)} \rightleftharpoons 2HI_{(g)}, \quad K_c = \dfrac{[HI]^2}{[H_2]^1[I_2]^1} = \dfrac{[HI]^2}{[H_2][I_2]}$

Calculate K_c by Putting **Numbers** into the **Expression**

If you know the **equilibrium concentrations**, just put them in your expression. Then you can work out the **value** of K_c.

Example: What is the equilibrium constant for the hydrogen iodide example above, at 640 K? The equilibrium concentrations are:

$[HI] = 0.80$ mol dm^{-3}, $[H_2] = 0.10$ mol dm^{-3}, and $[I_2] = 0.10$ mol dm^{-3}.

Just stick the concentrations into the **expression** for K_c: $\quad K_c = \dfrac{[HI]^2}{[H_2][I_2]} = \dfrac{0.80^2}{0.10 \times 0.10} = 64$

The **units** for K_c are a bit trickier — they **vary**, so you have to work them out after each calculation. You **don't** need to be able to work out the units for **AS** chemistry. But if you're interested, here's how it's done...

Put the units in the expression instead of the number: $\quad K_c = \dfrac{(\text{mol dm}^{-3})^2}{(\text{mol dm}^{-3})(\text{mol dm}^{-3})} = 0$

So there are **no units** for K_c because the concentration units cancel. So K_c for this reaction, at 640 K, is just **64**.

A **change in temperature** can change the **position of equilibrium** (see page 80) so K_c **varies** with temperature.

You can **Estimate** the **Position of Equilibrium** Using the Value of K_c

1) If K_c is **greater than 1**, there are **more products** than reactants and the equilibrium lies to the **right**. The higher above 1 K_c is, the **further to the right** equilibrium lies.

2) If K_c is **less than 1**, there are **more reactants** than products and the equilibrium lies to the **left**. The further below 1 K_c is, the **further to the left** equilibrium lies.

You can Investigate the **Equilibrium Position** with **Changing Temperature...**

In a closed system, the **brown** gas NO_2 exists in equilibrium with the **colourless** gas N_2O_4. This reversible reaction can be used to investigate the effect of **changing temperature** on **equilibrium position**. Here's how you do it...

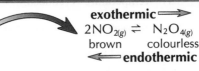

exothermic $\longrightarrow$
$2NO_{2(g)} \rightleftharpoons N_2O_{4(g)}$
brown $\qquad$ colourless
$\longleftarrow$ endothermic

1) Place two **sealed** tubes containing the equilibrium mixture in water baths — one in a **warm** water bath and one in a **cool** water bath, and **observe** the **colours** of the mixtures.

2) The tube in the **warm** water bath will change to a **darker brown** colour as the **endothermic** reaction **speeds up** to absorb the extra heat, pushing **equilibrium to the left**.

3) The tube in the **cool** water bath will **lose colour** as the **exothermic** reaction speeds up to try and replace the lost heat, pushing **equilibrium to the right**.

The Equilibrium Constant

... and with *Changing Concentration*

Mixing **iron(III) nitrate** (yellow) and **potassium thiocyanate** (colourless) results in a **reversible reaction** where the product is **iron(III) thiocyanate** (blood red). You end up with the following equilibrium...

$$Fe^{3+}_{(aq)} + 3SCN^-_{(aq)} \rightleftharpoons Fe(SCN)_{3(aq)}$$
yellow   colourless   blood red

The equilibrium mixture is a **reddish** colour. You can investigate what happens to the equilibrium position when the **concentrations** of reactants or products are changed by monitoring the **colour** of the solution.

Add equal amounts of the equilibrium mixture to four test tubes.

2) Add some iron(III) nitrate to test tube 2. The mixture turns a deep red colour.

3) Add some potassium thiocyanate to test tube 3. The mixture turns a deep red colour.

4) Add some iron(III) thiocyanate to test tube 4. The mixture turns a yellow colour.

1) Test tube 1 is the 'control' and nothing is added to it. It keeps its initial reddish colour.

- By adding more **reactants**, the **forward reaction speeds up** to produce more product (as seen by the deep red colour in test tubes 2 and 3) so **equilibrium moves to the right**.
- By adding more **product**, the **reverse reaction speeds up** to produce more reactants (as seen by the yellowish colour in test tube 4) so **equilibrium moves to the left**.

Practice Questions

Q1 Write an expression for the equilibrium constant of the reaction, $aA + bB \rightleftharpoons dD + eE$.

Q2 If K_c for a reaction has a value of 4, does the equilibrium lie to the right or the left?

Q3 What colour change would you expect in a NO_2/N_2O_4 gas mixture if you were to increase the temperature?

Q4 In which direction would equilibrium move if more product is added to a mixture?

Exam Questions

Q1   The concentrations of the species present in the following equilibrium mixture are
0.890 mol dm^{-3} N_2, 1.412 mol dm^{-3} H_2 and 1.190 mol dm^{-3} NH_3.

$$N_{2(g)} + 3H_{2(g)} \rightleftharpoons 2NH_{3(g)}$$

a)   Calculate the equilibrium constant, K_c.   [2 marks]

b)   The forward reaction in the above equilibrium is exothermic. If the equilibrium mixture was placed in a cool water bath, describe what would happen to the concentration of NH_3. Explain your answer.   [2 marks]

Q2   When a potassium chromate(VI) solution is mixed with sulfuric acid, the following equilibrium is established.

$$2CrO_4^{2-}_{(aq)} + 2H^+_{(aq)} \rightleftharpoons Cr_2O_7^{2-}_{(aq)} + H_2O_{(l)}$$
     yellow   orange

Describe an experiment to establish the effect on the equilibrium position of changing the concentration of chromate and dichromate ions. Describe what the results of the experiment would be.   [3 marks]

I'm constantly going on about equilibrium — that's what it feels like anyway...

Working out K_c is pretty straight forward once you've got the hang of it, although it may not seem like that to begin with. If you've not quite got it yet go back through these two pages until it all makes perfect sense. Once you've done that, there are just 6 more pages on equilibrium to go... ONLY JOKING! It's the end of the section. Hurrah hurrah hurrah :-)

Organic Chemistry — The Basics

This section's all about organic chemistry... carbon compounds, in other words. Read on...

There are **Loads of Ways** of **Representing** Organic Compounds

TYPE OF FORMULA	WHAT IT SHOWS YOU	FORMULA FOR BUTAN-1-OL
General formula	An algebraic formula that can describe **any member** of a family of compounds.	$C_nH_{2n+1}OH$ (for all alcohols)
Empirical formula	The **simplest whole number ratio** of atoms of each element in a compound (cancel the numbers down if possible). (So ethane, C_2H_6, has the empirical formula CH_3.)	$C_4H_{10}O$
Molecular formula	The **actual** number of atoms of each element in a molecule.	$C_4H_{10}O$
Structural formula	Shows the arrangement of atoms **carbon by carbon**, with the attached hydrogens and functional groups.	$CH_3CH_2CH_2CH_2OH$
Skeletal formula	Shows the **bonds** of the carbon skeleton **only**, with any functional groups. The hydrogen and carbon atoms aren't shown. This is handy for drawing large complicated structures, like cyclic hydrocarbons.	⌇OH
Displayed formula	Shows how all the atoms are **arranged**, and all the bonds between them.	H–C–C–C–C–O–H

This could also be written as $CH_3(CH_2)_3OH$

Members of **Homologous Series** Have the Same **General Formulas**

1) Organic chemistry is more about **groups** of similar chemicals than individual compounds.

2) These groups are called **homologous series**. A homologous series is a bunch of organic compounds that have the same **functional group** and **general formula**. Consecutive members of a homologous series differ by **$-CH_2-$**.

A functional group is a group of atoms in a molecule responsible for the characteristic reactions of that compound.

> **Example:**
>
> 1) The simplest homologous series is the **alkanes**. They're **straight chain** molecules that contain only **carbon** and **hydrogen** atoms. There's a lot more about the alkanes on pages 88-91.
>
> 2) The **general formula** for alkanes is C_nH_{2n+2}. So the first alkane in the series is $C_1H_{(2 \times 1)+2} = CH_4$ (you don't need to write the 1 in C_1), the second is $C_2H_{(2 \times 2)+2} = C_2H_6$, the seventeenth is $C_{17}H_{(2 \times 17)+2} = C_{17}H_{36}$, and so on...

3) Here are the homologous series you need to know about:

HOMOLOGOUS SERIES	PREFIX OR SUFFIX	EXAMPLE
alkanes	–ane	propane — $CH_3CH_2CH_3$
branched alkanes	alkyl– (–yl)	methylpropane — $CH_3CH(CH_3)CH_3$
alkenes	–ene	propene — $CH_3CH=CH_2$
haloalkanes	chloro–/bromo–/iodo–	chloroethane — CH_3CH_2Cl
alcohols	–ol	ethanol — CH_3CH_2OH
aldehydes	–al	ethanal — CH_3CHO
ketones	–one	propanone — CH_3COCH_3
cycloalkanes	cyclo– ... –ane	cyclohexane C_6H_{12}
carboxylic acids	–oic acid	ethanoic acid — CH_3COOH
esters	alkyl– ... –anoate	methyl propanoate — $CH_3CH_2COOCH_3$

Don't worry if you don't recognise all these series yet — you'll meet them all by the end of the module.

Organic Chemistry — The Basics

There Are Different **Types** of **Carbon Skeleton**

1) All organic compounds contain a **carbon skeleton**. This can be either **aromatic** or **aliphatic**.

2) **Aromatic** compounds contain a **benzene** ring. You can **draw** benzene rings in two ways:

Like this: or like this:

These are skeletal formulas — each point represents a carbon atom.

3) **Aliphatic** compounds contain carbon and hydrogen joined together in **straight** chains, **branched** chains or **non-aromatic rings**.

4) If an aliphatic compound contains a (non-aromatic) **ring**, then it can be called **alicyclic**.

5) Organic compounds may be saturated or unsaturated. **Saturated** compounds only contain carbon-carbon **single bonds** — like alkanes. **Unsaturated** compounds can have carbon-carbon **double** bonds, **triple** bonds or **aromatic** groups.

6) And finally... an **alkyl group** is a **fragment** of a molecule with general formula C_nH_{2n+1}.

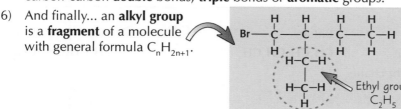

Ethyl group C_2H_5

The X-ray revealed a break in Timothy's carbon skeleton.

Nomenclature is a Fancy Word for the **Naming** of Organic Compounds

Organic compounds used to be given whatever names people fancied, but these names led to **confusion** between different countries.

The **IUPAC** system for naming organic compounds was invented as an **international language** for chemistry. It can be used to give any organic compound a **systematic name** using these **rules** of nomenclature...

1) Count the carbon atoms in the **longest continuous chain** — this gives you the stem.

No. of Carbons	1	2	3	4	5	6	7	8	9	10
Stem	meth-	eth-	prop-	but-	pent-	hex-	hept-	oct-	non-	dec-

2) The **main functional group** of the molecule usually tells you what **homologous series** the molecule is in, and so gives you the **prefix** or **suffix** — see the table on page 84.

3) Number the **longest** carbon chain so that the main functional group has the lowest possible number. If there's more than one longest chain, pick the one with the **most side-chains**.

4) Any side-chains or less important functional groups are added as prefixes at the start of the name. Put them in **alphabetical** order, after the **number** of the carbon atom each is attached to.

5) If there's more than one **identical** side-chain or functional group, use **di-** (2), **tri-** (3) or **tetra-** (4) before that part of the name — but ignore this when working out the alphabetical order.

Example: $CH_3CH(CH_3)CH(CH_2CH_3)C(CH_3)_2OH$

1) The longest chain is **5** carbons. So the stem is **pent-**.

2) The main functional group is **-OH** So the name will be based on '**pentanol**'.

3) **Numbering** the longest carbon chain so that -OH has the **lowest** possible number (and you have most side chains) puts -OH on carbon 2, so it's some sort of **pentan-2-ol**.

Longest chain with most side-chains

4) The other side chains are an **ethyl group** on carbon-3, and **methyl groups** on carbon-2 and carbon-4, so the systematic name for this molecule is: **3-ethyl-2,4-dimethylpentan-2-ol**.

Organic Chemistry — The Basics

Isomers Have the Same **Molecular Formula**

1) Two molecules are isomers of one another if they have the same **molecular formula** but the atoms are **arranged differently**.

2) There are two types of isomers you need to know about — **structural isomers** and **stereoisomers**. Structural isomers are coming right up, and you'll meet stereoisomers on pages 93-95.

Structural Isomers Have Different *Structural Arrangements* of Atoms

In structural isomers, the atoms are **connected** in different ways. So although the **molecular formula** is the same, the **structural formula** is different. There are **three** different types of structural isomer:

1. Chain Isomers

The **carbon skeleton** can be arranged differently — for example, as a **straight chain**, or **branched** in different ways.

These isomers have **similar chemical properties** — but their **physical properties**, like boiling point, will be **different** because of the change in shape of the molecule.

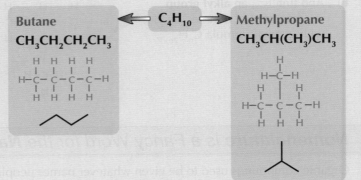

2. Positional Isomers

The **skeleton** and the **functional group** could be the same, only with the functional group attached to a **different carbon atom**.

These also have **different physical properties**, and the **chemical properties** might be **different** too.

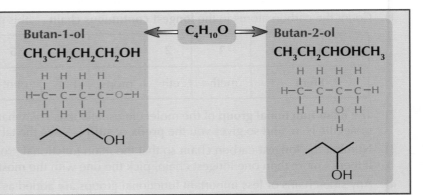

3. Functional Group Isomers

The same atoms can be arranged into **different functional groups**.

These have very **different physical** and **chemical** properties.

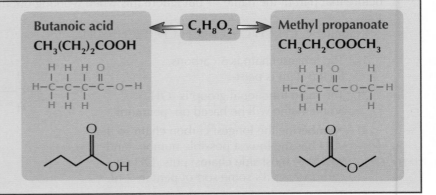

Organic Chemistry — The Basics

Don't be Fooled — What Looks Like an Isomer Might **Not** Be

Atoms can rotate as much as they like around single **C–C bonds**.
Remember this when you work out structural isomers — sometimes what looks like an isomer, isn't.

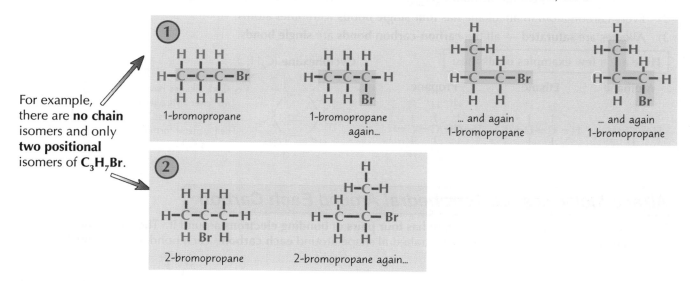

For example, there are **no chain** isomers and only **two positional** isomers of **C_3H_7Br**.

Practice Questions

Q1 Explain the difference between molecular formulas and structural formulas.

Q2 What is meant by the term 'homologous series'?

Q3 In what order should prefixes be listed in the name of an organic compound?

Q4 Draw the displayed formula of 3,4-diethylhexan-2-ol.

Q5 What are isomers?

Q6 Name the three types of structural isomerism.

Exam Questions

Q1 1-bromo-2-methylpentane is prepared from 2-methylpentan-1-ol in this reaction:

$$C_6H_{13}OH + NaBr + H_2SO_4 \rightarrow C_6H_{13}Br + NaHSO_4 + H_2O$$

a) Draw the displayed formulas for 1-bromo-2-methylpentane and 2-methylpentan-1-ol. [2 marks]

b) What is the functional group in 2-methylpentan-1-ol and why is it necessary
to state its position on the carbon chain? [2 marks]

Q2 Give the systematic names of the following compounds.

a) 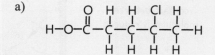   b)   c) 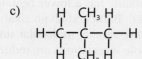 [3 marks]

Q3 a) How many chain isomers are there of the alkane C_6H_{14}?

   A 4   **B** 5   **C** 6   **D** 7 [1 mark]

b) Explain what is meant by the term 'chain isomerism'. [2 marks]

Human structural isomers...

Alkanes

Alkanes are your basic hydrocarbons — like it says on the tin, they've got hydrogen and they've got carbon.

Alkanes are **Saturated Hydrocarbons**

1) Alkanes have the **general formula C_nH_{2n+2}**. They've only got **carbon** and **hydrogen** atoms, so they're **hydrocarbons**.
2) Every carbon atom in an alkane has **four single bonds** with other atoms.
3) Alkanes are **saturated** — all the **carbon-carbon bonds** are **single bonds**.

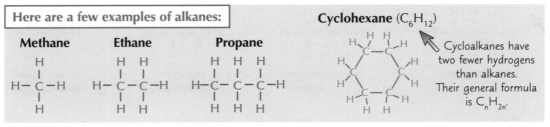

Here are a few examples of alkanes:

Methane   **Ethane**   **Propane**

Cyclohexane (C_6H_{12})

Cycloalkanes have two fewer hydrogens than alkanes. Their general formula is C_nH_{2n}.

Cyclohexane has the skeletal formula:

Alkane Molecules are **Tetrahedral** Around **Each Carbon**

In an alkane molecule, each carbon atom has **four pairs** of **bonding electrons** around it. They all repel each other **equally**. So the molecule forms a tetrahedral shape around **each carbon**. Each bond angle is **109.5°**

If you draw lines joining up the Hs in CH_4, the shape you get is a **tetrahedron**.

Methane
1 tetrahedral carbon

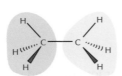

Ethane
2 tetrahedral carbons

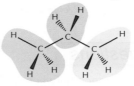

Propane
3 tetrahedral carbons

For more about the shapes of molecules, see pages 46-47.

The **Boiling Point** of an Alkane Depends on its **Size** and **Shape**

The smallest alkanes, like methane, are **gases** at room temperature and pressure — they've got very low boiling points. Larger alkanes are **liquids** — they have higher boiling points.

1) Alkanes have **covalent bonds** inside the molecules. **Between** the molecules, there are **induced dipole-dipole** interactions (also called **London forces**) which hold them all together.
2) The **longer** the carbon chain, the **stronger** the induced dipole-dipole interactions. This is because there's **more surface contact** and more electrons to interact.
3) As the molecules get longer, it takes **more energy** to overcome the induced dipole-dipole interactions, and the boiling point **rises**.
4) A **branched-chain** alkane has a **lower** boiling point than its straight-chain isomer. Branched-chain alkanes can't **pack closely** together and they have smaller **molecular surface areas** — so the induced dipole-dipole interactions are reduced.

Example: Isomers of C_4H_{10}

Butane, boiling point = 273 K

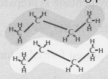

Molecules can pack closely so there is a lot of surface contact between them.

Methylpropane, boiling point = 261 K

Close packing isn't possible so surface contact between molecules is reduced

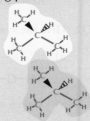

Alkanes Burn **Completely** in Oxygen

1) If you burn (**oxidise**) alkanes with **oxygen**, you get **carbon dioxide** and water — this is a **combustion reaction**.

Here's the equation for the combustion of propane — $C_3H_{8(g)} + 5O_{2(g)} \rightarrow 3CO_{2(g)} + 4H_2O_{(g)}$

2) Combustion reactions happen between **gases**, so liquid alkanes have to be **vaporised** first. Smaller alkanes turn into **gases** more easily (they're more **volatile**), so they'll **burn** more easily too.
3) Larger alkanes release heaps more **energy** per mole because they have more bonds to react.
4) Because they release so much energy when they burn, alkanes make excellent fuels.

MODULE 4: SECTION 1 — BASIC CONCEPTS AND HYDROCARBONS

Alkanes

You Can Use Volumes to Work Out Combustion Equations

Combustion reactions happen between **gases**. All gases at the same temperature and pressure have the same **molar volume**. This means you can use the **ratio** of the **volumes** of gases reacting together to calculate the **molar ratios**, and then work out what **hydrocarbon** is combusting.

Example: 30 cm³ of hydrocarbon X combusts completely with 240 cm³ oxygen.
150 cm³ carbon dioxide is produced. What is the molecular formula of hydrocarbon X?

- Using the volumes provided, the reaction equation can be written: $30X + 240O_2 \rightarrow 150CO_2 + ?H_2O$.
- This can be simplified by dividing everything by 30: $X + 8O_2 \rightarrow 5CO_2 + nH_2O$.
- 8 moles of oxygen reacts to form 5 moles of carbon dioxide and n moles of water. So any oxygen atoms that don't end up in CO_2 must be in H_2O. This means that $n = (8 \times 2) - (5 \times 2) = 6$.
- This means the combustion equation is: $X + 8O_2 \rightarrow 5CO_2 + 6H_2O$. You can use this to identify X.
- All the carbon atoms from X end up in carbon dioxide molecules, and all the hydrogen atoms from X end up in water, so the number of **carbon** atoms in X is **5** and the number of **hydrogen** atoms in X is **12**.
- The molecular formula of X is C_5H_{12}.

Burning Alkanes In Limited Oxygen Produces Carbon Monoxide

1) If there isn't much oxygen around, the alkane will still burn, but it will produce **carbon monoxide** and water.

For example, burning methane with not much O_2 — $2CH_{4(g)} + 3O_{2(g)} \rightarrow 2CO_{(g)} + 4H_2O_{(g)}$

2) This is a problem because **carbon monoxide is poisonous**.

1) The **oxygen** in your bloodstream is carried around by **haemoglobin**.
2) **Carbon monoxide** is **better** at binding to haemoglobin than oxygen is, so it binds to the haemoglobin in your bloodstream **before** the oxygen can.
3) This means that **less oxygen** can be carried around your body, leading to **oxygen deprivation**. At very high concentrations, carbon monoxide can be fatal.

Practice Questions

Q1 What's the general formula for alkanes?
Q2 What is the H-C-H bond angle in a molecule of methane?
Q3 What kind of intermolecular forces are there between alkane molecules?

Exam Questions

Q1 The alkane ethane is a saturated hydrocarbon.
It is mostly unreactive, but will react with oxygen in a combustion reaction.

   a) What is a saturated hydrocarbon?   [2 marks]

   b) Write a balanced equation for the complete combustion of ethane.   [2 marks]

Q2 Nonane is a hydrocarbon with the formula C_9H_{20}.

   a) Which would you expect to have a higher boiling point, nonane or 2,2,3,3-tetramethylpentane?
      Explain your answer.   [2 marks]

   b) When nonane burns in a limited air supply, the products are carbon monoxide and water.

      i) Write a balanced equation for the reaction.   [1 mark]

      ii) Explain why carbon monoxide is such a dangerous gas.   [2 marks]

Tetrahedra — aren't they those monsters from Greek mythology...

Alkanes are the simplest organic compounds you're going to meet. They're very stable so they don't get up to much. Make sure you can explain why different alkanes can have different boiling points — even if their molecular formulas are the same. It's all about the strength of the intermolecular forces and how closely the molecules can pack together.

Reactions of Alkanes

Alkanes react with particles that have unpaired electrons (called free radicals). These reactions happen in several steps, and a mechanism breaks reactions down to show you the steps. Watch out, there are a few coming up...

There are **Two Types** of Bond Fission — **Homolytic** and **Heterolytic**

Breaking a covalent bond is called **bond fission**. A single covalent bond is a shared pair of electrons between two atoms. It can break in two ways:

Heterolytic Fission:

In heterolytic fission the bond breaks **unevenly** with one of the bonded atoms receiving **both** electrons from the bonded pair. **Two different** substances are formed — a positively charged **cation** (X^+), and a negatively charged **anion** (Y^-).

$$X \overset{\frown}{\div} Y \rightarrow X^+ + Y^-$$

('hetero' means 'different')

A curly arrows shows the movement of an electron pair.

Homolytic Fission:

In homolytic fission, the bond breaks evenly and each bonding atom receives **one electron** from the bonded pair. Two electrically uncharged 'radicals' are formed. Radicals are particles that have an **unpaired electron**. They are shown in mechanisms by a big dot next to the molecular formula (the dot represents the unpaired electron.)

$$X \div Y \rightarrow X \cdot + Y \cdot$$

Because of the unpaired electron, radicals are very **reactive**.

Carl loved fission at the weekends.

Halogens React with **Alkanes**, Forming **Haloalkanes**

1) Halogens react with alkanes in **photochemical** reactions. Photochemical reactions are started by **light** — this reaction requires **ultraviolet light** to get going.

2) A hydrogen atom is **substituted** (replaced) by chlorine or bromine. This is a **free-radical substitution reaction**.

> **Example: Chlorine** and **methane** react with a bit of a bang to form **chloromethane**:
> $$CH_4 + Cl_2 \overset{UV}{\rightarrow} CH_3Cl + HCl$$

The **reaction mechanism** has three stages:

Initiation reactions — free radicals are produced.

1) Sunlight provides enough energy to break the Cl-Cl bond — this is **photodissociation**.
$$Cl_2 \overset{UV}{\rightarrow} 2Cl \cdot$$

2) The bond splits **equally** and each atom gets to keep one electron — **homolytic fission**. The atom becomes a highly reactive **free radical**, $Cl \cdot$, because of its **unpaired electron**.

Propagation reactions — free radicals are used up and created in a chain reaction.

1) $Cl \cdot$ attacks a **methane** molecule: $Cl \cdot + CH_4 \rightarrow \cdot CH_3 + HCl$
2) The new **methyl free radical**, $\cdot CH_3$, can attack another Cl_2 molecule: $\cdot CH_3 + Cl_2 \rightarrow CH_3Cl + Cl \cdot$
3) The new $Cl \cdot$ can attack **another** CH_4 molecule, and so on, until all the Cl_2 or CH_4 molecules are wiped out.

Termination reactions — free radicals are mopped up.

1) If two free radicals join together, they make a **stable molecule**.
2) There are **heaps** of possible termination reactions. Here are a couple of them to give you the idea:

$Cl \cdot + \cdot CH_3 \rightarrow CH_3Cl$ Some products formed will be trace impurities in the final sample.

$\cdot CH_3 + \cdot CH_3 \rightarrow C_2H_6$

The reaction between bromine and methane works in exactly the same way.
$$CH_4 + Br_2 \overset{UV}{\rightarrow} CH_3Br + HBr$$

Reactions of Alkanes

The Problem is — You End Up With a *Mixture of Products*

1) The big problem with free-radical substitution if you're trying to make a **particular product** is that you **don't only get** the product you're after, but a **mixture of products**.

2) For example, if you're trying to make chloromethane and there's **too much chlorine** in the reaction mixture, some of the remaining **hydrogen atoms** on the **chloromethane molecule** will be swapped for chlorine atoms. The propagation reactions happen again, this time to make **dichloromethane**.

$$Cl\bullet + CH_3Cl \rightarrow \bullet CH_2Cl + HCl$$
$$\bullet CH_2Cl + Cl_2 \rightarrow CH_2Cl_2 + Cl\bullet$$
dichloromethane

3) It doesn't stop there. Another substitution reaction can take place to form **trichloromethane**.

$$Cl\bullet + CH_2Cl_2 \rightarrow \bullet CHCl_2 + HCl$$
$$\bullet CHCl_2 + Cl_2 \rightarrow CHCl_3 + Cl\bullet$$
trichloromethane

4) **Tetrachloromethane** (CCl_4) is formed in the last possible substitution. There are no more hydrogens attached to the carbon atom, so the substitution process has to stop.

5) So the end product is a mixture of CH_3Cl, CH_2Cl_2, $CHCl_3$ and CCl_4. This is a nuisance, because you have to **separate** the **chloromethane** from the other three unwanted by-products.

6) The best way of reducing the chance of these by-products forming is to have an **excess of methane**. This means there's a greater chance of a chlorine radical colliding only with a **methane molecule** and not a **chloromethane molecule**.

7) Another problem with free radical substitution is that it can take place at any point along the **carbon chain**. So a mixture of **isomers** can be formed. For example, reacting **propane** with chlorine will produce a mixture of **1-chloropropane** and **2-chloropropane**.

Practice Questions

Q1 What's a free radical?
Q2 What's homolytic fission?
Q3 Write down the chemical equation for the free radical substitution reaction between methane and chlorine.
Q4 Write down three possible products, other than chloromethane, from the photochemical reaction between CH_4 and Cl_2.

Exam Question

Q1 When irradiated with UV light, methane gas will react with bromine to form a mixture of several organic compounds.

a) Name the type of mechanism involved in this reaction. [1 mark]

b) Write an overall equation to show the formation of bromomethane from methane and bromine. [1 mark]

c) Write down the two equations in the propagation step for the formation of CH_3Br. [2 marks]

d) i) Explain why a tiny amount of ethane is found in the product mixture. [1 mark]

ii) Name the mechanistic step that leads to the formation of ethane. [1 mark]

iii) Write the equation for the formation of ethane in this reaction. [1 mark]

e) Name the major product formed when a large excess of bromine reacts with methane in the presence of UV light. [1 mark]

This page is like... totally radical, man...

Mechanisms can be an absolute pain in the bum to learn, but unfortunately reactions are what Chemistry's all about. If you don't like it, you should have taken art — no mechanisms in that, just pretty pictures. Ah well, there's no going back now. You've just got to sit down and learn the stuff. Keep hacking away at it, till you know it all off by heart.

Alkenes

An alkene is like an alkane's wild younger brother. They look kinda similar, but alkenes are way more reactive.

Alkenes are **Unsaturated Hydrocarbons**

1) Alkenes have the **general formula C_nH_{2n}**. They're made of carbon and hydrogen atoms, so they're **hydrocarbons**.

2) Alkene molecules **all** have at least one **C=C double covalent bond**. Molecules with C=C double bonds are **unsaturated** because they can make more bonds with extra atoms in **addition** reactions.

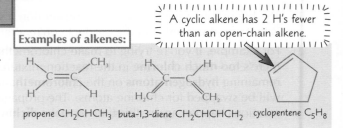

Examples of alkenes:

propene CH_2CHCH_3 buta-1,3-diene $CH_2CHCHCH_2$ cyclopentene C_5H_8

A cyclic alkene has 2 H's fewer than an open-chain alkene.

A **Double Bond** is made up of a **Sigma (σ) Bond** and a **Pi (π) Bond**

1) A σ **bond** (sigma bond) is formed when two **s orbitals overlap**.

2) The two s orbitals overlap in a straight line — this gives the **highest possible electron density** between the two nuclei. This is a **single** covalent bond.

3) The **high electron density** between the nuclei means there is a strong **electrostatic attraction** between the nuclei and the shared pair of electrons. This means that σ bonds have a high **bond enthalpy** — they are the **strongest** type of covalent bonds.

The C–C and C–H bonds in alkanes are all sigma bonds.

1) A π (pi) **bond** is formed by the sideways overlap of two adjacent **p orbitals**.

2) It's got **two parts** to it — one 'above' and one 'below' the molecular axis. This is because the p orbitals which overlap are **dumb-bell shaped**.

3) π bonds are much **weaker** than σ bonds because the electron density is **spread out** above and below the nuclei. This means that the **electrostatic attraction** between the nuclei and the shared pair of electrons is **weaker**, so π bonds have a **relatively low bond enthalpy**.

See page 40 for more on orbitals.

Alkenes are **Much More Reactive** than Alkanes

1) Alkanes only contain C–C and C–H σ **bonds**, which have a high bond enthalpy and so are difficult to break. The bonds are also **non-polar** so they don't attract **nucleophiles** or **electrophiles**. This means alkanes **don't react** easily.

2) Alkenes are **more reactive** than alkanes because the C=C bond contains both a σ bond and a π bond.

3) The C=C double bond contains four electrons so it has a **high electron density** and the π **bond** also sticks out above and below the rest of the molecule. These two factors mean the π **bond** is likely to be attacked by **electrophiles** (see p.96). The **low bond enthalpy** of the π bond also contributes to the reactivity of alkenes.

4) Because the double bond's so **reactive**, alkenes are handy **starting points** for making other organic compounds and for making **petrochemicals**.

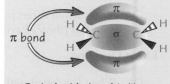

Each **double bond** is like a hot dog. The π **bond** is the bun and the σ **bond** is in the middle like the sausage.

Practice Questions

Q1 What is an alkene?

Q2 Describe the arrangement of electrons in a single bond and in a double bond.

Exam Question

Q1 Consider the hydrocarbons ethane and ethene.

a) Explain how the type of bonding differs in these two molecules. [2 marks]

b) Explain which of these molecules is more reactive. [2 marks]

Double, double toil and trouble. Alkene burn and pi bond bubble...

Double bonds are always made up of a σ bond and a π bond. So even though π bonds are weaker than σ bonds, double bonds will be stronger than single bonds because they have the combined strength of a σ and a π bond.

Stereoisomerism

The chemistry on these pages isn't so bad. And don't be too worried when I tell you that a good working knowledge of both German and Latin would be useful. It's not absolutely essential... and you'll be fine without.

Double Bonds Can't Rotate

1) Carbon atoms in a C=C double bond and the atoms bonded to these carbons all lie in the **same plane** (they're **planar**).
Because of the way they're arranged, they're actually said to be **trigonal planar** — the atoms attached to each double-bonded carbon are at the corners of an imaginary equilateral triangle.

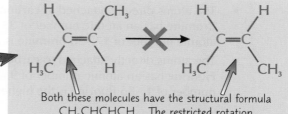

The bond angles in the planar unit are all 120°.

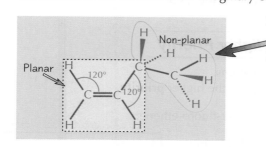

2) Ethene, C_2H_4 (like in the diagram above) is completely planar, but in larger alkenes, only the >C=C< unit is planar.

3) Another important thing about C=C double bonds is that atoms **can't rotate** around them like they can around single bonds (because of the way the p orbitals **overlap** to form a π **bond** — see p.92). In fact, double bonds are fairly **rigid** — they don't bend much either.

4) Even though atoms can't rotate about the **double bond**, things can still rotate about any **single bonds** in the molecule.

5) The **restricted rotation** around the C=C double bond is what causes **alkenes** to form **stereoisomers**.

Both these molecules have the structural formula $CH_3CHCHCH_3$. The restricted rotation around the double bond means you can't turn one into the other so they are isomers.

E/Z isomerism is a Type of Stereoisomerism

1) **Stereoisomers** have the same structural formula but a **different arrangement** in space.
(Just bear with me for a moment... that will become clearer, I promise.)

2) Because of the **lack of rotation** around the double bond, some **alkenes** can have stereoisomers.

3) Stereoisomers occur when the two double-bonded carbon atoms each have two **different atoms** or **groups** attached to them.

4) One of these isomers is called the **'E-isomer'** and the other is called the **'Z-isomer'**, (hence the name E/Z isomerism).

5) The **Z-isomer** has the same groups either **both above** or **both below** the double bond, whilst the **E-isomer** has the same groups positioned **across** the double bond.

When you're naming stereoisomers, you need to put 'E' or 'Z' at the beginning of the name.

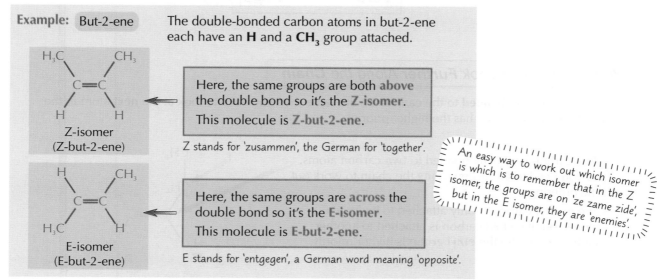

Example: But-2-ene — The double-bonded carbon atoms in but-2-ene each have an **H** and a **CH₃** group attached.

Z-isomer
(Z-but-2-ene)

Here, the same groups are both **above** the double bond so it's the **Z-isomer**.
This molecule is **Z-but-2-ene**.

Z stands for 'zusammen', the German for 'together'.

E-isomer
(E-but-2-ene)

Here, the same groups are **across** the double bond so it's the **E-isomer**.
This molecule is **E-but-2-ene**.

E stands for 'entgegen', a German word meaning 'opposite'.

An easy way to work out which isomer is which is to remember that in the Z isomer, the groups are on 'ze zame zide', but in the E isomer, they are 'enemies'.

Stereoisomerism

The E/Z System Works Even When All the Groups Are Different

1) When the carbons on either end of a double bond both have the **same groups** attached, then it's easy to work out which is the E-isomer and which is the Z-isomer (like in the example on page 93).

2) It only starts to get **problematic** if the carbon atoms both have **totally different groups** attached.

3) Fortunately, a clever person (well, three clever people — Mr Cahn, Mr Ingold and Mr Prelog) came up with a solution to this problem.

4) Using the **Cahn-Ingold-Prelog (CIP) rules** you can work out which is the E-isomer and which is the Z-isomer for any alkene. They're really simple, and they work every time.

Atoms With a Larger Atomic Number are Given a Higher Priority

1) Look at the atoms **directly bonded** to each of the C=C carbon atoms. The atom with the higher **atomic number** on each carbon is given the higher **priority**.

Example: Here's one of the stereoisomers of 1-bromo-1-chloro-2-fluoro-ethene:

- The atoms directly attached to **carbon-1** are bromine and chlorine. **Bromine** has an atomic number of **35** and **chlorine** has an atomic number of **17**. So **bromine** is the higher priority group.

- The atoms directly attached to **carbon-2** are fluorine and hydrogen. **Fluorine** has an atomic number of **9** and **hydrogen** has an atomic number of **1**. So **fluorine** is the higher priority group.

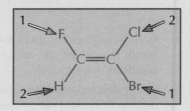

2) Now you can assign the isomers as E- and Z- as before, just by looking at how the groups of the **same priority** are arranged.

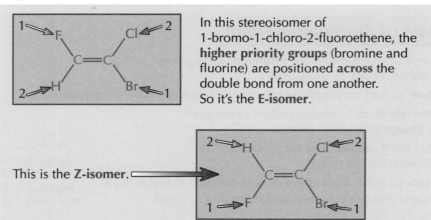

In this stereoisomer of 1-bromo-1-chloro-2-fluoroethene, the **higher priority groups** (bromine and fluorine) are positioned **across** the double bond from one another. So it's the **E-isomer**.

This is the Z-isomer.

You May Have to Look Further Along the Chain

If the atoms **directly bonded** to the carbon are the **same** then you have to look at the **next** atom in the groups to work out which has the higher priority.

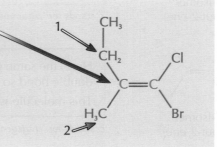

This carbon is directly bonded to **two carbon** atoms, so you need to go **further along** the chain to work out the ordering.

The methyl carbon is only attached to hydrogen atoms, but the ethyl carbon is attached to another carbon atom. So the **ethyl group** is higher priority.

Stereoisomerism

E/Z Isomers Can Sometimes Be Called Cis-Trans Isomers

1) If the carbon atoms have at least **one group in common** (like in but-2-ene), then you can call the isomers '**cis**' or '**trans**' (as well as E- or Z-) where...

- '**cis**' means the same groups are on the **same side** of the double bond,
- '**trans**' means the same groups are on **opposite sides** of the double bond.

So E-but-2-ene can be called **trans-but-2-ene**, and Z-but-2-ene can be called **cis-but-2-ene**.

We're talking Latin this time... 'cis' means 'on the same side', while 'trans' means 'across'.

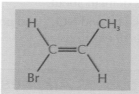

Here's an example:
The **H** atoms are on **opposite** sides of the double bond, so this is **trans-1-bromopropene**.
No problems there.

2) If the carbon atoms both have totally **different** groups attached to them, the cis-trans naming system can't cope.

Here, the **cis/trans** naming system doesn't work because the carbon atoms have **different groups** attached so there's no way of deciding **which isomer** is cis and which isomer is trans.

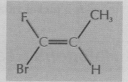

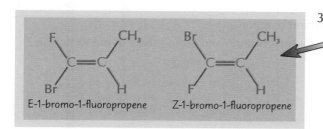

E-1-bromo-1-fluoropropene   Z-1-bromo-1-fluoropropene

3) The E/Z system keeps on working though — in the E/Z system, Br has a **higher priority** than F, so the names depend on where the Br atom is in relation to the CH₃ group.

Practice Questions

Q1 Why is an ethene molecule said to be planar?

Q2 Define the term 'stereoisomers'.

Q3 Which of the following is the Z-isomer of but-2-ene?

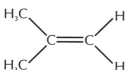 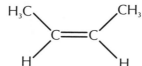 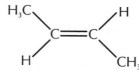

Q4 Is chlorine or bromine higher priority under the Cahn-Ingold-Prelog priority rules?

Q5 Which of the molecules in Question 3 is the trans-isomer of but-2-ene?

Exam Questions

Q1 a) Draw and name the E/Z isomers of pent-2-ene, using full systematic names. [2 marks]
   b) Explain why alkenes can have E/Z isomers but alkanes cannot. [2 marks]

Q2 How many stereoisomers are there of the molecule $CH_3CH=CHCH_2CH=C(CH_3)_2$?

   A. 1   B. 2   C. 3   D. 4 [1 mark]

You've reached the ausfahrt (that's German for exit)...

IMPORTANT FACT: If the two groups connected to one of the double-bonded carbons in an alkene are the same, then it won't have E/Z isomers. So neither propene nor but-1-ene have E/Z isomers. Try drawing them out if you're not sure. And then draw out all the structural isomers of butene. Just to prove you've got this completely sussed.

Reactions of Alkenes

I'll warn you now — some of this stuff gets a bit heavy — but stick with it, as it's pretty important.

Electrophilic Addition Reactions Happen to Alkenes

In an **electrophilic addition** reaction, the alkene **double bond** opens up and atoms are **added** to the carbon atoms.

1) Electrophilic addition reactions happen because the double bond has got plenty of **electrons** and is easily attacked by **electrophiles**.

2) **Electrophiles** are **electron-pair acceptors** — they're usually a bit short of electrons, so they're **attracted** to areas where there are lots of them about.

3) Electrophiles include **positively charged ions**, like H^+ and NO_2^+, and **polar molecules** (since the δ+ atom is attracted to places with lots of electrons).

Adding Hydrogen to C=C Bonds Produces Alkanes

Ethene will react with **hydrogen** gas in an addition reaction to produce ethane. It needs a **nickel catalyst** and a temperature of **150 °C** though.

$$H_2C{=}CH_2 + H_2 \xrightarrow[150\,°C]{Ni} CH_3CH_3$$

Halogens React With Alkenes to Form Dihaloalkanes

1) **Halogens** will react with alkenes to form **dihaloalkanes** — the halogens add **across** the **double bond**, and each of the carbon atoms ends up bonded to one halogen atom. It's an **electrophilic addition** reaction.

$$H_2C{=}CH_2 + X_2 \longrightarrow CH_2XCH_2X$$

2) Here's the mechanism — bromine is used as an example, but chlorine and iodine react in the same way.

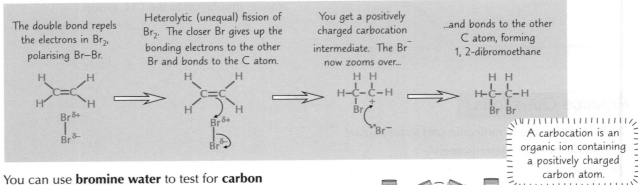

The double bond repels the electrons in Br_2, polarising Br–Br.

Heterolytic (unequal) fission of Br_2. The closer Br gives up the bonding electrons to the other Br and bonds to the C atom.

You get a positively charged carbocation intermediate. The Br^- now zooms over...

...and bonds to the other C atom, forming 1, 2-dibromoethane

A carbocation is an organic ion containing a positively charged carbon atom.

3) You can use **bromine water** to test for **carbon double bonds**. Here's how...

- When you shake an alkene with **orange bromine water**, the solution quickly **decolourises**.

- This is because bromine is added across the double bond to form a colourless **dibromoalkane**.

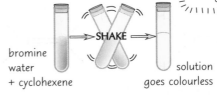

bromine water + cyclohexene → SHAKE → solution goes colourless

Alcohols Can be Made by Steam Hydration

1) Alkenes can be **hydrated** by **steam** at 300 °C and a pressure of 60-70 atm. The reaction needs a solid **phosphoric(V) acid catalyst**.

2) The reaction is used to manufacture **ethanol** from **ethene**:

$$H_2C{=}CH_{2\,(g)} + H_2O_{(g)} \underset{\substack{300\,°C \\ 60\,atm}}{\overset{H_3PO_4}{\rightleftharpoons}} CH_3CH_2OH_{(g)}$$

3) The reaction's **reversible** and the reaction yield is low — with ethene it's only about 5%. This sounds rubbish, but you can **recycle** the unreacted alkene gas, making the overall yield much better (you can get a yield of **95%** with ethene).

Reactions of Alkenes

Alkenes also Undergo **Addition** with **Hydrogen Halides**

Alkenes also undergo **addition** reactions with hydrogen halides — to form **haloalkanes**.
For example, this is the reaction between **ethene** and HBr:

$$H_2C=CH_2 + HBr \longrightarrow CH_2BrCH_3$$

Adding **Hydrogen Halides** to **Unsymmetrical Alkenes** Forms **Two Products**

1) If the hydrogen halide adds to an **unsymmetrical** alkene, there are two possible products.

2) The amount of each product depends on how **stable** the **carbocation** formed in the middle of the reaction is.

3) Carbocations with more **alkyl groups** are more stable because the alkyl groups feed **electrons** towards the positive charge. The **more stable carbocation** is much more likely to form.

Least Stable				Most Stable
primary carbocation (one R group)		secondary carbocation (two R groups)		tertiary carbocation (three R groups)

R = alkyl group
⇀ = electron donation

4) Here's how hydrogen bromide reacts with propene:

$$H_2C=CHCH_3 + HBr \longrightarrow CH_3CHBrCH_3$$
2-bromopropane (major product)

$$H_2C=CHCH_3 + HBr \longrightarrow CH_2BrCH_2CH_3$$
1-bromopropane (minor product)

This secondary carbocation's more stable because it's got two alkyl groups. This carbocation forms most of the time.

This primary carbocation's less stable as it's only got one alkyl group. It forms less often.

2-bromopropane (major product)

1-bromopropane (small amount only)

5) This can be summed up by **Markownikoff's rule** which says: ⟹

> The **major product** from addition of a hydrogen halide (HX) to an unsymmetrical alkene is the one where **hydrogen** adds to the carbon with the **most hydrogens** already attached.

Practice Questions

Q1 What is an electrophile?

Q2 Write an equation for the reaction of ethene with hydrogen.

Q3 What is Markownikoff's rule?

Exam Question

Q1 But-1-ene is an alkene. Alkenes contain at least one C=C double bond.

a) Describe how bromine water can be used to test for C=C double bonds. [2 marks]

b) Name the reaction mechanism involved in the above test. [1 mark]

c) Hydrogen bromide will react with but-1-ene by this mechanism, producing two isomeric products. Draw the displayed formulas of these two isomers and predict which will be the major product. [3 marks]

Electrophiles — they all want a piece of the pi...

Mechanisms are a classic that examiners just love. You need to know the electrophilic addition examples on these pages, so shut the book and scribble them out. And remember that sometimes the product has more than one isomer.

Polymers

Polymers are long, stringy molecules made by joining lots of alkenes together. They're made up of one unit repeated over and over and over and over and over and over and over and over again. Get the idea? OK, let's get started.

Alkenes **Join Up** to form **Addition Polymers**

1) The **double bonds** in alkenes can open up and join together to make long chains called **polymers**. It's kind of like they're holding hands in a big line. The individual, small alkenes are called **monomers**.

2) This is called **addition polymerisation**. For example, **poly(ethene)** is made by the **addition polymerisation** of **ethene**.

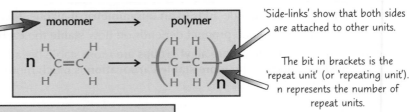

'Side-links' show that both sides are attached to other units.

The bit in brackets is the 'repeat unit' (or 'repeating unit'). n represents the number of repeat units.

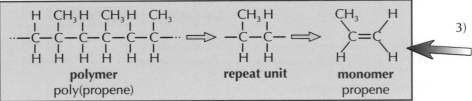

polymer
poly(propene)

repeat unit

monomer
propene

3) To find the **monomer** used to form an addition polymer, take the **repeat unit** and add a **double bond**.

Polymers — **Useful** but Difficult to **Get Rid Of**

1) Synthetic polymers have loads of **advantages**, so they're incredibly widespread these days — we take them pretty much for granted. Just imagine what you'd have to live without if there were no polymers...

2) One of the really useful things about many everyday polymers is that they're very **unreactive**. So food doesn't react with the PTFE coating on pans, plastic windows don't rot, and so on.

3) But this **lack** of reactivity also leads to a **problem**. Most polymers aren't **biodegradable**, and so they're really difficult to **dispose of**.

4) In the UK over **2 million** tonnes of plastic waste are produced each year. It's important to find ways to get rid of this waste while minimising **environmental damage**. There are various possible approaches...

Waste Plastics can be **Buried**

1) **Landfill** is one option for dealing with waste plastics. It's generally used when the plastic is:
   - difficult to separate from other waste,
   - not in sufficient quantities to make separation financially worthwhile,
   - too difficult technically to recycle.

2) But because the **amount of waste** we generate is becoming more and more of a problem, there's a need to **reduce** landfill as much as possible.

Waste Plastics can be **Reused**

Many plastics are made from non-renewable **oil-fractions**, so it makes sense to reuse plastics as much as possible.

There's more than one way to reuse plastics. After **sorting** into different types:

- some plastics (poly(propene), for example) can be **recycled** by **melting** and **remoulding** them,
- some plastics can be **cracked** into **monomers**, and these can be used as an **organic feedstock** to make more plastics or other chemicals.

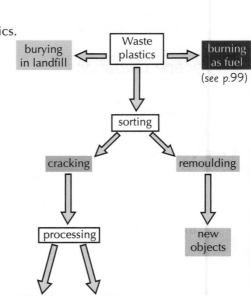

burying in landfill ← Waste plastics → burning as fuel (see p.99)

sorting

cracking

remoulding

processing

new objects

other chemicals

new plastics

Polymers

Waste Plastics can be **Burned**

1) If recycling isn't possible for whatever reason, waste plastics can be burned — and the heat can be used to generate **electricity**.

2) This process needs to be carefully **controlled** to reduce **toxic** gases. For example, polymers that contain **chlorine** (such as **PVC**) produce **HCl** when they're burned — this has to be removed.

3) Waste gases from the combustion are passed through **scrubbers** which can **neutralise** gases such as HCl by allowing them to react with a **base**.

Rex and Dirk enjoy some waist plastic.

Biodegradable Polymers **Decompose** in the **Right Conditions**

Scientists can now make **biodegradable** polymers — ones that naturally **decompose**.

1) **Biodegradable polymers** decompose pretty quickly in certain conditions — because organisms can digest them.

2) Biodegradable polymers can be made from **renewable** raw materials such as **starch** (from maize and other plants) or **oil fractions**, such as from the hydrocarbon **isoprene** (2-methyl-1,3-butadiene). But at the moment they're more **expensive** than non-biodegradable equivalents.

3) Even though they're biodegradable, these polymers still need the right conditions before they'll decompose. You **couldn't** necessarily just put them in a landfill and expect them to perish away because there's a lack of **moisture** and **oxygen** under all that compressed soil. You need to chuck them on a big compost heap.

4) This means that you need to **collect** and **separate** the biodegradable polymers from non-biodegradable plastics.

5) There are various potential uses — e.g. plastic sheeting used to protect plants from the frost can be made from poly(ethene) with **starch grains** embedded in it. In time the starch is broken down by **microorganisms** and the remaining poly(ethene) crumbles into dust. There's no need to collect and dispose of the old sheeting.

6) Scientists have also started developing **photodegradable** polymers. These are polymers that decompose when exposed to **sunlight**.

Practice Questions

Q1 What is the name of the reaction that turns alkenes into polymers?

Q2 Draw the monomer used to make the polymer poly(propene).

Q3 Many plastics are unreactive. Describe one benefit and one disadvantage of this.

Q4 Describe three ways in which used polymers such as poly(propene) can be disposed of.

Q5 What is a biodegradable polymer?

Exam Questions

Q1 Waste plastics can be disposed of by burning.

a) Describe one advantage of disposing of waste plastics by burning. [1 mark]

b) Describe a disadvantage of burning waste plastic that contains chlorine. [1 mark]

Q2 Give two ways that waste polymers can be reused. [2 marks]

Q3 Chloroethene $CH_2=CHCl$ forms the polymer poly(chloroethene), commonly known as PVC. Write an equation for the polymerisation of chloroethene, including a full displayed formula showing the repeating unit in poly(chloroethene). [2 marks]

Alkenes — *join up today, your polymer needs YOU...*

You may have noticed that all this recycling business is a hot topic these days. And not just in the usual places, such as Chemistry books. No, no, no... recycling even makes it onto the news as well. This suits examiners just fine — they like you to know how useful and important chemistry is. So learn this stuff, pass your exam, and do some recycling.

Alcohols

These two pages could well be enough to put you off alcohols for life...

Alcohols are **Primary**, **Secondary** or **Tertiary**

1) The alcohol homologous series has the **general formula $C_nH_{2n+1}OH$**.

2) An alcohol is **primary**, **secondary** or **tertiary**,
depending on which carbon atom the **-OH** group is bonded to.

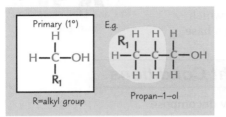

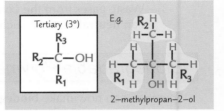

The Hydroxyl Group -OH Can Form **Hydrogen Bonds**

Alcohols are generally **polar molecules** due to the electronegative **hydroxyl group**
which pulls the electrons in the C–OH bond **away** from the **carbon atom**.

$$\overset{\delta+}{R_1}-\overset{\delta-}{O}-\overset{\delta+}{H}$$

The electronegative oxygen in the polar hydroxyl group draws electron density away from the hydrogen, giving it a
slightly positive charge. This positive charge can attract the **lone pairs** on an oxygen from a neighbouring molecule,
forming hydrogen bonds (see page 50). This gives alcohols certain properties...

1) When you mix an alcohol with water, hydrogen bonds
form between the **-OH** and **H_2O**. If it's a **small** alcohol
(e.g. methanol, ethanol or propan-1-ol), hydrogen bonding
lets it mix freely with water — it's **soluble** in water.

2) In **larger alcohols**, most of the molecule is a non-polar carbon chain,
so there's less attraction for the polar H_2O molecules. This means that
as alcohols **increase in size**, their solubility in water **decreases**.

3) Alcohols also form hydrogen bonds with **each other**.
Hydrogen bonding is the **strongest** kind of intermolecular force, so it gives alcohols a relatively **low volatility**
(they don't evaporate easily into a gas) compared to non-polar compounds, e.g. alkanes of similar sizes.

-OH can be **Swapped** for a Halogen to Make a **Haloalkane**

1) Alcohols will react with compounds containing **halide ions** (such as NaBr) in a **substitution reaction**.

2) The **hydroxyl (-OH)** group is **replaced** by the **halide**, so the alcohol is transformed into a **haloalkane**.

3) The reaction also requires an **acid catalyst**, such as H_2SO_4.

Example: To make 2-bromo-2-methylpropane you just need to shake 2-methylpropan-2-ol (a tertiary
alcohol) with sodium bromide and concentrated sulfuric acid at room temperature.

$$H_3C-\underset{\underset{OH}{|}}{\overset{\overset{CH_3}{|}}{C}}-CH_3 + NaBr \longrightarrow H_3C-\underset{\underset{Br}{|}}{\overset{\overset{CH_3}{|}}{C}}-CH_3 + NaOH$$

alcohol   haloalkane
(2-methylpropan-2-ol)   (2-bromo-2-methylpropane)

Alcohols

Alcohols can be **Dehydrated** to Form **Alkenes**

1) You can make alkenes by **eliminating** water from **alcohols** in an **elimination reaction**.

2) The alcohol is mixed with an **acid catalyst** — either **concentrated sulfuric acid** (H_2SO_4) or **concentrated phosphoric acid** (H_3PO_4). The mixture is then **heated**.

An elimination reaction where water is eliminated is called a dehydration reaction.

3) When an alcohol dehydrates it eliminates **water**.

> E.g. **Ethanol** dehydrates to form **ethene**.
> $$C_2H_5OH \rightarrow CH_2=CH_2 + H_2O$$

4) The water molecule is made up from the hydroxyl group and a hydrogen atom that was bonded to a carbon atom adjacent to the hydroxyl carbon.

5) This means that often there are **two possible** alkene products from one elimination reaction depending on **which side** of the hydroxyl group the **hydrogen** is **eliminated** from.

6) Also watch out for if any of the alkene products can form **E/Z isomers** (see pages 93-95) — if they can then a mixture of both isomers will form.

Example: When butan-2-ol is heated to 170 °C with concentrated phosphoric acid, it dehydrates to form a mixture of products. Give the names and structures of all the organic compounds in this mixture.

- Elimination can occur between the **hydroxyl group** and the hydrogen either on **carbon-1** or **carbon-3**. This results in two possible alkene products — **but-1-ene** and **but-2-ene**.
- In addition, **but-2-ene** can form E/Z isomers.
- So there are **3** possible products — but-1-ene, E-but-2-ene and Z-but-2-ene.

But-1-ene   E-But-2-ene   Z-But-2-ene

Practice Questions

Q1 What is the general formula for an alcohol?

Q2 How do the volatilities of alcohols compare with the volatilities of similarly sized alkanes?

Q3 What products are made when 2-methylpropan-2-ol is mixed with sodium bromide and concentrated sulfuric acid?

Exam Questions

Q1 a) Draw and name a primary alcohol, a secondary alcohol and a tertiary alcohol, each with the formula $C_5H_{12}O$.   [3 marks]

    b) Describe how ethanol could be converted into bromoethane   [1 mark]

Q2 When 3-methyl-pentan-3-ol is heated with concentrated sulfuric acid, it reacts to form a mixture of organic products.

    a) What is the name of this type of reaction?   [1 mark]

    b) How many organic compounds will be produced?

      A 4   **B** 3   **C** 2   **D** 1   [1 mark]

Euuurghh, what a page... I think I need a drink...

Not too much to learn here — a few basic definitions, some fiddly explanations of their properties in terms of their polarity and intermolecular bonding, a tricky little dehydration reaction, a substitution reaction...
As I was saying, not much here at all... Think I'm going to faint.   _[THWACK]_

Oxidation of Alcohols

Another two pages of alcohol reactions. Probably not what you wanted for Christmas...

The Simplest way to Oxidise Alcohols is to **Burn Them**

It doesn't take much to set ethanol alight and it burns with a **pale blue flame**. The C–C and C–H bonds are broken as the ethanol is **completely oxidised** to make carbon dioxide and water. This is a **combustion** reaction.

$$C_2H_5OH_{(l)} + 3O_{2(g)} \rightarrow 2CO_{2(g)} + 3H_2O_{(g)}$$

If you burn any alcohol along with plenty of oxygen, you get carbon dioxide and water as products.
But if you want to end up with something more interesting, you need a more sophisticated way of oxidising...

How Much an Alcohol can be **Oxidised** Depends on its **Structure**

You can use the **oxidising agent acidified dichromate(VI)** ($Cr_2O_7^{2-}$/H^+, e.g. $K_2Cr_2O_7$/H_2SO_4) to **mildly** oxidise alcohols.

- **Primary** alcohols are oxidised to **aldehydes** and then to **carboxylic acids**.
- **Secondary** alcohols are oxidised to **ketones** only.
- **Tertiary** alcohols won't be oxidised.

The orange dichromate(VI) ion is reduced to the green chromium(III) ion, Cr^{3+}.

Aldehydes and **ketones** are **carbonyl** compounds — they have the functional group C=O.
Their general formula is $C_nH_{2n}O$.

1) **Aldehydes** have a **hydrogen** and **one alkyl group** attached to the carbonyl carbon atom.
E.g.

propanal
CH_3CH_2CHO

2) **Ketones** have **two alkyl groups** attached to the carbonyl carbon atom.
E.g.

propanone
CH_3COCH_3

Primary Alcohols will Oxidise to **Aldehydes** and **Carboxylic Acids**

Primary alcohols can be oxidised **twice** — first to form **aldehydes** which can then be oxidised to form **carboxylic acids**.

$$R-CH_2-OH + [O] \xrightarrow{distil} R-C\!\!\begin{smallmatrix}O\\H\end{smallmatrix} + [O] \xrightarrow{reflux} R-C\!\!\begin{smallmatrix}O\\OH\end{smallmatrix}$$

+ H_2O

primary alcohol   aldehyde   carboxylic acid

[O] = oxidising agent
e.g. potassium dichromate(VI)

Distil for an **Aldehyde**, and **Reflux** for a **Carboxylic Acid**

You can control how **far** the alcohol is oxidised by controlling the **reaction conditions**. For example...

1) Gently heating ethanol with potassium dichromate(VI) solution and sulfuric acid in a test tube should produce "apple" smelling **ethanal** (an aldehyde). However, it's **really tricky** to control the amount of heat and the aldehyde is usually oxidised to form "vinegar" smelling **ethanoic acid**.

2) To get just the **aldehyde**, you need to get it out of the oxidising solution **as soon** as it's formed. You can do this by gently heating excess alcohol with a **controlled** amount of oxidising agent in **distillation apparatus**, so the aldehyde (which boils at a lower temperature than the alcohol) is distilled off **immediately**.

There's loads more about distillation and reflux on page 112.

3) To produce the **carboxylic acid**, the alcohol has to be **vigorously oxidised**. The alcohol is mixed with excess oxidising agent and heated under **reflux**.

Oxidation of Alcohols

Secondary Alcohols will Oxidise to Ketones

1) Refluxing a secondary alcohol, e.g. propan-2-ol, with acidified dichromate(VI) will produce a **ketone**.

2) Ketones can't be oxidised easily, so even prolonged refluxing won't produce anything more.

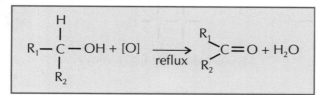

Monty and Bill were getting some much needed rest and refluxation.

Tertiary Alcohols can't be Oxidised Easily

1) Tertiary alcohols don't react with potassium dichromate(VI) at all — the solution stays orange.

2) The only way to oxidise tertiary alcohols is by **burning** them.

Practice Questions

Q1 What's the structural difference between an aldehyde and a ketone?

Q2 Why must you control the reaction conditions when oxidising a primary alcohol to an aldehyde?

Q3 How would you oxidise ethanol to ethanoic acid?

Q4 What will acidified potassium dichromate(VI) oxidise secondary alcohols to?

Q5 How would you oxidise a tertiary alcohol?

Exam Questions

Q1 A student wanted to produce the aldehyde propanal from propanol, and set up reflux apparatus using acidified potassium dichromate(VI) as the oxidising agent.

a) The student tested his product and found that he had not produced propanal.

   i) What is the student's product? [1 mark]

   ii) Write equations to show the two-stage reaction. You may use [O] to represent the oxidising agent. [2 marks]

   iii) What technique should the student have used and why? [1 mark]

b) The student also tried to oxidise 2-methylpropan-2-ol, unsuccessfully.

   i) Draw the full structural formula for 2-methylpropan-2-ol. [1 mark]

   ii) Why is it not possible to oxidise 2-methylpropan-2-ol with an oxidising agent? [1 mark]

Q2 What will be produced if 2-methylbutan-2-ol is heated under reflux with acidified dichromate(VI)?

A an aldehyde   **B** a carboxylic acid   **C** a ketone   **D** an unreacted alcohol   [1 mark]

Q3 Plan an experiment to prepare 2-methylpropanal ($CH_3CH(CH_3)CHO$) from an appropriate alcohol. Your plan should include details of the chemicals (including an alcohol that could be used as a starting material) and procedure used for the reaction. [2 marks]

I've never been very good at singing — I'm always in the wrong key-tone...

These alcohols couldn't just all react in the same way, could they? Nope — it seems like they're out to make your life difficult. So close the book and write down all the different ways of oxidising primary, secondary and tertiary alcohols, and what the different products are. And don't get caught out by those pesky primary alcohols getting oxidised twice.

Haloalkanes

*If you haven't had enough of organic chemistry yet, there's more. If you **have** had enough — there's still more.*

Haloalkanes are Alkanes with Halogen Atoms

A **haloalkane** is an alkane with at least one **halogen atom** in place of a hydrogen atom.
E.g.

Haloalkanes are special
amongst alkanes...

trichloromethane   2-iodo-propane   2-bromo-2-chloro-1,1,1-trifluoroethane

The Carbon–Halogen Bond in Haloalkanes is Polar

1) Halogens are generally much more **electronegative** than carbon.
   So, the **carbon–halogen bond** is **polar**.

2) The $\delta+$ **carbon** is electron deficient.
   This means it can be attacked by a **nucleophile**.

3) A nucleophile's an **electron pair donor**. It could be a **negative ion** or an atom with a **lone pair** of electrons. It donates an **electron pair** to somewhere without enough electrons.

4) **OH⁻**, **CN⁻** and **NH₃** are all **nucleophiles** which react with haloalkanes. **Water's** a nucleophile too, but it reacts slowly.

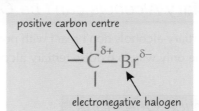

positive carbon centre

electronegative halogen

Haloalkanes can be Hydrolysed to make Alcohols

Haloalkanes can be **hydrolysed** to **alcohols**. This is a **nucleophilic substitution reaction**.
You have to use a **warm aqueous alkali**,
for example **sodium hydroxide** or **potassium hydroxide** or it won't work.
The general equation is...

Hydrolysis is when water breaks bonds.

$$R\text{–}X + OH^- \xrightarrow[\text{reflux}]{OH^- / H_2O} R\text{–}OH + X^-$$

Here's what happens. It's a nice simple **one-step mechanism**.
(We've used bromoethane as an example, but the mechanism's the same for all haloalkanes.)

This is a nucleophilic substitution reaction.

1) OH⁻ is the **nucleophile** which provides a **pair of electrons** for the $C^{\delta+}$.
2) The C–Br bond breaks **heterolytically** — **both** electrons from the bond are taken by **Br⁻**.
3) **Br⁻** falls off as **OH⁻** bonds to the carbon.

Water Can Act as a Nucleophile Too

1) The **water** molecule is a **weak nucleophile**, but it will eventually substitute for the halogen
   — it's just a much slower reaction than the one above.

2) You get an **alcohol** produced again. The general equation is:

$$R\text{–}X + H_2O \rightarrow R\text{–}OH + H^+ + X^-$$

3) Here's what would happen with bromoethane:

$$CH_3CH_2Br + H_2O \rightarrow C_2H_5OH + H^+ + Br^-$$

Haloalkanes

Iodoalkanes are Hydrolysed the Fastest

1) How quickly different haloalkanes are hydrolysed depends on **bond enthalpy** — see p.70 for more on this.

2) **Weaker** carbon-halogen bonds **break** more easily — so they react **faster**.

3) **Iodoalkanes** have the **weakest bonds**, so they hydrolyse the **fastest**.

4) **Fluoroalkanes** have the **strongest bonds**, so they're the **slowest** at hydrolysing.

bond	bond enthalpy kJ mol^{-1}
C–F	467
C–Cl	346
C–Br	290
C–I	228

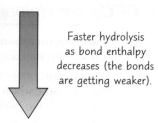

Faster hydrolysis as bond enthalpy decreases (the bonds are getting weaker).

5) You can **compare the reactivity** of chloroalkanes, bromoalkanes and iodoalkanes by doing an experiment:

1) When you mix a **haloalkane** with water, it reacts to form an **alcohol**.

$$R–X + H_2O \rightarrow R–OH + H^+ + X^-$$

2) If you put **silver nitrate solution** in the mixture too, the silver ions react with the **halide ions** as soon as they form, giving a **silver halide precipitate** (see page 63).

$$Ag^+_{(aq)} + X^-_{(aq)} \rightarrow AgX_{(s)}$$

3) To compare the reactivities, set up three test tubes each containing a different haloalkane, ethanol (as a solvent) and silver nitrate solution (this contains the water):

The haloalkanes should all have the same carbon skeleton to make it a fair test.

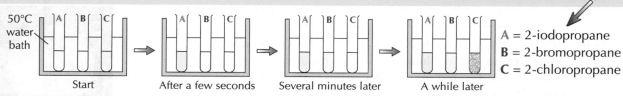

Start → After a few seconds → Several minutes later → A while later

A = 2-iodopropane
B = 2-bromopropane
C = 2-chloropropane

4) A pale yellow precipitate quickly forms with **2-iodopropane** — so iodoalkanes must be the **most reactive haloalkanes**. Bromoalkanes react slower than iodoalkanes to form a cream precipitate, and **chloroalkanes** form a white precipitate the slowest of all.

Practice Questions

Q1 Why is the carbon-halogen bond generally polar?

Q2 What is a nucleophile?

Q3 What is the product when bromoethane is reacted with warm aqueous sodium hydroxide?

Q4 Why does iodoethane react faster than chloro- or bromoethane with warm, aqueous sodium hydroxide?

Exam Questions

Q1 The haloalkane chloromethane is a substance that was formerly used as a refrigerant.

a) Draw the structure of this molecule. [1 mark]

b) Give the mechanism for the hydrolysis of this molecule by warm sodium hydroxide solution. [3 marks]

c) What would be observed if silver nitrate solution was added to the products of the reaction in part b)? [1 mark]

Q2 Which of the following compounds will react the fastest with aqueous potassium hydroxide?

A iodomethane **B** bromomethane **C** chloromethane [1 mark]

I got my tongue stuck on an ice cube last week...it was a polar bond...

Polar bonds manage to get in just about every area of Chemistry. If you still think they're something to do with either bears or mints, flick back and have a good read of page 48. Make sure you learn the mechanism of hydrolysis — including all the curly arrows and bond polarities— it could come up in exams. Ruin the examiner's day and get it right.

Haloalkanes and the Environment

Two pages on air pollution coming up, so take a deep breath...
unless you're hanging around somewhere with a lot of air pollution, that is...

CFCs are Haloalkanes

1) **Chlorofluorocarbons** (**CFCs**) are well-known haloalkanes.

2) They contain only chlorine, fluorine and carbon — all the hydrogens have been replaced.

3) They're very **stable**, **volatile**, **non-flammable** and **non-toxic**. They were used a lot — e.g. in **fridges**, **aerosol cans**, **dry cleaning** and **air-conditioning** — until scientists realised they were destroying the **ozone layer**.

trichlorofluoromethane

chlorotrifluoromethane

They're stable because of the strength of the carbon-halogen bonds.

Chlorine Atoms are Destroying The Ozone Layer

1) Ozone (O_3) in the upper atmosphere acts as a **chemical sunscreen**. It absorbs a lot of the **ultraviolet radiation** which can cause sunburn or even skin cancer.

2) Ozone's **formed naturally** when an **oxygen molecule** is **broken down** into **two free radicals** by **ultraviolet radiation**. The free radicals **attack** other oxygen molecules forming **ozone**. Just like this:

$$O_2 \xrightarrow{UV} O+O \Longrightarrow O_2+O \rightarrow O_3$$

3) In the 1970s and 1980s, scientists discovered that the **ozone layer** above **Antarctica** was getting **thinner** — in fact, it was decreasing very rapidly. The ozone layer over the **Arctic** has been found to be thinning too. These 'holes' in the ozone layer are bad because they allow more harmful **UV radiation** to reach the Earth.

4) The 'holes' are formed because **CFCs** in the upper atmosphere absorb UV radiation and split to form **chlorine free radicals**. These free radicals **catalyse** the destruction of ozone — they **destroy ozone molecules** and are then **regenerated** to destroy more ozone. One chlorine atom can destroy 10 000 ozone molecules before it forms a stable compound. Here's what happens:

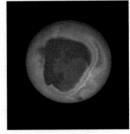

Here's a satellite map showing the 'hole' in the ozone layer over Antarctica. The 'hole' is shown by the blue area.

- **Chlorine free radicals**, Cl•, are formed when the C–Cl bonds in **CFCs** are broken down by **ultraviolet radiation**.

  E.g. $CF_2Cl_{2(g)} \xrightarrow{UV} \cdot CF_2Cl_{(g)} + Cl\cdot_{(g)}$

- These free radicals are **catalysts**. They react with **ozone** to form an **intermediate** (ClO•) and an oxygen molecule.

The O radical comes from the break down of oxygen by ultraviolet radiation.

$$Cl\cdot_{(g)} + O_{3\,(g)} \rightarrow O_{2\,(g)} + ClO\cdot_{(g)}$$
$$ClO\cdot_{(g)} + O_{(g)} \rightarrow O_{2\,(g)} + Cl\cdot_{(g)}$$

The chlorine free radical is regenerated. It goes straight on to attack another ozone molecule. It only takes one little chlorine free radical to destroy loads of ozone molecules.

- So the **overall reaction** is... $O_{3\,(g)} + O_{(g)} \rightarrow 2O_{2\,(g)}$ ... and Cl• is the catalyst.

Nitrogen Oxides Can Also Break Ozone Down

1) **NO•** free radicals from **nitrogen oxides** destroy ozone too. Nitrogen oxides are produced by **car and aircraft engines** and **thunderstorms**. NO• free radicals affect ozone in the **same way** as chlorine radicals.

2) The reactions can be represented by these equations, where **R** represents either Cl• or NO•. In both cases, the free radicals act as **catalysts** for the destruction of the ozone. The overall reaction is:

$$O_3 + O \rightarrow 2O_2$$

$$R + O_3 \rightarrow RO + O_2$$
$$RO + O \rightarrow R + O_2$$

Formed when UV breaks down O_2.

The harmful radical is regenerated.

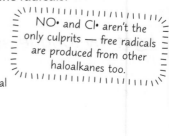

NO• and Cl• aren't the only culprits — free radicals are produced from other haloalkanes too.

Haloalkanes and the Environment

Chemists Developed **Alternatives** to **CFCs**

1) In the 1970s scientists discovered that CFCs were causing **damage** to the **ozone layer**. The **advantages** of CFCs couldn't outweigh the **environmental problems** they were causing, so they were **banned**.

2) The **Montreal Protocol** of 1989 was an **international treaty** to phase out the use of CFCs and other ozone-destroying haloalkanes by the year 2000. There were a few **permitted uses** such as in medical inhalers and in fire extinguishers used in submarines.

3) Scientists supported the treaty, and worked on finding **alternatives** to CFCs.

- **HCFCs (hydrochlorofluorocarbons)** and **HFCs (hydrofluorocarbons)** are being used as temporary alternatives to CFCs until safer products are developed.
- **Hydrocarbons** are also used.
- **HCFCs** are broken down in the atmosphere in 10-20 years. They still damage the ozone layer, but their effect is much smaller than CFCs.
- **HFCs** are also broken down in the atmosphere. Unlike HCFCs, they **don't** contain **chlorine**, so they don't affect the ozone layer.
- Unfortunately, **HFCs and HCFCs are greenhouse gases** (see page 108) — they're 1000 times worse than carbon dioxide.
- Some **hydrocarbons** are being used in fridges but these are greenhouse gases too.
- Nowadays, most aerosols have been replaced by **pump spray systems** or use **nitrogen** as the propellant. Many industrial fridges and freezers now use **ammonia** as the coolant gas, and **carbon dioxide** is used to make foamed polymers.

4) These substances do have **drawbacks**, but they're currently the **least environmentally damaging** of all the alternatives.

5) The ozone holes **still** form in the spring but are slowly shrinking — so things are looking up.

Practice Questions

Q1 What is a CFC?
Q2 Describe how ozone is beneficial.
Q3 Write equations to show how ozone is formed.
Q4 Write out equations to show how ozone is destroyed, using R to represent the radical.
Q5 Name two alternatives to CFCs.

Exam Questions

Q1 Trichlorofluoromethane ($CFCl_3$) is a CFC that was once used widely as an aerosol propellant.

a) What are two useful properties of CFCs? [1 mark]

b) Give equations to show how trichlorofluoromethane catalyses the breakdown of ozone in the upper atmosphere. Your answer should include an equation for the overall reaction. [3 marks]

c) Name another species of free radical responsible for destroying ozone. [1 mark]

Q2 Nitric oxide radicals (NO•) are destructive radicals that can form in the atmosphere. These radicals act as catalysts in the breakdown of ozone. Give equations to show how nitric oxide radicals catalyse the break down of ozone. [2 marks]

WANTED for vandalism — CFCs. Highly volatile, approach with caution...

How scientists found the hole in the ozone layer and used their evidence to instigate government legislation is a great example of How Science Works. The alternatives to CFCs we use now are less stable, so they don't hang around for as long and are less likely to make it to the upper atmosphere. This gives the ozone layer a chance to replenish. Phew.

The Greenhouse Effect & Global Warming

The greenhouse effect keeps Earth warm, and that's great. Unfortunately, humans are pumping loads of greenhouse gases into the atmosphere, so the greenhouse effect is being enhanced. And that's where it all goes wrong.

The **Greenhouse Effect** Keeps Us **Alive**

1) Various gases in the atmosphere that contain C=O, C–H or O–H bonds are able to **absorb infrared radiation** (heat)... and **re-emit** it in **all directions** — including back towards Earth, keeping us warm. This is called the '**greenhouse effect**' (even though a real greenhouse doesn't actually work like this).

2) The main greenhouse gases are **water vapour**, **carbon dioxide** and **methane**.

An **Enhanced Greenhouse Effect** Causes **Global Warming**

1) Over the last 150 years or so, the world's **population** has increased, and we've become more **industrialised**. This means we've been **burning fossil fuels**, releasing tons of CO_2 and **chopping down forests** which absorb CO_2. We've also been growing more **food**, and cows and paddy fields release lots of **methane**.

2) Higher concentrations of greenhouse gases mean **more heat** is being trapped and the Earth is getting **warmer** — this is **global warming**. Global warming is thought to be responsible for recent **changes to climates** — such as the shrinking of the **polar ice caps** and **less predictable weather**.

There's **Scientific Evidence** for the Increase in Global Warming

1) Scientists have collected data to confirm whether or not climate change is happening, e.g. from analysing air samples and sea water samples.

2) The evidence shows that the Earth's average temperature has increased **dramatically** in the last 50 years, and that CO_2 levels have increased at the same time.

3) The **correlation** between CO_2 and temperature is pretty clear, but just showing a correlation doesn't prove that one thing **causes** another — there has to be a plausible mechanism for how one change causes the other (here, the explanation is the enhanced greenhouse effect).

4) There's now a consensus among climate scientists that the link **is** causal, and that recent warming is **anthropogenic** — **human activities** are to blame.

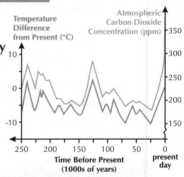

Governments are Working to **Reduce** their Greenhouse Gas Emissions

1) Scientific evidence has persuaded governments to form a **global agreement** that climate change could be damaging for people, the environment and economies, and that we should try to **limit** it.

2) In 1997 the **Kyoto protocol** was signed — industrialised countries (including the UK) promised to reduce their greenhouse gas emissions to agreed levels. This agreement came to an end in 2012, and currently has no replacement, though many governments agree that they need to reduce CO_2 emissions by around 50% by 2050.

3) The UK government has created policies to use more **renewable energy supplies**, such as wind and solar farms, in order to reduce their emissions.

Practice Questions

Q1 Name three greenhouse gases.

Q2 What's the difference between the greenhouse effect and global warming?

Exam Question

Q1 The concentration of carbon dioxide in the Earth's atmosphere has increased over the last 50 years.

a) Give two reasons for this increase. [2 marks]

b) How do governments know that global warming is happening? [1 mark]

c) Describe how governments are acting to reduce greenhouse gas emissions. [1 mark]

Eating ice cream causes sunburn (well, they correlate)...

Global warming doesn't just affect the temperature. The climate depends on a complicated system of ocean currents and winds etc. As the atmosphere warms up, these factors could change, leading to much less predictable weather.

Analytical Techniques

If you've got some stuff and don't know what it is, don't taste it. Stick it in an infrared spectrometer or a mass spectrometer instead. You'll wind up with some scary looking graphs. But just learn the basics, and you'll be fine.

Infrared Spectroscopy Helps You Identify Organic Molecules

1) In infrared (IR) spectroscopy, a beam of **IR radiation** is passed through a sample of a chemical.

2) The IR radiation is absorbed by the **covalent bonds** in the molecules, increasing their **vibrational** energy (i.e. they vibrate more).

3) **Bonds between different atoms** absorb **different frequencies** of IR radiation. Bonds in different **places** in a molecule absorb different frequencies too — so the O–H bond in an **alcohol** and the O–H bond in a **carboxylic acid** absorb different frequencies. This table shows what **frequencies** different bonds absorb:

Functional Group	Where it's found	Frequency/ Wavenumber (cm⁻¹)
C–H	alkyl groups, alkenes, arenes	2850 – 3100
O–H	alcohols	3200 – 3600
O–H	carboxylic acids	2500 – 3300 (broad)
C=O	aldehydes, ketones, carboxylic acids, esters	1630 – 1820

You don't need to learn this data, but you do need to understand how to use it.

4) An infrared spectrometer produces a **spectrum** that shows you what frequencies of radiation the molecules are absorbing. You can use it to identify the **functional groups** in a molecule:

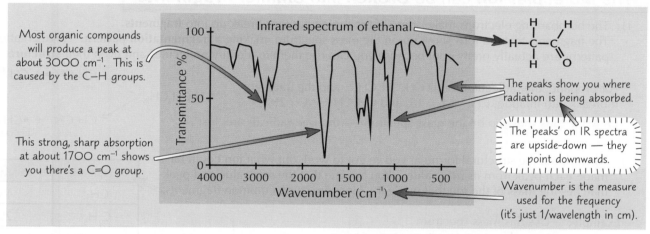

Most organic compounds will produce a peak at about 3000 cm⁻¹. This is caused by the C–H groups.

This strong, sharp absorption at about 1700 cm⁻¹ shows you there's a C=O group.

The peaks show you where radiation is being absorbed.

The 'peaks' on IR spectra are upside-down — they point downwards.

Wavenumber is the measure used for the frequency (it's just 1/wavelength in cm).

5) This also means that you can tell if a functional group has **changed** during a reaction. For example, if you **oxidise** an **alcohol** to an **aldehyde** you'll see the O–H absorption **disappear** from the spectrum, and a C=O absorption **appear**. If you then oxidise it further to a **carboxylic acid** an O–H peak at a slightly lower frequency than before will appear, alongside the C=O peak.

There Are Lots of Uses for Infrared Spectroscopy

1) Infrared spectroscopy is used in **breathalysers** to work out if a driver is over the drink-drive limit. The **amount** of **ethanol vapour** in the driver's breath is found by measuring the **intensity** of the peak corresponding to the **C–H bond** in the IR spectrum. It's chosen because it's **not affected** by any **water vapour** in the breath.

2) Infrared spectroscopy is also used to monitor the concentrations of **polluting gases** in the atmosphere. These include **carbon monoxide** (CO) and **nitrogen monoxide** (NO), which are both present in **car emissions**. The intensity of the peaks corresponding to the C≡O or N=O bonds can be studied to monitor their levels.

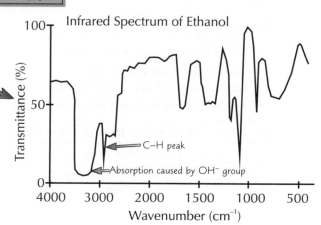

MODULE 4: SECTION 2 — ALCOHOLS, HALOALKANES & ANALYSIS

Analytical Techniques

Mass Spectrometry Can Help to Identify Compounds

1) You saw on page 15 how you can use a mass spectrum showing the relative isotopic abundances of an element to work out its relative atomic mass. You need to make sure you can remember how to do this. You can also get mass spectra for **molecular samples**.

2) A mass spectrum is produced by a mass spectrometer. The molecules in the sample are bombarded with electrons, which remove an electron from the molecule to form a **molecular ion, $M^+_{(g)}$**.

3) To find the relative molecular mass of a compound you look at the **molecular ion peak** (the **M peak**). The mass/charge value of the molecular ion peak is the **molecular mass**. ← Assuming the ion has a 1+ charge, which it normally will have.

The **y-axis** gives the **abundance of ions**, often as a percentage.

The **x-axis** units are given as a 'mass/charge' ratio.

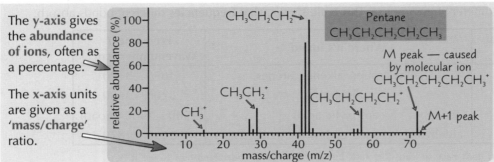

Here's the mass spectrum of pentane. Its M peak is at 72 — so the compound's M_r is 72.
For most <u>organic compounds</u> the M peak is the one with the second highest mass/charge ratio.
The smaller peak to the right of the M peak is called the M+1 peak — it's caused by the presence of the carbon isotope ^{13}C.

The Molecular Ion can be Broken into Smaller Fragments

1) The bombarding electrons make some of the molecular ions break up into **fragments**. The fragments that are ions show up on the mass spectrum, making a **fragmentation pattern**. Fragmentation patterns are actually pretty cool because you can use them to identify **molecules** and even their **structure**.

For propane, the molecular ion is $CH_3CH_2CH_3^+$, and the fragments it breaks into include CH_3^+ ($M_r = 15$) and $CH_3CH_2^+$ ($M_r = 29$).

Only the **ions** show up on the mass spectrum — the **free radicals** are 'lost'.

$$CH_3CH_2CH_3^+ \nearrow CH_3CH_2\bullet + CH_3^+ \quad \text{(free radical) (ion)}$$
$$\searrow CH_3CH_2^+ + \bullet CH_3 \quad \text{(ion) (free radical)}$$

2) To work out the structural formula, you've got to work out what **ion** could have made each peak from its **m/z value**. (You assume that the m/z value of a peak matches the **mass** of the ion that made it.) Here are some common fragments:

Fragment	Molecular Mass
CH_3^+	15
$C_2H_5^+$	29
$CH_3CH_2CH_2^+$ or $CH_3CHCH_3^+$	43
OH^+	17

Example: Use this mass spectrum to work out the structure of the molecule:

It's only the m/z values you're interested in — ignore the heights of the bars.

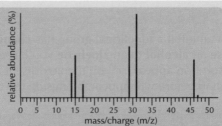

1. Identify the fragments

This molecule's got a peak at 15 m/z, so it's likely to have a **CH₃** group.

It's also got a peak at 17 m/z, so it's likely to have an **OH** group.

Other ions are matched to the peaks here:

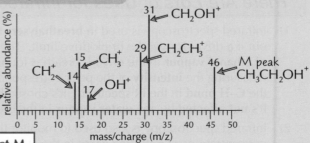

2. Piece them together to form a molecule with the correct M_r

Ethanol has all the fragments on this spectrum.

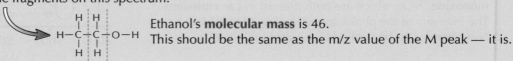

Ethanol's **molecular mass** is 46. This should be the same as the m/z value of the M peak — it is.

Analytical Techniques

Mass Spectrometry is Used to *Differentiate* Between *Similar Molecules*

1) Even if two **different compounds** contain **the same atoms**, you can still tell them apart with mass spectrometry because they won't produce exactly the same set of fragments.

2) The formulas of **propanal** and **propanone** are shown on the right. They've got the same M_r, but different structures, so they produce some **different fragments**. For example, propanal will have a C_2H_5 fragment but propanone won't.

3) Every compound produces a different mass spectrum — so the spectrum's like a **fingerprint** for the compound. Large computer **databases** of mass spectra can be used to identify a compound from its spectrum.

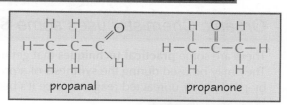

propanal   propanone

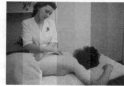

A massage spectrum

You Can *Combine Techniques* to *Identify* a Compound

In the exam, you may be asked to identify a compound from its **mass or percentage composition**, **IR spectrum** and **mass spectrum**. Here's what you should do:

1) Use the **composition** to work out the **molecular formula** of the compound.

2) Work out what **functional groups** are in the compound from its **infrared spectrum**.

3) Use the **mass spectrum** to work out the **structure** of the molecule.

Have a look at pages 22-23 if you're not sure how to work out a compound's molecular formula from its composition.

Practice Questions

Q1 Which parts of a molecule absorb infrared energy?

Q2 Why do most infrared spectra of organic molecules have a strong, sharp peak at around 3000 cm⁻¹?

Q3 Give two uses of infrared spectroscopy.

Q4 What is meant by the molecular ion?

Q5 What is the M peak?

Exam Questions

Use the infrared absorption data on p.109.

Q1 The molecule that produces the IR spectrum shown on the right has composition by mass of:
C: 48.64%, H: 8.12%, O: 43.24%.

a) Which functional groups are responsible for peaks A and B? [2 marks]

b) Give the molecular formula and name of this molecule. Explain your answer. [3 marks]

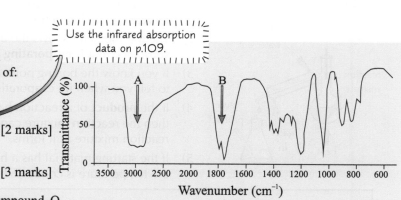

Q2 Below is the mass spectrum of an organic compound, Q.

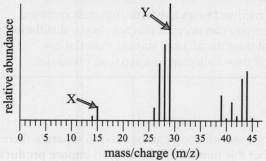

a) What is the M_r of compound Q? [1 mark]

b) What fragments are the peaks marked X and Y most likely to correspond to? [2 marks]

c) Suggest a structure for this compound. [1 mark]

d) Why is it unlikely that this compound is an alcohol? [1 mark]

Use the clues, identify a molecule — mass spectrometry my dear Watson...

Luckily you don't have to remember where any of the infrared peaks are. But you do need to be able to identify them using your data sheet. It's handy if you can learn the molecular masses of the common mass spec fragments, but if you do forget them, then you can just work them out from the relative atomic masses of the atoms in each fragment.

Organic Synthesis — Practical Skills

*I'm sure learning all this organic chemistry has got you itching to get into the lab and do some experiments.
Well, hold your horses and read these pages before you go throwing chemicals around willy-nilly...*

Organic Chemistry uses some **Specific Techniques**

There are some **practical techniques** that get used a lot in organic chemistry.
They may be used during the **synthesis** of a product, or to **purify** it from unwanted
by-products or unreacted reagents once it's been made.

Refluxing Makes Sure You Don't Lose Any **Volatile** Organic Substances

1) **Organic reactions** are **slow** and the substances are usually
   flammable and **volatile** (they've got **low boiling points**).
   If you stick them in a beaker and heat them with a Bunsen burner
   they'll **evaporate** or **catch fire** before they have **time to react**.

2) You can **reflux** a reaction to get round this problem.

3) The mixture's **heated in a flask** fitted with a **vertical Liebig condenser**
   — this continuously boils, evaporates and condenses the vapours
   and **recycles** them back into the flask, giving them **time to react**.

4) The **heating** is usually **electrical** — hot plates, heating mantles,
   or electrically controlled water baths are normally used.
   This **avoids naked flames** that might ignite the compounds.

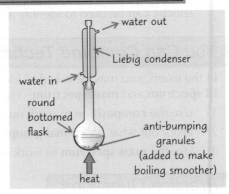

Distillation Separates Substances With Different **Boiling Points**

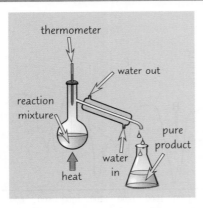

1) Distillation works by **gently heating** a mixture in a distillation apparatus.
   The substances will evaporate out of the mixture in order of
   increasing boiling point.

2) The thermometer shows the **boiling point** of the
   substance that is **evaporating** at any given time.

3) If you know the boiling point of your **pure product**, you can use the thermometer
   to tell you when it's evaporating and therefore when it's condensing.

4) If the **product** of a reaction has a **lower boiling point** than the **starting materials**
   then the reaction mixture can be **heated** so that the product **evaporates** from the
   reaction mixture as it forms.

5) If the starting material has a **higher boiling point** than the product, so as long as
   the temperature is controlled, it won't evaporate out from the reaction mixture.

- Sometimes, a product is formed that will go on to **react further** if it's left in the reaction mixture.

- For example, when you oxidise a **primary alcohol**, it is first oxidised to an **aldehyde** and then oxidised
  to a **carboxylic acid**. If you want the **aldehyde product**, then you can do your reaction in the **distillation
  equipment**. The aldehyde product has a **lower boiling point** than the alcohol starting material, so
  will distil out of the reaction mixture **as soon** as it forms. It is then collected in a separate container.

Volatile Liquids Can be Purified by **Redistillation**

1) If a product and its impurities have **different boiling points**, then redistillation can be used to **separate** them.
   You just use the same distillation apparatus as shown above, but this time you're heating an **impure product**,
   instead of the reaction mixture.

2) When the liquid you want **boils** (this is when the thermometer is at the boiling point of the
   liquid), you place a flask at the open end of the condenser ready to collect your product.

3) When the thermometer shows the temperature is changing, put another flask
   at the end of the condenser because a **different liquid** is about to be delivered.

Organic Synthesis — Practical Skills

Separation Removes Any Water Soluble Impurities From the Product

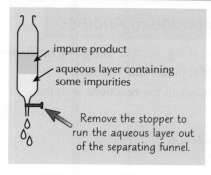

impure product

aqueous layer containing
some impurities

Remove the stopper to
run the aqueous layer out
of the separating funnel.

1) If the product is **insoluble** in water then you can use **separation** to remove any impurities that **do dissolve** in water, such as **salts** or water soluble organic compounds (e.g. alcohols).

2) Once the reaction is completed, the mixture is poured into a **separating funnel**, and **water** is added.

3) The funnel is **shaken** and then allowed to settle. The **organic layer** is **less dense** than the **aqueous layer** so should float on top. Any water soluble impurities should have dissolved in the lower **aqueous layer**. You can then open the stopper on the separating funnel, run off the aqueous layer and collect your product.

- If you use separation to purify a product, the organic layer will end up containing **trace amounts** of **water**, so it has to be **dried**.
- To do this you can add an **anhydrous salt** such as **magnesium sulfate** ($MgSO_4$) or **calcium chloride** ($CaCl_2$). The salt is used as a **drying agent** — it **binds** to any water present to become **hydrated**.
- When you first add the salt to the organic layer it will be **lumpy**. This means you need to add more. You know that all the water has been removed when you can swirl the mixture and it looks like a snow globe.
- You can **filter** the mixture to remove the solid **drying agent**.

Practice Questions

Q1 Draw a labelled diagram to show the apparatus used in a reflux reaction.

Q2 Why might you want to avoid naked flames when performing an experiment with organic substances?

Q3 Name two ways of purifying organic products.

Q4 Name two drying agents.

Exam Question

Q1 a) A student carried out an experiment to make hex-1-ene from hexan-1-ol using the following procedure:

$$HO\diagdown\diagup\diagdown\diagup\diagdown \xrightarrow[\text{heat}]{H_3PO_4} \diagup\diagdown\diagup\diagdown\diagup$$

1) Mix 1 mL hexan-1-ol with concentrated phosphoric acid in a reflux apparatus, and reflux for 30 minutes.

2) Once the mixture has cooled, separate the alkene from any aqueous impurities.

3) Dry the organic layer. with anhydrous magnesium sulfate.

i) What is meant by reflux and why is it a technique sometimes used in organic chemistry? [2 marks]

ii) What organic compound is removed in the separating step? [1 mark]

iii) Describe, in detail, how the student would carry out the separation in step 2). [3 marks]

b) In another experiment, the student decides to make 1-hexen-6-ol by carrying out a single dehydration reaction of the diol 1,6-hexanediol.

$$HO\diagdown\diagup\diagdown\diagup\diagdown\diagup^{OH} \xrightarrow[\text{heat}]{H_3PO_4} \diagup\diagdown\diagup\diagdown\diagup^{OH}$$

i) If the student follows the procedure in part a), why might he produce a mixture of products? [1 mark]

ii) How could the procedure in part a) be adapted to prevent a mixture of products being formed? [2 marks]

___

Thought this page couldn't get any drier? Try adding anhydrous $MgSO_4$...

Scientists need to know why they do the sythings they do — that way they can plan new experiments to make new compounds. Learning the fine details of how experiments are carried out may not be the most interesting thing in the world, but you should get to try out some of these methods in practicals, which is a lot more fun.

Organic Synthesis — Synthetic Routes

There's lots of information on these pages, but you've seen most of it before. It's really just a great big round-up of all the organic reactions you've met in this module. (Maybe not the most exciting thing in the world, but really useful).

Chemists Use **Synthetic Routes** to Get from One Compound to Another

1) Chemists need to be able to make one compound from another. It's vital for things such as **designing medicines**.

2) It's not always possible to synthesise a desired product from a starting material in **just one** reaction.

3) A **synthetic route** shows how you get from one compound to another. It shows all the **reactions** with the **intermediate products**, and the **reagents** needed for each reaction.

Example: You can't produce **propanone** from **2-bromopropane** via one reaction. Instead you first have to make **propan-2-ol**. The synthetic route is:

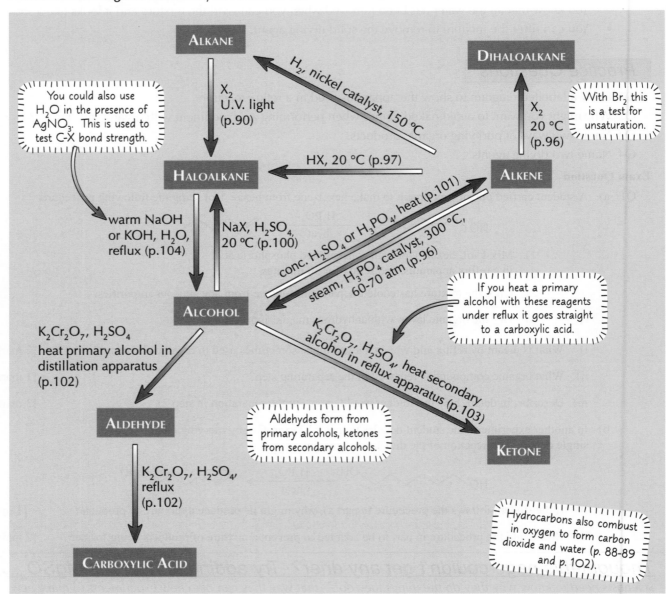

4) Here are all the **organic reactions** you've met so far:

Organic Synthesis — Synthetic Routes

Different *Functional Groups* are Involved in Different *Types* of *Reactions*

1) The different **properties** of functional groups influence their **reactivity** — **nucleophiles** don't react with the **electron-rich double bond** in **alkenes**, but they do attack the δ+ carbon in **haloalkanes**.

2) Here are all the functional groups you've studied so far and how they'll typically react:

Homologous series	Functional group	Properties		Typical reactions
Alkane	C–C	Non-polar, unreactive		Radical substitution
Alkene	C=C	Non-polar, electron-rich double bond		Electrophilic addition
Alcohol	C–OH	Polar C–OH bond		Nucleophilic substitution Dehydration/elimination
Haloalkane	C–X	Polar C–X bond		Nucleophilic substitution
Aldehyde/Ketone	C=O	Polar C=O bond		Aldehydes will oxidise.
Carboxylic acid	-COOH	Electron deficient carbon centre		—

3) Sometimes a compound will have **more than one** functional group. Make sure you can identify **all** of them.

Make Sure You Give *All* the Information

If you're asked how to make one compound from another in the exam, make sure you include:

1) Any **special procedures**, such as refluxing.
2) The **conditions** needed, e.g. high temperature or pressure, or the presence of a catalyst.

Practice Questions

Q1 Why might a chemist want to devise a synthetic route?

Q2 Write a reaction scheme to show how propanone could be formed from 2-bromopropane.

Q3 Name three types of compound that can react to form a haloalkane.

Q4 What is the name for the typical reaction of alkenes?

Exam Questions

Q1 The following flowchart shows some of the reactions of 2-methylpropan-1-ol:

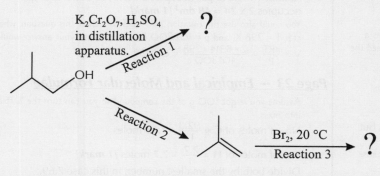

a) Give the skeletal formula of the product of Reaction 1. [1 mark]

b) What are the reagents and conditions needed for Reaction 2? [2 marks]

c) i) Draw the displayed formula of the product of Reaction 3. [1 mark]

   ii) What would be observed during the reaction? [1 mark]

Q2 Devise a two step synthetic route for the formation of butanal from but-1-ene. Include all reagents and reaction conditions in your scheme. [3 marks]

Last week I dyed my hair bright pink... I've got synthetic roots...

Woah, there's a lot of information on these pages. But before you go for a well-deserved cuppa, have another look at that big spider diagram on the other page. It links up all the reactions and organic compounds you've met, and it'll be super useful to know in the exam. So draw it out with all the reagents and conditions. And then go and have a break.

Answers

Module 1 — Development of Practical Skills

Page 5 — Planning Experiments

1 Using litmus paper is not a particularly accurate method of measuring pH / not very sensitive equipment *[1 mark]*. It would be better to use a pH meter *[1 mark]*.

Page 7 — Practical Techniques

1 a) The student measured the level of the liquid from the top of the meniscus, when he should have measured it from the bottom *[1 mark]*.
   b) B *[1 mark]*.

Page 9 — Presenting Results

1 a) mean volume $= \dfrac{7.30 + 7.25 + 7.25}{3} = 7.26666...$ cm^3
   $= \textbf{0.00727 dm}^3$ or $\textbf{7.27} \times \textbf{10}^{-3}$ dm^3 (3 s.f.) *[1 mark]*
   b) $0.50 \div 1000 = \textbf{0.00050 mol cm}^{-3}$ or $\textbf{5.0} \times \textbf{10}^{-4}$ mol cm^{-3} *[1 mark]*

Page 11 — Analysing Results

1 a) 15 °C and 25 °C *[1 mark]*.
   b) Positive correlation *[1 mark]*.
   c) C *[1 mark]*

Page 13 — Evaluating Experiments

1 a) The volumetric flask reads to the nearest 0.5 cm^3, so the uncertainty is ±0.25 cm^3.
   percentage error $= \dfrac{\text{uncertainty}}{\text{reading}} \times 100 = \dfrac{0.25}{25} \times 100 = \textbf{1.0 \%}$
   [1 mark]
   b) E.g. The student should add the thermometer to the citric acid solution and allow it to stabilise before adding the sodium bicarbonate to give an accurate value for the initial temperature *[1 mark]*. The student should then measure the temperature change until the solution stops reacting to give a valid result for the temperature change of the entire reaction *[1 mark]*.

Module 2: Section 1 — Atoms and Reactions

Page 15 — The Atom

1 a) Similarity — They've all got the same number of protons/electrons *[1 mark]*. Difference — They all have different numbers of neutrons *[1 mark]*.
   b) 1 proton, 1 neutron (2 – 1), 1 electron *[1 mark]*.
   c) ^{3}H *[1 mark]*
   Since tritium has 2 neutrons in the nucleus and also 1 proton, it has a mass number of 3. You could also write $^3_1$H but you don't really need the atomic number.

2 a) i) They both have 18 electrons *[1 mark]*.
      ii) They both have 16 protons (the atomic number of S must always be the same) *[1 mark]*.
      iii) They both have 22 neutrons *[1 mark]*.
   b) A and C *[1 mark]*. They have the same number of protons but different numbers of neutrons *[1 mark]*.
   It doesn't matter that they have a different number of electrons because they are still the same element.

Page 17 — Atomic Models

1 a) Bohr knew that if an electron was freely orbiting the nucleus it would spiral into it, causing the atom to collapse *[1 mark]*. His model only allowed electrons to be in fixed shells and not in between them *[1 mark]*.
   b) When an electron moves from one shell to another electromagnetic radiation is emitted or absorbed *[1 mark]*.

c) Atoms react in order to gain full shells of electrons *[1 mark]*. Noble gases have full shells and so do not react *[1 mark]*. (Alternatively: a full shell of electrons makes an atom stable *[1 mark]*; noble gases have full shells and do not react because they are stable *[1 mark]*.)

Page 19 — Relative Mass

1 a) First multiply each relative abundance by the relative mass —
   $120.8 \times 63 = 7610.4$, $54.0 \times 65 = 3510.0$
   Next add up the products: $7610.4 + 3510.0 = 11\ 120.4$ *[1 mark]*
   Now divide by the total abundance ($120.8 + 54.0 = 174.8$)
   $A_r(Cu) = \dfrac{11120.4}{174.8} \approx \textbf{63.6}$ *[1 mark]*
   You can check your answer by seeing if $A_r(Cu)$ is in between 63 and 65 (the lowest and highest relative isotopic masses).
   b) A sample of copper is a mixture of 2 isotopes in different abundances *[1 mark]*. The relative atomic mass is an average mass of these isotopes which isn't a whole number *[1 mark]*.

2 You use pretty much the same method here as for question 1 a).
   $93.1 \times 39 = 3630.9$, $0.120 \times 40 = 4.8$, $6.77 \times 41 = 277.57$
   $3630.9 + 4.8 + 277.57 = \textbf{3913.27}$ *[1 mark]*
   This time you divide by 100 because they're percentages.
   $A_r(K) = \dfrac{3913.27}{100} \approx \textbf{39.1}$ *[1 mark]*
   Again check your answer's between the lowest and highest relative isotopic masses, 39 and 41. $A_r(K)$ is closer to 39 because most of the sample (93.1 %) is made up of this isotope.

Page 21 — The Mole

1 Molar mass of HCl = 1.0 + 35.5 = 36.5 g mol^{-1}
   No. moles in 7.3 g HCl $= \dfrac{7.3}{36.5} = 0.2$ mol
   No. molecules of HCl in 0.2 mol $= 0.2 \times 6.02 \times 10^{23}$
   $= 1.204 \times 10^{23}$ *[1 mark]*
   There are 2 atoms in each molecule of HCl, so
   No. atoms $= 2 \times 1.204 \times 10^{23} = \textbf{2.4} \times \textbf{10}^{23}$ atoms (2 s.f) *[1 mark]*

2 $M(CH_3COOH) = (2 \times 12.0) + (4 \times 1.0) + (2 \times 16.0) = 60.0$ g mol^{-1} *[1 mark]* so mass of 0.360 moles $= 60.0 \times 0.360 = \textbf{21.6 g}$ *[1 mark]*

3 Moles of $Cl_2 = \dfrac{1.28}{35.5 \times 2} = 0.0180$ moles *[1 mark]*
   Rearranging pV = nRT to find T gives $T = \dfrac{pV}{nR}$.
   So, $T = \dfrac{175 \times (98.6 \times 10^{-3})}{0.0180 \times 8.314} = \textbf{115 K}$ *[1 mark]*

4 M of $C_3H_8 = (3 \times 12.0) + (8 \times 1.0) = 44.0$ g mol^{-1}
   No. of moles of $C_3H_8 = \dfrac{88}{44.0} = 2$ moles *[1 mark]*
   At r.t.p. 1 mole of gas occupies 24 dm^3, so 2 moles of gas occupies $2 \times 24 = \textbf{48 dm}^3$ *[1 mark]*
   You could also use the equation pV = nRT to answer this question, where at r.t.p, T = 298 K, and p = 101 300 Pa. In this case, your answer would be $V = \dfrac{nRT}{p} = \dfrac{2 \times 8.314 \times 298}{101300} = 0.0489$ m$^3 = 49$ dm^3.

Page 23 — Empirical and Molecular Formulae

1 Assume you've got 100 g of the compound so you can turn the % straight into mass.
   No. of moles of C $= \dfrac{92.3}{12} = 7.69$ moles
   No. of moles of H $= \dfrac{7.7}{1} = 7.7$ moles *[1 mark]*
   Divide both by the smallest number, in this case 7.69.
   So ratio C : H = 1 : 1
   So, the empirical formula = CH *[1 mark]*
   The empirical mass = 12.0 + 1.0 = 13.0
   No. of empirical units in molecule $= \dfrac{78}{13} = 6$
   So the molecular formula = $\textbf{C}_6\textbf{H}_6$ *[1 mark]*

Answers

2 The magnesium is burning, so it's reacting with oxygen and the product is magnesium oxide. First work out the number of moles of each element.

No. of moles Mg $= \frac{1.2}{24.3} = 0.05$ moles

Mass of O is everything that isn't Mg: $2 - 1.2 = 0.8$ g

No. of moles O $= \frac{0.8}{16} = 0.05$ moles *[1 mark]*

Ratio Mg:O $= 0.05:0.05$

Divide both by the smallest number, in this case 0.05.

So ratio Mg:O $= 1:1$

So the empirical formula is **MgO** *[1 mark]*

3 First calculate the no. of moles of each product and then the mass of C and H:

No. of moles of $CO_2 = \frac{33}{44.0} = 0.75$ moles

Mass of C $= 0.75 \times 12.0 = 9$ g

No. of moles of $H_2O = \frac{10.8}{18.0} = 0.6$ moles

0.6 moles $H_2O = 1.2$ moles H

Mass of H $= 1.2 \times 1.0 = 1.2$ g *[1 mark]*

Organic acids contain C, H and O,
so the rest of the mass must be O.

Mass of O $= 19.8 - (9 + 1.2) = 9.6$ g

No. of moles of O $= \frac{9.6}{16.0} = 0.6$ moles *[1 mark]*

Mole ratio $= $ C:H:O $= 0.75:1.2:0.6$

Divide by smallest $1.25:2:1$

This isn't a whole number ratio, so you have to multiply them all up until it is. Multiply them all by 4.

So, mole ratio $= $ C:H:O $= 5:8:4$

Empirical formula $= C_5H_8O_4$ *[1 mark]*

Empirical mass $= (5 \times 12.0) + (8 \times 1.0) + (4 \times 16.0) = 132$ g

This is the same as what we're told the molecular mass is, so the molecular formula is also $C_5H_8O_4$ *[1 mark]*.

Page 25 — Equations and Calculations

1 $2KI_{(aq)} + Pb(NO_3)_{2\,(aq)} \rightarrow PbI_{2\,(s)} + 2KNO_{3\,(aq)}$ *[1 mark]*

In this equation, the NO_3 group remains unchanged, so it makes balancing much easier if you treat it as one indivisible lump.

2 M of $C_2H_5Cl = (2 \times 12) + (5 \times 1) + (1 \times 35.5) = 64.5$ g mol^{-1}

Number of moles of $C_2H_5Cl = \frac{258}{64.5} = 4$ moles *[1 mark]*

From the equation, 1 mole C_2H_5Cl is made from 1 mole C_2H_4

so, 4 moles C_2H_5Cl is made from 4 moles C_2H_4.

M of $C_2H_4 = (2 \times 12) + (4 \times 1) = 28$ g mol^{-1}

so, the mass of 4 moles $C_2H_4 = 4 \times 28 = $ **112 g** *[1 mark]*

3 Start by writing the balanced equation for the combustion of butane:

$C_4H_{10} + 6\tfrac{1}{2}O_2 \rightarrow 4CO_2 + 5H_2O$ *[1 mark]*

So, moles of O_2 required $= 3.50 \times 10^{-2} \times 6.5 = 0.2275$ mol

At room temperature and pressure, 1 mole of gas occupies 24 dm^3. So $0.2275 \times 24 = $ **5.46 dm^3** *[1 mark]*.

4 a) M of $CaCO_3 = 40.1 + 12 + (3 \times 16) = 100.1$ g mol^{-1}

Number of moles of $CaCO_3 = \frac{15.0}{100.1} = 0.150$ moles

From the equation, 1 mole $CaCO_3$ produces 1 mole CaO

so, 0.150 moles of $CaCO_3$ produces 0.150 moles of CaO *[1 mark]*.

M of CaO $= 40.1 + 16 = 56.1$ g mol^{-1} so, mass of 0.150 moles of CaO $= 56.1 \times 0.150 = $ **8.42 g** *[1 mark]*

b) From the equation, 1 mole $CaCO_3$ produces 1 mole CO_2

so, 0.150 moles of $CaCO_3$ produces 0.150 moles of CO_2.

1 mole gas occupies 24.0 dm^3, so, 0.150 moles occupies $24.0 \times 0.150 = $ **3.60 dm^3** *[1 mark]*

Page 27 — Formulae of Ionic Compounds

1 $Sc_2(SO_4)_3$ *[1 mark]*

Scandium has a charge of +3. Sulfate has a charge of −2. So, for every 2 scandium atoms, you will need three sulfate ions to balance the charge.

2 Na_2O *[1 mark]*

Sodium is in group 1, so forms ions with a charge of +1.

In compounds, oxygen usually has a charge of −2.

3 a) M of $CaSO_4 = 40.1 + 32.1 + (4 \times 16.0) = 136.2$ g mol^{-1} *[1 mark]*

no. moles $= \frac{1.133}{136.2} = $ **0.008319 moles** *[1 mark]*

b) mass of water = difference in mass between hydrated and anhydrous salt $= 1.883 - 1.133 = 0.7500$ g *[1 mark]*

no. moles of water $= \frac{mass}{molar\ mass} = \frac{0.7500}{18.0} = 0.04167$ *[1 mark]*

$X = $ ratio of no. moles water to no. moles salt $= \frac{0.04167}{0.008319} = 5.009$.

Rounded to nearest whole number, $X = $ **5** *[1 mark]*

Page 29 — Acids and Bases

1 a) One of: magnesium ($Mg_{(s)}$), magnesium hydroxide ($Mg(OH)_2$), magnesium oxide (MgO) or magnesium carbonate ($MgCO_3$) *[1 mark]*

b) One of: $Mg + 2HCl \rightarrow MgCl_2 + H_2$,

$Mg(OH)_2 + 2HCl \rightarrow MgCl_2 + 2H_2O$,

$MgO + 2HCl \rightarrow MgCl_2 + H_2O$,

$MgCO_3 + 2HCl \rightarrow MgCl_2 + CO_2 + H_2O$ *[1 mark]*

2 a) $NaOH_{(aq)} + HNO_{3\,(aq)} \rightarrow H_2O_{(l)} + NaNO_{3\,(aq)}$ *[1 mark]*

b) neutralisation *[1 mark]*

Page 31 — Titrations

1 $n = 0.600 \times \left(\frac{250}{1000}\right) = 0.150$ moles *[1 mark]*

$M(NaHSO_4) = (23 + 1 + 32.1 + (4 \times 16)) = 120.1$

So mass of $NaHSO_4$ needed $= 0.150 \times 120.1 = $ **18.0 g** *[1 mark]*.

2 *5-6 marks:*

The answer explains how indicators are used and includes at least one suitable and one unsuitable indictor for acid/alkali titrations, with reasoning. The answer has a clear and logical structure. The information given is relevant and detailed.

3-4 marks:

The answer explains how indicators are used and includes one example of a suitable or unsuitable indicator for acid/alkali titrations. The answer has some structure. Most of the information given is relevant and there is some detail involved.

1-2 marks:

The answer contains some explanation of how indicators are used but gives no examples of indicators for acid/alkali titrations. The answer has no clear structure. The information given is basic and lacking in detail. It may not all be relevant.

0 marks:

No relevant information is given.

Here are some points your answer may include:

Indicators change colour at an end point. They are used in acid/alkali titrations to mark an end point. Indicators used in titrations need to change colour quickly over a very small pH range. A few drops of indicator solution are added to the analyte. The analyte/indicator solution can be placed on a white surface to make a colour change easy to see. Methyl orange turns from yellow to red when adding acid to alkali. Phenolphthalein turns from pink to colourless when adding acid to alkali. Universal indicator is a poor indicator to use for titrations as the colour changes gradually over a wide pH range.

Page 33 — Titration Calculations

1 First write down what you know:

$CH_3COOH + NaOH \rightarrow CH_3COONa + H_2O$

$\quad$ 25.4 cm^3 $\quad$ 14.6 cm^3

$\quad\quad$? $\quad\quad$ 0.500 mol dm^{-3}

No. of moles of NaOH $= \frac{0.500 \times 14.6}{1000} = 0.00730$ moles *[1 mark]*

From the equation, you know 1 mole of NaOH neutralises 1 mole of CH_3COOH, so if you've used 0.00730 moles NaOH you must have neutralised 0.00730 moles CH_3COOH *[1 mark]*.

Concentration of $CH_3COOH = \frac{0.00730 \times 1000}{25.4} = $ **0.287 mol dm^{-3}** *[1 mark]*

Answers

2   First write down what you know again:

$$CaCO_3 \;+\; H_2SO_4 \;\rightarrow\; CaSO_4 \;+\; H_2O \;+\; CO_2$$

0.750 g   0.250 mol dm^{-3}

M of $CaCO_3$ = 40.1 + 12.0 + (3 × 16.0) = 100.1 g mol^{-1}

Number of moles of $CaCO_3 = \dfrac{0.750}{100.1}$ = 7.49 × 10^{-3} moles *[1 mark]*

From the equation, 1 mole $CaCO_3$ reacts with 1 mole H_2SO_4 so, 7.49 × 10^{-3} moles $CaCO_3$ reacts with 7.49 × 10^{-3} moles H_2SO_4 *[1 mark]*.

The volume needed is = $\dfrac{(7.49 \times 10^{-3}) \times 1000}{0.250}$ = **30.0 cm^3** *[1 mark]*

If the question mentions concentration or molarities, you can bet your last clean pair of underwear that you'll need to use the formula number of moles = $\dfrac{concentration \times volume}{1000}$. Just make sure the volume's in cm^3 though.

3 a) $Ca(OH)_2 + 2HCl \rightarrow CaCl_2 + 2H_2O$ *[1 mark]*

  b)   Number of moles of HCl = $\dfrac{0.250 \times 17.1}{1000}$

    = 4.275 × 10^{-3} moles *[1 mark]*

    From the equation in a), 2 moles HCl reacts with 1 mole $Ca(OH)_2$, so, 4.275 × 10^{-3} moles HCl reacts with 2.1375 × 10^{-3} moles $Ca(OH)_2$ *[1 mark]*.

    So concentration of $Ca(OH)_2$ solution =

    $\dfrac{2.1375 \times 10^{-3} \times 1000}{25.0}$ = **0.0855 mol dm^{-3}** *[1 mark]*.

Page 35 — Atom Economy and Percentage Yield

1 a)   2 is an addition reaction *[1 mark]*

  b)   For reaction 1: % atom economy

    = $M_r(C_2H_5Cl)$ ÷ $[M_r(C_2H_5Cl) + M_r(POCl_3) + M_r(HCl)]$ × 100% *[1 mark]*

    = [(2 × 12.0) + (5 × 1.0) + 35.5] ÷ [(2 × 12.0) + (5 × 1.0) + 35.5 + 31.0 + 16.0 + (3 × 35.5) + 1.0 + 35.5] × 100%

    = (64.5 ÷ 254.5) × 100% = **25.3%** *[1 mark]*

  c)   The atom economy is 100% because there is only one product (there are no by-products) *[1 mark]*

2 a)   Number of moles = mass ÷ molar mass

    Moles PCl_3 = 0.275 ÷ 137.5 = 0.002 moles

    Chlorine is in excess, so there must be 0.002 moles of product *[1 mark]*. Mass of PCl_5 = 0.002 × 208.5 = **0.417 g** *[1 mark]*

  b)   percentage yield = (0.198 ÷ 0.417) × 100% = **47.5%** *[1 mark]*

  c)   Changing reaction conditions will have no effect on atom economy *[1 mark]*. Since the equation shows that there is only one product, the atom economy will always be 100% *[1 mark]*. *Atom economy is related to the type of reaction — addition, substitution, etc. — not to the quantities of products and reactants.*

Page 37 — Oxidation Numbers

1   SO_4^{2-} contains sulfur and oxygen so it's a sulfate.

  It has an overall charge of –2.

  Total charge from the SO_4^{2-} ions = 3 × –2 = –6.

  For the overall charge to be 0, the total charge from chromium ions = +6. 6 ÷ 2 = +3.

  So the systematic name is **chromium(III) sulfate** *[1 mark]*.

2   Oxidation number of iron = +2. Charge of nitrate = –1.

  You will need a ratio of 1:2 of iron:nitrate to make the compound neutral. So the formula is **$Fe(NO_3)_2$** *[1 mark]*.

3 a)   Since lead oxide and sulfuric acid react in a ratio of 1:1, the formula for lead sulfate must be **$PbSO_4$** *[1 mark]*.

  b) i) Oxygen has an oxidation number of –2, so lead must be **+2** *[1 mark]*.

    ii) Sulfate has a charge of –2, so lead must have an oxidation number of **+2**. *[1 mark]*

Page 39 — Redox Reactions

1   redox reaction *[1 mark]*

2   D *[1 mark]*

3 a)   When metals and acids react, they produce hydrogen and a salt.

    $Fe_{(s)} + H_2SO_{4(aq)} \rightarrow FeSO_{4(aq)} + H_{2(g)}$ *[1 mark]*

  b)   Hydrogen has been reduced from oxidation number +1 to 0. Hydrogen is the oxidising agent.

    Iron has been oxidised from oxidation number 0 to +2.

    Iron is the reducing agent *[1 mark]*.

4   At the start of the reaction, Al has an oxidation number of 0.

  In AlI_3, each I ion has an oxidation number of –1. Therefore, Al has an oxidation number of +3 (since (–1 × 3) + 3 = 0).

  Al has lost electrons, so it has been oxidised *[1 mark]*.

Module 2: Section 2 — Electrons, Bonding & Structure

Page 41 — Electronic Structure

1 a)   K atom: 1s^2 2s^2 2p^6 3s^2 3p^6 4s^1 *[1 mark]*.

    K$^+$ ion: 1s^2 2s^2 2p^6 3s^2 3p^6 *[1 mark]*.

             1s   2s   2p

  b)   O^{2-} ion: [↑↓] [↑↓] [↑↓|↑↓|↑↓] *[1 mark]*.

2 a)   Germanium (1s^2 2s^2 2p^6 3s^2 3p^6 3d^{10} 4s^2 4p^2) *[1 mark]*.

  b)   Ar (atom) *[1 mark]*, K$^+$ (positive ion) *[1 mark]*, Cl$^-$ (negative ion) *[1 mark]*. You also could have suggested Ca^{2+}, S^{2-} or P^{3-}.

  c)   1s^2 2s^2 2p^6 *[1 mark]*

3 a)   1s^{2}2s^{2}2p^{6}3s^{2}3p^2 *[1 mark]*

  b)   Two *[1 mark]*

Page 43 — Ionic Bonding

1 a)   Giant ionic lattice *[1 mark]*

  b)   You'd expect it to have a high melting point *[1 mark]*, because a lot of energy is required to overcome the strong electrostatic attraction between the positive and negative ions *[1 mark]*.

2 a)

calcium ion   oxide ion

[2 marks]

1 mark for correct electron arrangement, 1 mark for correct charges

  b)   In a solid, ions are held in place by strong ionic bonds *[1 mark]*. When molten, the ions are mobile *[1 mark]* and so carry charge (and hence electricity) through the substance *[1 mark]*.

Page 45 — Covalent Bonding

1 a)   The electrostatic attraction between a shared pair of electrons and the nuclei of the bonded atoms. *[1 mark]*

  b)

    Your diagram should show the following —

    •   a completely correct electron arrangement *[1 mark]*

    •   all 4 overlaps correct (one dot + one cross in each) *[1 mark]*

2 a)   Covalent bonding and dative covalent/coordinate bonding *[1 mark]*

  b)   One atom donates a pair of/both the electrons to the bond *[1 mark]*.

Answers

Page 47 — Shapes of Molecules

1 a) i) *[1 mark]*

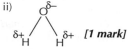

shape: pyramidal *[1 mark]*,
bond angle: 107° (accept between 106° and 108°) *[1 mark]*.

ii) *[1 mark]*

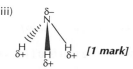

shape: trigonal planar *[1 mark]*
bond angle: 120° exactly *[1 mark]*.

b) BCl_3 has three electron pairs only around B. *[1 mark]*
NCl_3 has four electron pairs around N *[1 mark]*, including one lone pair. *[1 mark]*

2 Atom A: shape: trigonal planar, bond angle: 120° *[1 mark]*
Atom B: shape: tetrahedral, bond angle: 109.5° *[1 mark]*
Atom C: shape: non-linear/bent, bond angle: 104.5° *[1 mark]*

Page 51 — Polarity and Intermolecular Forces

1 a) An atom's ability to attract the electron pair in a covalent bond *[1 mark]*.

b) i) Br —— Br *[1 mark]*   ii) *[1 mark]*

iii) *[1 mark]*

2 a) Induced dipole-dipole OR London (dispersion) forces. *[1 mark]*
Permanent dipole-dipole interactions/forces. *[1 mark]*
Hydrogen bonding. *[1 mark]*

b) i) Water contains hydrogen covalently bonded to oxygen, so it is able to form hydrogen bonds *[1 mark]*. These hydrogen bonds are stronger than the other types of intermolecular forces, so more energy is needed to break them *[1 mark]*.

ii)

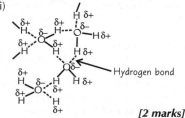

Hydrogen bond

[2 marks]

Your diagram should show the following —
- Labelled hydrogen bonds between the water molecules.
- At least two hydrogen bonds between an oxygen atom and a hydrogen atom on adjacent molecules.

Module 3: Section 1 — The Periodic Table

Page 53 — The Periodic Table

1 B *[1 mark]*
2 D *[1 mark]*
3 The p-block *[1 mark]*.
4 Aluminium atoms have one more proton than magnesium atoms *[1 mark]*.

Page 56 — Ionisation Energies

1 a) Group 3 *[1 mark]*
There are three electrons removed before the first big jump in energy.

b) The electrons are being removed from an increasingly positive ion *[1 mark]* so more energy is needed to remove an electron / the force of attraction that has to be broken is greater *[1 mark]*.

c) When an electron is removed from a different shell there is a big increase in the energy required (since that shell is closer to the nucleus) *[1 mark]*.

d) There are 3 shells (because there are 2 big jumps in energy) *[1 mark]*.

2 **5-6 marks:**
The answer correctly describes the general trend in the first ionisation energies across Period 3 and gives an explanation AND the exceptions to the trend are also described and explained. The answer has a clear and logical structure. The information given is relevant and detailed.
3-4 marks:
The answer describes the general trend in the first ionisation energies across Period 3 with some explanation of the trend. Exceptions to the trend are referenced briefly. The answer has some structure. Most of the information given is relevant and there is some detail involved.
1-2 marks:
The answer describes the general trend in the first ionisation energies across Period 3. Exceptions to the trend are not mentioned. The answer has no clear structure. The information given is basic and lacking in detail. It may not all be relevant.
0 marks:
No relevant information is given.
Here are some points your answer may include:
Generally the first ionisation energy increases across Period 3. The number of protons / positive charge of the nucleus increases, so the atomic radius decreases. Also, the number of electrons in the outer shell increases but there is no extra shielding. Both of these factors strengthen the attraction between the nucleus and the outer electrons. The first ionisation energy decreases slightly between magnesium and aluminium. This is because aluminium's outer electron is in a p orbital rather than an s orbital, so it is slightly further away from the nucleus (so it is less strongly attracted). The first ionisation energy also decreases slightly between phosphorous and sulfur. This is because sulfur's outer electron is being removed from an orbital containing two electrons. The (p orbital) repulsion between the electrons makes it easier to remove one of them.

Page 59 — Structure, Bonding and Properties

1 Mg has more delocalised electrons per atom *[1 mark]* and a smaller ionic radius *[1 mark]*. So the electrostatic attraction between the metal ions and the delocalised electrons is stronger *[1 mark]*.

2 a) Si has a giant covalent lattice structure *[1 mark]* consisting of lots of very strong covalent bonds *[1 mark]*.

b) Sulfur (S_8) is a larger molecule than phosphorus (P_4) *[1 mark]* which results in stronger induced dipole-dipole forces of attraction between molecules *[1 mark]*.

3 **5-6 marks:**
The answer describes in detail the relative abilities of diamond, graphite and graphene to conduct electricity AND includes correct references to their structure and its impact on the availability of delocalised electrons. The answer has a clear and logical structure. The information given is relevant.
3-4 marks:
The answer describes in some detail the abilities of diamond, graphite and graphene to conduct electricity. Their structures are described AND delocalised electrons are identified. The answer has some structure and most of the information given is relevant.

Answers

1-2 marks:
The answer describes briefly the ability of diamond, graphite or graphene to conduct electricity. There is some link to their structure. The information given is basic and lacking in detail. It may not all be relevant.
0 marks:
No relevant information is given.
Here are some points your answer may include:
Diamond has all of its outer electrons in localised covalent bonds, so it is a poor electrical conductor. Graphite has delocalised electrons between the sheets which can flow, so it is a good electrical conductor. Graphene also has delocalised electrons which can flow. It is a better electrical conductor than graphite because it has no other layers to slow the electrons down.

Page 61 — Group 2 — The Alkaline Earth Metals

1    $CaCO_{3(s)} + 2HCl_{(aq)} \rightarrow CaCl_{2(aq)} + CO_{2\,(g)} + H_2O_{(l)}$ *[1 mark]*
2 a) $2Ba_{(s)} + O_{2(g)} \rightarrow 2BaO_{(s)}$ *[1 mark]*
  b) From 0 to +2 *[1 mark]*
  c) Strongly alkaline / pH 12-13 *[1 mark]*
3 a) Z *[1 mark]*
  b) Z has the largest radius *[1 mark]* so it will be furthest down the group / have the smallest ionisation energy *[1 mark]*.

Page 63 — Group 7 — The Halogens

1 a) $I_2 + 2At^- \rightarrow 2I^- + At_2$ *[1 mark]*
  b) astatide *[1 mark]*
2   A *[1 mark]*
3   C *[1 mark]*

Page 65 — Disproportionation and Water Treatment

1 a) $2OH^- + Br_2 \rightarrow OBr^- + Br^- + H_2O$ *[1 mark]*
  b) A disproportionation reaction *[1 mark]*.
2 a) $2I^- + ClO^- + H_2O \rightarrow I_2 + Cl^- + 2OH^-$ *[1 mark]*
  b) Iodine: –1 to 0 — oxidation
     Chlorine: +1 to –1 — reduction *[1 mark]*

Page 67 — Tests for Ions

1   B *[1 mark]*
2   **5-6 marks:**
The answer describes all of the tests and provides observations to correctly identify each compound. The answer has a clear and logical structure. The information given is relevant and detailed.
3-4 marks:
The answer describes most of the tests with some detail and provides observations to correctly identify each compound. The answer has some structure. Most of the information given is relevant and there is some detail involved.
1-2 marks:
The answer describes some of the tests but lacks description of any observations. The answer has no clear structure. The information given is basic and lacking in detail. It may not all be relevant.
0 marks:
No relevant information is given.
Here are some points your answer may include:
Add dilute hydrochloric acid to a sample of each solution to identify the carbonates. Two solutions should produce a gas/ CO_2 which turns limewater cloudy. Add sodium hydroxide to samples of these two solutions, warm them and test for ammonia with damp red litmus paper. One solution should turn the litmus paper blue — this is ammonium carbonate, and the other solution is calcium carbonate. Add barium chloride solution to each of the remaining samples to identify sodium sulfate — it should form a white precipitate. Add silver nitrate solution to identify magnesium chloride — it should form a white precipitate.

Module 3: Section 2 — Physical Chemistry

Page 69 — Enthalpy Changes

1
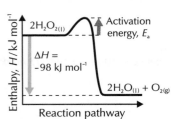

[1 mark for having reactants lower in energy than products. 1 mark for labelling activation energy correctly. 1 mark for labelling ΔH correctly, with arrow pointing downwards.]
For an exothermic reaction, the ΔH arrow points downwards, but for an endothermic reaction it points upwards. The activation energy arrow always points upwards though.
2 a) $CH_3OH_{(l)} + 1\frac{1}{2}O_{2(g)} \rightarrow CO_{2(g)} + 2H_2O_{(l)}$ *[1 mark]*
Make sure that only 1 mole of CH_3OH is combusted, as it says in the definition for $\Delta_c H^{\ominus}$.
  b) $C_{(s)} + 2H_{2(g)} + \frac{1}{2}O_{2(g)} \rightarrow CH_3OH_{(l)}$ *[1 mark]*
  c) Only 1 mole of C_3H_8 should be shown according to the definition of $\Delta_c H^{\ominus}$ *[1 mark]*.
You really need to know the definitions of the standard enthalpy changes off by heart. There are loads of nit-picky little details they could ask you questions about.
3 a) $C_{(s)} + O_{2(g)} \rightarrow CO_{2(g)}$ *[1 mark]*
  b) It has the same value because it is the same reaction *[1 mark]*.
  c) 1 tonne = 1 000 000 g
     1 mole of carbon is 12.0 g
     so 1 tonne is 1 000 000 ÷ 12.0 = 83 333 moles *[1 mark]*
     1 mole releases 393.5 kJ
     so 1 tonne will release 83 333 × 393.5 = **32 800 000 kJ** (3 s.f.)
     [1 mark]
The final answer is rounded to 3 significant figures because the number with the fewest significant figures in the whole calculation is 12.0.

Page 71 — More on Enthalpy Changes

1   No. of moles of $CuSO_4 = (0.200 \times 50.0) \div 1000 = 0.0100$ mole
     [1 mark]
     From the equation, 1 mole of $CuSO_4$ reacts with 1 mole of Zn.
     So, 0.0100 mole of $CuSO_4$ reacts with 0.0100 mole of Zn
     [1 mark].
     Heat produced by reaction $= mc\Delta T$
                                  $= 50.0 \times 4.18 \times 2.60 = 543.4$ J
                                  [1 mark]
     0.0100 mole of zinc produces 543.4 J of heat, therefore 1 mole of zinc produces 543.4 ÷ 0.0100 = 54 340 J = 54.340 kJ
     So the enthalpy change is **–54.3 kJ mol⁻¹** (3 s.f.) *[1 mark]*
You need the minus sign because it's exothermic.
2 a) A chemical reaction always involves bond breaking which needs energy / is endothermic and bond making which releases energy / is exothermic *[1 mark]*. Whether the reaction is exothermic or endothermic depends on whether more energy is used to break bonds or released by forming new bonds over the whole reaction *[1 mark]*.
  b) $q = mc\Delta T$
     m = 1.000 kg = 1000 g
     no. of moles carbon = $m \div M_r = 6.000 \div 12.0 = 0.5000$ mole
     [1 mark]
     So $q = 0.5000 \times 393.5 = 196.75$ kJ = 196 750 J *[1 mark]*
     So 196 750 = 1000 × 4.18 × ΔT
     $\Delta T = 196\,750 \div (1000 \times 4.18) = $ **47.1 K** (3 s.f.) *[1 mark]*

Answers

Page 73 — Enthalpy Calculations

1 $\Delta_r H^{\ominus}$ = sum of $\Delta_f H^{\ominus}$(products) − sum of $\Delta_f H^{\ominus}$(reactants)
[1 mark]
$\Delta_r H^{\ominus}$ = [0 + (3 × −602)] − [−1676 + 0]
$\Delta_r H^{\ominus}$ = **−130 kJ mol⁻¹** *[1 mark]*
Don't forget the units. It's a daft way to lose marks.

2 $\Delta_r H^{\ominus} = \Delta_c H^{\ominus}$(glucose) − 2 × $\Delta_c H^{\ominus}$(ethanol) *[1 mark]*
$\Delta_r H^{\ominus}$ = [−2820] − [(2 × −1367)]
$\Delta_r H^{\ominus}$ = **−86 kJ mol⁻¹** *[1 mark]*

3 $\Delta_r H^{\ominus}$ = sum of $\Delta_c H^{\ominus}$(reactants) − $\Delta_c H^{\ominus}$(propane) *[1 mark]*
$\Delta_r H^{\ominus}$ = [(3 × −394) + (4 × −286)] − [−2220]
$\Delta_r H^{\ominus}$ = **−106 kJ mol⁻¹** *[1 mark]*

4 Total energy required to break bonds = (4 × 435) + (2 × 498)
= 2736 kJ
Energy released when bonds form = (2 × 805) + (4 × 464)
= 3466 kJ *[1 mark]*
Net energy change = 2736 + (−3466) = **−730 kJ mol⁻¹** *[1 mark]*

Page 75 — Reaction Rates

1 Increasing the pressure will increase the rate of reaction
[1 mark] because the molecules will be closer together, so they
will collide more frequently and therefore are more likely to
react *[1 mark]*.

2 a) X *[1 mark]*
The X curve shows the same total number of molecules as the 25 °C
curve, but more of them have lower energy.

b) The shape of the curve shows fewer molecules have the required
activation energy *[1 mark]*.

Page 77 — Catalysts

1 a)
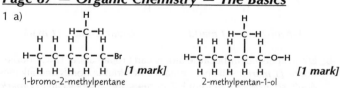
$$2SO_{2(g)} + O_{2(g)} \xrightarrow{V_2O_{5(s)}} 2SO_{3(g)}$$
[1 mark]
You could also write the reaction as $SO_{2(g)} + \frac{1}{2}O_{2(g)} \rightarrow SO_{2(g)}$.

b) A *[1 mark]*
A catalyst only lowers activation energy. It doesn't affect the enthalpy
change.

c) The vanadium(V) oxide catalyst is heterogenous because it's in a
different physical state to the reactants *[1 mark]*.

Page 79 — Calculating Reaction Rates

1 a) E.g.
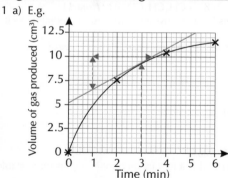

[1 mark for tangent drawn at 3 mins.]
rate of reaction = gradient of tangent at 3 mins
gradient = change in y ÷ change in x
e.g.   = (10.00 − 6.50) ÷ (3.40 − 1.00)
          = **1.46 (± 0.3) cm³ min⁻¹**
[1 mark for answer within margin of error. 1 mark for units.]
Different people will draw slightly different tangents and pick different
spots on the tangent so there's a margin of error in this answer.
1.45 (± 0.3) cm³ min⁻¹ means any answer between 1.15 cm³ min⁻¹ and
1.75 cm³ min⁻¹ is worth the mark.

b) E.g. the volume of gas produced could be measured using a gas
syringe *[1 mark]*.

c) One of the reactants is a gas *[1 mark]*.

Page 81 — Dynamic Equilibrium

1 a) i) There's no change as there's the same number of molecules/
moles on each side of the equation *[1 mark]*.
ii) Reducing temperature removes heat. The equilibrium
shifts in the exothermic direction to release heat, so the
position of equilibrium shifts left *[1 mark]*.
iii) Removing nitrogen monoxide reduces its concentration.
The equilibrium position shifts right to try and increase the
nitrogen monoxide concentration again *[1 mark]*.

b) No effect *[1 mark]*.
Catalysts don't affect the equilibrium position.
They just help the reaction to get there sooner.

2 For an exothermic reaction, a low temperature means a high
yield *[1 mark]*. But a low temperature also means a slow
reaction rate, so moderate temperatures are chosen as a
compromise *[1 mark]*.

Page 83 — The Equilibrium Constant

1 a) $K_c = [NH_3]^2 \div ([N_2] \times [H_2]^3)$ *[1 mark]*
= $(1.190)^2 \div ((0.890) \times (1.412)^3)$
= **0.565 mol⁻² dm⁶** *[1 mark]*
To work out the units...
$(mol\ dm^{-3})^2 \div (mol\ dm^{-3})^4$
= $(mol^2\ dm^{-6}) \div (mol^4\ dm^{-12})$
= $mol^{-2}\ dm^6$ (but you don't need to give units with this answer to get the
marks).

b) The concentration of NH_3 would increase *[1 mark]*. Exothermic
reactions speed up when the temperature in decreased *[1 mark]*.

2 E.g. equal amounts of the equilibrium mixture should be added
to three test tubes. The first test tube is a control and should be
orangey/yellow in colour. Add some chromate solution
to test tube 2 and note any colour change. Add some
dichromate solution to test tube 3 and note any colour change
[1 mark for description of experiment]. Test tube 2 should turn
more orange as the forward reaction speeds up to produce more
dichromate ions, pushing equilibrium to the right *[1 mark]*.
Test tube 3 should turn more yellow as the reverse reaction
speeds up to produce more chromate ions, pushing equilibrium
to the left *[1 mark]*.

Module 4: Section 1 — Basic Concepts and Hydrocarbons

Page 87 — Organic Chemistry — The Basics

1 a)

1-bromo-2-methylpentane *[1 mark]*   2-methylpentan-1-ol *[1 mark]*

b) −OH (hydroxyl) *[1 mark]*.
It could be attached to any of the five carbons OR because the
position of the −OH group affects its chemistry *[1 mark]*.

2 a) 4-chloro-pentanoic acid *[1 mark]*

b) methylbutane *[1 mark]*
There's only actually one type of methylbutane. You can't have
1-methylbutane — it'd be exactly the same as pentane.

c) dimethylpropane *[1 mark]*
There's only one type of dimethylpropane — 1,1-dimethylpropane and
1,2-dimethylpropane are actually methylbutane.

3 a) B *[1 mark]*

b) The same molecular formula *[1 mark]* but different arrangements
of the carbon skeleton *[1 mark]*.

Answers

Page 89 — Alkanes

1 a) One with no double bonds OR all the carbon-carbon bonds are single bonds *[1 mark]*. It contains only hydrogen and carbon atoms *[1 mark]*.
  b) $C_2H_{6(g)} + 3\frac{1}{2}O_{2(g)} \rightarrow 2CO_{2(g)} + 3H_2O_{(g)}$ *[2 marks]*
  1 mark for correct symbols, 1 mark for balancing

2 a) Nonane will have a higher boiling point than 2,2,3,3-tetramethylpentane *[1 mark]* because the molecules of branched-chain alkanes like 2,2,3,3-tetramethylpentane are less closely packed together than their straight-chain isomers, so they have fewer induced dipole-dipole interactions holding them together *[1 mark]*.
  b) i) $C_9H_{20} + 9\frac{1}{2}O_2 \rightarrow 9CO + 10H_2O$ *[1 mark]*
    ii) Carbon monoxide binds to haemoglobin in the blood in preference to oxygen *[1 mark]*, so less oxygen can be carried around the body, leading to oxygen deprivation *[1 mark]*.

Page 91 — Reactions of Alkanes

1 a) Free radical substitution. *[1 mark]*
  b) $CH_4 + Br_2 \xrightarrow{U.V.} CH_3Br + HBr$ *[1 mark]*
  c) $Br\bullet + CH_4 \rightarrow HBr + \bullet CH_3$ *[1 mark]*
    $\bullet CH_3 + Br_2 \rightarrow CH_3Br + Br\bullet$ *[1 mark]*
  d) i) Two methyl radicals bond together to form an ethane molecule. *[1 mark]*
    ii) Termination step *[1 mark]*
    iii) $\bullet CH_3 + \bullet CH_3 \rightarrow CH_3CH_3$ *[1 mark]*
  e) Tetrabromomethane *[1 mark]*

Page 92 — Alkenes

1 a) Ethane is an alkane, so has a single C–C bond made up of a σ bond *[1 mark]*. Ethene is an alkene, so has a C=C double bond made up of a σ bond and a π bond *[1 mark]*.
  b) Ethene will be more reactive than ethane because the double bond has a high electron density / the π bond sticks out above and below the plane of the molecule, so it attracts electrophiles *[1 mark]* and because the π bond has a low bond enthalpy so is more easily broken than the C–C σ bond in ethane *[1 mark]*.

Page 95 — Stereoisomerism

1 a)

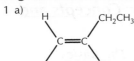 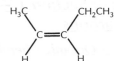

E-pent-2-ene *[1 mark]*   Z-pent-2-ene *[1 mark]*

  b) E/Z isomers occur because atoms can't rotate about C=C double bonds *[1 mark]*. Alkenes contain C=C double bonds and alkanes don't, so alkenes can form E/Z isomers and alkanes can't *[1 mark]*.

2 B *[1 mark]*

Page 97 — Reactions of Alkenes

1 a) Shake the alkene with bromine water *[1 mark]*, and the solution goes colourless if a double bond is present *[1 mark]*.
  b) Electrophilic addition *[1 mark]*.
  c)

2-bromobutane *[1 mark]*   1-bromobutane *[1 mark]*
  The major product will be 2-bromobutane *[1 mark]*.

Page 99 — Polymers

1 a) Energy can be used to generate electricity *[1 mark]*
  b) Toxic gases produced *[1 mark]*.

2 Used as an organic feedstock to produce plastics and other organic chemicals *[1 mark]* or melted and remoulded *[1 mark]*.

3

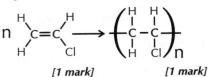

[1 mark]   *[1 mark]*

Module 4: Section 2 — Alcohols, Haloalkanes & Analysis

Page 101 — Alcohols

1 a) primary: e.g.

pentan-1-ol   *[1 mark]*

  secondary: e.g

pentan-2-ol   *[1 mark]*

  tertiary:

2-methylbutan-2-ol   *[1 mark]*

  b) React ethanol with sodium bromide (NaBr) with a concentrated sulfuric acid catalyst *[1 mark]*.

2 a) Elimination reaction OR dehydration reaction *[1 mark]*.
  b) C *[1 mark]*

Page 103 — Oxidation of Alcohols

1 a) i) Propanoic acid (CH_3CH_2COOH) *[1 mark]*
    ii) $CH_3CH_2CH_2OH + [O] \rightarrow CH_3CH_2CHO + H_2O$ *[1 mark]*
      $CH_3CH_2CHO + [O] \rightarrow CH_3CH_2COOH$ *[1 mark]*
    iii) Distillation. This is so aldehyde is removed immediately as it forms *[1 mark]*.
    If you don't get the aldehyde out quick-smart, it'll be a carboxylic acid before you know it.
  b) i)

    ii) 2-methylpropan-2-ol is a tertiary alcohol (which is more stable) *[1 mark]*.

2 D *[1 mark]*

3 React 2-methylpropan-1-ol ($CH_3CH(CH_3)CH_2OH$) *[1 mark]* with a controlled amount of acidified potassium dichromate(VI) and heat gently in distillation apparatus to distil off the aldehyde *[1 mark]*.

Answers

Page 105 — Haloalkanes

1 a)
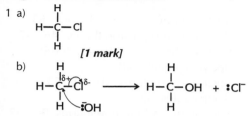
[1 mark]

b)
Your diagram should show:
- Curly arrow from lone pair on OH⁻ to δ+ on carbon *[1 mark]*.
- Curly arrow and dipole on C–Cl bond *[1 mark]*.
- Correct products *[1 mark]*.

c) A white precipitate *[1 mark]*.

2 A *[1 mark]*

Page 107 — Haloalkanes and the Environment

1 a) Any two from: stable/volatile/non-flammable/non-toxic *[1 mark]*.

b) $CFCl_{3(g)} \xrightarrow{U.V.} \cdot CFCl_{2(g)} + Cl\cdot_{(g)}$ *[1 mark]*
$Cl\cdot_{(g)} + O_{3\,(g)} \rightarrow O_{2\,(g)} + ClO\cdot_{(g)}$ and
$ClO\cdot_{(g)} + O_{(g)} \rightarrow O_{2\,(g)} + Cl\cdot_{(g)}$ *[1 mark]*
Overall reaction: $O_{3(g)} + O_{(g)} \rightarrow 2O_{2(g)}$ *[1 mark]*

c) NO• free radicals *[1 mark]*

2 $NO\bullet + O_3 \rightarrow NO_2 + O_2$ *[1 mark]*
$NO_2 + O \rightarrow NO\bullet + O_2$ *[1 mark]*

Page 108 — The Greenhouse Effect & Global Warming

1 a) Any two from: increased use of fossil fuels/increased deforestation/increased food production *[2 marks]*.

b) Scientists collected data which shows that the Earth's average temperature has dramatically increased in recent years *[1 mark]*.

c) Creating policies to use more renewable energy sources, such as wind and solar farms *[1 mark]*.

Page 111 — Analytical Techniques

1 a) A: O–H group in a carboxylic acid *[1 mark]*.
B: C=O as in an aldehyde, ketone, carboxylic acid, ester or acid anhydride *[1 mark]*.

b) From the percentage composition data, the ratio of elements in the compound, C:H:O is 3:6:2 *[1 mark]* so the empirical formula is $C_3H_6O_2$ *[1 mark]*. The spectrum suggests that the compound is a carboxylic acid, so it must be propanoic acid (CH_3CH_2COOH) *[1 mark]*.

2 a) 44 *[1 mark]*

b) X has a mass of 15. It is probably a methyl group/CH_3^+ *[1 mark]*.
Y has a mass of 29. It is probably an ethyl group/$C_2H_5^+$ *[1 mark]*.

c)
$$H-\overset{\overset{\displaystyle H}{|}}{\underset{\underset{\displaystyle H}{|}}{C}}-\overset{\overset{\displaystyle H}{|}}{\underset{\underset{\displaystyle H}{|}}{C}}-\overset{\overset{\displaystyle H}{|}}{\underset{\underset{\displaystyle H}{|}}{C}}-H$$
[1 mark]

d) If the compound was an alcohol, you would expect a peak with m/z ratio of 17, caused by the OH fragment *[1 mark]*.

Page 113 — Organic Synthesis — Practical Skills

1 a) i) Reflux is continuous boiling/evaporation and condensation *[1 mark]*. It's done to prevent loss of volatile liquids while heating *[1 mark]*.

ii) Unreacted hexan-1-ol *[1 mark]*

iii) Pour the reaction mixture into a separating funnel and add water *[1 mark]*. Shake the funnel and allow the layers to settle. The lower layer is the denser aqueous layer and contains water soluble impurities *[1 mark]*. This can be run off, so only the organic layer, containing the product and other organic impurities, remains *[1 mark]*.

b) i) The alkene product may dehydrate again to form a diene *[1 mark]*.

ii) Carry out the experiment in a distillation apparatus *[1 mark]* so the singly dehydrated product is removed immediately from the reaction mixture and doesn't react a second time *[1 mark]*.

Page 115 — Organic Synthesis — Synthetic Routes

1 a)
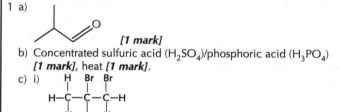
[1 mark]

b) Concentrated sulfuric acid (H_2SO_4)/phosphoric acid (H_3PO_4) *[1 mark]*, heat *[1 mark]*.

c) i)
$$H-\overset{\overset{\displaystyle H}{|}}{\underset{\underset{\underset{\underset{\displaystyle H}{|}}{\underset{\displaystyle C-H}{}}}{|}{\displaystyle H}}}{C}-\overset{\overset{\displaystyle Br}{|}}{\underset{\underset{\displaystyle H}{|}}{C}}-\overset{\overset{\displaystyle Br}{|}}{\underset{\underset{\displaystyle H}{|}}{C}}-H$$
[1 mark]

ii) The mixture would turn from orange/brown to colourless *[1 mark]*.

2
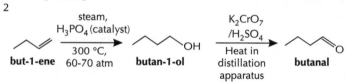

[3 marks — 2 marks for correct reagents and conditions, 1 mark for intermediate butan-1-ol product.]

Index

Index

Index

This revision guide is matched to the new **OCR GCSE Additional Science Specification A (J631)**, from the Twenty First Century Science Suite.

It is designed to build on the basic scientific ideas covered in *The Essentials of OCR GCSE Science A*, also published by Lonsdale. In doing so it provides full coverage of all the scientific explanations and models you need to know, along with their practical applications and impact on society.

As a revision guide, this book focuses on the skills and material on which you will be examined. It does not cover the practical skills and case study, which are assessed by your science teacher.

You will have to sit four exams in total. An overview of these exams is provided in the table below, with details of where the relevant material can be found in this guide:

- The **contents list and page headers** in this revision guide clearly identify the separate modules, to help you revise for the different exam papers.

- The **Ideas in Context** paper will focus on the ideas covered in three of the modules you have already studied (one each from biology, chemistry and physics). It will test your understanding of the content and your ability to apply that knowledge, for example, to evaluate information about a current social-science issue effectively. This paper is looked at in more detail on pages 86–91 of this revision guide.

- This guide can be used to revise for both the Foundation and Higher Tier exam papers.

> (HT) Content that will only be tested on the Higher Tier papers appears in a coloured box, and can easily be identified by the symbol (HT).*

- You will find a **glossary** at the back, providing clear definitions of essential words and phrases, and a copy of the Periodic Table for reference. (The Periodic Table corresponds with the one issued by OCR. Some details may differ from other published versions.)

- Don't just read the information in this guide – **learn actively!** Jot down anything you think will help you to remember, no matter how trivial it may seem and constantly test yourself without looking at the text.

Good luck with your exams.

* Higher tier material correct at time of going to print

Title	What is Being Assessed?	Duration	Weighting	Total Mark	Page Numbers
Unit 1	Modules B4, C4 and P4	40 minutes	16.7%	42	4–30
Unit 2	Modules B5, C5 and P5	40 minutes	16.7%	42	31–56
Unit 3	Modules B6, C6 and P6	40 minutes	16.7%	42	57–85
Unit 4	Ideas in Context	45 minutes	16.7%	42	86–91

Contents

Contents

Homeostasis

Module B4

The correct balance of fluids, temperature and waste products in our bodies is very important for survival. This module looks at…

- what homeostasis is
- why homeostasis is important for cells
- how our bodies maintain a constant temperature
- how our bodies control water balance.

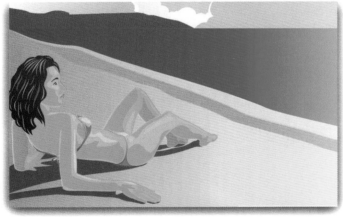

Homeostasis

Homeostasis is the maintenance of a constant internal environment. It is achieved by balancing bodily inputs and outputs and removing waste products.

The body has automatic control systems in place which ensure that the correct, steady levels of **temperature** and **water** are maintained.

These factors are essential in order for cells to be able to function properly.

Factors Affecting Homeostasis

Homeostasis can be affected by changes to **temperature**, and **hydration levels**.

If a person is doing strenuous exercise, or lives in a very hot or cold climate, the systems in the body have to work extra hard to ensure homeostasis.

If homeostasis fails then death rapidly follows.

Exercise

When a person is doing **strenuous exercise**, the temperature inside the body increases and the body loses water through sweat. If the body cannot get rid of the excess heat then the body temperature would reach a critical level where different systems would stop working.

If the water is not replaced then vital chemical reactions would also stop. These effects, if not corrected, will lead to death.

Hot Climates

In very hot climates survival is dependent upon homeostasis. As with strenuous exercise, controlling temperature and hydration is extremely important. Body temperature can quickly escalate to critical levels and water levels can drop rapidly.

Cold Climates

In very cold climates heat is lost to the surroundings rapidly and this can lead to a condition called hypothermia. The body becomes too cold and chemical reactions stop.

Homeostasis can also be affected by changes in **blood oxygen levels** and **salt levels**.

If too much water is lost to the environment, then the balance of essential salts will change – their concentration will increase.

Scuba divers dive to depths where homeostasis would normally fail. Therefore, they rely on equipment to overcome these problems.

The scuba equipment controls the gases which enter the body, ensuring that dissolved oxygen is kept at the correct level.

A wetsuit traps a layer of water between the body and the inner of the suit. This layer of water warms up, insulating the body and preventing it from cooling down too much.

Mountain climbers at high altitudes have to contend with a change in air pressure. The higher up they go, the lower the air pressure becomes. This means that the amount of oxygen that can be inhaled decreases and climbers can suffer (and possibly die) from altitude sickness.

Climbers wear breathing apparatus to ensure that the correct blood oxygen level is maintained.

Artificial Homeostasis

Some individuals' homeostatic mechanisms may not work correctly and may need to be artificially supported, e.g. premature babies or patients with kidney disease.

A premature baby may not have fully functioning systems, so an **incubator** helps the baby to survive by controlling temperature and oxygen levels.

Artificial systems and body systems have similarities in that they have…

* receptors (sensors) to detect stimuli
* processing centres to receive information and coordinate responses
* effectors which produce the response automatically.

Negative Feedback

The temperature inside an incubator fluctuates naturally, but it is important that the temperature is maintained within the correct range to support the life of the baby inside.

When the temperature inside the incubator exceeds a set level, it is detected by a sensor (receptor). The processing centre in the computer responds to this by sending a signal to the heater (effector) to turn the heat off.

If the temperature drops below a set level it is detected by the sensor and the processing centre sends another signal to switch the heater on; this will increase the temperature. This process is an example of **negative feedback**; the receptor and effector reverse any changes to the system's steady state.

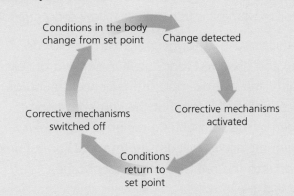

Conditions in the body change from set point

Change detected

Corrective mechanisms activated

Conditions return to set point

Corrective mechanisms switched off

Antagonistic Effectors

In many systems there are effectors which act **antagonistically** (i.e. as opposites) to one another.

An increase in the activity of one effector is accompanied by a decrease in the activity of an antagonistic effector, e.g. one effector is responsible for increasing temperature whilst another carries out the opposite, decreasing the temperature.

This method of control is far more sensitive and accurate.

Homeostasis

Homeostasis in Cells

Homeostasis also takes place at a cellular level (i.e. inside cells). Chemical reactions taking place inside a cell need raw materials which must enter across the membrane of the cell.

Some products, including water, gases (oxygen and carbon dioxide) and other compounds, also need to be transported away from the cell.

Diffusion

Diffusion is the spontaneous and passive overall (net) movement of substances from regions where the concentration is high, to regions where the concentration is low. It is spontaneous and passive because no energy input is needed by cells to make the process work. The process is random which means that some particles can move back to where the particles are in a high concentration. However, the overall movement is from a high to low concentration.

Chemicals such as oxygen (O_2), carbon dioxide (CO_2) and dissolved food move in and out of cells by diffusion. For example, if the concentration of oxygen in a cell is low but the concentration of oxygen in the surrounding region is high, then oxygen molecules will diffuse from the surrounding region into the cell (see diagram opposite).

Osmosis

Osmosis is the diffusion of water from a dilute solution (i.e. with a high water to solute ratio) to a more concentrated solution (i.e. with a low water to solute ratio) through a partially permeable membrane.

The membrane allows the water molecules through but not solute molecules because they are too large (see Osmosis diagram ❶ opposite).

The effect of osmosis is to gradually dilute the concentrated solution. This is what happens at root hair cells, where water moves from the soil into the cell by osmosis, along a concentration gradient (see Osmosis diagram ❷ opposite).

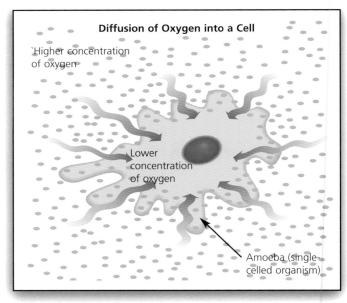

Diffusion of Oxygen into a Cell

Higher concentration of oxygen

Lower concentration of oxygen

Amoeba (single-celled organism)

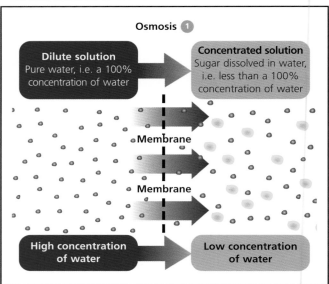

Osmosis ❶

| Dilute solution
Pure water, i.e. a 100% concentration of water | Concentrated solution
Sugar dissolved in water, i.e. less than a 100% concentration of water |

Membrane

Membrane

| High concentration of water | Low concentration of water |

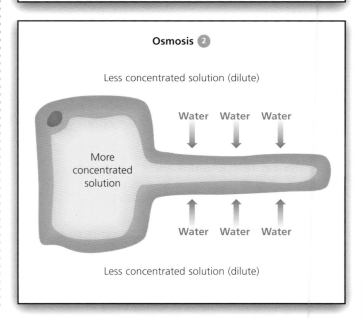

Osmosis ❷

Less concentrated solution (dilute)

Water Water Water

More concentrated solution

Water Water Water

Less concentrated solution (dilute)

More on Osmosis

Animal cells, unlike plant cells, have no cell wall to support the cell membrane, so osmosis can have serious effects. There is the possibility that cells could rupture if too much water enters them. On the other hand, if a cell loses a lot of water it will be unable to carry out chemical reactions.

Animals which live in salt water (such as the sea) must conserve water because they will have a tendency to lose water through osmosis.

Animals which live in freshwater have the opposite problem – the solute concentration is greater inside their cells compared to the external water. This means that they must quickly get rid of excess water, otherwise the cells will burst.

Active Transport

Active transport is the movement of a chemical substance against a concentration gradient. This requires energy.

If a cell produces glucose then the concentration of glucose inside the cell will be higher than the concentration outside. If the glucose were able to diffuse it would leave the cell along the concentration gradient.

Cells use active transport to bring the glucose outside the cell back inside against the concentration gradient, for example in the villi in the small intestine.

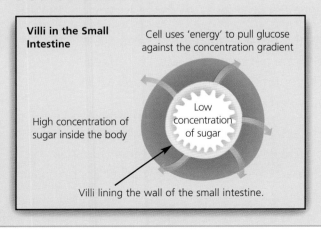

Villi in the Small Intestine

Cell uses 'energy' to pull glucose against the concentration gradient

High concentration of sugar inside the body

Low concentration of sugar

Villi lining the wall of the small intestine.

Enzymes

Enzymes are organic catalysts. They are **protein molecules** that speed up the rate of chemical reactions in living organisms. These reactions take place in cells in order to produce new materials.

Activity and Temperature

The graph below shows the effect of temperature on enzyme activity.

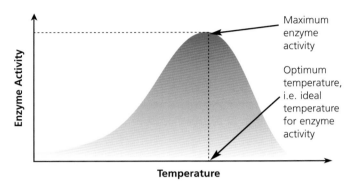

Maximum enzyme activity

Optimum temperature, i.e. ideal temperature for enzyme activity

Enzyme Activity

Temperature

At low temperatures, small increases in temperature cause an increase in the frequency and energy of collisions between reactants and enzymes, so the rate of reaction increases.

The enzyme activity increases until the **optimum temperature** is reached. After this, the increase in temperature continues to cause increased collisions, but the enzyme molecules become permanently damaged by the heat, resulting in either decreased enzyme activity, or no activity at all.

Different enzymes have different optimum working temperatures. For example, enzymes in the human body work best at about 37°C. Below this temperature the rate of reaction is **slow** whilst above 40°C the enzyme becomes **denatured**. Denaturing means the enzyme is permanently destroyed and stops working.

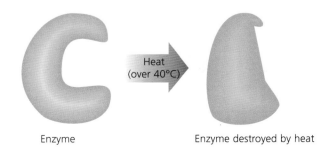

Heat (over 40°C)

Enzyme

Enzyme destroyed by heat

Homeostasis

The Lock and Key Model

Only a molecule with the correct shape can fit into an enzyme. This is a bit like a key (the molecule) fitting into a lock (the enzyme). Once the enzyme and molecule are linked the reaction takes place, the products are released and the process is able to start again.

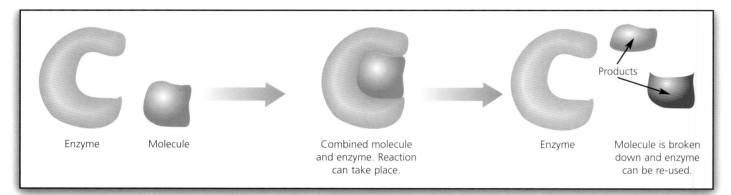

Enzyme   Molecule   Combined molecule and enzyme. Reaction can take place.   Enzyme   Products   Molecule is broken down and enzyme can be re-used.

The Active Site

The place where the molecule fits is called the **active site**.

Each enzyme has a different **shape**, so it is highly specific; only certain molecules will fit into its active site.

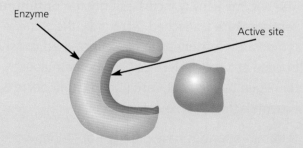

Enzyme   Active site

If an enzyme becomes denatured by being heated above a certain temperature or by being subjected to extreme pH levels, then the shape of the active site is **changed irreversibly**. This means the molecules can no longer fit and the reaction cannot take place.

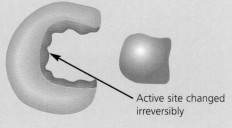

Active site changed irreversibly

The graph below shows how changes in pH levels affect enzyme activity.

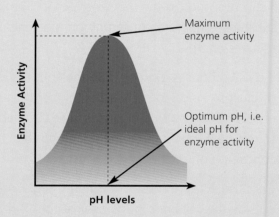

Maximum enzyme activity

Optimum pH, i.e. ideal pH for enzyme activity

Enzyme Activity

pH levels

Note that, as with temperature, there is an optimum pH level at which the enzyme works best.

As the pH level increases or decreases, the enzyme becomes less and less effective. The optimum pH of different enzymes can vary considerably.

The enzyme in human saliva works best at about pH 7.3 whilst the enzyme, pepsin, found in the stomach, needs to be in very acidic conditions in order to work well.

Maintaining Constant Body Temperature

Since enzymes work best at 37°C in humans, it is essential that the body temperature remains very close to this. In order to maintain this constant temperature, energy loss and energy gain from the body must be balanced.

The temperature of the body's extremities tends to be cooler than the core body temperature. Energy is transferred from the blood to the tissues when it reaches the cooler parts.

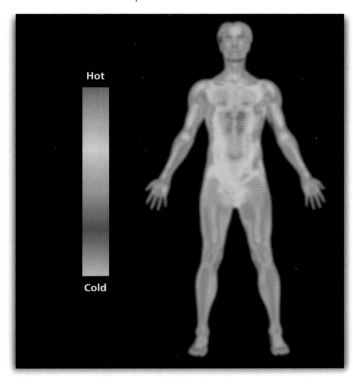

Hot

Cold

Controlling body temperature requires...
- temperature detectors in the skin to detect the external temperature
- a temperature detector in the brain to measure the temperature of the blood
- the brain, which acts as a processing centre, to receive information from the temperature receptors in the skin and in the brain
- effectors (sweat glands and muscles) which carry out the response.

The response to any change in temperature is triggered automatically.

If the temperature of the body is too high then heat needs to be transferred to the environment. This is done by sweating, since evaporation from the skin requires heat energy from the body.

If the temperature of the body is too low then the body starts to shiver. Shivering is the rapid contraction and release of muscles. These contractions require energy from increased respiration, and heat is released as a by-product, warming surrounding tissue.

Heat Stroke

Heat stroke is an uncontrolled increase in body temperature – the body cannot lose heat fast enough. A core body temperature of 40°C is life threatening. At 41°C, brain death starts to occur – the brain stops functioning properly and so cannot trigger the effectors that would normally lead to heat loss.

Increased sweating due to very hot temperatures can lead to dehydration. Dehydration stops sweating from occurring which leads to the core temperature increasing still further. If the body is not cooled down, then death will occur.

Common causes of heat stroke include exercising in very warm conditions, very high humidity, and dehydration.

Symptoms of Heat Stroke

- Confusion.
- Red / dry skin.
- Low blood pressure.
- Convulsions.
- Fainting.
- Rapid heartbeat.

Initial Treatment of Heat Stroke

- Remove clothes and bathe in cool water.
- Cool body using wet towels.
- Use a fan.
- Put ice packs on the neck, head and groin.
- Elevate (raise) legs.

Homeostasis

Vasodilation and Vasoconstriction

Vasodilation is the widening, and vasoconstriction is the narrowing, of the blood vessels (capillaries) which run very close to the surface of the skin.

Blood temperature is monitored by a centre in the brain called the **hypothalamus**. The hypothalamus constantly monitors temperature and switches various temperature control mechanisms on and off.

In **hot conditions** blood vessels in the skin dilate causing greater heat loss – more heat is lost from the surface of the skin by radiation.

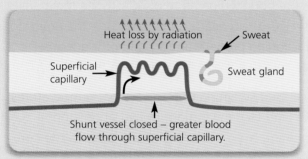

Heat loss by radiation
Sweat
Superficial capillary
Sweat gland
Shunt vessel closed – greater blood flow through superficial capillary.

In **cold conditions** blood vessels in the skin constrict reducing heat loss – less heat is lost from the surface of the skin by radiation.

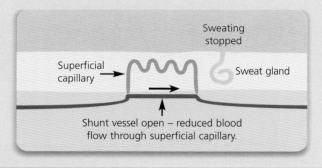

Sweating stopped
Superficial capillary
Sweat gland
Shunt vessel open – reduced blood flow through superficial capillary.

Hypothermia

Hypothermia occurs when the body is exposed to low temperatures for a long period of time. The body's heat is not replaced fast enough and, if untreated, this can lead to death.

The common cause of hypothermia is when the core body temperature falls below 35°C because it cannot get enough energy in cold conditions, and is unable to respond to the drop in body temperature.

Symptoms of Hypothermia

- Grey skin colour.
- Amnesia (memory loss).
- Shivering.
- Slurred speech.
- Confusion.
- Loss of coordination.
- Cold skin.

Initial Treatment of Hypothermia

- Raise the core body temperature.
- Insulate the body (particularly the armpits, head and groin).
- Give warm drinks, but not alcohol.
- Do not rub or massage, (this brings blood to the surface meaning even more heat is lost which can lead to heart failure).

Water Balance

Water is input (gained) from drinks, food and respiration. It is output (lost) through sweating, breathing and the excretion of faeces and urine. The body has to balance these different inputs and outputs to ensure that there is enough water inside cells for cell activity to take place.

Most people have two **kidneys**, one situated on either side of the spine on the back wall of the abdomen. It is the kidneys' job to control the balance of water in the body.

This is achieved by adjusting the amount of urine that is excreted from the body.

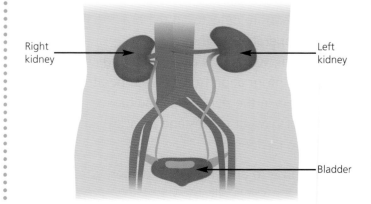

Right kidney
Left kidney
Bladder

The kidneys filter the blood to remove all waste (urea) and to balance levels of other chemicals (including water). They achieve this by:

1. Filtering small molecules from the blood to form urine (water, salt and urea).
2. Absorbing all the sugar for respiration.
3. Absorbing as much salt as the body requires.
4. Absorbing as much water as the body requires.
5. Excreting the remaining urine, which is stored in the bladder.

The brain monitors water content constantly and causes the kidneys to adjust the concentration and volume of urine produced.

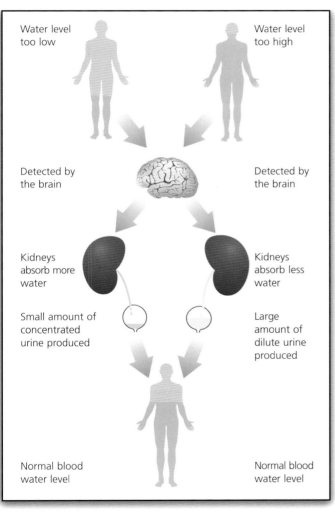

Water level too low — Detected by the brain — Kidneys absorb more water — Small amount of concentrated urine produced — Normal blood water level

Water level too high — Detected by the brain — Kidneys absorb less water — Large amount of dilute urine produced — Normal blood water level

Low water urine level

Normal urine level

Excess water urine level

The amount of water that needs to be absorbed depends on a number of factors:

- **External temperature**
  If the temperature is hot then extra water will be lost as sweat. As a result, more water will need to be absorbed in the body. The urine will be a dark yellow colour with a high salt content. On colder days, less water will be lost as sweat and the urine will be a pale straw colour.

- **Amount of exercise**
  More sweat is produced during exercise, so once again the urine will be dark and will contain more dissolved salts.

- **Fluid intake**
  If not enough fluids are drunk then the urine produced will be more concentrated. Some drinks (such as coffee and tea) cause more water to be excreted. This is due to the chemical **caffeine**. Caffeine is a **diuretic** which means it increases the amount of urine produced.

  Alcohol is an even stronger diuretic than caffeine, and it causes a larger volume of more dilute urine to be produced. This then causes dehydration (one of the causes of a hangover).

- **Drugs**
  Drugs, such as Ecstasy, can interfere with the brain, causing the body to stop excreting water into the urine. A small quantity of concentrated urine is produced (whilst the blood plasma has more water than it should). If the user then drinks too much water (in response to getting hot) the water level increases in the blood. The consequence of this is that the cells rupture and, if this occurs in the brain, brain damage or death can result.

- **Salt intake**
  The consumption of too many salty snacks (with not enough water intake) can increase the levels of salt in the urine.

Homeostasis

Urine Concentration

The concentration of urine is controlled by a hormone called anti-diuretic hormone (ADH).

ADH is released into the blood via the pituitary gland. Controlling water balance is an example of negative feedback (see diagram below).

Drugs such as alcohol and Ecstasy affect the production of ADH in different ways. Alcohol causes ADH to be suppressed and, therefore, more water leaves the body in the urine. Ecstasy causes too much ADH to be produced leading to too much water in the blood. Osmosis then causes the water to leave the blood causing brain cells to swell and burst.

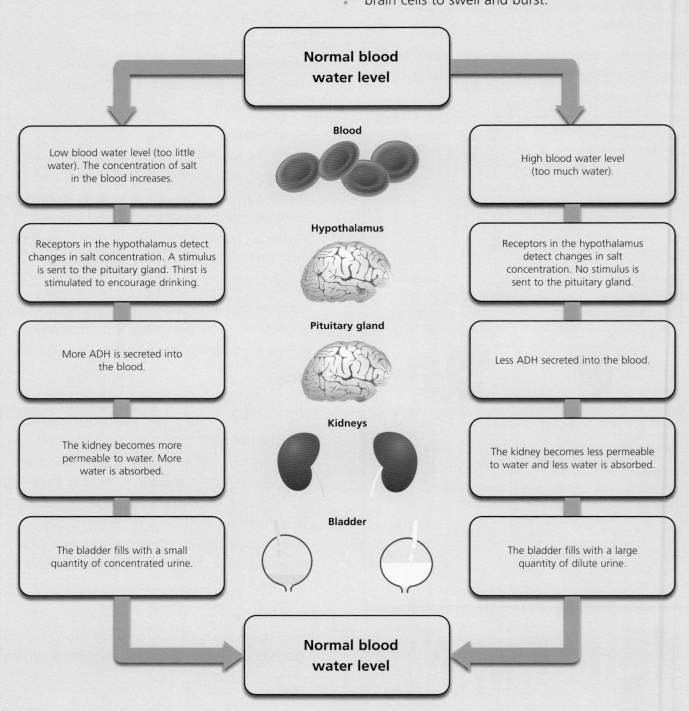

Normal blood water level

Blood

Low blood water level (too little water). The concentration of salt in the blood increases.

High blood water level (too much water).

Hypothalamus

Receptors in the hypothalamus detect changes in salt concentration. A stimulus is sent to the pituitary gland. Thirst is stimulated to encourage drinking.

Receptors in the hypothalamus detect changes in salt concentration. No stimulus is sent to the pituitary gland.

Pituitary gland

More ADH is secreted into the blood.

Less ADH secreted into the blood.

Kidneys

The kidney becomes more permeable to water. More water is absorbed.

The kidney becomes less permeable to water and less water is absorbed.

Bladder

The bladder fills with a small quantity of concentrated urine.

The bladder fills with a large quantity of dilute urine.

Normal blood water level

Module C4

Theories of atomic structure can be used to explain the properties and behaviour of elements. This module looks at...

- the pattern of properties in elements
- the Periodic Table
- alkali metals and halogens
- ionic bonding.

The Periodic Table

Elements are the 'building blocks' of all materials.

The atoms of each of the 100 or so elements have a different proton number. The elements are arranged in order of ascending **atomic** (or **proton**) **number**, which gives repeating patterns in the properties of elements.

Groups

A **vertical column** of elements is called a **group**. For example, lithium (Li), sodium (Na) and potassium (K) are all elements found in Group 1.

Elements in the same group have the same number of electrons in their outermost shell (see p.14) (except helium). This number also coincides with the group number, e.g. Group 1 elements have 1 electron in their outer shell, and Group 7 elements have 7 electrons in their outer shell. Elements in the same group have similar properties.

Periods

A **horizontal row** of elements is called a **period**. For example, lithium (Li), carbon (C) and neon (Ne) are all elements in the same period.

The period to which an element belongs corresponds to the number of shells of electrons it has, e.g. sodium (Na), aluminium (Al) and chlorine (Cl) all have three shells of electrons, and so they are found in the third period.

The Periodic Table can be used as a reference table to obtain important information about the elements. For example:

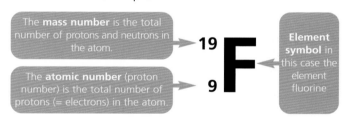

The **mass number** is the total number of protons and neutrons in the atom. → 19 **F**

The **atomic number** (proton number) is the total number of protons (= electrons) in the atom. → 9

Element symbol in this case the element fluorine

You can also tell if elements are metals or non-metals by looking at their position in the table.

You will be given a copy of the Periodic Table in the exam.

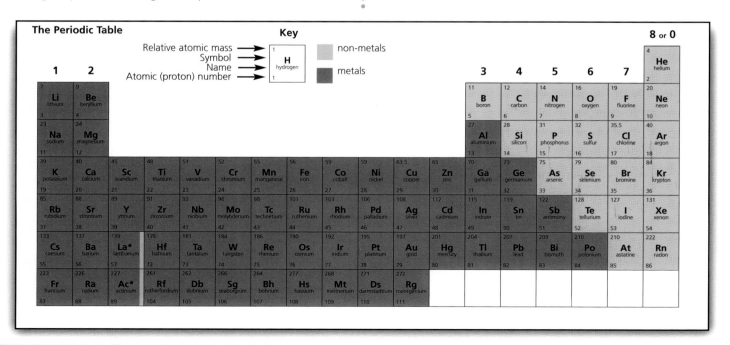

The Periodic Table

Key

Relative atomic mass → 1
Symbol → H
Name → hydrogen
Atomic (proton) number → 1

non-metals

metals

8 or 0

Chemical Patterns

Atoms

All substances are made up of **atoms** (very small particles). Each atom has a small central nucleus, made up of **protons** and **neutrons** (with the exception of hydrogen), which is surrounded by **electrons** arranged in **shells** (or **energy levels**).

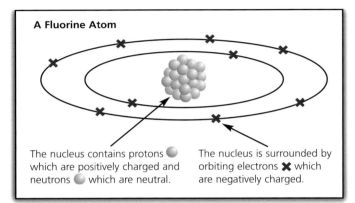

A Fluorine Atom

The nucleus contains protons ● which are positively charged and neutrons ● which are neutral.

The nucleus is surrounded by orbiting electrons ✖ which are negatively charged.

Atomic Particle	Relative Mass	Relative Charge
Proton ●	1	+1
Neutron ●	1	0
Electron ✖	0 (nearly)	-1

- An atom has the same number of protons as electrons, so the atom as a whole is neutral (i.e. it has no electrical charge).
- A proton has the same mass as a neutron.
- The mass of an electron is negligible, i.e. nearly nothing, when compared to a proton or neutron.
- A substance which contains only one sort of atom is called an element.
- All atoms of the same element have the same number of protons.
- Atoms of different elements have different numbers of protons.
- The elements are arranged in the Periodic Table in order of increasing atomic (proton) number.

Spectroscopy

When some elements are heated they emit distinctive coloured flames. Lithium, sodium, and potassium compounds can be recognised by the distinctive colours they produce in a flame test.

A piece of nichrome (a nickel-chromium alloy) wire is dipped in the compound and then put into a Bunsen flame to produce the following distinctive colours:

Lithium Red **Sodium** Yellow **Potassium** Lilac

The light emitted from the flame of an element produces a characteristic line spectrum. Each line in the spectrum represents an energy change as excited electrons fall from high energy levels to lower energy levels. The study of spectra has helped chemists to discover new elements.

High energy level

Low energy level

Moving electrons

Electron Configuration

Electron configuration tells us how the electrons are arranged around the nucleus of an atom in shells (energy levels).

- The electrons in an atom occupy the lowest available shells (i.e. shells closest to the nucleus).
- The first level (or shell) can only contain a maximum of 2 electrons.
- The shells after this can hold a maximum of 8 electrons.
- The electron configuration is written as a series of numbers, e.g. oxygen is 2.6; aluminium is 2.8.3; and potassium is 2.8.8.1.

There is a connection between the number of outer electrons and the position of an element in a group, (see p.13). You can also deduce the period to which an element belongs from its electron configuration, e.g. oxygen is 2.6, which means it is found in the second period, potassium is 2.8.8.1, which means it is found in the fourth period, and so on (i.e. the number of energy levels occupied by electrons equals the number of the period).

Chemical Patterns

Electron Configuration of the First 20 Elements

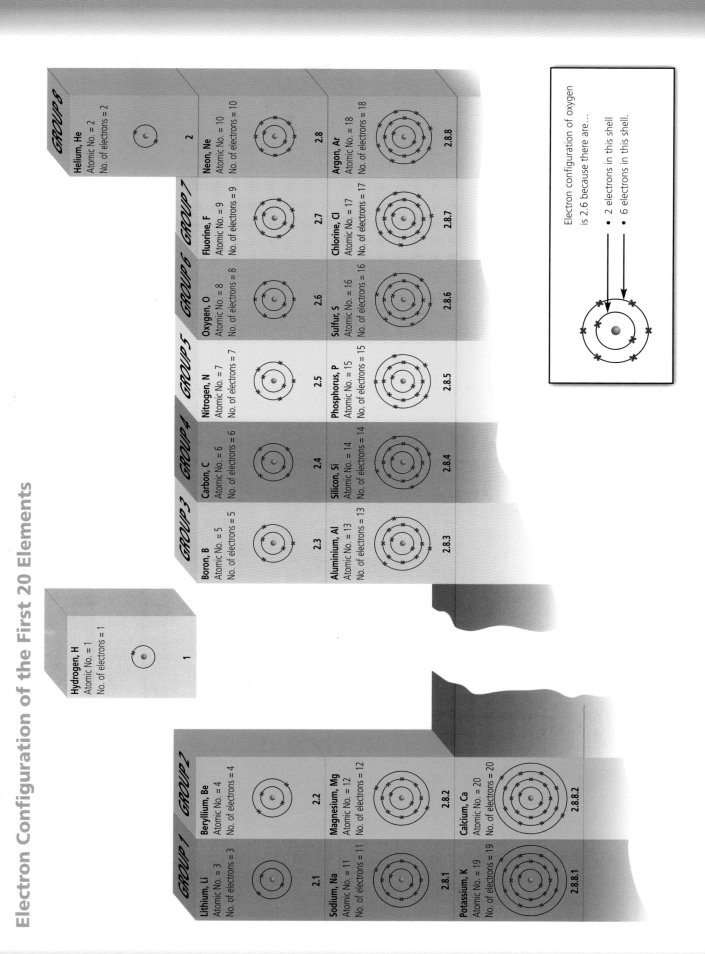

Electron configuration of oxygen is 2.6 because there are...

- 2 electrons in this shell.
- 6 electrons in this shell.

Hydrogen, H
Atomic No. = 1
No. of electrons = 1

1

GROUP 1

Lithium, Li
Atomic No. = 3
No. of electrons = 3

2.1

Sodium, Na
Atomic No. = 11
No. of electrons = 11

2.8.1

Potassium, K
Atomic No. = 19
No. of electrons = 19

2.8.8.1

GROUP 2

Beryllium, Be
Atomic No. = 4
No. of electrons = 4

2.2

Magnesium, Mg
Atomic No. = 12
No. of electrons = 12

2.8.2

Calcium, Ca
Atomic No. = 20
No. of electrons = 20

2.8.8.2

GROUP 3

Boron, B
Atomic No. = 5
No. of electrons = 5

2.3

Aluminium, Al
Atomic No. = 13
No. of electrons = 13

2.8.3

GROUP 4

Carbon, C
Atomic No. = 6
No. of electrons = 6

2.4

Silicon, Si
Atomic No. = 14
No. of electrons = 14

2.8.4

GROUP 5

Nitrogen, N
Atomic No. = 7
No. of electrons = 7

2.5

Phosphorus, P
Atomic No. = 15
No. of electrons = 15

2.8.5

GROUP 6

Oxygen, O
Atomic No. = 8
No. of electrons = 8

2.6

Sulfur, S
Atomic No. = 16
No. of electrons = 16

2.8.6

GROUP 7

Fluorine, F
Atomic No. = 9
No. of electrons = 9

2.7

Chlorine, Cl
Atomic No. = 17
No. of electrons = 17

2.8.7

GROUP 8

Helium, He
Atomic No. = 2
No. of electrons = 2

2

Neon, Ne
Atomic No. = 10
No. of electrons = 10

2.8

Argon, Ar
Atomic No. = 18
No. of electrons = 18

2.8.8

Chemical Patterns

Balanced Equations

The total mass of the products of a chemical reaction is always equal to the total mass of the reactants.

This is because the products of a chemical reaction are made up from the atoms of the reactants – no atoms are lost or made. So, chemical symbol equations must always be balanced: there must be the same number of atoms of each element on the reactant side of the equation as there is on the product side (see Example 1).

Writing Balanced Equations

Follow these steps to write a balanced equation (see Example 2):

1. Write a word equation for the chemical reaction.
2. Substitute in formulae for the elements or compounds involved.
3. Balance the equation by adding numbers in front of the reactants and/or products.
4. Write a balanced symbol equation.

Example 1

Word equation...

Symbol equation...

This means that...

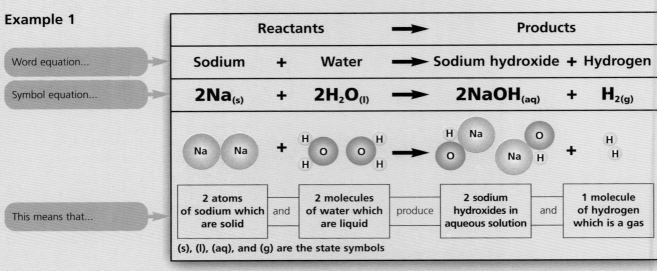

Example 2

1. Write a word equation
2. Substitute in formulae
3. Balance the equation

- There are 2 **O**s on the reactant side, but only 1 **O** on the product side. We need to add another **MgO** to the product side to balance the **O**s.
- We now need to add another **Mg** on the reactant side to balance the **Mg**s.
- There are 2 Mg atoms and 2 O atoms on each side – **it is balanced**.

4. Write a balanced symbol equation

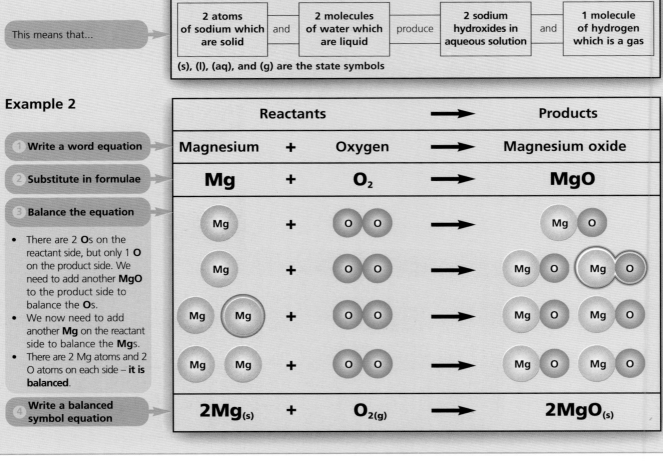

Chemical Patterns

Hazard Symbols

Hazardous materials will have one of the following hazard symbols on their packaging.

Toxic
These substances can kill when swallowed, breathed in or absorbed through the skin.

Oxidising
These substances provide oxygen, which allows other substances to burn more fiercely.

Harmful
These substances are similar to toxic substances but they are less dangerous.

Highly Flammable
These substances will catch fire easily. They pose a serious fire risk.

Corrosive
These substances attack living tissue, including eyes and skin, and can damage materials.

Irritant
These substances are not corrosive but they can cause blistering of the skin.

Environmental Hazard
These substances may present a danger to the environment.

Safety Precautions

Some common safety precautions are…

- wearing gloves and eye protection, and washing hands after handling chemicals
- using safety screens
- using small amounts and low concentrations of the chemicals
- working in a fume cupboard or ventilating the room
- not eating or drinking when working with chemicals
- not working near naked flames.

Group 1 – The Alkali Metals

There are six metals in Group 1. As we go down the group, the alkali metals become more reactive.

Alkali metals have low melting points. The melting and boiling points decrease as we go down the group.

Physical Properties of the Alkali Metals

Element	Melting Point (°C)	Boiling Point (°C)	Density (g/cm³)
Lithium, Li	180	1340	0.53
Sodium, Na	98	883	0.97
Potassium, K	64	760	0.86
Rubidium, Rb	39	688	1.53
Caesium, Cs	29	671	1.90

Alkali Metal Compounds

When alkali metals react they form compounds that are similar. The reactivity of the reaction increases as we go down the group. The table below shows the compounds formed when alkali metals react with water, oxygen and chlorine.

Element	+ Water	+ Oxygen	+ Chlorine
Lithium, Li	LiOH	Li_2O	LiCl
Sodium, Na	NaOH	Na_2O	NaCl
Potassium, K	KOH	K_2O	KCl

Reaction of Alkali Metals with Chlorine

Chlorine reacts vigorously with alkali metals to form colourless crystalline salts called metal chlorides, for example:

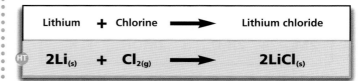

Lithium + Chlorine ⟶ Lithium chloride

$$2Li_{(s)} + Cl_{2(g)} \longrightarrow 2LiCl_{(s)}$$

Chemical Patterns

Reaction of Alkali Metals with Oxygen

The alkali metals are stored under oil because they react very vigorously with oxygen and water. When freshly cut they are shiny. However, they quickly tarnish in moist air, go dull and become covered in a layer of metal oxide. For example:

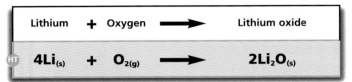

| Lithium | + | Oxygen | → | Lithium oxide |

HT $$4Li_{(s)} + O_{2(g)} \longrightarrow 2Li_2O_{(s)}$$

Reaction of Alkali Metals with Water

Lithium, sodium and potassium float on top of cold water (due to their low density). They melt because the heat from the reaction is great enough to turn them into liquids. Lithium reacts gently, sodium more aggressively and potassium so aggressively it melts and catches fire.

Li   Na   K

When alkali metals react with water, a metal hydroxide and hydrogen gas are formed. The metal hydroxide dissolves in water to form an alkaline solution, for example:

| Potassium | + | Water | → | Potassium hydroxide | + | Hydrogen |

HT $$2K_{(s)} + 2H_2O_{(l)} \longrightarrow 2KOH_{(aq)} + H_{2(g)}$$

Since all the reactions of alkali metals are similar, a general equation or formula is sometimes used. In each case M refers to the alkali metal.

HT

Alkali metal reacting with chlorine:

$$2M_{(s)} + Cl_{2(g)} = 2MCl_{(s)}$$

Alkali metal reacting with oxygen:

$$4M_{(s)} + O_{2(g)} = 2M_2O_{(s)}$$

Alkali metal reacting with water:

$$2M_{(s)} + 2H_2O_{(l)} = 2MOH_{(aq)} + H_{2(g)}$$

Follow these steps to check the pH level of the solution formed when an alkali metal is added to water.

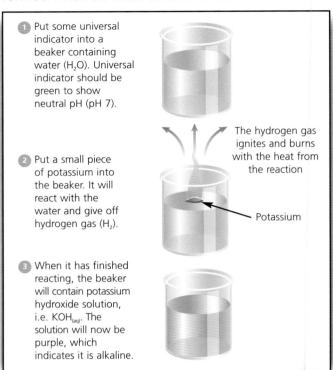

1. Put some universal indicator into a beaker containing water (H_2O). Universal indicator should be green to show neutral pH (pH 7).

2. Put a small piece of potassium into the beaker. It will react with the water and give off hydrogen gas (H_2).

Potassium

The hydrogen gas ignites and burns with the heat from the reaction

3. When it has finished reacting, the beaker will contain potassium hydroxide solution, i.e. $KOH_{(aq)}$. The solution will now be purple, which indicates it is alkaline.

The alkali metals carry the following hazard symbols:

Chemical	Hazard Symbol
Lithium	🔥 ⚗️
Lithium chloride	✖ i
Sodium	🔥 ⚗️
Sodium hydroxide	⚗️
Potassium	🔥 ⚗️

When working with Group 1 metals, the following precautions should be taken:

- use small amounts of very dilute concentrations
- wear safety glasses and use safety screens
- watch teacher demonstrations carefully
- avoid working near naked flames.

Group 7 – The Halogens

There are five non-metals in this group.

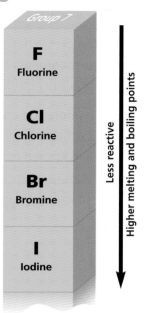

At room temperature and room pressure, chlorine is a green gas, bromine is an orange liquid and iodine is a grey solid.

Chlorine is used to sterilise water and to make pesticides and plastics.

Iodine is used as an antiseptic to sterilise wounds.

All halogens consist of **diatomic molecules** (i.e. they only exist in pairs of atoms), e.g. Cl_2, Br_2, I_2, and they can be used to bleach dyes and kill bacteria in water.

Physical Properties of the Halogens

The physical properties of the halogens alter as we go down the group. The table below shows their melting points, boiling points and densities:

Element	Melting Point (°C)	Boiling Point (°C)	Density (g/cm³)
Fluorine, F	-220	-188	0.0016
Chlorine, Cl	-101	-34	0.003
Bromine, Br	-7	59	3.12
Iodine, I	114	184	4.95
Astatine, At	302 (estimated)	337 (estimated)	not known

- The melting points and boiling points of the halogens increase as we go down the group. Astatine is estimated to have the highest melting point and boiling point.
- The densities increase as we go down the group. (However, due to the unstable nature of astatine, its density is not known.)

The halogens carry the following hazard symbols:

Element	Hazard Symbol
Fluorine, F	🔥 ⚗️ 🐟🌳
Chlorine, Cl	✖ 🐟🌳
Bromine, Br	🔥 ⚗️ 🐟🌳

When working with halogens, the following precautions should be taken:
- wear safety glasses
- work in a fume cupboard
- make sure the room is well ventilated
- use small amounts of very dilute concentrations
- avoid working near naked flames
- watch teacher demonstrations carefully.

Displacement Reactions of Halogens

A more reactive halogen will displace a less reactive halogen from an aqueous solution of its salt. Therefore, chlorine will displace both bromine and iodine, while bromine will displace iodine.

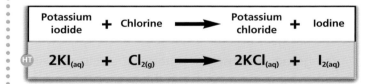

| Potassium iodide | + | Chlorine | → | Potassium chloride | + | Iodine |

$$2KI_{(aq)} + Cl_{2(g)} \longrightarrow 2KCl_{(aq)} + I_{2(aq)}$$

Halogen Compounds

When halogens react they form compounds that are similar. The reactivity decreases as we go down the group. The table below shows the compounds that are formed when halogens react with Group 1 metals and metal hydroxides.

	Chlorine	Bromine	Iodine	Metal Hydroxide
Lithium	LiCl	LiBr	LiI	LiOH
Sodium	NaCl	NaBr	NaI	NaOH
Potassium	KCl	KBr	KI	KOH

Chemical Patterns

Trends in Group 1

Alkali metals have similar properties because they have the same number of electrons in their outermost shell, i.e. the highest occupied energy level contains 1 electron.

The alkali metals become more reactive as we go down the group because the outermost electron shell gets further away from the influence of the nucleus and so an electron is more easily lost.

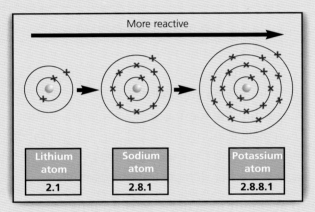

More reactive

Lithium atom	Sodium atom	Potassium atom
2.1	2.8.1	2.8.8.1

Trends in Group 7

The halogens have similar properties, because they have the same number of electrons in their outermost shell, i.e. the highest occupied energy level contains 7 electrons.

The halogens become less reactive as we go down the group, because the outermost electron shell gets further away from the influence of the nucleus and so an electron is less easily gained.

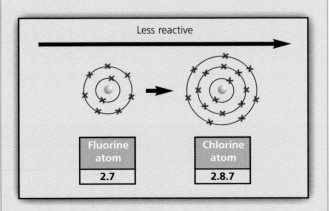

Less reactive

Fluorine atom	Chlorine atom
2.7	2.8.7

The Properties of Compounds

Chemists use their observations to develop theories to explain the properties of different compounds. For example, experiments show that molten compounds, such as lithium chloride, conduct electricity.

It can, therefore, be concluded that there must be charged particles in molten compounds. These particles are known as **ions**.

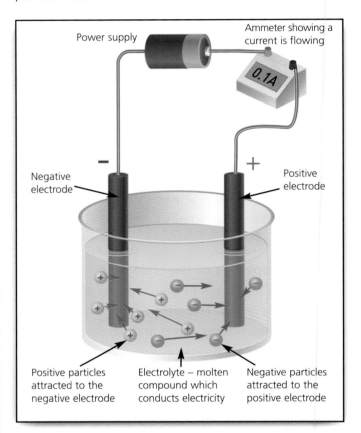

Power supply

Ammeter showing a current is flowing

0.1A

Negative electrode

Positive electrode

Positive particles attracted to the negative electrode

Electrolyte – molten compound which conducts electricity

Negative particles attracted to the positive electrode

Ions

If an atom loses or gains one or more electrons it will carry an overall charge because the proton and electron numbers are no longer equal. When this happens, the atom becomes an ion.

If the ion has been formed by an atom losing electron(s), it will have an overall positive (+) charge because it now has more protons that electrons. It is called a **cation,** e.g. Na^+. If the ion has been formed by an atom gaining an electron(s), it will have an overall negative (–) charge because it now has more electrons than protons. It is called an **anion** e.g. Cl^-.

The Ionic Bond

An ionic bond occurs between a metal and a non-metal and involves the transfer of electrons from one atom to another to form electrically charged ions. Each electrically charged ion has a complete outermost energy level or shell, i.e. the first shell has 2 electrons and each outer shell has 8 electrons. Compounds of Group 1 metals and Group 7 elements are **ionic compounds**.

Example 1

Sodium and chlorine bond ionically to form sodium chloride, NaCl. The sodium (Na) atom has 1 electron in its outer shell which is transferred to the chlorine (Cl) atom so they both have 8 electrons in their outer shell. The atoms become ions, Na^+ and Cl^-, and the compound formed is sodium chloride, NaCl.

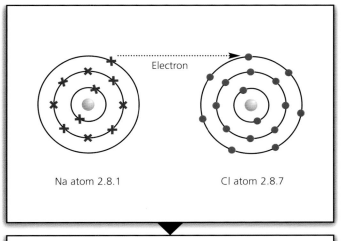

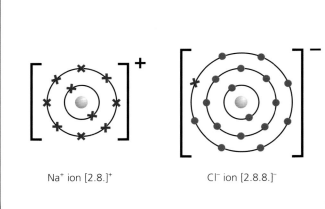

The positive ion and the negative ion are then electrostatically attracted to each other to form a giant crystal lattice.

Sodium Chloride

- ● Na^+ ion, i.e. a sodium atom that has lost 1 electron
- ● Cl^- ion, i.e. a chlorine atom that has gained 1 electron

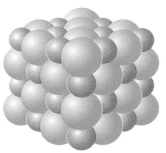

Sodium chloride has a high melting point and dissolves in water. It conducts electricity when it is in solution or is molten, but not when it is a solid.

Example 2

Sodium and oxygen bond ionically to form sodium oxide, Na_2O. Each sodium (Na) atom has 1 electron in its outer shell. An oxygen (O) atom wants 2 electrons, therefore 2 Na atoms are needed. The atoms become ions (Na^+, Na^+ and O^{2-}) and the compound formed is sodium oxide, Na_2O.

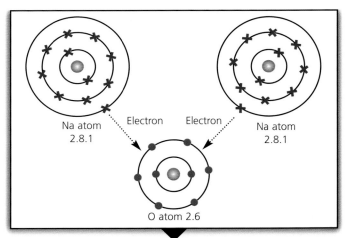

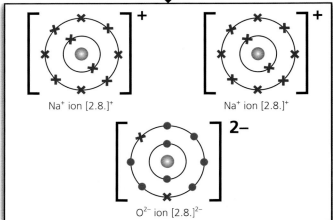

Chemical Patterns

Example 3

Magnesium and oxygen bond ionically to form magnesium oxide, MgO. The magnesium (Mg) atom has 2 electrons in its outer shell. The oxygen atom only has 6 electrons in its outer shell so the 2 electrons from the Mg atom are transferred to the O atom, so they both have 8 electrons in their outer shell. The atoms become ions Mg^{2+} and O^{2-} and the compound formed is magnesium oxide, MgO.

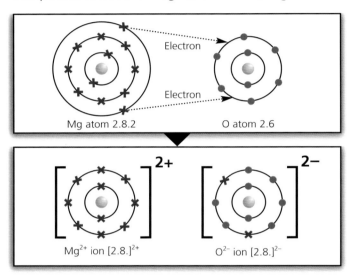

Many ionic compounds have properties similar to those of sodium chloride. They form crystals because the ions are arranged into a regular lattice.

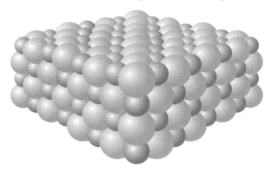

Magnesium Oxide

- ○ Mg^{2+} ion, i.e. a magnesium atom that has lost 2 electrons
- ○ O^{2-} ion, i.e. an oxygen atom that has gained 2 electrons

HT There is a strong force of attraction between the ions, which takes a lot of energy to break, so ionic compounds have high melting and boiling points. When the compound is molten or dissolved, the charged ions are free to move around the liquid. This means they can conduct electricity.

HT Deducing the Formula of an Ionic Compound

If you know the charge given on both ions you can work out the formula, or if you know the formula and the charge on one of the ions, you can work out the charge on the other ion.

This is because all ionic compounds are neutral substances where the charge on the positive ion(s) is equal to the charge on the negative ion(s). (See table below.)

Positive Ions		Negative Ions	
		1− e.g. Cl^-, OH^-	**2−** e.g. SO_4^{2-}, O^{2-}
1+ e.g. K^+, Na^+		KCl ↙ ↘ 1+ 1−	K_2SO_4 ↙ ↘ 2 x 1+ 2− = 2+
		NaOH ↙ ↘ 1+ 1−	Na_2O ↙ ↘ 2 x 1+ 2− = 2+
2+ e.g. Mg^{2+}, Cu^{2+}		$MgCl_2$ ↙ ↘ 2+ 2 x 1− = 2−	$MgSO_4$ ↙ ↘ 2+ 2−
		$Cu(OH)_2$ ↙ ↘ 2+ 2 x 1− = 2−	CuO ↙ ↘ 2+ 2−
3+ e.g. Al^{3+}, Fe^{3+}		$AlCl_3$ ↙ ↘ 3+ 3 x 1− = 3−	$Al_2(SO_4)_3$ ↙ ↘ 2 x 3+ 3 x 2− = 6+ = 6−
		$Fe(OH)_3$ ↙ ↘ 3+ 3 x 1− = 3−	Fe_2O_3 ↙ ↘ 2 x 3+ 3 x 2− = 6+ = 6−

Explaining Motion

Module P4

An understanding of the rules that govern forces and motion has led to the development of numerous modern technologies, from aeroplanes and spacecraft to sports equipment and theme park rides. This module looks at…
- how we can describe motion
- what forces are
- what the connection is between forces and motion
- how we can describe motion in terms of energy changes.

Speed and Velocity

Speed tells you how far an object will travel in a certain time. However, it does not tell you the direction of travel.

Velocity tells you an object's speed *and* gives an indication of its direction of travel.

Example

A lorry is travelling along a straight road. The speed of the lorry is 15m/s (metres per second).

In the morning, travelling in one direction (from the warehouse to the supermarket), the velocity is +15m/s. At night, travelling in the opposite direction (from the supermarket back to the warehouse) the velocity is -15m/s.

It does not matter which direction is called positive or negative as long as opposite directions have opposite signs.

This idea is also used when describing distance; changes in distance in one direction are described as positive, and in the opposite direction they are described as negative.

Calculating Speed

To calculate the speed of an object we need to know two things about its motion:
- the distance it has travelled
- the time it took to travel that distance.

Speed is calculated using the formula:

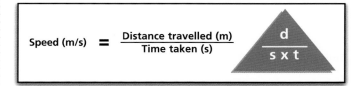

$$\text{Speed (m/s)} = \frac{\text{Distance travelled (m)}}{\text{Time taken (s)}}$$

The scientific unit for speed is metres per second (m/s), so the distance should be in metres and the time in seconds.

A speed of 4m/s means that the object travels 4 metres every second. At this speed, in 5 seconds, the object would travel a total of 20 metres.

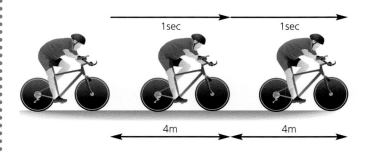

Speed can also be calculated in miles per hour, mph.

Explaining Motion

Calculating Speed (cont.)

The formula calculates an average speed over the total distance travelled, even if the speed of an object is not constant.

Example

An object travels 10 metres in 5 seconds. Use the formula to calculate its average speed.

$$\text{Speed} \; = \; \frac{\text{Distance travelled}}{\text{Time taken}} \; = \; \frac{10\text{m}}{5\text{s}} = \textbf{2m/s}$$

However, during those 5 seconds the object could have been moving at different speeds.

For example, the object could have moved at 5m/s for 1 second, stopped for 3 seconds, and then moved at 5m/s for 1 second. The object would still have an average speed of 2m/s, because it took 5 seconds to travel 10 metres.

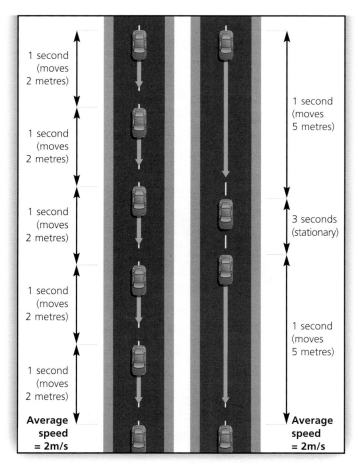

The speed of an object at a particular point in time is called the **instantaneous speed**.

Distance–Time Graphs

The slope or gradient of a distance–time graph is a measure of the speed of the object. The steeper the slope, the greater the speed.

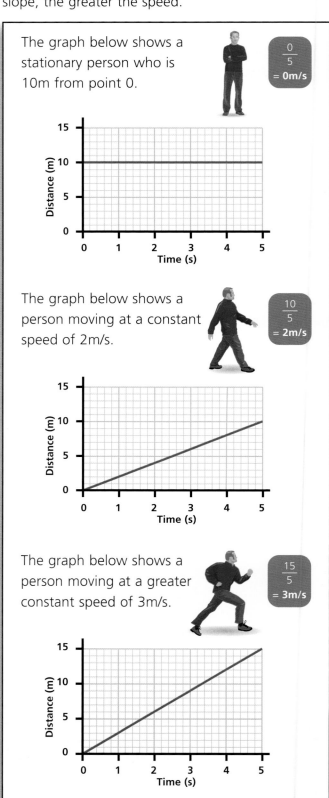

The graph below shows a stationary person who is 10m from point 0.

$$\frac{0}{5} = \textbf{0m/s}$$

The graph below shows a person moving at a constant speed of 2m/s.

$$\frac{10}{5} = \textbf{2m/s}$$

The graph below shows a person moving at a greater constant speed of 3m/s.

$$\frac{15}{5} = \textbf{3m/s}$$

Calculating Speed

The speed of an object can be calculated by working out the gradient of a distance–time graph. The steeper the gradient, the faster the speed. All we have to do is take any point on the gradient and read off the distance travelled at this point, and the time taken to get there.

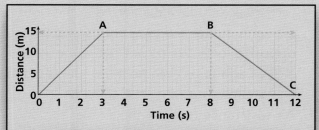

0 to A: Substitute figures into the formula…

$$\text{Speed from 0 to A} = \frac{15m}{3s} = \textbf{5m/s}$$

A to B: A horizontal line means the object is stationary.

$$\text{Speed from A to B} = \frac{15m - 15m}{5s} = \textbf{0m/s}$$

B to C: Substitute figures into the formula…

$$\text{Speed from B to C} = \frac{15m}{4s} = \textbf{3.75m/s}$$

So, the object travelled at 5m/s for 3 seconds, remained stationary for 5 seconds then travelled at 3.75m/s for 4 seconds back to the starting point.

The example above illustrates how to calculate speed from a graph but remember...

- this only works when looking at straight line sections
- the average velocity for this journey is 0 because the object ends up back where it started
- if you are asked to give velocity you need to indicate the direction. If the velocity in the first section is positive the velocity in the last section will be negative because the object is moving in the opposite direction.

Curvy Distance–Time Graphs

The slope or gradient of a distance–time graph represents how quickly an object is moving; the steeper the slope, the faster its speed. When the gradient is changing, its speed is changing.

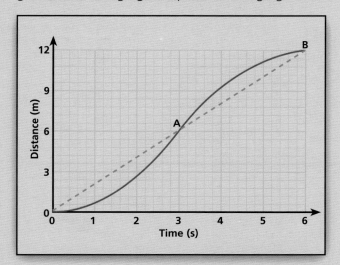

In section 0 to A the line is curved. This tells us that the object is speeding up because the gradient is increasing.

Between A and B the line curves the other way. The gradient is decreasing so the object must be slowing down.

Because the graph is curved it is difficult to work out the instantaneous speed at a particular point but we can work out the average speed. The average speed is simply the total distance divided by the total time; it is shown by the dotted line.

$$\text{Speed} = \frac{\text{Distance}}{\text{Time}}$$
$$= \frac{12m}{6s}$$
$$= \textbf{2m/s}$$

Where the gradient is steeper than the dotted line, the object is travelling faster than the average speed. Where the gradient is less steep than the line, the object is travelling slower than the average speed.

Explaining Motion

Velocity–Time Graphs

The slope or gradient of a velocity–time graph represents how quickly an object is increasing in speed (i.e. accelerating); the steeper the slope, the faster its speed is increasing.

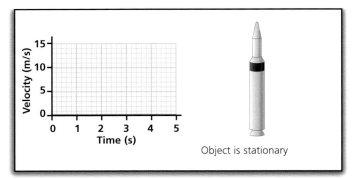

Object is stationary

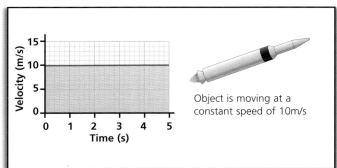

Object is moving at a constant speed of 10m/s

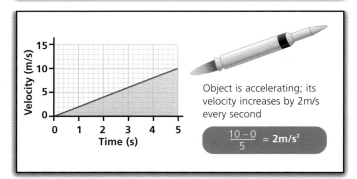

Object is accelerating; its velocity increases by 2m/s every second

$$\frac{10-0}{5} = 2m/s^2$$

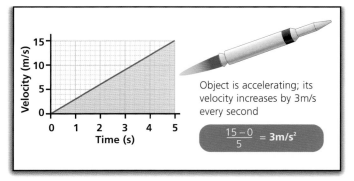

Object is accelerating; its velocity increases by 3m/s every second

$$\frac{15-0}{5} = 3m/s^2$$

Velocity–time graphs are used in lorry tachographs to make sure that drivers do not exceed the speed limit, and that they rest for suitable amounts of time.

Forces

A force occurs when two objects interact with each other. Whenever one object exerts a force on another it always experiences an equal and opposite force in return. The forces in an **interaction pair** are equal in size and opposite in direction.

Examples

- **Gravity (weight)** – two masses are attracted to each other, e.g. we are attracted to the Earth and the Earth is attracted to us with an **equal** and **opposite** force. We do not notice the attraction of the Earth to us because it has such a big mass that the force has very little effect on it.
- **Air resistance (drag)** – the air tries to slow down a skydiver by pushing upwards against him / her. The skydiver pushes the air out of the way with an equal and opposite force.
- If two people are standing on skateboards and one pushes the other, both skateboards will move away from each other.

- The rocket's engines push gas backwards (action) and the gas pushes the rocket forwards (reaction), thrusting it through the atmosphere. A jet engine works in a similar way.

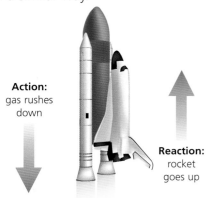

Action: gas rushes down

Reaction: rocket goes up

Friction and Reaction

Some forces, such as friction and reaction (of a surface), only occur as a response to another force.

A force occurs when an object is resting on a surface. The object is being pulled down to the surface by gravity and the surface pushes up with an equal force called the **reaction of the surface**.

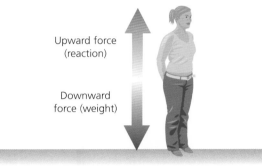

Upward force
(reaction)

Downward
force (weight)

Upward force
(reaction)

Downward
force (weight)

When two objects try to slide past one another both objects experience a force that tries to stop them moving. This interaction is called **friction**.

A moving object experiences friction. However, an object does not have to be moving to experience friction. For example, a car parked on a slope is trying to roll down the hill but there is enough friction from the brakes (hopefully) to stop it.

Forces and Motion

Arrows are used when drawing diagrams of forces. The size and direction of the arrow represents the size of the force, and the direction that it is acting in. Force arrows are always drawn with the tail of the arrow touching the object even if the force is pushing the object.

If more than one force acts on an object, the forces will add up if they are acting in the same direction, or subtract if they are acting in opposite directions.

The overall effect of adding (or subtracting) these forces is called the **resultant** force. The diagrams below show the overall effect of various push and friction forces on the movement of a trolley.

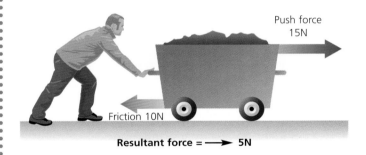

Push force
15N

Friction 10N

Resultant force = ⟶ 5N

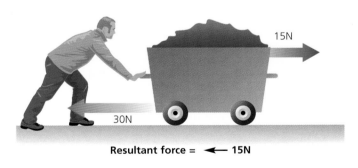

15N

30N

Resultant force = ⟵ 15N

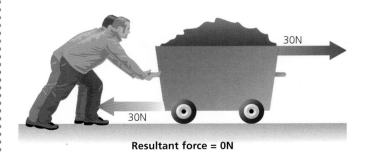

30N

30N

Resultant force = 0N

Explaining Motion

Momentum

Momentum is a measure of the motion of an object. The momentum of an object is calculated using the following formula:

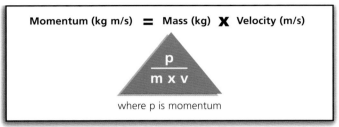

Momentum (kg m/s) **=** Mass (kg) **X** Velocity (m/s)

$$\frac{p}{m \times v}$$

where p is momentum

Example

A car has a mass of 1200kg. It is travelling at a velocity of 30m/s. Calculate its momentum.

Using the formula…

Momentum = Mass x Velocity

= 1200kg x 30m/s

= **36 000kg m/s**

Change in Momentum

If the resultant force acting on an object is zero its momentum will not change. If the object…

- is stationary, it will remain stationary
- is already moving, it will continue moving in a straight line at a steady speed.

If the resultant force acting on an object is not zero, it causes a change in momentum in the direction of the force. This could…

- give a stationary object momentum (i.e. make it move)
- increase or decrease the speed, or change the direction of a moving object, i.e. change its velocity.

The size of the change in momentum depends on…

- the size of the resultant force
- the length of time the force is acting on the object.

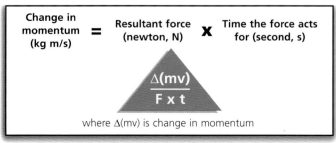

Change in momentum (kg m/s) **=** Resultant force (newton, N) **X** Time the force acts for (second, s)

$$\frac{\Delta(mv)}{F \times t}$$

where Δ(mv) is change in momentum

Speeding Up and Slowing Down

Cars and bicycles have a **driving force** produced by the engine (car) or the energy of the cyclist (bicycle). This force has the effect of making the vehicle move or accelerate.

However, there is also a **counter force** caused by friction and air resistance, which has the effect of making the vehicle slow down or stop.

If the driving force is bigger than the counter force the vehicle accelerates.

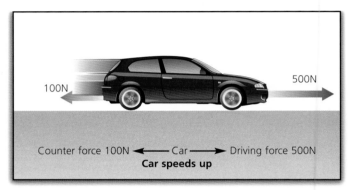

100N · · · · · 500N

Counter force 100N ◄——— Car ——► Driving force 500N

Car speeds up

If the driving force and counter force are equal the vehicle travels at a constant speed in a straight line.

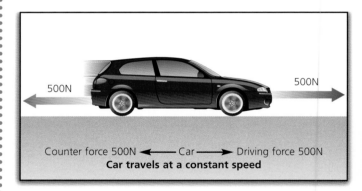

500N · · · · · 500N

Counter force 500N ◄——— Car ——► Driving force 500N

Car travels at a constant speed

If the counter force is bigger than the driving force the vehicle decelerates.

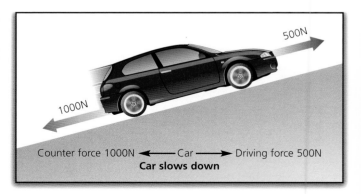

500N

1000N

Counter force 1000N ◄——— Car ——► Driving force 500N

Car slows down

Collisions

If a car is involved in a collision it comes to a sudden stop, i.e. it undergoes a change in momentum. If this change in momentum is spread out over a longer period, the average resultant force acting on the car will be smaller.

Example

A car with a mass of 1000kg, travelling at 10m/s, has a momentum of 10 000kg m/s. If the car is involved in a collision and comes to a sudden stop, it would experience a change in momentum of 10 000kg m/s.

This sudden change in momentum will affect not only the car, but its passengers. If the car stops in a very short time, then the occupants of the car will experience a large force which can lead to serious injuries.

If the car stops in 5 seconds the force acting on it would be 2000N, but if the car stops in 10 seconds the force would be 1000N.

All car safety devices, such as seat-belts, crumple zones and air bags, are designed to reduce the force of the impact on the human body. They do this by increasing the time of the impact.

For example, a crumple zone is an area designed to 'crumple' on impact. This helps to increase the time during which the car changes momentum, i.e. instead of coming to an immediate halt there will be a few seconds during which the momentum is reduced. This means that the force exerted on the people inside the car will be reduced, resulting in fewer injuries.

Motorcycle and bicycle helmets work on the same principle – they crumple slightly on impact, absorbing some of the energy of the collision and spreading the force out over a longer period.

Kinetic Energy

A moving object has **kinetic** energy. The amount of kinetic energy an object has depends on…
- the mass of the object
- the velocity of the object.

The greater the mass and velocity of an object, the more kinetic energy it has. Therefore, it takes a longer time to stop a heavy, fast-moving object, than a light, slow-moving object.

Car brakes convert the kinetic energy into heat energy. As with all energy transfers the total amount of energy remains the same (energy is conserved).

Kinetic energy is calculated using the following formula:

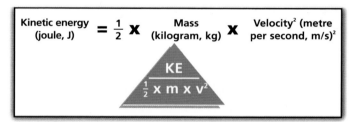

$$\text{Kinetic energy (joule, J)} = \frac{1}{2} \times \text{Mass (kilogram, kg)} \times \text{Velocity}^2 \text{ (metre per second, m/s)}^2$$

$$\frac{\text{KE}}{\frac{1}{2} \times m \times v^2}$$

Example

A bicycle of mass 50kg is moving at a velocity of 8m/s. How much kinetic energy does it have?

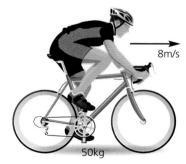

Using the formula…

Kinetic energy $= \frac{1}{2} \times \text{Mass} \times \text{Velocity}^2$

$\qquad = \frac{1}{2} \times 50\text{kg} \times (8\text{m/s})^2$

$\qquad = \frac{1}{2} \times 50 \times 64$

$\qquad = \textbf{1600J}$

Explaining Motion

Gravitational Potential Energy

An object lifted above the ground gains potential energy (PE), often called gravitational potential energy (GPE). The additional height gives it the potential to do work when it falls, e.g. a diver standing on a diving board has gravitational potential energy. It is calculated by the following formula...

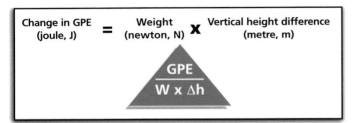

If an object is dropped, its gravitational potential energy decreases and is converted into kinetic energy.

Example

On Earth, an object of mass 2kg weighs 20N. How much kinetic energy does the object gain if it is dropped from a height of 5m?

N.B. Remember, to find the GPE you use the weight (20N) not the mass.

Change in GPE = Weight x Height difference
           = 20N x 5m = **100J**

If the object loses 100J of gravitational potential energy when it falls, it must have gained 100J of kinetic energy.

> **HT** To work out the velocity of a falling object you need to use the mass. In the example above, we know that the object has gained 100J of kinetic energy.
>
> Kinetic energy $= \frac{1}{2} \times$ Mass $\times$ Velocity^2
>
> $100 = \frac{1}{2} \times 2 \times$ velocity^2
>
> $100 = 1 \times$ velocity^2
>
> $100 =$ velocity^2
>
> velocity $= \sqrt{100}$
>
> $= \textbf{10m/s}$

Work and Energy

When a force moves an object, work is done on the object resulting in the transfer of energy.

When work is done *by* an object it loses energy, and when work is done *on* an object it gains energy according to the relationship:

> Change in Energy (joule, J) = Work done (joule, J)

When a force acting on an object causes it to accelerate, work is done on the object to increase its kinetic energy (see p.29). A falling object has work done on it by the force of gravity and this causes it to accelerate.

Ignoring the effects of air resistance and friction, the increase in kinetic energy will be equal to the amount of work done. However, in reality some of the energy will be dissipated (lost) as heat, and the increase in kinetic energy will, therefore, be less than the work done.

When a car is travelling at a constant speed the driving force from the engine is balanced by the counter force (see p.28). All of the work being done by the engine is used to overcome friction and there is no increase in kinetic energy.

Work done is calculated by the following formula:

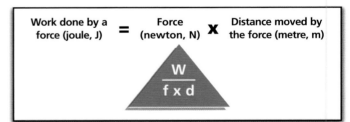

Example

A car needs to be pushed with a force of 100N to overcome friction. If the car is pushed for 5m, calculate the work done.

Work done = Force x Distance moved
         = 100N x 5m
         = **500J**

Growth and Development

Module B5

Genetic technologies such as stem cell research and cellular growth control are an important part of modern medical science. This module looks at...

- how organisms produce new cells
- how genes control growth and development within the cell
- how new organisms develop from a single cell.

Cells

Cells are the building blocks of all living things. All cells contain **DNA**, which is a nucleic acid (i.e. it is found mainly in the nucleus).

DNA molecules are in the form of a double helix and contain the genetic code. DNA determines the biological development of all cellular life forms, from single-celled organisms to complex organisms.

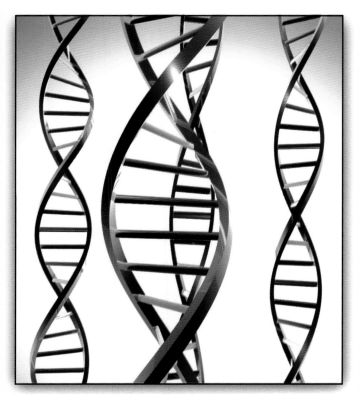

All cells contain **organelles** (different parts of the cell's structure). In general, plant and animal cells have the following structures:

Plant Cell – Palisade Cell From a Leaf

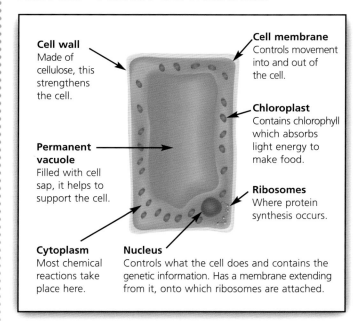

Cell wall
Made of cellulose, this strengthens the cell.

Cell membrane
Controls movement into and out of the cell.

Chloroplast
Contains chlorophyll which absorbs light energy to make food.

Permanent vacuole
Filled with cell sap, it helps to support the cell.

Ribosomes
Where protein synthesis occurs.

Cytoplasm
Most chemical reactions take place here.

Nucleus
Controls what the cell does and contains the genetic information. Has a membrane extending from it, onto which ribosomes are attached.

Animal Cell – Cheek Cell From a Human

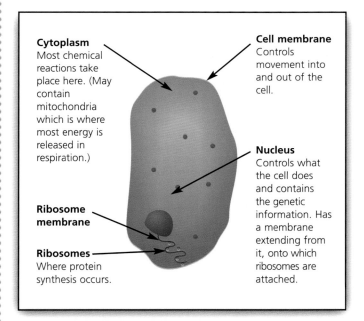

Cytoplasm
Most chemical reactions take place here. (May contain mitochondria which is where most energy is released in respiration.)

Cell membrane
Controls movement into and out of the cell.

Nucleus
Controls what the cell does and contains the genetic information. Has a membrane extending from it, onto which ribosomes are attached.

Ribosome membrane

Ribosomes
Where protein synthesis occurs.

The organelles do different jobs within the cell. For example...

- the nucleus contains the DNA
- the chloroplasts in plant cells are where photosynthesis takes place
- mitochondria are where respiration takes place
- the ribosomes interpret the coded instructions carried by DNA to make host proteins.

The organelles work together to allow the cell to perform a specific function.

Growth and Development

Mitosis

Mitosis is the process by which a cell divides to produce two new cells with identical sets of chromosomes, and the same number of chromosomes as the parent cell. They will also have all the necessary organelles. The purpose of mitosis is to produce new cells for growth and repair and to replace old tissues.

The Cell Cycle

To enable mitosis to take place, cells go through a cycle of growth and division. The cycle repeats itself until the cell can no longer divide. (In humans this is after approximately 70 cell divisions.)

Cell Growth

When a cell enters the growth phase of the cycle…
- the numbers of organelles increase
- the chromosomes are copied.

This happens because the cell is preparing to divide. Copies of all the cell's organelles and chromosomes need to be produced otherwise one daughter cell would be left incomplete and would not be able to function.

Duplicate chromosomes are produced when the two strands in each DNA molecule separate and new strands form alongside them.

Meiosis

Meiosis only takes place in the testes and ovaries. It is a special type of cell division that produces gametes (sex cells, i.e. eggs and sperm) for sexual reproduction.

Gametes contain **half** the number of chromosomes of the parent cell.

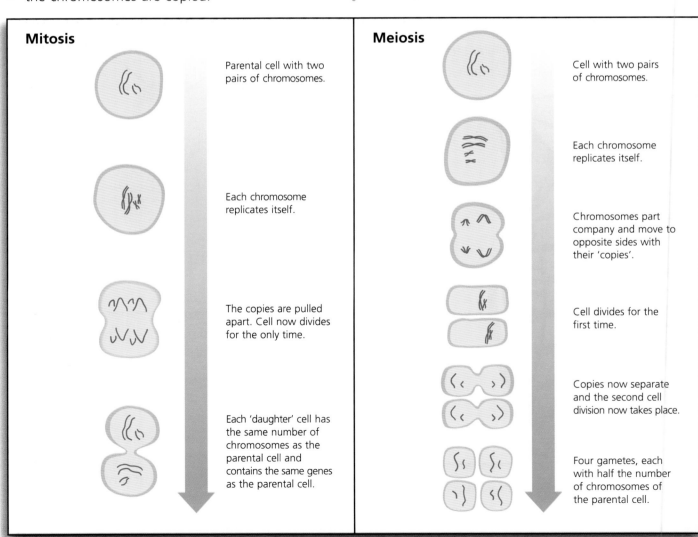

Mitosis

Parental cell with two pairs of chromosomes.

Each chromosome replicates itself.

The copies are pulled apart. Cell now divides for the only time.

Each 'daughter' cell has the same number of chromosomes as the parental cell and contains the same genes as the parental cell.

Meiosis

Cell with two pairs of chromosomes.

Each chromosome replicates itself.

Chromosomes part company and move to opposite sides with their 'copies'.

Cell divides for the first time.

Copies now separate and the second cell division now takes place.

Four gametes, each with half the number of chromosomes of the parental cell.

Fertilisation

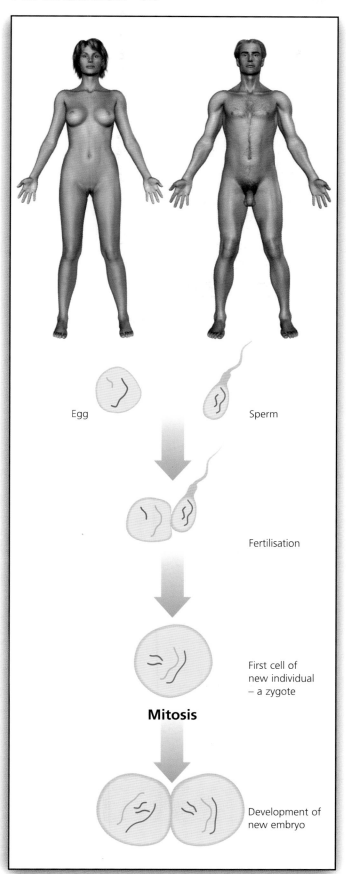

Egg

Sperm

Fertilisation

First cell of new individual – a zygote

Mitosis

Development of new embryo

During fertilisation, a male gamete (sperm) and a female gamete (egg) fuse together.

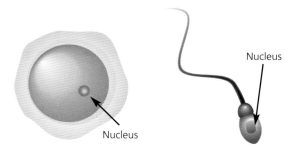

Nucleus

Nucleus

It is important that the cells produced during meiosis only have half the number of chromosomes as the parent cell, so when they fuse they produce a single body cell, called a **zygote**, with one whole set of chromosomes. In each pair of chromosomes, one chromosome comes from the father and one chromosome comes from the mother.

The zygote divides by mitosis to produce a cluster of cells called an embryo. The cells of the embryo all contain the same DNA. These cells will eventually differentiate into bone, muscle and nerve cells, etc.

The cells of the embryo also have to ensure that different tissues develop at the correct stages.

The embryo continues to develop by mitosis (from 1 cell to 2, to 4, to 8, etc.) to eventually become an adult individual. An adult human contains approximately 1×10^{14} (100 trillion) cells.

Each cell has the same information copied inside the nucleus.

Variation

Meiosis and sexual reproduction produce variation between offspring and parents because, when the gametes fuse, genetic information from two individuals is combined.

For each gene, just one of each parent's two alleles is passed on. This means that each offspring can have a different combination of alleles from either parent and, therefore, different characteristics.

This process is completely random.

Growth and Development

Controlling Growth and Development

Growth and development in organisms are governed by genes present on the chromosomes in each cell nucleus. Genes determine characteristics (e.g. the ability to roll your tongue) by providing instructions for the production of proteins, and therefore control the development of the whole organism.

The instructions are in the form of a code, made up of four bases which hold the two strands of the molecule together. These bases always pair up in the same way (i.e. form the same base pairs):

- adenine (A) pairs with thymine (T)
- cytosine (C) pairs with guanine (G).

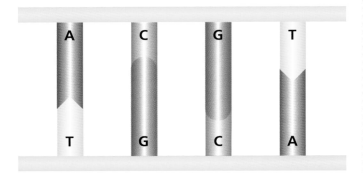

The chromosomes (and the genes that are on them) always stay inside the nucleus. However, the production of proteins takes place outside the nucleus, in the cytoplasm.

Therefore, there is a mechanism for transferring the information stored in the genes into the cytoplasm.

Imagine the nucleus is a reference library, from which you are not allowed to remove the books. You would need to copy down any information you needed so that you could take it away with you.

The DNA cannot leave the cell because it is too large. So, the relevant section of DNA is unzipped and the instructions are copied onto smaller molecules called **messenger RNA** (mRNA). These leave the nucleus and carry the instructions to the **ribosomes** which follow the instructions to make the relevant protein.

The sequence of bases in a gene determines the order in which amino acids are joined together to make a particular protein. A group of three base pairs codes for one amino acid in a protein chain (this is called a triplet code). There are 20 different amino acids that can be used.

The process culminates in a protein, its structure is dependent upon the amino acids that make it up.

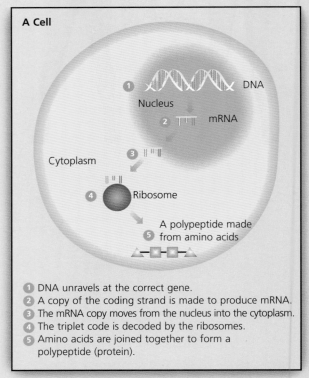

A Cell

1. DNA unravels at the correct gene.
2. A copy of the coding strand is made to produce mRNA.
3. The mRNA copy moves from the nucleus into the cytoplasm.
4. The triplet code is decoded by the ribosomes.
5. Amino acids are joined together to form a polypeptide (protein).

The diagram below shows an example of a protein. The different coloured shapes represent different amino acid chains which give the protein its characteristic shape.

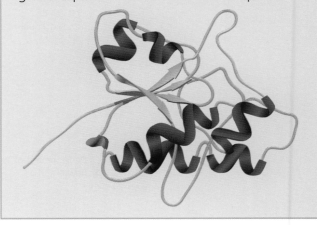

Growth and Development

Development of New Organisms

In a human embryo, all the cells are identical up to the 8 cell stage and could potentially develop into any sort of cell required by the organism, including neurons, blood cells, liver cells or muscle cells. These identical cells are known as **embryonic stem cells**.

At the 16 cell stage (approximately 4 days after fertilisation) the cells in an embryo begin to specialise and form different types of tissue. The cells contain the same genetic information, but each cell's position relative to the others is different. The distribution of various proteins in the egg cell is also different, so although embryonic cells contain the same genes, the cells are already different from one another. At the time of specialisation, these differences determine what specific function a cell will have.

The only genes that are active in a cell are the ones that are needed by that cell. The cell only produces the specific proteins it needs to enable it to carry out its role. Some proteins are needed by all cells, whilst others will only be needed in specific cells.

In human DNA, there are approximately 20 000 to 25 000 genes. This means that a similar number of proteins can be manufactured in the human body.

Stem Cells

Stem cells could potentially be used to help treat diseases and disorders, and to repair damage to various tissues. Although there are lots of benefits associated with stem cell technology, there are also a number of **ethical issues** (previously covered in B1, GCSE Science).

There are three sources of stem cells – embryos, blood from the umbilical cord and **adult stem cells**. Only the embryonic stem cells are completely unspecialised and can be used to form any cell type.

Therapeutic cloning is a process which involves removing the nucleus from an egg cell and replacing it with a nucleus from one of the patient's cells. The egg cell is then stimulated so that it starts to divide (as if it were a zygote).

At the 8 cell stage, cells can be removed as they are still unspecialised. However, this technique is highly controversial because, effectively, a clone of the adult patient is being created, although it is prevented from developing to adult form.

Adult stem cells are not like embryonic stem cells – they will only produce cells of a certain type (rather than any cell), e.g. cells for creating blood cells in bone marrow would have to be encouraged to grow more of that type of cell by reactivating inactive genes in the nuclei.

The problem here is that there is only a small proportion of these cells amongst lots of non-stem cells so they are difficult to harvest. The reactivation process itself is also difficult.

To date, scientists have successfully grown ears, skin and, most recently, a bladder, using the patients' own cells. They can either be grown in a laboratory, or by using a 'host animal' to maintain a blood supply during growth.

The advantage of using adult cells is that they can be taken from the patient, so the patient's immune system will not reject the transplant.

Human ear grown on the back of a mouse. The mouse provides all the blood vessels needed to keep the ear alive.

Growth and Development

Differentiation in Plants

Plant cells, as with animal cells, divide by the process of mitosis. The cells then specialise into the cells of roots, leaves or flowers. Unlike animals, most plants continue to grow in height and width throughout their lives.

Meristems

Plant growth occurs in areas called **meristems**, which are sites where unspecialised cells divide repeatedly (mitosis). These cells then differentiate, and become specialised in relation to the function they will perform.

There are two types of meristems: those that result in increased girth (**lateral**) and those that result in increased height and longer roots (**apical**).

Cells from the meristem behave like embryonic stem cells in animals – they can develop into any type of plant cell. The presence of these unspecialised cells is what enables clones of plants with desirable features to be produced from cuttings.

Clones can be produced by growing cells from the meristem in a special culture medium (jelly containing relevant nutrients) to produce a **callus**, which is a cluster of undifferentiated cells containing the same genetic information as the parent plant.

If the hormonal conditions in their environment are changed, these unspecialised plant cells can develop into a range of other tissues such as xylem and phloem (see p.37), or organs such as leaves, roots and flowers.

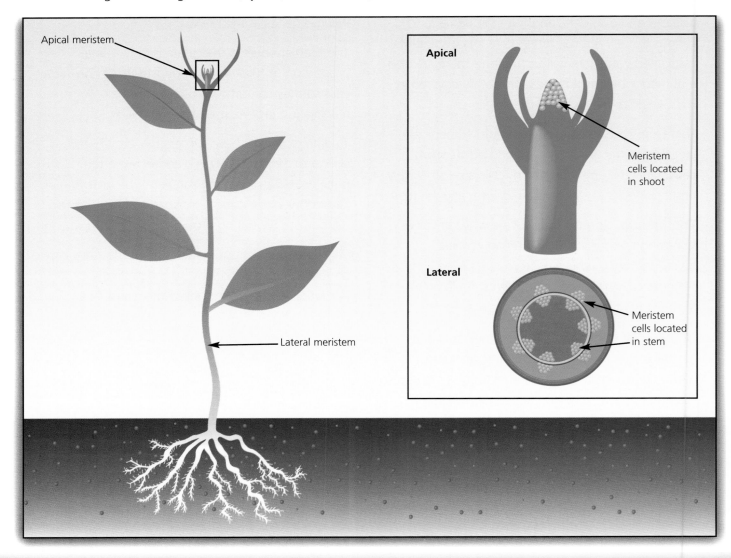

Apical meristem

Lateral meristem

Apical

Meristem cells located in shoot

Lateral

Meristem cells located in stem

Growth and Development

Xylem and Phloem

Xylem are used by the plant to transport water and soluble mineral salts from the roots to the stem and leaves, and to replace water lost during transpiration and photosynthesis. By adding certain plant hormones to unspecialised plant cells, xylem tissue can be formed.

Phloem, the tubes used by the plant to transport dissolved food to the whole plant for respiration or storage, can be generated in a similar way to xylem (see diagram opposite).

Cuttings

Plants can be reproduced by taking a cutting and putting it in a rooting hormone which causes roots to form. Because the cutting already has a stem and leaves it will develop into a complete new plant, which is genetically identical to the parent plant (i.e. it is a clone).

> **HT** There are a wide range of plant hormones. The main group that is used in horticulture is called **auxins**. Auxins mainly affect cell division at the tip of a shoot, because this is where cell division mainly occurs. Just under the tip, the cells grow in size under the influence of auxins, causing the stem or root to grow longer.

Responding to Stimuli

All living organisms possess sensitivity. For example, plants are able to respond to changes in their environment. They can respond to external stimuli such as gravity or light by changing the direction of growth.

The mechanism by which plants respond to light is called **phototropism**. A plant's survival depends on its ability to photosynthesise; it needs light to grow. Plants, therefore, need strategies to detect light and respond to changes in intensity. This is demonstrated by the way in which plants will grow towards a light source (see diagram opposite).

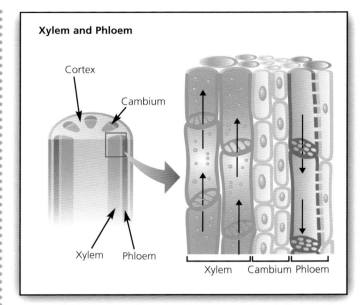

Xylem and Phloem

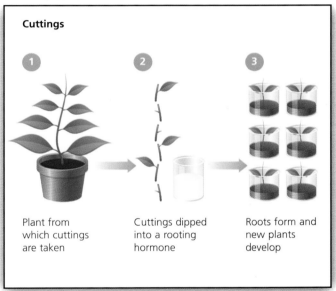

Cuttings

1	2	3
Plant from which cuttings are taken	Cuttings dipped into a rooting hormone	Roots form and new plants develop

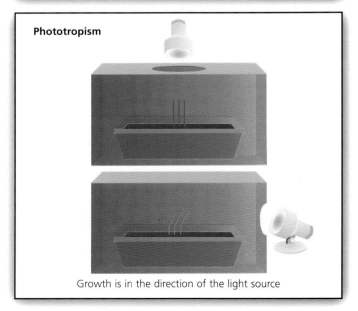

Phototropism

Growth is in the direction of the light source

Growth and Development

How Phototropism Works

The cells which are furthest away from a light source grow more, due to the presence of auxin, which is sensitive to light.

Auxin is produced at the shoot tip and migrates down the shoot.

If a light source is directly overhead, then the distribution of auxin would be the same on both sides of the plant shoot.

Charles Darwin carried out some simple experiments that demonstrated the role played by plant hormones produced in the shoot tip.

As we have seen, light causes the shoot to bend towards the source. If the tip of the shoot is removed or covered in opaque material then the plant will continue to grow upwards – as if the light source was not there.

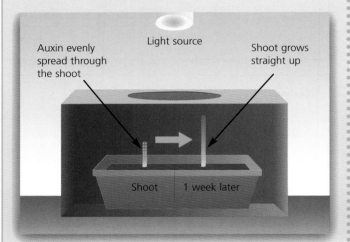

If a light source shines onto the shoot at an angle, the auxin at the tip moves away from the light source.

As a result, the concentration of auxin on the side furthest away from the light increases, causing the cells there to elongate, and the shoot begins to bend towards the light.

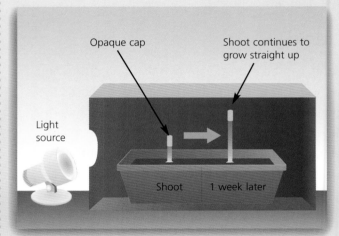

If the tip is covered with a transparent cap then it will still grow towards the light source. The same thing will happen if an opaque cylinder is wrapped around the stem leaving the tip exposed.

This experiment proves it is a substance produced in the tip that caused the cells further down the shoot to grow.

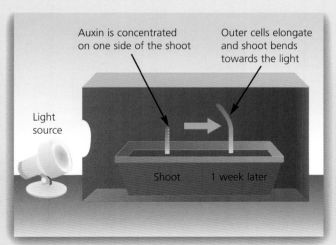

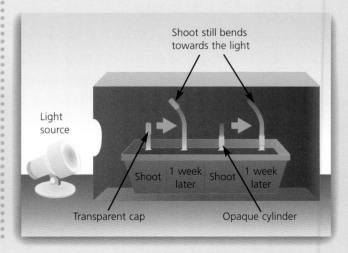

Chemicals of the Natural Environment

Module C5

We can get a better understanding of the impact human activity can have on the natural environment by knowing more about the chemicals that make up our planet. This module looks at…

- the structure of the Earth and the properties of the chemicals found in the atmosphere, hydrosphere, lithosphere and biosphere
- the natural cycle of elements between the spheres
- how to extract useful minerals
- properties of metals.

The Earth's Resources

1 Atmosphere – a layer of gas surrounding the Earth. It is made up of the elements nitrogen (N), oxygen (O), traces of argon (Ar) and some compounds, e.g. carbon dioxide (CO_2) and water vapour (H_2O).

2 Hydrosphere – all the water on the Earth, including oceans, rivers, lakes and underground reserves. The water contains dissolved compounds.

3 Biosphere – all living organisms on the Earth, including plants, animals and microorganisms. They are all made up of compounds containing the elements carbon (C), hydrogen (H), oxygen (O) and nitrogen (N), with small amounts of phosphorus (P) and sulfur (S).

4 Lithosphere – the rigid outer layer of the Earth made up of the crust and the part of the mantle just below it. It is a mixture of minerals, such as silicon dioxide. Abundant elements in the lithosphere include silicon (Si), oxygen (O) and aluminium (Al).

Chemicals of the Natural Environment

Chemical Cycles

In order to sustain life, chemicals constantly move between the different spheres. For example, carbon dioxide in the atmosphere is moved into the biosphere by green plants during photosynthesis. During respiration it is returned to the atmosphere.

Sometimes human activity upsets the balance of natural cycles, e.g. burning fossil fuels puts carbon dioxide into the atmosphere more quickly than it is removed.

N.B. You need to be able to interpret the type of diagram shown below.

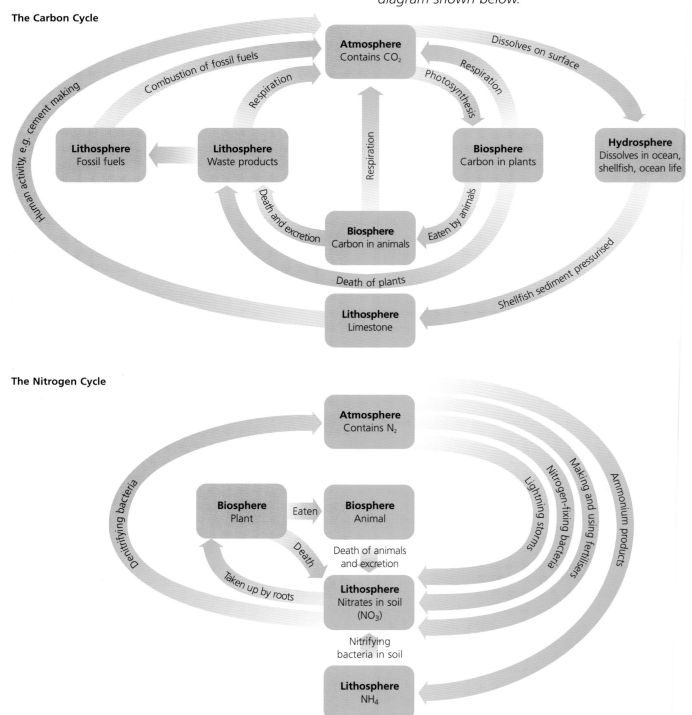

The Carbon Cycle

The Nitrogen Cycle

Chemicals of the Natural Environment

Chemicals of the Atmosphere

Chemical	2-D Molecular Diagram	3-D Molecular Diagram	Boiling Point (°C)	Melting Point (°C)
Oxygen O_2	O=O		−182.9	−218.3
Nitrogen N_2	N≡N		−195.8	−210.1
Carbon dioxide CO_2	O=C=O		−78	Sublimes (no liquid state)
Water vapour H_2O	H–O–H		100	0
Argon Ar	Ar		−185.8	−189.3

The chemicals that make up the atmosphere consist of non-metal elements and molecular compounds made up from non-metal elements.

From the information in the table above we can deduce that the molecules (with the exception of water) that make up the atmosphere are gases at 20°C because they have very low boiling points, i.e. they boil below 20°C. This can be explained by looking at the structure of the molecules.

Gases consist of small molecules with weak forces of attraction between the molecules. Only small amounts of energy are needed to break these forces, which allows the molecules to move freely through the air.

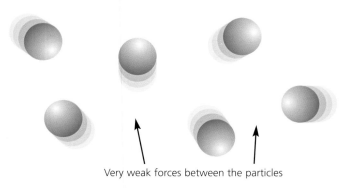

Very weak forces between the particles

HT The atoms within molecules (e.g. hydrogen) are connected by strong covalent bonds that arise because the electrons are shared between the nuclei. This causes a strong, electrostatic attraction between the nuclei and shared electrons.

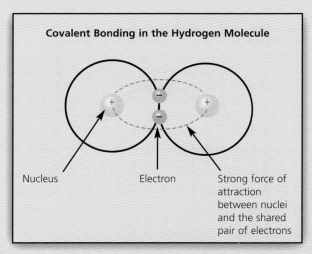

Covalent Bonding in the Hydrogen Molecule

Nucleus   Electron   Strong force of attraction between nuclei and the shared pair of electrons

Unlike ionic compounds (see p.21), pure molecular compounds do not conduct electricity because their molecules are not charged.

Chemicals of the Natural Environment

Chemicals of the Hydrosphere

Sea water in the hydrosphere is 'salty' because it contains dissolved ionic compounds called **salts**. A litre of sea water contains approximately 40g of salts. These salts include...

- sodium chloride, NaCl
- magnesium chloride, $MgCl_2$
- magnesium sulfate, $MgSO_4$
- potassium chloride, KCl
- potassium bromide, KBr.

HT When given a table of charges, you must be able to work out the formulae for the following ionic compounds: sodium chloride, magnesium sulfate, potassium chloride and potassium bromide (see method on p.22).

The Water Molecule

Water has some unexpected properties. For example, the table on p.41 shows that the boiling point of water is 100°C. This is a much higher boiling point than for the other molecules listed. Water is also a good **solvent** for salts. The properties can be explained by its structure.

The water molecule is bent, because the electrons in the covalent bond are nearer to the oxygen atom than the hydrogen atoms. The result is a **polar molecule**.

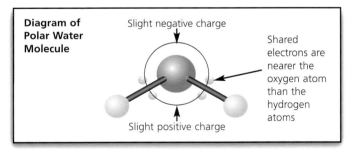

Diagram of Polar Water Molecule

Slight negative charge

Shared electrons are nearer the oxygen atom than the hydrogen atoms

Slight positive charge

The small charges on the atoms mean that the forces between the molecules are slightly stronger than in other covalent molecules. More energy is therefore needed to separate them.

The small charges also help water to **dissolve** ionic compounds as the water molecules attract the charges on the ions. The ions can then move freely through the liquid (see p.21 for ionic bonding).

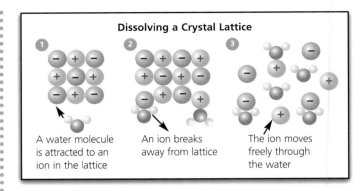

Dissolving a Crystal Lattice

A water molecule is attracted to an ion in the lattice

An ion breaks away from lattice

The ion moves freely through the water

Chemicals of the Lithosphere

Element	Abundance in Lithosphere (ppm)
Oxygen, O	455 000
Silicon, Si	272 000
Aluminium, Al	83 000
Iron, Fe	62 000
Calcium, Ca	46 600
Magnesium, Mg	27 640
Sodium, Na	22 700
Potassium, K	18 400
Titanium, Ti	6 320
Hydrogen, H	1 520

N.B. You may be asked to interpret data like this in your exam.

The table shows that the three most abundant elements in the Earth's crust are oxygen, silicon and aluminium. Much of silicon and oxygen is present as the compound silicon dioxide (SiO_2). Silicon dioxide exists in different forms, such as **quartz** in granite, and it is the main constituent of sandstone.

Silicon dioxide forms a **giant covalent structure**, where each silicon atom is covalently bonded to four oxygen atoms. Each oxygen atom is bonded to two silicon atoms. The result is a very strong, rigid 3-dimensional structure, which is very difficult to break down. It does not conduct electricity, as there are no ions or free electrons in the structure, or dissolve in water because there are no charges to attract the water molecules.

Silicon dioxide is very hard, has high melting and boiling points, is an electrical insulator and is insoluble in water.

Chemicals of the Natural Environment

Chemicals of the Lithosphere (cont.)

These properties can be explained by looking at the structure of silicon dioxide.

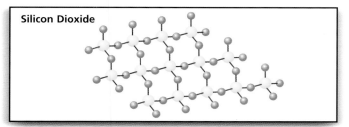

Silicon Dioxide

Amethyst is a form of quartz that is used as a **gemstone**. It is cut, polished and used in jewellery. The violet colour comes from traces of manganese and iron oxides found in the quartz. Some gemstones are very valuable because of their rarity, hardness and shiny appearance.

HT By understanding giant covalent structures, we can explain why we use different materials for certain jobs. The table gives some examples:

Element / Compound	Property	Use	Explanation
Carbon – diamond	Very hard	Drill tips	A lot of energy is needed to break the strong covalent bonds between the atoms.
Silicon dioxide	High melting point (1610°C)	Furnace linings	A lot of energy is needed to break the strong covalent bonds between the atoms.
Silica glass	Does not conduct electricity	Insulator in electrical devices	No free electrons or ions to carry electrical charge.

Chemicals of the Biosphere

Carbohydrates, proteins and DNA are three very important groups of molecules that make up a large part of the biosphere.

Glucose is a carbohydrate because it contains carbon, oxygen and hydrogen (see above opposite).

Glucose, $C_6H_{12}O_6$

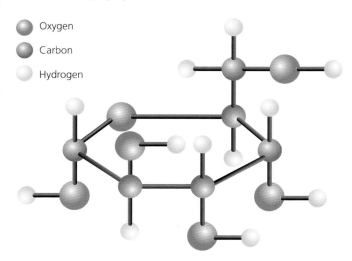

- Oxygen
- Carbon
- Hydrogen

Proteins are polymers made from amino acid monomers joined together. One of the simplest amino acids is glycine.

Glycine, $NH_2CH_2CO_2H$

- Oxygen
- Carbon
- Hydrogen
- Nitrogen

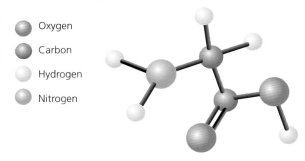

DNA is a large complex molecule.

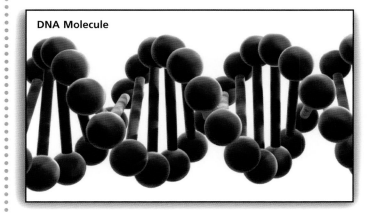

DNA Molecule

N.B. From a diagram of a molecule, you must be able to identify the elements in the compound and write the formula, as shown in glucose and glycine above.

Chemicals of the Natural Environment

	% Carbon	% Oxygen	% Hydrogen	% Nitrogen	% Phosphorus
Carbohydrate	40.0	53.3	6.7	0	0
Protein 1	32.0	42.7	6.7	18.7	0
Protein 2	40.4	36.0	7.9	15.7	0
Fat	39.0	52.0	8.7	0	0
DNA	41.0	30.7	4.6	29.0	4.2

Chemicals of the Biosphere (cont.)

Carbohydrates, fats, proteins and DNA are made up of different elements. The actual composition of the elements varies as there are many different molecules of carbohydrates, fats, proteins and DNA.

The table above lists the percentage composition of some elements. You must be able to interpret this type of data. For example, the data tells us that Protein 2 contains more carbon than Protein 1; DNA is the only molecule to contain phosphorus, etc.

Balancing Equations

All chemical reactions follow the same simple rule: the mass of the reactants is equal to the mass of the products. This means there must be the same number of atoms on both sides of the equation.

You do not have to do anything if the equation is already balanced. If the equation needs balancing, follow this method:

1. Write a number in front of one or more of the formulae. This increases the number of all of the atoms in that formula.
2. Include the state symbols: (s) = solid, (l) = liquid, (g) = gas and (aq) = dissolved in water (aqueous solution).

Example
Balance the reaction between calcium carbonate and hydrochloric acid.

Calcium carbonate	+	Hydrochloric acid	→	Calcium chloride	+	Carbon dioxide	+	Water

$$CaCO_3 + HCl \longrightarrow CaCl_2 + CO_2 + H_2O$$

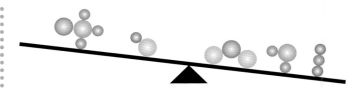

There are more chlorine atoms and hydrogen atoms on the products side than on the reactants side, so balance chlorine by doubling the amount of hydrochloric acid.

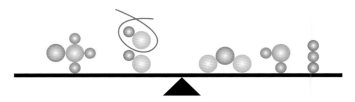

The amount of chlorine and hydrogen on both sides is now equal. This gives you a balanced equation.

$$CaCO_{3(s)} + 2HCl_{(aq)} \longrightarrow CaCl_{2(aq)} + CO_{2(g)} + H_2O_{(l)}$$

Relative Atomic Mass

Atoms are too small for their actual atomic mass to be of much use to us. We therefore use the **relative atomic mass, A_r**. This is a number that compares the mass of one atom to the mass of other atoms.

Each element in the Periodic Table has two numbers. The larger of the two (at the top of the symbol) is the mass number, which also doubles up as the relative atomic mass, A_r.

Example

$$^{65}_{30}\text{Zn}$$ Relative atomic mass of zinc is 65.

$$^{16}_{8}\text{O}$$ Relative atomic mass of oxygen is 16.

Chemicals of the Natural Environment

Extracting Useful Materials

The lithosphere contains many naturally occurring elements and compounds called **minerals**. Ores are rocks that contain varying amounts of minerals from which metals can be extracted.

Sometimes very large amounts of ores need to be mined in order to recover a small percentage of valuable minerals, e.g. copper. The method of extraction depends on the metal's position in the reactivity series.

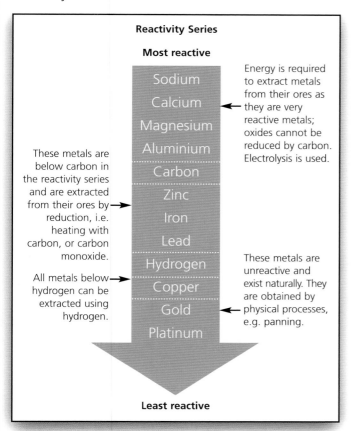

Reactivity Series

Most reactive

Sodium
Calcium
Magnesium
Aluminium
Carbon
Zinc
Iron
Lead
Hydrogen
Copper
Gold
Platinum

Least reactive

Energy is required to extract metals from their ores as they are very reactive metals; oxides cannot be reduced by carbon. Electrolysis is used.

These metals are below carbon in the reactivity series and are extracted from their ores by reduction, i.e. heating with carbon, or carbon monoxide.

All metals below hydrogen can be extracted using hydrogen.

These metals are unreactive and exist naturally. They are obtained by physical processes, e.g. panning.

Example of Extraction by Reduction

Zinc can be extracted from zinc oxide by heating it with carbon. Zinc oxide is reduced because it has lost oxygen. Carbon is oxidised because it has gained oxygen.

$$2ZnO_{(s)} + C_{(s)} = 2Zn_{(s)} + CO_{2(g)}$$

```
       ┌──── Reduction ────┐
Zinc oxide + Carbon ──→ Zinc + Carbon dioxide
       └──── Oxidation ────┘
```

Calculating a Metal's Mass

If you are given its formula, you can calculate the mass of metal that can be extracted from a substance. Follow these steps:

1. Write down the formula.
2. Work out the relative formula mass (see p.71).
3. Work out the percentage mass of metal in the formula.
4. Work out the mass of metal.

Example

Find the mass of Zn that can be extracted from 100g of ZnO.

1. ZnO

2. Relative formula mass = 65 + 16
$$= 81$$

3. Percentage of zinc present
$$= \frac{A_r\ Zn}{M_r\ ZnO} \times 100$$
$$= \frac{65}{81} \times 100 = 80\%$$

4. In 100g of ZnO, there will be $\frac{80}{100} \times 100$
$$= \textbf{80g of Zn}$$

If you were given the equation, you could find the ratio of the mass of the reactant to the mass of the product.

Equation: $2ZnO + C \longrightarrow 2Zn + CO_2$

Relative formula mass:

Work out the M_r of each substance

$$(2 \times 81) + 12 = (2 \times 65) + 44$$
$$162 + 12 = 130 + 44$$
$$174 = 174\ ✔$$

Therefore, 162g of ZnO produces 130g of Zn.

So, 1g of ZnO = $\frac{130}{162}$ = 0.8g of Zn

and 100g of Zn = 0.8 x 100 = 80g of Zn.

Chemicals of the Natural Environment

Metals and the Environment

In order to assess the impact on the environment of extracting and using metals, a life cycle analysis of metal products needs to be carried out. You need to be able to understand and evaluate the sort of data in the table below:

Stage of Life Cycle	Process	Environmental Impact
Manufacture	Mining	• Lots of rock wasted. • Leaves a scar on the landscape. • Air pollution. • Noise pollution.
	Processing	• Pollutants caused by transportation. • Energy usage.
	Extracting the metal	• Electrolysis uses more energy than reduction.
	Manufacturing products	• Energy usage in processing and transportation.
Use	Transport to shops / home	• Pollutants caused by transportation.
	Running product	• Energy usage.
Disposal	Reuse	• No impact.
	Recycle	• Uses a lot less energy than the initial manufacturing.
	Throw away	• Landfill – increase in methane gas.

Extraction by Electrolysis

Electrolysis is the decomposition of an **electrolyte** (solution that conducts electricity) using an electric current. The process is used in industry to extract reactive metals from their ores. Ionic compounds will only conduct electricity when their ions are free to move. This occurs when the compound is either molten or dissolved in solution. During melting of an ionic compound, the electrostatic forces between the charged ions are broken. The crystal lattice is broken down and the ions are free to move.

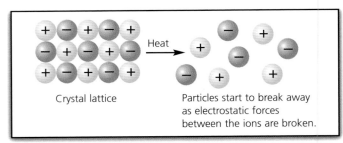

Crystal lattice   Particles start to break away as electrostatic forces between the ions are broken.

Molten lead bromide is a liquid containing positive lead ions and negative bromide ions that are free to move throughout the liquid. When a direct current is passed through the molten salt, the positively charged lead ions are attracted towards the negative electrode. The negatively charged bromide ions are attracted towards the positive electrode.

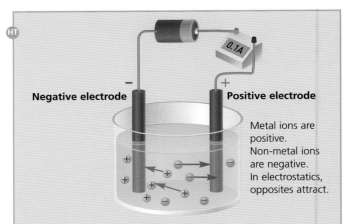

Negative electrode   **Positive electrode**

Metal ions are positive. Non-metal ions are negative. In electrostatics, opposites attract.

When the ions get to the oppositely charged electrode they are **discharged**, (i.e. they lose their charge).

- The bromide ion loses electrons to the positive electrode to form a bromine atom. The bromine atom then bonds with a second atom to form a bromine molecule.
  $2Br^- = Br_2 + 2e^-$
- The lead ions gain electrons from the negative electrode to form a lead atom.
  $Pb_2+ +2e^- = Pb$

This process completes the circuit as the electrons are exchanged at the electrodes.

Chemicals of the Natural Environment

Extracting Aluminium by Electrolysis

Aluminium must be obtained from its ore by electrolysis because it is too reactive to be extracted by heating with carbon. (Look at its position in the Reactivity Series, see p.45.)

The steps in the process are as follows:

1. Aluminium ore (bauxite) is purified to leave aluminium oxide.
2. Aluminium oxide is mixed with cryolite (a compound of aluminium) to lower its melting point.
3. The mixture of aluminium oxide and cryolite is melted so that the ions can move.
4. When a current passes through the molten mixture, positively charged aluminium ions move towards the negative electrode (the cathode), and aluminium is formed. Negatively charged oxide ions move towards the positive electrode (the anode), and oxygen is formed.
5. This causes the positive electrodes to burn away quickly. They frequently have to be replaced.

Electrolysis of bauxite to obtain aluminium is quite an expensive process because of the cost of the large amounts of electrical energy needed to carry it out. The equation for this reaction is...

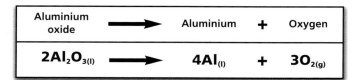

Aluminium oxide	$\longrightarrow$	Aluminium	+	Oxygen
$2Al_2O_{3(l)}$	$\longrightarrow$	$4Al_{(l)}$	+	$3O_{2(g)}$

HT The reactions at the electrodes can be written as half equations. This means that we write separate equations for what is happening at each of the electrodes during electrolysis.

At the cathode...

$$Al^{3+}_{(l)} + 3e^- \xrightarrow{\text{Reduction}} Al_{(l)}$$

At the anode...

$$2O^{2-}_{(l)} - 4e^- \xrightarrow{\text{Oxidation}} O_{2(g)}$$

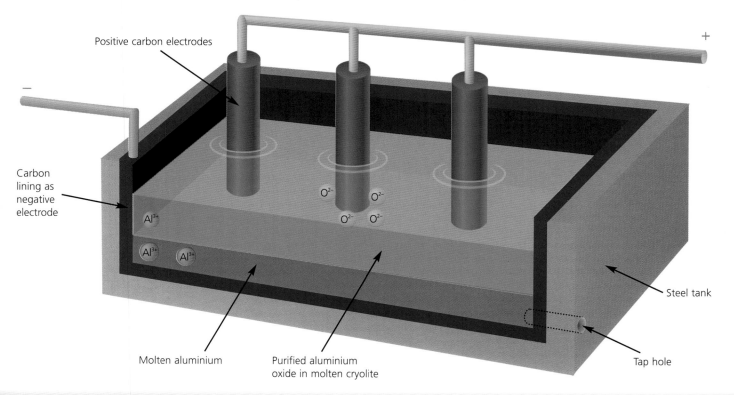

Electrolysis of Bauxite (Aluminium Oxide)

Positive carbon electrodes

Carbon lining as negative electrode

Al^{3+} Al^{3+} Al^{3+}

O^{2-} O^{2-} O^{2-} O^{2-}

Steel tank

Molten aluminium

Purified aluminium oxide in molten cryolite

Tap hole

Chemicals of the Natural Environment

Properties of Metals

Generally, metals are strong and malleable, have high melting points and can conduct electricity. Their properties determine how each particular metal can be used. For example…

Metal	Property	Use
Titanium	• Very strong • Lightweight • Resistant to corrosion	• Replacement hip joints • Bicycles • Submarines
Aluminium	• Malleable • Lightweight • Resistant to corrosion	• Drink cans • Window frames
Iron	• High melting point • Strong	• Saucepans • Cars
Copper	• Conducts electricity • Conducts heat	• Cables, e.g. kettle cable • Electromagnets • Electrical switches

HT In a metal crystal the positively charged metal ions are held closely together by a 'sea' of electrons that are free to move.

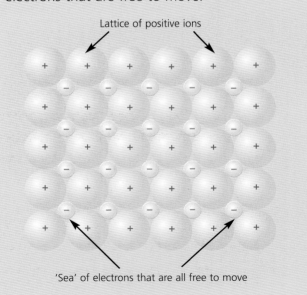

Lattice of positive ions

'Sea' of electrons that are all free to move

The properties of a metal can be explained by its structure. The force of attraction that keeps the structure together is known as the **metallic bond**. The metallic bond can be used to explain the properties of metals.

Structure	Property and Explanation
The ions are arranged in a lattice form	**Very strong** Metal ions are closely packed in a lattice structure.
Force applied Rows of ions slide over each other. Result: The metal is 'bendy' and can be dented	**Malleable** External forces cause layers of metal ions to move by sliding over other layers.
	High melting point A lot of energy is needed to break the strong force of attraction between the metal ions and the sea of electrons.
Moving electrons can carry the electric charge (or thermal energy)	**Conducts electricity** Electrons are free to move throughout the structure. When an electrical force is applied the electrons move along the metal in one direction.

Module P5

When electrical charges move, they create a current. Different types of current have different uses. This module looks at…

- static electricity
- electric currents
- electromagnetic induction
- electrical generators
- the use of transformers.

Static Electricity

Some insulating materials can become electrically charged when they are rubbed against each other. The electrical charge (static) then stays on the material, i.e. it does not move.

Static builds up when electrons (which have a negative charge) are 'rubbed off' one material onto another. The material receiving the electrons becomes negatively charged and the one giving up electrons becomes positively charged.

If a Perspex rod is rubbed with a cloth, the rod loses electrons to become positively charged. The cloth gains electrons to become negatively charged.

If an ebonite rod is rubbed with fur, the ebonite gains electrons to become negatively charged. The fur loses electrons to become positively charged.

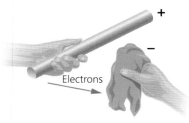

Perspex rod rubbed with cloth

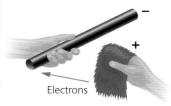

Ebonite rod rubbed with fur

Repulsion and Attraction

When two charged materials are brought together, they exert a force on each other so they are attracted or repelled. Two materials with the same type of charge repel each other; two materials with different charges attract each other.

If a positively charged Perspex rod is moved near to another positively charged Perspex rod suspended on a string, the suspended rod will be repelled. We would get the same result with two positively charged ebonite rods.

If a negatively charged ebonite rod is moved near to a positively charged suspended Perspex rod, the suspended Perspex rod will be attracted. We would get the same result if the rods were the other way round.

Example

When cars are spray painted, a panel of the car is positively charged and the paint is negatively charged. The paint particles repel each other, but are attracted to the positively charged panel. This causes the paint to be applied evenly.

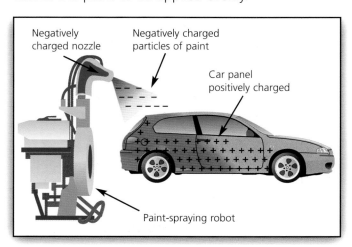

Negatively charged nozzle

Negatively charged particles of paint

Car panel positively charged

Paint-spraying robot

Electric Circuits

Electric Circuits

An **electric current** is a **flow of charge**. It is measured in **amperes** (amps).

In an electric circuit the components and wires are full of charges that are free to move. When a circuit is made, the battery causes these charges to move in a continuous loop. The charges are not used up.

In metal **conductors** there are lots of charges free to move. **Insulators**, on the other hand, have few charges that are free to move. Remember, metals contain free electrons in their structure (see p.48). The movement of these electrons creates the flow of charge (electric current).

Direction of current

Circuit Symbols

You need to know the following standard symbols used to represent components in circuits:

Cell	⊣⊢
Power supply (battery)	⊣⊢--⊣⊢
Filament lamp	—⊗—
Switch (open)	—∘ ∘—
Switch (closed)	—∘—∘—
Light dependent resistor (LDR)	
Fixed resistor	—▭—
Variable resistor	
Thermistor	
Voltmeter	—Ⓥ—
Ammeter	—Ⓐ—

Currents

A **direct current** (d.c) always flows in the same direction. Cells and batteries supply direct current.

An **alternating current** (a.c.) changes the direction of flow back and forth continuously. An alternating current is used for **mains electricity.** The mains supply has a voltage of 230 volts.

> **HT** Alternating current is used for our mains supply because it is easier to generate than direct current and can be distributed more efficiently.

Current Size

The amount of current flowing in a circuit depends on the resistance of the components in the circuit and the **potential difference** (p.d) across them. Potential difference tells us the energy given to the charge and is another name for **voltage**. It is a measure of the 'push' of the battery on the charges in the circuit.

For example, a 12 volt battery will transfer 12 joules of energy to every unit of charge. A potential difference of 3 volts across a bulb means that the bulb is taking 3 joules of energy from every unit of charge; this energy is given off as heat and light.

The Potential Difference Across the Component
The greater the potential difference (or voltage) across a component, the greater the current that flows through the component. Two cells together provide a bigger potential difference across a lamp than one cell. This makes a bigger current flow.

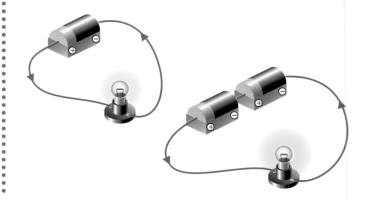

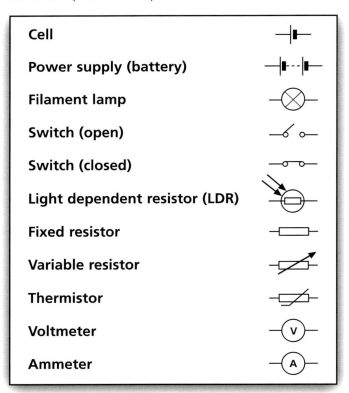

Resistance and Current

Components such as resistors, lamps and motors resist the **flow** of **charge** through them, i.e. they have **resistance**.

The greater the resistance of a component or components, the smaller the current that flows for a particular voltage, or the greater the voltage needed to maintain a particular current.

Even the connecting wires in the circuit have some resistance but it is such a small amount that it is usually ignored.

Two lamps together in a circuit with one cell have a certain resistance. Including another cell in the circuit provides a greater potential difference so a larger current flows.

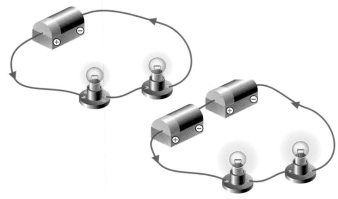

Adding resistors in series increases the resistance because the battery has to push charges through all of the resistors.

Adding resistors in parallel reduces the total resistance and increases the total current because this provides more paths for the charges to flow along.

When an electric current flows through a component it causes the component to heat up. In a filament lamp this heating effect is large enough to make the filament in the lamp glow.

HT As the current flows, the moving charges collide with the stationary atoms in the wire giving them energy; this increase in energy causes the component to become hot.

Resistance, which is measured in ohms, Ω, is a measure of how hard it is to get a current though a component at a particular potential difference or voltage. Resistance can be calculated by the following formula:

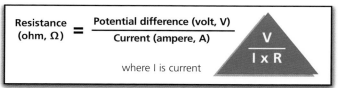

Example

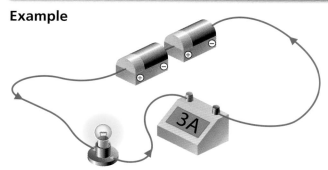

The circuit above has a current of 3 amps and a potential difference of 6V. What is the resistance?

$$\text{Resistance} = \frac{\text{Potential difference}}{\text{Current}} = \frac{6V}{3A} = 2\Omega$$

HT The resistance formula can be rearranged using the formula triangle to work out the voltage or current.

Example
Calculate the reading on the voltmeter in this circuit if the bulb has a resistance of 15 ohms.

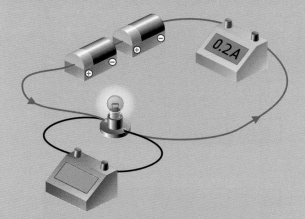

Rearranging the formula...
Potential difference = Current x Resistance
$$= 0.2A \times 15\Omega = 3V$$

Electric Circuits

Current–Potential Difference Graphs

As long as the temperature of a resistor stays constant, the current through the resistor is directly proportional to the voltage across the resistor, regardless of which direction the current is flowing, i.e. if one doubles, the other also doubles.

This means that a graph showing current through the component and voltage across the component will be a straight line through 0. (If there is no voltage, then there is nothing to push the current around.)

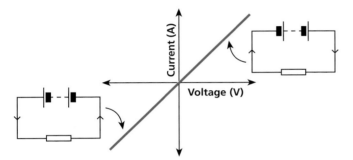

Thermistors and Light Dependent Resistors (LDRs)

The resistance of some materials depends on environmental conditions.

The resistance of a **thermistor** depends on its temperature. Its resistance decreases as the temperature increases; this allows more current to flow.

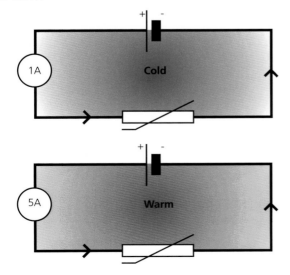

The resistance of a **light dependent resistor (LDR)** depends on light intensity. Its resistance decreases as the amount of light falling on it increases; this allows more current to flow.

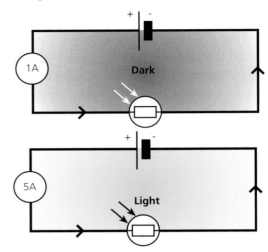

Potential Difference and Current

The potential difference across a component in a circuit is measured in volts (V) using a voltmeter connected in parallel across the component.

The current flowing through a component in a circuit is measured in amperes (A), using an ammeter connected in series.

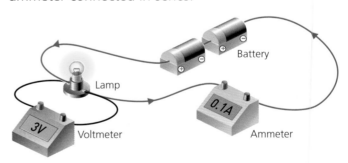

When batteries are added in series, the total potential difference is the sum of all the individual potential differences.

> **HT** When batteries are added in parallel, the total potential difference and current through the circuit remains the same, but each battery supplies less current.
>
> This sharing of the load makes the batteries last longer.

Series and Parallel Circuits

Components in Series

In a series circuit all components are connected one after another in one loop going from one terminal of the battery to the other.

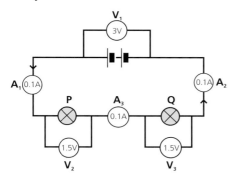

- The current flowing through each component is the same, i.e. $A_1 = A_2 = A_3$.
- The potential difference across the components adds up to the potential difference across the battery, i.e. $V_1 = V_2 + V_3$.

> **HT** The total energy transferred to each unit charge by the battery must equal the total amount of energy transferred from the charge by the component because energy cannot come from nowhere and it cannot disappear.

- If another battery was added to the above circuit, it would have the effect of increasing the voltage and current.
- The potential difference is largest across components with the greatest resistance.

> **HT** More energy is transferred from the charge flowing through a greater resistance because it takes more energy to push the current through the resistor.
>
> If a circuit has two identical components, they will have the same potential difference across them. If the components are different, the one with the greatest resistance will have the greatest potential difference across it, and vice versa.

Components Connected in Parallel

Components connected in parallel are connected separately in their own loop going from one terminal of the battery to the other.

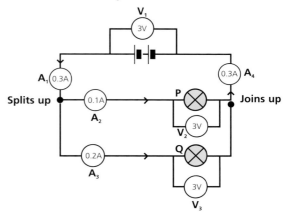

- The amount of current which passes through each component depends on the resistance of each component. The greater the resistance, the smaller the current. In the circuit above, bulb Q has half the resistance of bulb P so twice as much current flows through it.
- The total current running from (and back to) the battery is equal to the sum of the current through each of the parallel components, i.e. $A_1 = A_2 + A_3 = A_4$. In the circuit above, 0.3A = 0.1A + 0.2A = 0.3A.
- The current is smallest through the component with the largest resistance.

> **HT** The same voltage causes more current to flow through a smaller resistance than a bigger one.
>
> The potential difference across each component is equal to the potential difference of the battery.
>
> The current through each component is the same as if it was the only component present. For example, a circuit with a battery and a bulb has a 1 amp current. If a second identical component is added in parallel, the current through each would be 1 amp. The total current through the battery will increase.

Electric Circuits

Electromagnetic Induction

In electromagnetic induction, **movement produces current**. If a wire or a coil of wire cuts through the lines of force of a magnetic field (or vice versa) then a voltage is induced (produced) between the ends of the wire. If the wire is part of a complete circuit, a current will be induced.

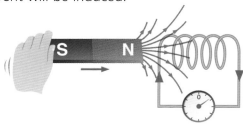

Moving the magnet into the coil induces a current in one direction. A current can be induced in the opposite direction by...

- moving the magnet out of the coil

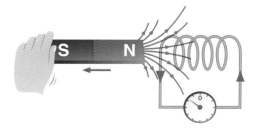

- moving the other pole of the magnet into the coil.

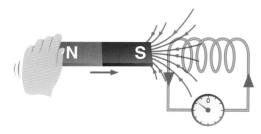

Both of these involve a magnetic field being cut by a coil of wire, creating an induced voltage. If there is no movement of the magnet or coil there is no induced current, because the magnetic field is not being cut.

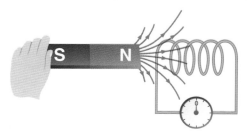

The Electric Generator

Mains electricity is produced by generators. Generators use the principle of electromagnetic induction to generate electricity by rotating a magnet inside a coil.

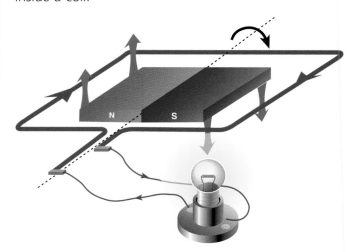

The size of the induced voltage follows the same rules as with the magnet and coil. The voltage will be increased by...

- increasing the speed of rotation of the magnet
- increasing the strength of the magnetic field
- increasing the number of turns on the coil
- placing an iron core inside the coil.

HT The voltage induced in the coil by the rotating magnetic field is cut as the stationary wire changes direction and size, as seen below.

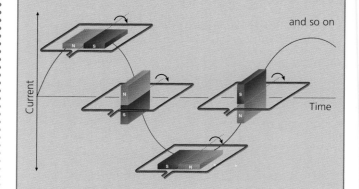

The induced current reverses its direction of flow every half turn of the magnet and is therefore alternating current (see p.50).

Power

When charge flows through a component, energy is transferred to the component. Power, measured in watts (W), is a measure of how much energy is transferred every second, i.e. **the rate of energy transfer.**

Power can be calculated using the following equation.

| Power (watt, W) | = | Potential difference (volt, V) | X | Current (ampere, A) | $\dfrac{P}{V \times I}$ |

where I is the current

Example

An electric motor works at a current of 3A and a potential difference of 24V. What is the power of the motor?

Power = Potential Difference x Current
= 24V x 3A
= 72W

The power formula can be rearranged using the formula triangle to work out the potential difference or current.

Example

A 4W light bulb works at a current of 2A. What is the potential difference?

$$\text{Potential difference} = \frac{\text{Power}}{\text{Current}}$$

$$= \frac{4W}{2A}$$

= 2V

Transformers

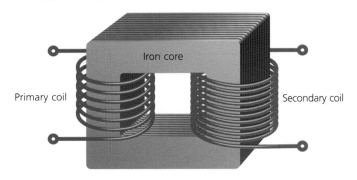

Iron core

Primary coil

Secondary coil

Transformers are used to change the voltage of an alternating current. They consist of two coils, called the **primary** and **secondary** coils, wrapped around a soft iron core.

When two coils of wire are close to each other, a changing magnetic field in one coil can induce a voltage in the other. Alternating current flowing through the primary coil creates an alternating magnetic field. This changing field then induces an alternating current in the secondary coil.

HT The amount by which a transformer changes the voltage depends on the number of turns on the primary and secondary coils. If the number of turns on each coil is the same, the voltage does not change. If there are more turns on the secondary coil, the voltage goes up; if there are fewer turns the voltage goes down.

You need to be able to use this equation.

| $\dfrac{\text{Voltage on primary coil } (V_p)}{\text{Voltage on secondary coil } (V_s)}$ | = | $\dfrac{\text{Number of turns on primary coil, } N_p}{\text{Number of turns on secondary coil, } N_s}$ |

Example

A transformer has 1000 turns on the primary coil and 200 turns on the secondary coil.

If a voltage of 250V is applied to the primary coil, what is the voltage across the secondary coil?

Using our formula... $\dfrac{V_p}{V_s} = \dfrac{N_p}{N_s}$

$$\frac{250}{V_s} = \frac{1000}{200}$$

$$250 = 5V_s$$

$$V_s = \frac{250}{5}$$

$$V_s = \textbf{50V}$$

Electric Circuits

Energy

Energy is measured is joules (J). A joule is a very small amount of energy so a domestic electricity meter measures the energy transfer in a much larger unit, the kilowatt hour (kWh).

The amount of energy transferred for either joules or kilowatt hours can be calculated by the following equation:

Energy transferred (joule, J)	=	Power (watt, W)	X	Time (second, s)
Energy transferred (kilowatt hour, kWh)	=	Power (kilowatt, kW)	X	Time (hour, h)

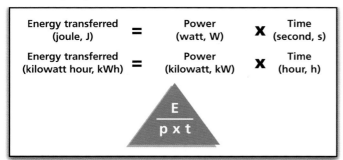

$$\frac{E}{p \times t}$$

Examples

1. A 30W light bulb is switched on for 45 seconds. What is the energy transferred in joules?

   Energy transferred = Power x Time

   = 30W x 45s

   = **1350J**

2. A 2000W electric hot plate is switched on for 90 minutes. What is the energy transferred in kilowatt hours?

   Energy transferred = 2kW x 1.5h ← *power in kW and time in hours*

   = **3kWh**

HT The energy transfer formula can be rearranged using the formula triangle to work out power or time.

Example

A hairdryer is switched on for 6 minutes and the total energy transferred is 0.2kWh. What is the power rating of the hairdryer?

$$\text{Power} = \frac{\text{Energy transferred}}{\text{Time}} = \frac{0.2\text{kWh}}{0.1\text{h}} = \mathbf{2kW}$$

Cost of Electricity

The cost of the electrical energy used can be calculated if the power, time and cost per kilowatt hour are known.

The formula for cost of energy is as follows:

Total cost	=	Number of units (kWh)	X	Cost per unit

Example

A 2000W electric fire is switched on for 30 minutes. How much does it cost if electricity is 8p per unit (kWh)?

Energy transferred = 2kW x 0.5h

= 1kWh (or 1 unit)

Cost = 1kWh x 8p

= **8 pence**

Efficiency of Appliances

The greater the proportion of energy that is usefully transferred, the more efficient we say an appliance is. Efficiency can be calculated using the following formula:

$$\text{Efficiency (\%)} = \frac{\text{Energy usefully transferred}}{\text{Total energy supplied}} \ X \ 100$$

Examples

Electrical Appliance	Energy In	Useful Energy Out	Efficiency
Light bulb	100 joules/sec	Light: 20 joules/sec	$\frac{20}{100}$ x 100% = **20%**
Kettle	2000 joules/sec	Heat (in water): 1800 joules/sec	$\frac{1800}{2000}$ x 100% = **90%**
Electric motor	500 joules/sec	Kinetic: 300 joules/sec	$\frac{300}{500}$ x 100% = **60%**
Television	200 joules/sec	Light: 20 joules/sec Sound: 30 joules/sec	$\frac{50}{200}$ x 100% = **25%**

Brain and Mind

Module B6

How the human brain functions remains largely unknown. Neuroscience (the study of the nervous system, including the brain) is an area at the forefront of medical research, as developments and discoveries in this field have a huge potential impact for society. This module looks at...

- how organisms respond to changes in their environment
- how information is passed through the nervous system
- what reflex actions are
- how humans develop more complex behaviour
- what we know about the way in which the brain coordinates our senses
- how drugs affect our nervous system
- stem cells, and their role in treating disease.

Changes in Environment

Most living organisms can detect and respond to **stimuli**, i.e. changes, in their environment.

Animals respond to stimuli in order to keep themselves in conditions that will ensure their survival. These responses are coordinated by the **central nervous system (CNS)**.

The pathway for receiving information and then acting upon it is...

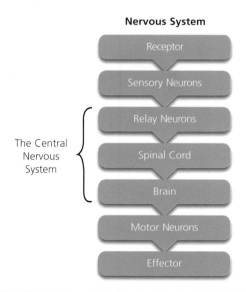

Nervous System

Receptor → Sensory Neurons → Relay Neurons → Spinal Cord → Brain → Motor Neurons → Effector

The Central Nervous System: Relay Neurons, Spinal Cord, Brain

The Central Nervous System

The central nervous system allows organisms to react to their surroundings and coordinates their responses.

Remember, the central nervous system (brain and spinal cord) is connected to the body via sensory and motor neurons, which make the **peripheral nervous system** (**PNS**).

The peripheral nervous system is the second major division of the nervous system.

Its sensory and motor neurons transmit messages all over the body, for example, to the limbs and organs.

They also transmit messages to and from the central nervous system.

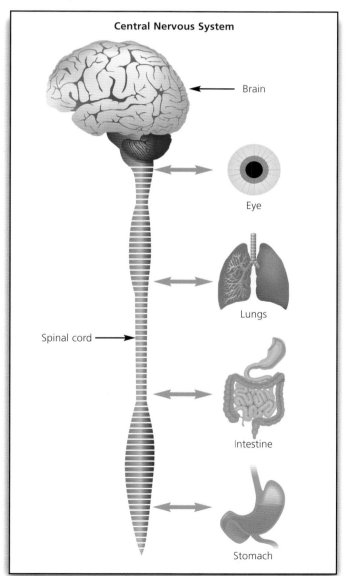

Central Nervous System

- Brain
- Eye
- Lungs
- Spinal cord
- Intestine
- Stomach

Brain and Mind

Sensory neurons carry nervous impulses (electrical signals) from receptors to the CNS.

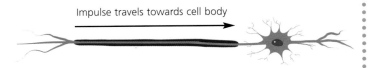

Impulse travels towards cell body

Motor neurons carry impulses from the CNS to effectors.

Impulse travels away from cell body

Types of Receptor

- **Light** – receptors in the eyes.
- **Sound** – receptors in the ears.
- **Change of position** – receptors in the ears (balance).
- **Taste** – receptors on the tongue.
- **Smell** – receptors in the nose.
- **Touch, pressure and temperature** – receptors in the skin.

Receptors and Effectors

Receptors and effectors can form part of complex organs:

1 **Muscle cells in muscle tissue**

The specialised cells that make up muscle tissues are effectors. Impulses travel along motor neurons and terminate at the muscle cells. These impulses cause the muscle cells to contract.

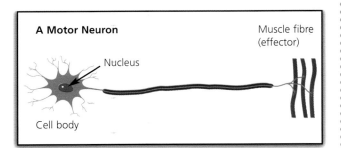

A Motor Neuron

Muscle fibre (effector)

Nucleus

Cell body

2 **Light receptors in the retina of the eye**

The eye is a complex sense organ. The lens focuses light onto receptor cells in the retina which are sensitive to light. The receptor cells are then stimulated and send impulses along sensory neurons to the brain.

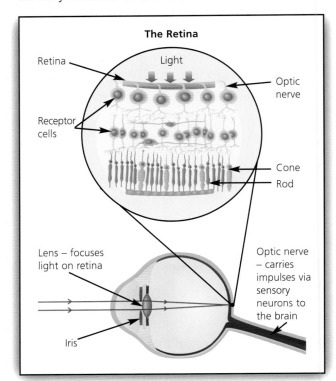

The Retina

Retina

Light

Optic nerve

Receptor cells

Cone

Rod

Lens – focuses light on retina

Optic nerve – carries impulses via sensory neurons to the brain

Iris

3 **Hormone-secreting cells in a gland**

The hormone-secreting cells in glands are effectors. They are activated by an impulse, which travels along a motor neuron from the CNS and terminates at the gland. The impulse triggers the release of the hormone into the bloodstream, which transports it to the site where it is required.

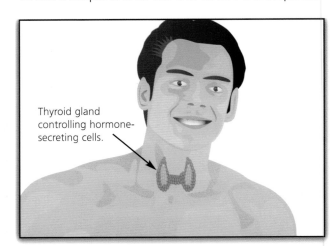

Thyroid gland controlling hormone-secreting cells.

Neurons

Neurons are specially adapted cells that can carry an **electrical signal** when stimulated, e.g. a **nerve impulse**. They are **elongated** (lengthened) to make connections from one part of the body to another. They have **branched endings** which allow a single neuron to act on many other neurons or effectors, e.g. muscle fibres.

In **motor neurons** the cytoplasm forms a long fibre surrounded by a cell membrane called an **axon**.

Some axons are surrounded by a fatty sheath, which insulates the neuron from neighbouring cells (a bit like the plastic coating on an electrical wire) and increases the speed at which the nerve impulse is transmitted.

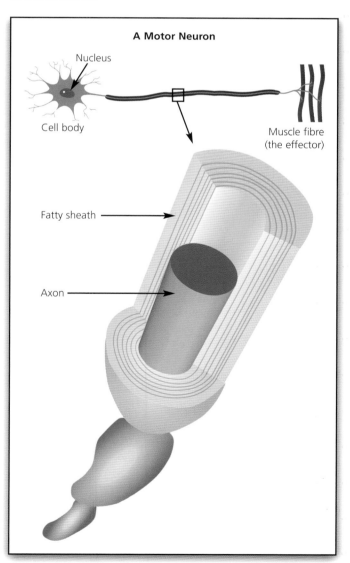

A Motor Neuron

Nucleus

Cell body

Muscle fibre (the effector)

Fatty sheath

Axon

Synapses

Synapses are the gaps between adjacent neurons. They allow the brain to form interconnected neural circuits. The human brain contains a huge number of synapses. There are approximately 1000 trillion in a young child. This number decreases with age, stabilising by adulthood. The estimated number of synapses for an adult human varies between 100 and 500 trillion.

HT When an impulse reaches the end of a sensory neuron, it triggers the release of chemicals, called neurotransmitters, into the synapse. They diffuse across the synapse and bind with receptor molecules on the membrane of a motor neuron.

The receptor molecules bind with certain chemicals to initiate a nerve impulse in the motor neuron so the signal can continue on its way. Meanwhile, the neurotransmitter is reabsorbed back into the sensory neuron, to be used again.

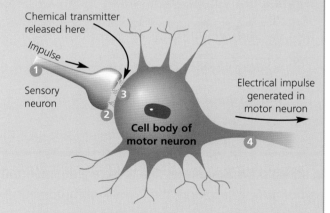

Chemical transmitter released here

Impulse

1

Sensory neuron

3

2

Cell body of motor neuron

Electrical impulse generated in motor neuron

4

The sequence is as follows.
1. Electrical signal (nerve impulse) moves through sensory neuron.
2. Chemicals (neurotransmitters) are released into synapse.
3. Neurotransmitters bind with receptors on motor neuron.
4. Electrical signal (nerve impulse) is sent through motor neuron.

Brain and Mind

Reflex Actions

When certain receptors are stimulated they cause a very fast, involuntarily (automatic) response.

These simple reflexes involve both sensory and motor neurons. The basic pathway for a simple reflex arc is shown below:

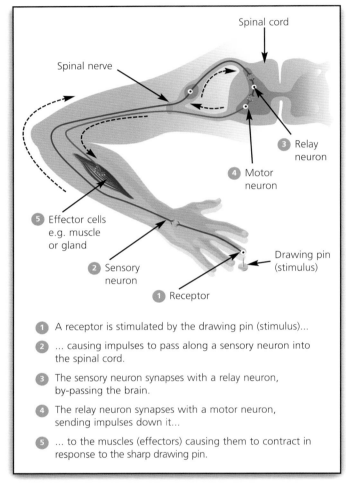

1. A receptor is stimulated by the drawing pin (stimulus)...

2. ... causing impulses to pass along a sensory neuron into the spinal cord.

3. The sensory neuron synapses with a relay neuron, by-passing the brain.

4. The relay neuron synapses with a motor neuron, sending impulses down it...

5. ... to the muscles (effectors) causing them to contract in response to the sharp drawing pin.

In animals, simple reflexes like these are an important part of self-preservation; the animal will automatically respond to a stimulus in a way that helps it to survive, for example, by finding food, sheltering from predators, finding a mate or avoiding injury.

A majority of the behaviour displayed by simple animals, e.g. insects, is the result of reflex actions. For example, a woodlouse responds to changes in light and humidity by automatically moving towards damp, dark places. The disadvantage of this type of behaviour is that the animals have difficulty responding to new situations.

Simple Reflexes in Humans

Newborn babies exhibit a range of simple reflexes for a short time after birth. The absence of these reflexes, or their failure to disappear, might indicate that the nervous system is not developing properly.

- **Stepping reflex** – when held under its arms in an upright position with feet on a firm surface, a baby makes walking movements with legs.
- **Startle (or moro) reflex** – baby shoots out arms and legs when startled, e.g. by a loud noise.
- **Grasping reflex** – baby tightly grasps a finger that is placed in its hand.
- **Rooting reflex** – baby turns head and opens mouth ready to feed when its cheek is stroked.
- **Sucking reflex** – baby sucks on a finger (or mother's nipple) that is put in its mouth.

Adults also display a range of simple reflexes. For example, the pupil reflex in the eye stops bright light from damaging the very sensitive cells that line the retina.

The iris of an eye consists of muscle tissue and, by contracting various muscle fibres, it can control the size of the pupil and, therefore, the amount of light entering the eye.

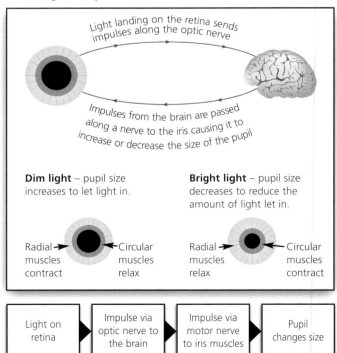

Conditioned Reflexes

Although they are not conscious actions, reflex responses to a new stimulus can be learnt. Through a process called conditioning, the body learns to produce a specific reflex response when a certain stimulus is detected. Conditioning works by building an association between the new stimulus (the **secondary stimulus**) and the stimulus that naturally triggers the response (the **primary stimulus**). This resulting reflex is called a **conditioned reflex action**.

This effect was discovered at the beginning of the 20th century by a Russian Scientist named Pavlov, who received the Nobel prize for his work.

Pavlov observed that whenever a dog sees and smells a piece of meat, it starts to salivate (produce saliva). In his experiment, a bell was rung repeatedly whenever meat was shown and given to the dog. Eventually, simply ringing the bell, without any meat present, caused the dog to salivate. This classic experiment is known as Pavlov's dog experiment.

In a conditioned reflex the final response has no direct connection to the stimulus.

For example, the ringing bell in Pavlov's experiment is a stimulus that has *nothing* to do with feeding; it is just a sound. However, the association between the sound of the bell and meat is strong enough to induce the dog to salivate.

Some conditioned reflexes can increase a species' chance of survival:

Example

The caterpillar of the cinnabar moth is black and orange in colour, to warn predators that it is poisonous. After eating a few cinnabar caterpillars, a bird will start to associate these colours with a very unpleasant taste and avoid eating anything that is black and orange in colour.

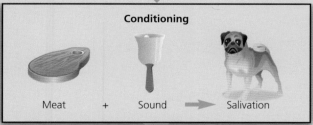

Simple Reflex

Meat → Salivation

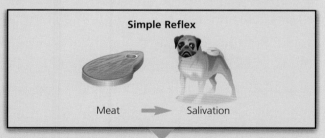

Conditioning

Meat + Sound → Salivation

Conditioned Response

Sound → Salivation

In some situations the brain can override or modify a reflex action.

For example, when the hand comes into contact with something that is hot, the body's natural reflex response is to pull away or drop the object.

However, you might know an object is hot but still want to pick it up, e.g. a hot potato or a dinner plate. To allow you to do this, the brain sends a signal, via a neuron, to the motor neuron in the reflex arc, modifying the reflex so that you do not drop the potato or plate.

Brain and Mind

Complex Behaviour

Mammals have a **complex brain** which contains billions of neurons (nerve cells). This allows them to learn from experience, including how to respond to different situations (social behaviour).

Rabbits learn quite quickly that eating stinging nettles is painful; dogs can be trained to respond to instructions or to hunt for explosives; horses or cattle that are reared alone will often be vicious fighters when mixed with other animals – they adapt to being alone rather than part of a herd. All these aspects of behaviour are due to the ability of the brain to adapt and respond.

In mammals, **neuron pathways** are formed in the brain during development. The way in which the animal interacts with its environment determines what pathways are formed.

During the first few years after birth, the brain grows extremely rapidly. As each neuron matures, it sends out multiple branches, increasing the number of synapses (junctions between neurons).

At birth, in humans, the cerebral cortex (see p.63) has approximately 2 500 synapses per neuron. By the time an infant is two or three years old, the number of synapses is approximately 15 000 synapses per neuron.

Each time an individual has a new experience, a different pathway between neurons is stimulated. Every time the experience is repeated after that, the pathway is strengthened. Pathways which are not used regularly are eventually deleted. Only the pathways that are activated most frequently are preserved.

These modifications mean that certain pathways of the brain become more likely to transmit impulses than others and the individual will become better at a given task. This is why some skills may be learnt through repetition. For example, riding a bicycle, revising for an exam, learning to ski or playing a musical instrument.

The average adult brain has approximately half the amount of synapses of an infant brain.

The brain's ability to reorganise neural pathways in this way throughout its lifetime is called **plasticity**.

A PET scan (an imaging technique which produces 3-D images) shows neuron activity in parts of the brain in response to learning words through speaking, hearing and seeing them. The areas which are stimulated the most will develop a greater number of synapses between neurons.

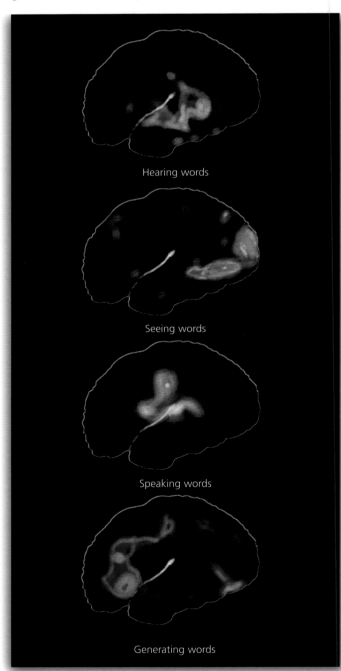

Hearing words

Seeing words

Speaking words

Generating words

Feral Children

If neural pathways are not used then they are destroyed. There is evidence to suggest that because of this, if a new skill, e.g. language, has not been learnt by a particular stage in development, an animal or child might not be able to learn it in the same way as normal.

One example of evidence showing this comes from the study of so-called 'feral children' (feral means wild).

Feral children are children who have been isolated from society in some way, so they do not go through the normal development process. This can be deliberate (e.g. inhumanely keeping a child in isolation in a cellar or locked room) or it can be accidental (e.g. through being shipwrecked).

In the absence of any other humans, the children do not ever gain the ability to talk (or may lose any ability already gained) other than to make rudimentary grunting noises. Learning a language later in development is a much harder and slower process.

Child Development

After children are born there are a series of developmental milestones which can be checked to see if development is following normal patterns.

If they are missing or late it could mean that there are neurological problems, or it could mean that the child is lacking stimulation (is not being exposed to the necessary experiences). For example, at three months, babies should be able to lift their heads when held to someone's shoulder, or grasp a rattle when it is given to them.

By 12 months, babies should be able to hold a cup and drink from it, and walk when one of their hands is held.

Adapting

The variety of potential pathways in the brain makes it possible for animals to adapt to new situations. For example, dogs can be trained to follow spoken commands and even sniff out drugs and explosives.

Marine animals in captivity such as dolphins and killer whales can be trained to collect food from a person's hand or to push underwater buttons that will release food.

Coordination of Senses

The cerebral cortex is the part of the human brain that is most concerned with intelligence, memory, language and consciousness.

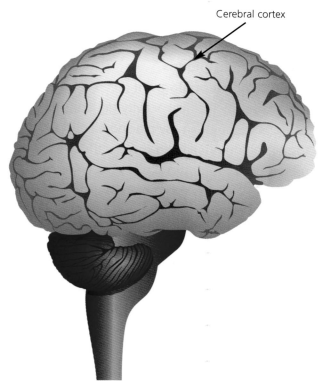

Cerebral cortex

Brain and Mind

Mapping the Cortex

Scientists have used a variety of methods to map the different regions of the cerebral cortex:

- **Physiological Techniques**
  Damage to different parts of the brain can produce different problems, e.g. long-term memory loss, short-term memory loss, paralysis in one or more parts of the body, speech loss, etc. Therefore, studying the effects of accidents or illnesses on the brain has led to an understanding of which parts of the brain control different functions:

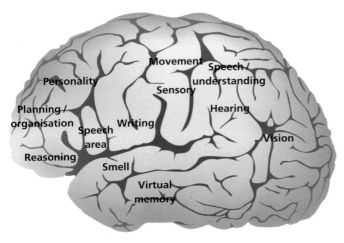

N.B. You do not need to learn the different parts of the brain.

- **Electronic Techniques**
  An **electroencephalogram** (EEG) is a visual record of the electrical activity generated by neurons in the brain. By placing electrodes on the scalp and amplifying the electrical signals picked up through the skull, a trace can be produced showing the rise and fall of electrical potentials called brain waves.

  By stimulating the patient's receptors (e.g. by flashing lights or making sounds), the parts of the brain which respond can be mapped.

  Magnetic Resonance Imaging (MRI) scanning is a relatively new technique that can be used to produce images of different cross-sections of the brain. The computer-generated picture uses colour to represent different levels of electrical activity. The activity in the brain changes depending on what the person is doing or thinking.

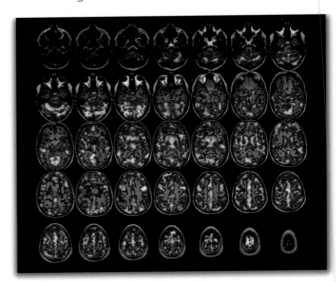

Memory

Memory is the ability to store and retrieve information. Scientists have produced models to try to explain how the brain facilitates this but, so far, none have been able to provide an adequate explanation.

Verbal memory (words and labels) can be divided into **short-term memory** and **long-term memory**. Short-term memory is capable of storing a limited amount of information for a limited amount of time (roughly 15–30 seconds). Long-term memory can store a seemingly unlimited amount of information indefinitely.

When using short-term memory, it is believed that up to 7 (+/-2) separate pieces of information can be stored (e.g. a number with seven digits like 6421978). This capacity can be increased by dividing information into small chunks, e.g. (213) (645) (978) could be stored as 3 out of the possible 7 units of storage.

Long-term memory is where information is stored in the brain through repetition, which strengthens and builds up the neuron pathway.

More on Memory

Humans are more likely to remember information when…

- it is repeated (especially over an extended period of time), e.g. going over key points several times as a method of revising for exams
- there is a strong stimulus associated with it, including colour, light, smell or sound (the more senses involved the better)
- there is a pattern to it (or if a pattern can be artificially imposed on it). For example, people find remembering the order of the planets difficult, so a sentence where there is a logical relationship between the words (unlike the names of the planets themselves) can be remembered as a prompt instead: **m**y **v**ery **e**asy **m**ethod **j**ust **s**peeds **u**p **n**aming **p**lanets – **M**ercury, **V**enus, **E**arth, **M**ars, **J**upiter, **S**aturn, **U**ranus, **N**eptune and **P**luto. This is called a mnemonic and is an example of an artificially imposed pattern.

Drugs and the Nervous System

Many drugs cause changes in the speed at which nerve impulses travel to the brain, speeding them up or slowing them down. False signals are sometimes sent.

Drugs and toxins (poisons) can prevent impulses from travelling across synapses, or they can cause the nervous system to become overloaded with too many impulses.

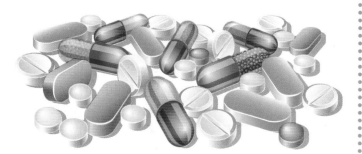

For example, alcohol has a direct effect on chemical transmitters in the brain. The more alcohol that is consumed, the slower the chemical signals are sent, and so coordination and reaction times decrease. Caffeine, in low doses, causes nerve impulses to be sent faster and therefore increases reaction times.

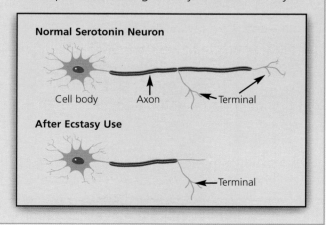

HT **Serotonin** is a chemical transmitter (neurotransmitter) used in the central nervous system. It is associated with feeling happy. The drug Ecstasy (MDMA) blocks the sites in the brain's synapses where the chemical serotonin is removed. As a result, serotonin concentrations in the brain increase and the user experiences feelings of elation. However, the neurons are harmed in this process and a long-term consequence of taking Ecstasy can be memory loss.

Normal Serotonin Neuron

Cell body   Axon   Terminal

After Ecstasy Use

Terminal

Chemical Synthesis

Module C6

Chemical synthesis provides the chemicals needed for food processing, health care, and many other products. This module looks at...

* chemicals, and why we need them
* relative formula mass
* calculating the mass of products and reactants
* how titrations are used
* measuring the rate of a reaction.

Chemicals

Chemicals are all around us and we depend on them daily. **Chemical synthesis** is the process by which raw materials are made into useful products such as...

* food additives
* fertilizers
* dyestuffs
* pigments
* pharmaceuticals
* cosmetics
* paints.

The chemical industry makes **bulk chemicals** such as sulfuric acid and ammonia on a very large scale (millions of tonnes per year). **Fine chemicals** such as drugs and pesticides are made on a much smaller scale.

The range of chemicals made in industry and laboratories in the UK is illustrated in the pie chart below.

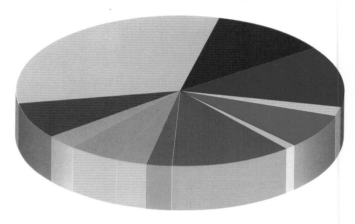

Key:

Pharmaceuticals 31.5%

Paint, varnishes and printing inks 8%

Agrochemicals 3%

Industrial glass 5%

Dyes and pigments 3%

Basic inorganics 2.5%

Basic organics 12%

Fertilizers 1%

Plastic and synthetic rubber 7.5%

Synthetic fibres 2%

Other specialities 13%

Soaps, toiletries and cleaning preparations 11.5%

Many of the raw materials are hazardous, therefore it is important to recognise the standard hazard symbols and understand the necessary precautions that need to be taken (see p.17).

The pH Scale

The pH scale is a measure of the acidity or alkalinity of an aqueous solution, across a 14-point scale.

Acids are substances that have a pH less than 7.

Bases are the oxides and hydroxides of metals. Those which are soluble are called **alkalis** and they have a pH greater than 7.

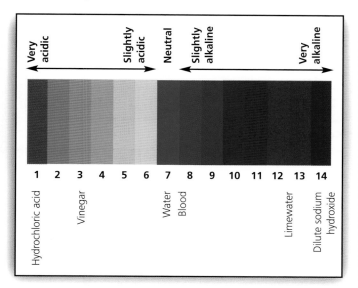

The pH of a substance is measured using an indicator, such as universal indicator solution, or a pH meter.

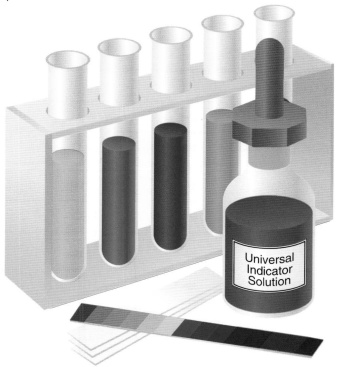

Acidic compounds produce aqueous **hydrogen ions**, $H^+_{(aq)}$, when they dissolve in water.

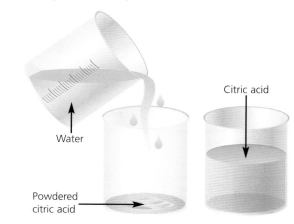

Common Acids	Formulae to Remember	State at Room Temp.
Citric acid	–	Solid
Tartaric acid	–	Solid
Nitric acid	HNO_3	Liquid
Sulfuric acid	H_2SO_4	Liquid
Ethanoic acid	–	Liquid
Hydrogen chloride (hydrochloric acid)	HCl	Gas

Alkali compounds produce aqueous **hydroxide ions**, $OH^-_{(aq)}$, when they dissolve in water.

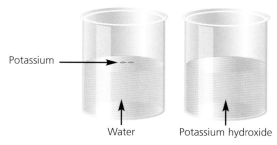

Common Alkalis	Formulae to Remember
Sodium hydroxide	NaOH
Potassium hydroxide	KOH
Magnesium hydroxide	$Mg(OH)_2$
Calcium hydroxide	$Ca(OH)_2$

Chemical Synthesis

Neutralisation

When an acid and a base are mixed together in the correct amounts they 'cancel' each other out. This reaction is called **neutralisation** because the solution which remains has a neutral pH of 7.

Acid	+	Base	→	Neutral salt solution	+	Water

Example

Hydrochloric acid	+	Potassium hydroxide	→	Potassium chloride	+	Water

$$HCl_{(aq)} + KOH_{(aq)} \longrightarrow KCl_{(aq)} + H_2O_{(l)}$$

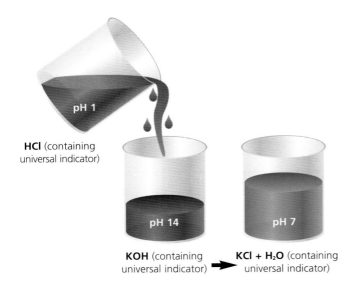

HCl (containing universal indicator)

pH 1

KOH (containing universal indicator)

KCl + H₂O (containing universal indicator)

pH 14

pH 7

N.B. A balanced equation for a chemical reaction shows the relative numbers of atoms and molecules of reactants and products taking part in the reaction.

During neutralisation, the hydrogen ions from the acid react with the hydroxide ions from the alkali to make water. The simplest way of writing a neutralisation equation is…

$$H^+_{(aq)} + OH^-_{(aq)} \longrightarrow H_2O_{(l)}$$

You need to remember this

The salt produced during neutralisation depends on the metal in the base and the acid used. Hydrochloric acid produces chloride salts, sulfuric acid produces sulfate salts, and nitric acid produces nitrate salts.

Hydrochloric Acid

Hydrochloric acid	+	Sodium hydroxide	→	Sodium chloride	+	Water

$$HCl_{(aq)} + NaOH_{(aq)} \longrightarrow NaCl_{(aq)} + H_2O_{(l)}$$

Hydrochloric acid	+	Potassium hydroxide	→	Potassium chloride	+	Water

$$HCl_{(aq)} + KOH_{(aq)} \longrightarrow KCl_{(aq)} + H_2O_{(l)}$$

Hydrochloric acid	+	Copper oxide	→	Copper chloride	+	Water

$$2HCl_{(aq)} + CuO_{(s)} \longrightarrow CuCl_{2(aq)} + H_2O_{(l)}$$

Hydrochloric acid	+	Calcium carbonate	→	Calcium chloride	+	Water	+	Carbon dioxide

$$2HCl_{(aq)} + CaCO_{3(s)} \longrightarrow CaCl_{2(aq)} + H_2O_{(l)} + CO_{2(g)}$$

Sulfuric Acid

Sulfuric acid	+	Sodium hydroxide	→	Sodium sulfate	+	Water

$$H_2SO_{4(aq)} + 2NaOH_{(aq)} \longrightarrow Na_2SO_{4(aq)} + 2H_2O_{(l)}$$

Sulfuric acid	+	Potassium hydroxide	→	Potassium sulfate	+	Water

$$H_2SO_{4(aq)} + 2KOH_{(aq)} \longrightarrow K_2SO_{4(aq)} + 2H_2O_{(l)}$$

Sulfuric acid	+	Copper oxide	→	Copper sulfate	+	Water

$$H_2SO_{4(aq)} + CuO_{(s)} \longrightarrow CuSO_{4(aq)} + H_2O_{(l)}$$

Sulfuric acid	+	Calcium carbonate	→	Calcium sulfate	+	Water	+	Carbon dioxide

$$H_2SO_{4(aq)} + CaCO_{3(s)} \longrightarrow CaSO_{4(aq)} + H_2O_{(l)} + CO_{2(g)}$$

Nitric Acid

Nitric acid	+	Sodium hydroxide	→	Sodium nitrate	+	Water

$$HNO_{3(aq)} + NaOH_{(aq)} \longrightarrow NaNO_{3(aq)} + H_2O_{(l)}$$

Nitric acid	+	Potassium hydroxide	→	Potassium nitrate	+	Water

$$HNO_{3(aq)} + KOH_{(aq)} \longrightarrow KNO_{3(aq)} + H_2O_{(l)}$$

Nitric acid	+	Copper oxide	→	Copper nitrate	+	Water

$$2HNO_{3(aq)} + CuO_{(s)} \longrightarrow Cu(NO_3)_{2(aq)} + H_2O_{(l)}$$

Nitric acid	+	Calcium carbonate	→	Calcium nitrate	+	Water	+	Carbon dioxide

$$2HNO_{3(aq)} + CaCO_{3(s)} \longrightarrow Ca(NO_3)_{2(aq)} + H_2O_{(l)} + CO_{2(g)}$$

Writing Formulae

In the Chemical Patterns module we looked at how to write formulae for ionic compounds. Given the formula of the salts listed below, you need to be able to work out the charge of both ions. See p.22 for the method.

Group 1 Salts	Formula
Sodium chloride	NaCl
Potassium chloride	KCl
Sodium carbonate	Na_2CO_3

Group 2 Salts	Formula
Magnesium sulfate	$MgSO_4$
Magnesium carbonate	$MgCO_3$
Magnesium oxide	MgO
Calcium carbonate	$CaCO_3$
Calcium chloride	$CaCl_2$

It is important to know the formulae of the common gases, which occur as covalently bonded (diatomic) molecules.

Gas	Formula
Chlorine	Cl_2
Hydrogen	H_2
Nitrogen	N_2
Oxygen	O_2

Oxygen

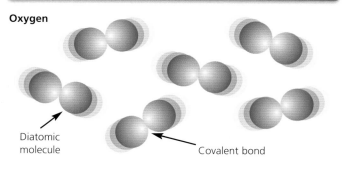

Diatomic molecule

Covalent bond

Chemical Synthesis

Whenever chemical synthesis takes place, the starting materials (reactants) react to produce new substances (products). The greater the amount of reactants used, the greater the amount of product formed. The **percentage yield** can be calculated by comparing the actual amount of product made (actual yield) with the amount of product you would expect to get if the reaction goes to completion (theoretical yield).

$$\text{Percentage yield} = \frac{\text{Actual yield}}{\text{Theoretical yield}} \times 100$$

There are a number of different stages to any chemical synthesis of an inorganic compound. Look at the flow chart below.

1. Establish the reaction or series of reactions that are needed in order to produce the product.

2. Carry out a risk assessment.

3. Calculate the quantities of reactants to use.

4. Carry out the reaction under suitable conditions, e.g. temperature, concentration and presence of catalyst.

5. Separate the product from the reaction mixture.

6. Purify the product to ensure it is not contaminated by other products or reactants.

7. Measure the yield.

8. Check the purity.

Chemical Synthesis

Chemical Synthesis (cont.)

Example
The following steps show how to make **magnesium sulfate**.

1. $Mg_{(g)} + H_2SO_{4(aq)} \longrightarrow MgSO_{4(aq)} + H_{2(g)}$
2. Wear safety glasses and use dilute sulfuric acid.

HT **3** To calculate the quantities of reactants you need to use, see example on p.72

4. Measure out the sulfuric acid, and add magnesium until no more hydrogen is formed. This indicates that the reaction is complete.

5. Filter to remove any excess magnesium that has not reacted.

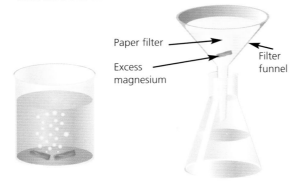

Paper filter
Excess magnesium
Filter funnel

6. Remove the water by gently heating the solution. It will evaporate slowly to form crystals that will cling to the end of a cold glass rod. Leave them to cool and crystallise. Filter to separate the crystals from any solution left behind.

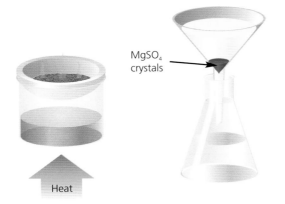

$MgSO_4$ crystals

Heat

7. Wash crystals and dry in a dessicator or oven. Weigh the mass and calculate the percentage yield (see p.69).

Distilled water

Actual yield = 8g

Theoretical yield = 10g

Percentage yield = $\dfrac{8}{10}$ x 100 = **80%**

8. Check the purity by measuring the melting point.

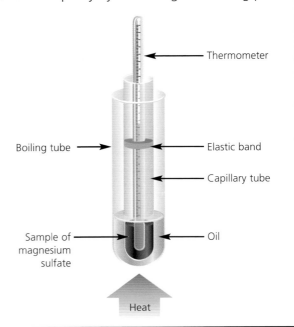

Thermometer
Boiling tube
Elastic band
Capillary tube
Sample of magnesium sulfate
Oil

Heat

Quantity of Products

In order to work out how much of each reactant is required to make a known amount of product, you must understand…

- how to calculate its relative atomic mass
- how to calculate its relative formula mass
- that a balanced equation shows the number of atoms or molecules taking part in the reaction
- how to work out the ratio of the mass of reactants to the mass of products
- how to apply the ratio to the question.

Relative Atomic Mass, A_r

To compare the mass of one atom to the mass of other atoms, we use the **relative atomic mass, A_r** (see p.44).

We can obtain this by looking at the Periodic Table below.

Examples

A_r of Mg = 24
A_r of Cu = 63.5
A_r of C = 12
A_r of K = 39

Relative Formula Mass, M_r

The **relative formula mass, M_r**, of a compound is the relative atomic masses of all its elements added together. To calculate M_r we need to know the formula of the compound and the A_r of each of the atoms involved.

Example 1

Calculate the M_r of water, H_2O.

The formula	H_2O
Substitute the A_rs	$(2 \times 1) + 16$
The M_r	$2 + 16 = \mathbf{18}$

Since water has an M_r of 18, it is 18 times heavier than a hydrogen atom ($M_r = 1$), or one and a half times heavier than a carbon atom ($M_r = 12$), or two thirds as heavy as an aluminium atom ($M_r = 27$).

Example 2

Calculate the M_r of potassium carbonate, K_2CO_3.

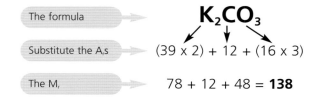

The formula	K_2CO_3
Substitute the A_rs	$(39 \times 2) + 12 + (16 \times 3)$
The M_r	$78 + 12 + 48 = \mathbf{138}$

Key

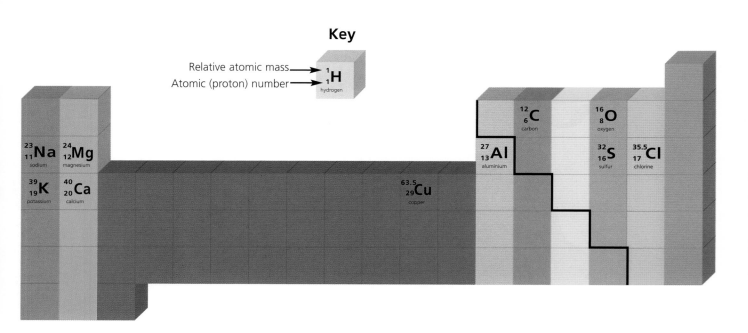

Chemical Synthesis

Calculating a Product's Mass

Example

Calculate how much calcium oxide can be produced from 50kg of calcium carbonate. (Relative atomic masses: Ca = 40, C = 12, O = 16).

> Write down the equation

$$CaCO_3 \rightarrow CaO + CO_2$$

> Work out the M_r of each substance

$$40 + 12 + (3 \times 16) \rightarrow (40 + 16) + [12 + (2 \times 16)]$$

> Check that the total mass of reactants equals the total mass of the products. If they are not the same, check your work

$$100 \rightarrow 56 + 44 \quad ✔$$

> Since the question only mentions calcium oxide and calcium carbonate, you can now ignore the carbon dioxide. You just need the ratio of mass of reactant to mass of product.

$$100 : 56$$

If 100kg of $CaCO_3$ produces 56kg of CaO, then 1kg of $CaCO_3$ produces $\frac{56}{100}$ kg of CaO, and 50kg of $CaCO_3$ produces $\frac{56}{100} \times 50$ = **28kg** of CaO.

Calculating a Reactant's Mass

Example

Calculate how much aluminium oxide is needed to produce 540 tonnes of aluminium. (Relative atomic masses: Al = 27, O = 16).

> Write down the equation

$$2Al_2O_3 \rightarrow 4Al + 3O_2$$

> Work out the M_r of each substance

$$2[(2 \times 27) + (3 \times 16)] \rightarrow (4 \times 27) + [3 \times (2 \times 16)]$$

> Check that the total mass of reactants equals the total mass of the products

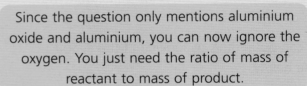

$$204 \rightarrow 108 + 96 \quad ✔$$

> Since the question only mentions aluminium oxide and aluminium, you can now ignore the oxygen. You just need the ratio of mass of reactant to mass of product.

$$204 : 108$$

If 204 tonnes of Al_2O_3 produces 108 tonnes of Al, then $\frac{204}{108}$ tonnes is needed to produce 1 tonne of Al, and $\frac{204}{108}$ x 540 tonnes is needed to produce 540 tonnes of Al, i.e. 1020 tonnes of Al_2O_3 is needed.

Titration

Titration can be used to calculate the concentration of an acid, such as citric acid, by finding out how much alkali is needed to neutralise it.

1 Fill a burette with the alkali sodium hydroxide (the concentration of the alkali must be known) and take an initial reading of the volume.

2 Accurately weigh out a 4g sample of solid citric acid and dissolve it in 100cm³ of distilled water.

3 Use a pipette to measure 25cm³ of the aqueous citric acid and put it into a conical flask.

Add a few drops of the indicator, phenolphthalein, to the conical flask. The indicator will stay colourless.

Place the flask on a white tile under the burette.

4 Add the alkali from the burette to the acid in the flask drop by drop.

- Swirl the flask to ensure it mixes well. Near the end of the reaction, the indicator will start to turn pink.
- Keep swirling and adding the alkali until the indicator is completely pink, showing that the citric acid has been neutralised.
- Record the volume of alkali added by subtracting the amount in the burette at the end from the starting value.

Repeat the whole procedure until you get two results that are the same.

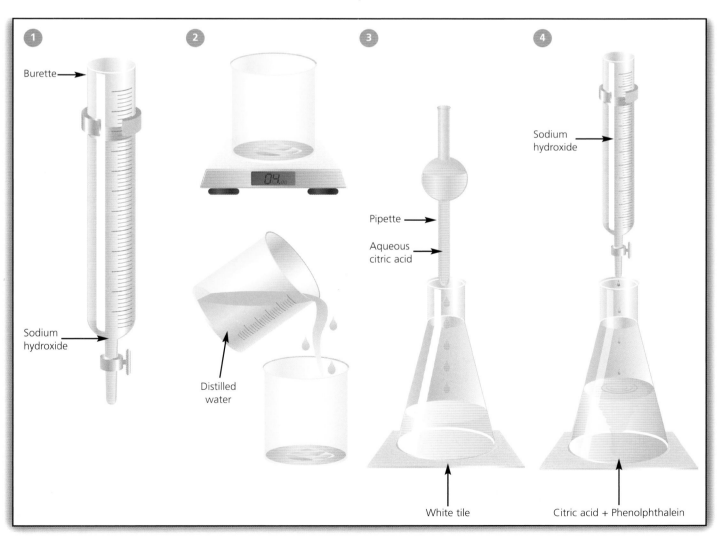

1 Burette → Sodium hydroxide

2 04

3 Pipette → Aqueous citric acid → White tile

4 Sodium hydroxide → Distilled water → Citric acid + Phenolphthalein

Chemical Synthesis

Interpreting Results

Example
For the titration example on p.73:
Concentration of sodium hydroxide = 40g/dm^3
Mass of citric acid = 4g
Volume of citric acid solution = 25cm^3

1. Work out the average volume of sodium hydroxide used, e.g. 8cm^3.

2. Using the given formula, calculate the concentration of citric acid by substituting the values.

$$\text{Concentration of acid} = 3 \times \frac{\text{Volume x Conc. NaOH}}{\text{Volume citric acid}}$$

1 molecule of citric acid reacts with 3 molecules of sodium hydroxide

N.B. Units – you must work in dm^3 when doing the calculations. To convert cm^3 to dm^3, divide by 1000.

$$= 3 \; \frac{\left(\frac{8}{1000} \times 40\right)}{\left(\frac{25}{1000}\right)}$$

$$= \textbf{38.4g/dm}^3$$

3. Work out the actual mass of citric acid in the sample.

Mass = Concentration x Volume

$$= 38.4\text{g/dm}^3 \times \left(\frac{25\text{cm}^3}{1000}\right)$$

$$= \textbf{0.96g}$$

4. The mass of citric acid dissolved in 100cm^3 of water is 4 x 0.96 = 3.84g

5. % of purity $= \dfrac{\text{Calculated mass}}{\text{Mass weighed out at start}} \times 100$

$$= \frac{3.84}{4.0} \times 100$$

$$= \textbf{96\%}$$

Rates of Reactions

The rate of a **chemical reaction** is the amount of reaction that takes place in a given unit of time. Chemical reactions only occur when the reacting particles collide with each other with sufficient energy to react.

These reactions can proceed at different speeds, e.g. rusting is a slow reaction whereas burning is a fast reaction.

Measuring the Rate of Reaction

The rate of a chemical reaction can be found in three different ways:

1. **Weighing the reaction mixture.**
   If one of the products is a gas, you could weigh the reaction mixture at timed intervals. The mass of the mixture will decrease.

2. **Measuring the volume of gas produced.**
   You could use a gas syringe to measure the total volume of gas produced at timed intervals.

Observing the formation of a precipitate.

This can be done by either watching a cross (on a tile underneath the jar to see when it is no longer visible), to measure the formation of a precipitate, or by maintaining a colour change using a light sensor. The light sensor will lead to more reliable and accurate results as there is a definite end point. There are also more data points collected, especially if it is interfaced with a computer.

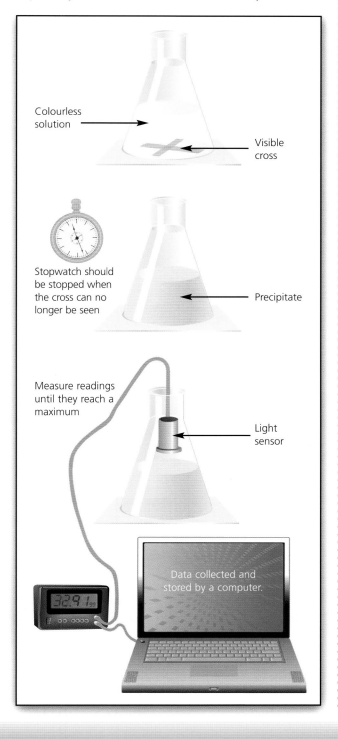

Colourless solution

Visible cross

Stopwatch should be stopped when the cross can no longer be seen

Precipitate

Measure readings until they reach a maximum

Light sensor

Data collected and stored by a computer.

Analysing the Rate of Reaction

Graphs can be plotted to show the progress of a chemical reaction – there are three things to remember:

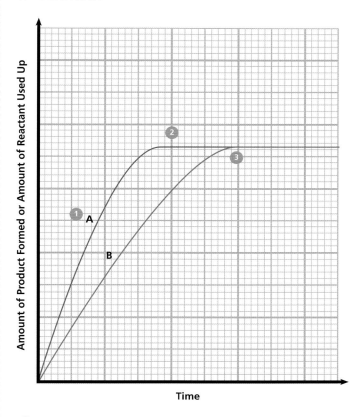

Amount of Product Formed or Amount of Reactant Used Up

Time

1. The steeper the line, the faster the reaction.

2. When one of the reactants is used up the reaction stops (line becomes flat).

3. The same amount of product is formed from the same amount of reactants, irrespective of rate.

Reaction A is faster than reaction B. This could be because…

- the surface area of the solid reactants in reaction A is greater than in reaction B (i.e. smaller particles are used)
- the temperature of reaction A is greater than reaction B
- the concentration of the solution in reaction A is greater than in reaction B
- a catalyst is used in reaction A but not in reaction B.

Chemical Synthesis

Changing the Rate of the Reaction

There are four important factors which affect the rate of reaction – temperature, concentration of dissolved reactants, surface area and the use of a catalyst.

1 Temperature of the Reactants

In a cold reaction mixture, the particles move quite slowly. They will collide less often, with less energy, so fewer collisions will be successful.

In a hot reaction mixture, the particles move more quickly. They will collide more often, with greater energy, so many more collisions will be successful.

Low Temperature	High Temperature

2 Concentration of the Dissolved Reactants

In a low concentration reaction, the particles are spread out. The particles will collide with each other less often resulting in fewer successful collisions.

In a high concentration reaction, the particles are crowded close together. The particles will collide with each other more often, resulting in many more successful collisions.

Low Concentration	High Concentration

3 Surface Area of Solid Reactants

Large particles (e.g. of powdered solids) have a small surface area in relation to their volume, meaning fewer particles are exposed and available for collisions. This means fewer collisions and a slower reaction.

Small particles (e.g. of powdered solids) have a large surface area in relation to their volume, so more particles are exposed and available for collisions. This means more collisions and a faster reaction.

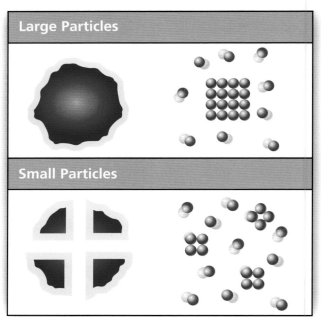

Large Particles

Small Particles

4 Using a Catalyst

A catalyst is a substance which increases the rate of a chemical reaction, without being changed during the process.

If we consider the decomposition of hydrogen peroxide...

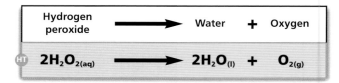

Hydrogen peroxide $\longrightarrow$ Water + Oxygen

HT $2H_2O_{2(aq)} \longrightarrow 2H_2O_{(l)} + O_{2(g)}$

We can measure the rate of this reaction by measuring the amount of oxygen given off at one-minute intervals. This reaction happens very slowly unless we add a catalyst of manganese (IV) oxide. With a catalyst, plenty of fizzing can be seen as the oxygen is given off.

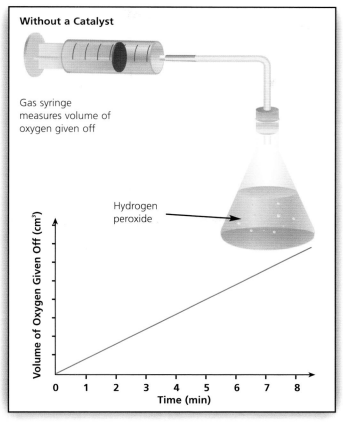

Without a Catalyst

Gas syringe measures volume of oxygen given off

Hydrogen peroxide

Volume of Oxygen Given Off (cm³)

Time (min)
0 1 2 3 4 5 6 7 8

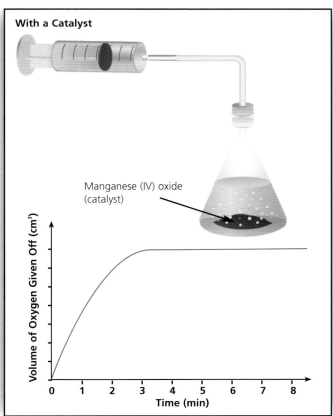

With a Catalyst

Manganese (IV) oxide (catalyst)

Volume of Oxygen Given Off (cm³)

Time (min)
0 1 2 3 4 5 6 7 8

The same amount of gas is given off, but it takes a far shorter time when a catalyst is present.

⊞ Collision Theory

Chemical reactions only occur when particles collide with each other with sufficient energy. Increasing temperature causes an increase in the kinetic energy of the particles, i.e. they move a lot faster. This results in more energetic collisions happening more frequently. The minimum energy required for a reaction will therefore be achieved more often, resulting in a greater rate of reaction.

An increase in concentration or surface area results in more frequent collisions and therefore more collisions which are sufficiently energetic for a reaction to occur.

Catalysts work by lowering the amount of energy needed for a successful collision. They are specific to a particular reaction and are not used up during the reaction. Consequently, only small amounts are needed.

Controlling a Chemical Reaction

When carrying out a chemical synthesis on an industrial scale there are also economic, safety and environmental factors to consider:

- The rate of manufacture must be high enough to produce a sufficient daily yield of product.
- Percentage yield must be high enough to produce a sufficient daily yield of product.
- A low percentage yield is acceptable providing the reaction can be repeated many times with recycled starting materials.
- Optimum conditions should be used that give the lowest cost rather than the fastest reaction or highest percentage yield.
- Care must be taken when using any of the reactants or products that could harm the environment if there was a leak.
- Care must be taken to avoid putting any harmful by-products into the environment.
- A complete risk assessment must be carried out, and the necessary precautions taken.

The Wave Model of Radiation

Different waves, both natural and artificial, have common properties. This module looks at…
- how waves travel
- the characteristics of light and sound waves
- reflection, refraction and diffraction
- how electromagnetic radiations behave
- how information is added to a wave.

Types of Waves

Waves are regular patterns of disturbance that transfer energy in the direction that the wave travels, without transferring matter. There are two types of wave – **longitudinal** and **transverse**.

All waves transfer energy from one point to another without transferring particles of matter. If we consider that each coil of the slinky spring in the following diagrams represents one particle, then we can show the movement of the particles in each type of wave.

Longitudinal Waves

Each particle moves backwards and forwards in the same plane as the direction of wave movement. Each particle simply vibrates to and fro about its normal position.

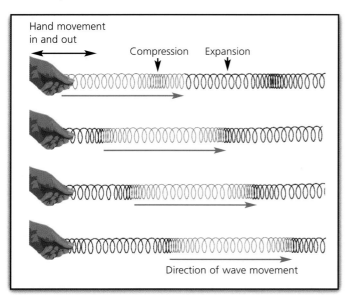

Transverse Waves

Sound travels as longitudinal waves.

Each particle moves up and down at right angles (90°) to the direction of wave movement. Each particle simply vibrates up and down about its normal position.

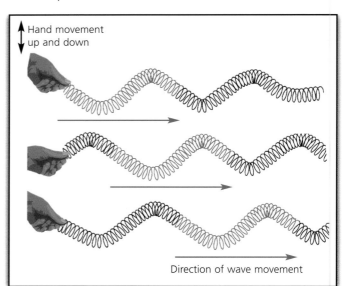

Light and water ripples both travel as transverse waves.

The Wave Model of Radiation

Wave Features

All waves have several important features:
- **Amplitude** – the maximum disturbance caused by a wave. It is measured by the distance from a crest or trough of the wave to the undisturbed position.
- **Wavelength** – the distance between corresponding points on two adjacent disturbances.
- **Frequency** – the number of waves produced, (or passing a particular point) in one second. Frequency is measured in hertz (Hz).

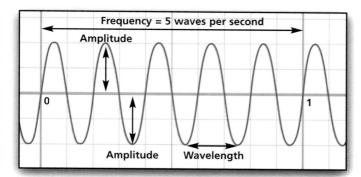

Wave Speed, Wavelength and Frequency

If a wave travels at a **constant speed** (i.e. its speed does not change), then...
- increasing its frequency will decrease its wavelength
- decreasing its frequency will increase its wavelength.

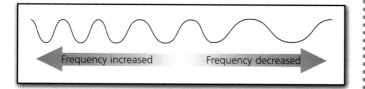

If a wave has a **constant frequency**, (i.e. its frequency does not change), then...
- decreasing its wave speed will decrease its wavelength
- increasing its wave speed will increase its wavelength.

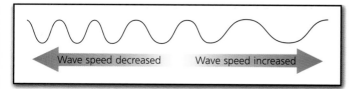

N.B. The speed of a wave is usually independent of its frequency and amplitude.

The Wave Equation

Wave speed, frequency and wavelength are related by the following formula:

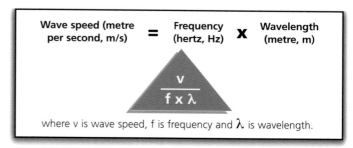

where v is wave speed, f is frequency and λ is wavelength.

Example

A tapped tuning fork of frequency 480Hz produces sound waves with a wavelength of 70cm. What is the speed of the wave?

Using our relationship...

Wave speed = Frequency x Wavelength

= 480Hz x 0.7m ← Wavelength must be in metres.

= **336m/s**

HT The wave speed formula can be rearranged using the formula triangle to work out the frequency or wavelength.

Example

Radio 5 Live transmits on a frequency of 909 000Hz. If the speed of radio waves is 300 000 000m/s, on what wavelength does it transmit?

Rearrange the formula...

$$\text{Wavelength} = \frac{\text{Wave speed}}{\text{Frequency}}$$

$$= \frac{300\,000\,000\text{m/s}}{909\,000\text{Hz}} = \textbf{330m}$$

The Wave Model of Radiation

Behaviour of Waves

Waves, including light, water and sound waves, can be reflected, refracted or diffracted (see diagram opposite).

Reflection

Waves are reflected when a barrier is placed in their path. This effect can be seen in water waves.

Refraction

When waves cross a boundary between one medium and another (of a different density) the frequency remains the same but there is a change in wavelength. This leads to a change in wave speed, which causes the wave to change direction. If the waves meet a boundary along a normal (at 90°), the speed still changes but the direction does not.

With water waves, refraction occurs when waves pass from deep into more shallow water, or vice versa.

Diffraction

When waves move through a narrow gap or past an obstacle they spread out from the edges. This is diffraction. Diffraction is most obvious in two instances:

1. When the size of the gap is similar to the wavelengths of the wave.
2. When the waves which pass obstacles have long wavelengths.

Light can be diffracted, but the waves need a small gap. The fact that light and sound can be diffracted provides evidence of their wave natures.

Reflection of Light

When light strikes a surface it changes direction; it is **reflected**. The diagram opposite shows light being reflected in a plane mirror (flat, smooth and shiny).

> **Angle of incidence = Angle of reflection**

The **normal** line is perpendicular to the reflecting surface at the point of incidence. It is used to calculate the angles of incidence and reflection. The **incident ray** is the light ray travelling towards the mirror. The **reflected ray** is the light ray travelling away from the mirror.

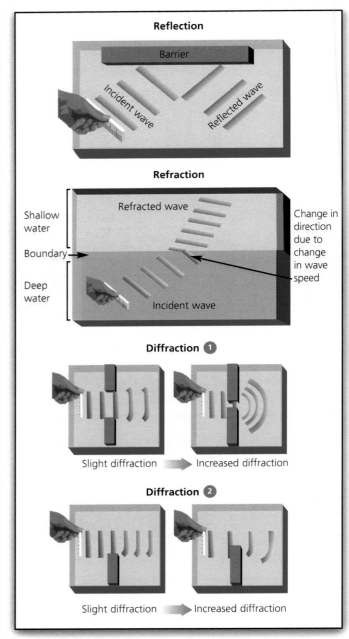

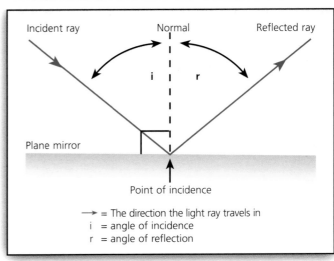

The Wave Model of Radiation

Refraction of Light at an Interface

Light changes direction when it crosses an interface, i.e. a boundary between two transparent materials (media) of different densities, unless it meets the boundary at an angle of 90° (i.e. along the normal).

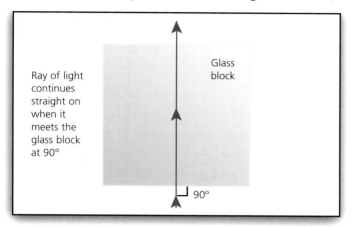

Ray of light continues straight on when it meets the glass block at 90°

Glass block

90°

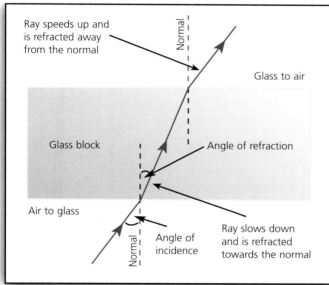

Ray speeds up and is refracted away from the normal

Normal

Glass to air

Glass block

Angle of refraction

Air to glass

Normal

Angle of incidence

Ray slows down and is refracted towards the normal

Total Internal Reflection

When the angle of refraction is greater than 90° the light cannot escape from the medium and is reflected. This is called **total internal reflection.**

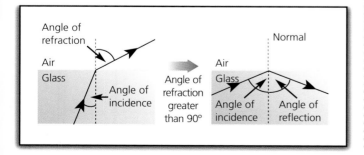

Angle of refraction

Air

Glass

Angle of incidence

Angle of refraction greater than 90°

Normal

Air

Glass

Angle of incidence

Angle of reflection

Interference

When two waves meet, their effects can add up; this is called **interference**.

If the peak of one wave coincides with the peak of another they are said to be in step. When this happens they reinforce each other and their amplitudes add up; this is called **constructive interference**.

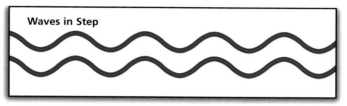

Waves in Step

If the two waves arrive out of step, the peak of one can meet the trough of another and they cancel each other out; this is called **destructive interference**.

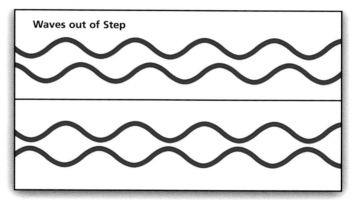

Waves out of Step

Two rays of light can be shown to produce an interference pattern. If the light from one ray arriving at the screen is either in step or out of step with the other ray, it produces the pattern shown below. The interference of light and sound provides further evidence of their wave nature.

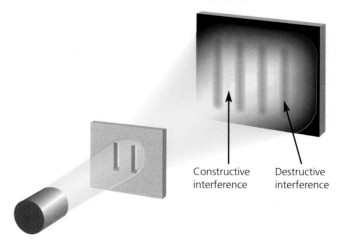

Constructive interference

Destructive interference

The Wave Model of Radiation

Electromagnetic Radiation

Light is one type of electromagnetic radiation which, together with the other types of radiation, form the **electromagnetic spectrum**. The seven 'colours of the rainbow' form the **visible spectrum** which, as the name suggests, is the only part of the electromagnetic spectrum we can see.

The visible spectrum is produced because white light is made up of many different colours. The colours are refracted by different amounts as they pass through a prism – red light is refracted the least and violet is refracted the most. This is because the different colours have different frequencies and, therefore, different wavelengths.

Electromagnetic radiations can be reflected and refracted, which supports the idea that they travel as waves.

The intensity of a beam of radiation depends on the number of **photons** (packets of energy) it delivers every second.

> **HT** The intensity of the beam also depends on the amount of energy carried by each photon.

All electromagnetic waves travel through space (a vacuum) at the same very high speed (300 000 000m/s).

Electromagnetic waves are very different from sound waves:
- Sound waves are longitudinal; electromagnetic waves are transverse.
- Electromagnetic waves are much faster than sound waves.
- Electromagnetic waves can travel through empty space but sound waves need a medium (solid, liquid or gas) to travel through.

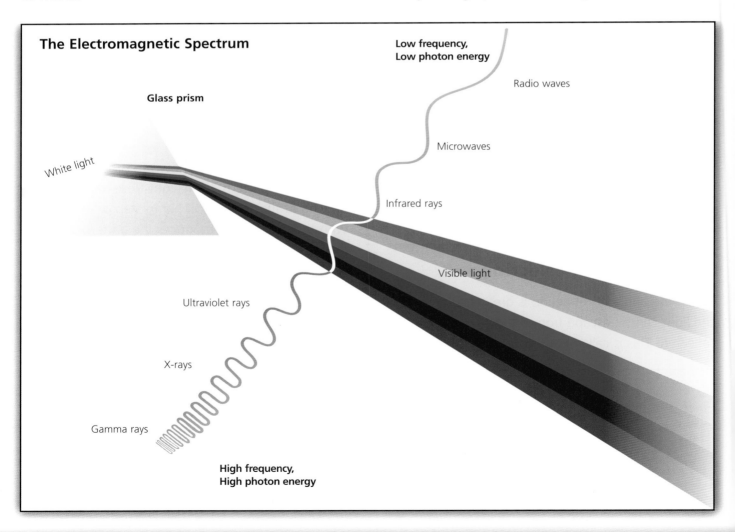

The Electromagnetic Spectrum

Low frequency, Low photon energy

Radio waves

Microwaves

Glass prism

Infrared rays

White light

Visible light

Ultraviolet rays

X-rays

Gamma rays

High frequency, High photon energy

The Wave Model of Radiation

Uses of Electromagnetic Waves

Different electromagnetic waves have different frequencies. This affects their properties and the effect that other materials have on them.

They can be used for different purposes depending on how much they are reflected, absorbed or transmitted by different materials.

Electromagnetic waves are very useful. Their signals can be carried by...
- radio waves (television signals) and microwaves (mobile phones) through the Earth's atmosphere and space
- light waves and infrared waves through optical fibres.

Electromagnetic Waves	Properties and Uses
Radio Waves	• They are used for transmitting radio and television programmes because they are not strongly absorbed by the atmosphere. • Radio telescopes are used in astronomy to pick up radio waves from stars.
Microwaves	• They are reflected well by metals so satellite dishes are made of metal and shaped to reflect the signal onto the receiver. • Some microwave frequencies are strongly absorbed by water molecules so they are used to heat objects containing water (usually food in a microwave oven).
Light and infrared radiation	• They will travel huge distances down optical fibres without becoming significantly weaker. This makes them very useful for carrying information, e.g. computer networks and telephone conversations.
X-rays	• They are absorbed by dense materials which makes them very useful for seeing inside bodies and objects. They are used to produce shadow pictures of bones and to 'see' inside luggage at airport security checks.

The Wave Model of Radiation

Modulation

For a wave to carry a signal it must be **modulated**. This process involves making the wave vary either in amplitude or frequency to create a variation in the original wave. It is this pattern of variation which carries the information.

The pattern of variation is decoded by the receiver to reproduce the original sound, e.g. sound from a radio wave.

Analogue Signals

In amplitude modulation or frequency modulation (AM or FM) the amplitude of the carrier wave is changed by the input signal.

With frequency modulation the input signal causes the frequency of the carrier wave to change.

In both these cases the signal is called an **analogue** signal because it varies in exactly the same way as the information it is carrying. Analogue signals can have almost any value.

Digital Signals

Information, including sound, can also be transmitted digitally. The signal is not sent as a continually varying transmission, but is first converted into a digital code that uses just two symbols: 0 and 1.

Example

The number 25 can be digitally encoded as 11001, which can then be transmitted as a series of short bursts of waves called pulses (0 = no pulse, 1 = pulse). So, 25 would be: pulse, pulse, no pulse, no pulse, pulse.

Digital radio signals are encoded in the same way – different sequences of 0s and 1s correspond to different sounds. When the digital signal is received, the pulses are decoded to produce the original sound wave.

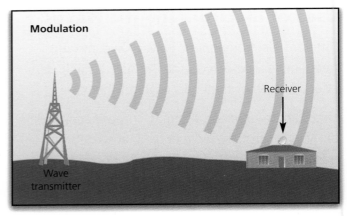

Modulation

Wave transmitter — Receiver

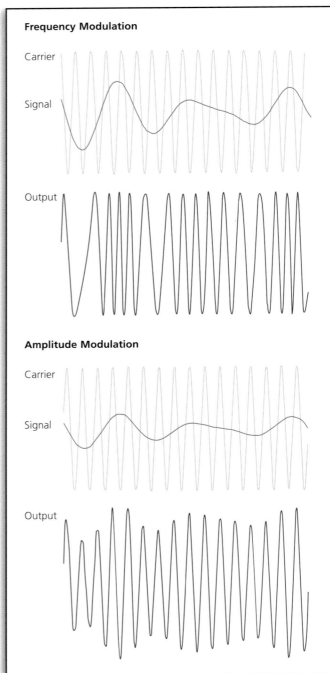

Frequency Modulation

Carrier

Signal

Output

Amplitude Modulation

Carrier

Signal

Output

The Wave Model of Radiation

Benefits of Digital

Both digital and analogue signals become weaker (their amplitude becomes smaller) as they travel and they can also pick up random variations, called **noise**, which reduce the quality of the sound.

Therefore, the transmitted signals have to be amplified at selected intervals to counteract the effects of the weakening.

Analogue signals can have many different values so it is hard to distinguish between noise and the original signal. This means that noise cannot be completely removed and, when the signal is amplified, any noise which has been picked up is also amplified.

With analogue signals you are often left with a noisy signal. With music this can make it sound 'hissy'.

Digital signals, which have two states, on (1) or off (0), can still be recognised despite any noise that is picked up. Therefore, it is easy to remove the noise and clean up the signal, restoring the on / off pattern. So, when it is amplified, the quality of the digital signal is retained.

The signal is less affected by the transmission process, which gives digital signals an important advantage over analogue signals; they can be sent over long distances without a noticeable loss in quality.

> **HT** Information transmitted digitally can travel long distances and is received at a higher quality than analogue signals because any interference can be removed.

Analogue signals

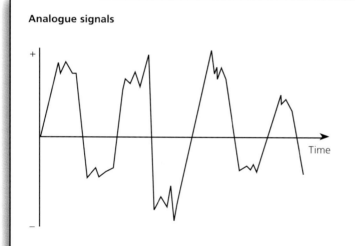

Digital signals

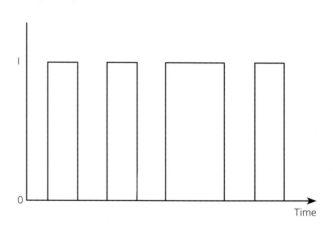

Analogue signals – poor signal quality due to interference

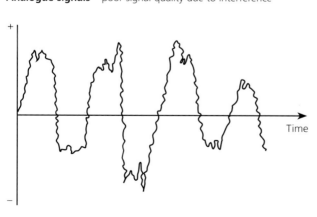

Digital signals – high signal quality as interference is easily removed

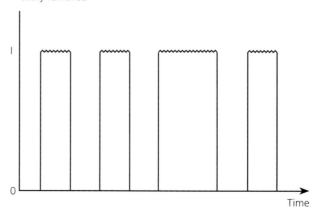

Ideas in Context

EXAM ROOM

The Exam Paper

One of the aims of OCR GCSE Additional Science A is to develop your knowledge and understanding of key scientific explanations and ideas, so that you can evaluate information about important science-based issues and make informed personal decisions where necessary.

In addition to your practical investigation, which is assessed by your teacher, you will have to sit four exams.

The first three papers will focus on the scientific explanations and ideas covered in Units 4, 5 and 6 respectively (covered on pages 4–85 of this revision guide).

The fourth paper will test your understanding of ideas in context. The questions will be based on current science-based issues (which you may well be aware of from coverage in the media). To answer them you will have to recall relevant scientific facts and draw upon your knowledge of how science works, i.e. the practices and procedures involved in collecting scientific evidence, and its impact on society.

This section of the revision guide looks at the Ideas in Context exam paper in more detail so you will know exactly what to expect.

It clarifies how many marks the paper represents and looks at the type of questions that may come up, the format they are likely to take, and what skills you will need to use to answer them.

Exam Details

Title: OCR Additional Science A
          Unit 4 – Ideas in Context

Duration: 45 minutes

Total Mark: 40

Weighting: 16.7% (of total mark for course)

The paper will consist of three structured questions (i.e. questions with several parts) and you must answer all of them.

You will sit either the foundation paper or the higher paper. This will be decided with your teacher during the build up to the exams.

Question Format

Each of the three questions will be based on a different topic from the specification. Each year, the topics featured in the exam are chosen at random. However, they are always taken from the three separate subject areas, so there will be one biology question, one chemistry question and one physics question.

Do not worry, you will not be asked questions relating to any topics other than those on the specification.

At the start of each question you will be presented with some facts and information about a science-based issue connected to the chosen topic. This could be written information, data (i.e. tables and graphs), or a combination of both.

The same information will be sent to your school before the exam. Your teachers will give you the information in a science lesson a set number of days before the exam. You will be able to read through the text in class and look up any technical terms or phrases that you do not understand. You are not expected to do further research but you should revise any of the relevant scientific explanations or ideas.

You will not be able to take the original articles or any notes into the exam.

In the exam, you will be presented with the information and a series of questions relating to that issue. The questions can take a variety of formats, from multiple choice and matching questions to data analysis and questions that require a written response.

The questions will be designed to test...
- your understanding of the information
- your understanding of related scientific explanations
- your understanding of the practices and procedures used in scientific investigations
- your ability to identify the benefits and drawbacks of the science and technology involved
- your ability to identify the different arguments surrounding the issue (i.e. for and against)
- your ability to evaluate the impact of the technology involved on the environment and society.

The next few pages include an exam-style question, with model answers and handy hints on how to approach the different parts of the question.

Ideas in Context

The information below is based on the content in Module B4: Homeostasis. Make sure you read all the information below carefully before you even attempt to answer the questions.

1

Answer all questions.

Question 1

Homeostasis is the process whereby the body prevents the outside environment from changing things inside the body.

It is important that the body stays at 37°C and keeps the same level of water in the blood no matter what is happening outside the body.

Read the following article about what happens to the human body when mountaineers attempt to climb Mount Everest.

INTO THE DEATH ZONE

Climbers call mountains over 26000 feet, the death zone. Mount Everest is 29035 feet high. Over 90 climbers have climbed Mount Everest.

Climbers can suffer from frostbite, when fingers and toes freeze. They also have to survive winds of over 90 miles per hour. Above 25000 feet, the air is so dry, that climbers can breathe out 5 litres of water in their breath every day.

Ultraviolet radiation increases by 4% for every thousand feet and Everest is over 29000 feet high. These levels of ultraviolet radiation can cause blindness.

The following data show what happens to the body at higher altitudes.

29000 feet
Air pressure 30%.
Climber may hallucinate.
Resting heart rate 123 beats per minute.

18000 feet
Air pressure 50%.
No one on Earth has a home above this height.
Lungs breathe out too much carbon dioxide turning blood alkaline.
Kidneys excrete more water.

9000 feet
Air pressure 75%.
People get out of breath.
People get headaches as brain starts to swell.
Body starts to make more red blood cells.
Resting heart rate 85 beats per minute.

Specimen paper: Additional Science A

Reproduced from an OCR specimen exam paper

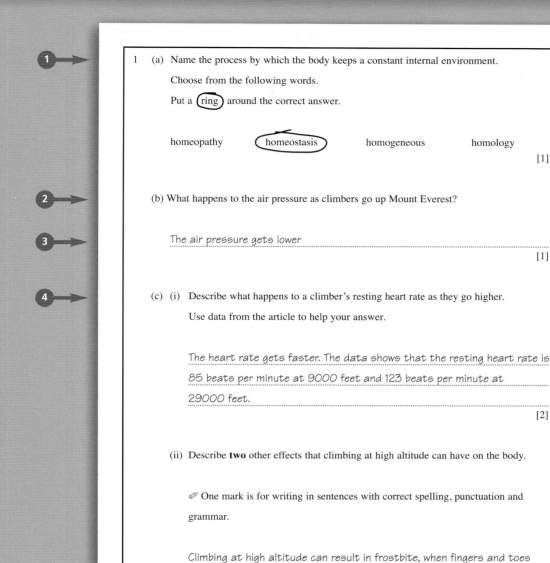

1 (a) Name the process by which the body keeps a constant internal environment.

Choose from the following words.

Put a (ring) around the correct answer.

homeopathy   (homeostasis)   homogeneous   homology

[1]

(b) What happens to the air pressure as climbers go up Mount Everest?

The air pressure gets lower

[1]

(c) (i) Describe what happens to a climber's resting heart rate as they go higher.

Use data from the article to help your answer.

The heart rate gets faster. The data shows that the resting heart rate is
85 beats per minute at 9000 feet and 123 beats per minute at
29000 feet.

[2]

(ii) Describe **two** other effects that climbing at high altitude can have on the body.

✎ One mark is for writing in sentences with correct spelling, punctuation and grammar.

Climbing at high altitude can result in frostbite, when fingers and toes
freeze due to the cold conditions. Headaches can also occur due to
swelling of the brain.

[2+1]

1 This is a multiple choice question. You can answer this correctly by referring back to the information. With a multiple choice question like this, even if you do not know it immediately, you can sometimes arrive at the correct answer by eliminating the wrong answers one at a time.

2 This part of the question is testing how carefully you have read the information. The answer is in the text, but you might have missed it if you were skim-reading.

3 Your answer does not have to be word perfect; there are several different wordings that are acceptable as an answer here, i.e. gets less / lower / drops. The most important thing is that your answer clearly states that air pressure is decreasing.

4 Read the question carefully – there are two parts to this question. You must describe what happens to a climber's resting heart rate AND include relevant data from the article to support your answer to get full marks.

5 This question is worth two marks, one for each correct effect you describe. The pencil symbol (✎) means that an extra mark is available for a clear, well ordered answer.

To earn this extra mark, make sure you write in clear sentences and order them in a logical way. Finally, make sure your spelling, punctuation and grammar are all correct.

Ideas in Context

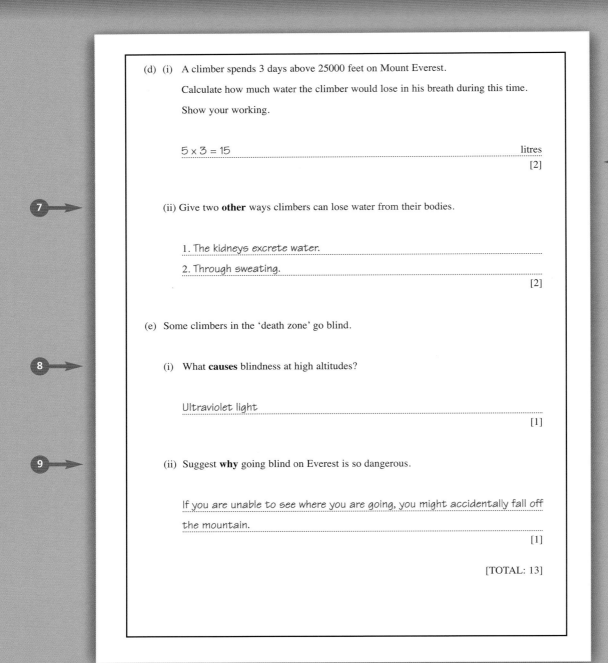

(d) (i) A climber spends 3 days above 25000 feet on Mount Everest.

Calculate how much water the climber would lose in his breath during this time.

Show your working.

5 x 3 = 15   litres

[2]

← 6

7 →

(ii) Give two **other** ways climbers can lose water from their bodies.

1. The kidneys excrete water.

2. Through sweating.

[2]

(e) Some climbers in the 'death zone' go blind.

8 →

(i) What **causes** blindness at high altitudes?

Ultraviolet light

[1]

9 →

(ii) Suggest **why** going blind on Everest is so dangerous.

If you are unable to see where you are going, you might accidentally fall off

the mountain.

[1]

[TOTAL: 13]

6 Look at the marks for each question (given on the right-hand side of the question paper) – they will give you a clue as to how much information you need to give. This question is worth two marks: one for the correct answer, and one for showing the working out. The amount of water lost through breathing each day is given in the text.

7 This question requires you to recall information from module B4, which is why it is important for you to revise thoroughly before the exam.

8 This question is testing your understanding of the information given. By referring back to the text you should find the answer in the third paragraph of the article.

9 This question is a bit harder than the rest, because the answer is not in the text or the specification. But do not be put off – it just requires a bit of careful thinking and common sense.

Exam and Revision Tips

- Try to watch the news and read newspapers and publications like *New Scientist, BBC Focus* and *Flipside* whenever you can – this will alert you to any topical science-based issues that might come up on the exam paper. You should be able to find these in your school library or resource centre. You can also find websites for these publications with up-to-date information.
- It may sound obvious, but make sure you read the information carefully before attempting to answer any of the questions. Underline key words and try breaking up sentences into clauses. This will help you to focus on the content.
- The answers to many of the questions will be in the information, so keep referring back to it.
- The total marks available for each question are shown in the right-hand margin. The marks allocated and the space provided should give you a clue as to the length of answer required and how much information you need to give.

For example, if a question is worth two marks, the examiner is likely to be looking for two key points in your answer.

- If you are asked to make a calculation, always show your working. Marks are often given if you use the correct method, even if the answer is incorrect.
- If you are giving a measurement, make sure you remember to include the units and use the correct abbreviation.
- For some questions, an extra mark may be awarded for the quality of written communication of your answer. If this is the case, a pencil icon (✐) will be shown and it will say so clearly on the paper. This means you should…
  - write in clear sentences
  - order your sentences in a logical way
  - use correct spelling, punctuation and grammar
  - use the correct scientific words.

Glossary

Acid – a compound with a pH lower than 7

Alkali – a compound with a pH higher than 7

Alternating current – a current that changes direction continuously

Amplitude – the maximum disturbance caused by a wave

Analogue – a signal which can take any value

Atmosphere – layer of gas surrounding the Earth

Atom – the smallest part of an element which can enter into chemical reactions

Attraction – the drawing together of two materials with different charges

Biosphere – all living organisms on Earth

Central Nervous System – the brain and spinal cord; allows organisms to react to the surroundings and coordinates their responses

Clone – a genetically identical descendent of an organism

Compound – a substance consisting of two or more elements chemically combined together

Constructive interference – when the peaks of waves are in step; they reinforce each other

Covalent bonding – a bond between two atoms in which the atoms share one or more electrons

Denatured enzyme – an enzyme that has had its shape destroyed by heat and can no longer catalyse reactions

Deoxyribonucleic acid (DNA) – nucleic acid which contains the genetic information carried by every cell in an organism

Destructive interference – when the peaks of waves are out of step; they cancel each other out

Diffraction – the change in the direction of a wave at the edge of an obstacle in its path

Diffusion – the movement of a substance from a region of high concentration to a region of low concentration down a concentration gradient.

Digital – a signal which has an on / off state

Direct current – current flowing in one direction

Distance–time graph – shows distance travelled against time taken; gradient represents speed

Effector – the part of the body, e.g. a muscle or a gland, which produces a response to a stimulus

Electrolysis – the process by which an electric current causes a solution to undergo chemical decomposition

Electron – a negatively charged particle in orbit around the nucleus of an atom

Element – a substance that consists of only one type of atom

Enzymes – organic catalysts; protein molecules which speed up the rate of reactions in living organisms

Fertilisation – the fusion of the male nucleus with the female nucleus

Force – a push or pull acting upon an object

Frequency – the number of waves produced (or passing a particular point) in one second

Friction – a force which opposes movement

Gravitational potential energy (GPE) – the energy an object has because of its height and mass

Group – a vertical column of elements in the Periodic Table

Heat stroke – the result of an uncontrolled increase in body temperature

Homeostasis – the maintenance of a constant internal environment

Hormone – a regulatory substance which stimulates cells or tissues into action

Hydrosphere – all the water on Earth including rivers, oceans, lakes, etc.

Hypothermia – an uncontrolled decrease in body temperature

Instantaneous speed – the speed of an object at a particular point

Ion – a charged particle formed when an atom gains or loses electrons

Ionic bonding – the process by which two or more atoms lose or gain electrons to become charged ions which are held together by forces of attraction

Kinetic energy – the energy possessed by a body due to its movement

Lithosphere – rigid outer layer of the Earth made up of the crust and the part of the mantle just below it

Longitudinal – an energy-carrying wave in which the movement of the particles is in line with the direction in which the energy is being transferred

Meiosis – cell division that forms daughter cells that have half the number of chromosomes of the parent cell

Meristems – areas where unspecialised cells divide producing plant growth

Mitosis – cell division that forms two daughter cells, each with the same number of chromosomes as the parent cell

Momentum – a measure of the state of motion of a body as a product of its mass and velocity

Neuron – a specialised cell which transmits electrical messages or nerve impulses when stimulated

Neutralisation – reaction between an acid and a base which forms a neutral solution

Neutron – a particle found in the nucleus of atoms that has no electrical charge

Organelles – different parts of a cell's structure

Osmosis – the movement of water from a high concentration to a low concentration

Parallel circuit – a circuit where there are two (or more) paths for the current to take

Period – a horizontal row of elements in the Periodic Table

Photon – a 'packet of' energy

Phototropism – a plant's response to light

Pituitary – small gland at the base of the brain that produces hormones

Potential difference / voltage – the difference in electrical charge between two charged points

Proton – a positively charged particle found in the nucleus of atoms

Reaction – a force which occurs when an object is pushing against a surface

Receptor – a sense organ, e.g. eye, ear, nose, etc.

Reflection – a wave that is thrown back from a surface

Reflex action – a fast, automatic response

Refraction – the change in direction of a wave as it passes from one medium to another

Relative atomic mass (A$_r$) – the mass of an atom compared to the mass of a hydrogen atom

Relative formula mass (M$_r$) – the sum of the atomic masses of all atoms in a molecule

Repulsion – the pushing away of two materials with the same type of charge

Resistance – the measure of how hard it is to get a current through a component at a particular potential difference

Resultant force – the total force acting on an object (the effect of all the forces combined)

Ribosome – a particle involved in protein synthesis

Series circuit – a circuit where there is only one path for the current to take

Specialised – adapted for a particular purpose

Speed – how far an object travels in a given time

Static electricity – electricity that is produced by friction and does not move

Synapses – gaps between adjacent neurons; allow the brain to form interconnected neural circuits

Titration – chemical analysis used to determine the concentration of a known element

Transformer – an electrical device used to change the voltage of alternating current

Transverse – a wave in which the vibrations are at 90° to the direction of energy transfer

Velocity – an object's speed and direction

Velocity–time graph – shows velocity against time taken; gradient represents acceleration

Voltage / potential difference – the difference in electrical charge between two charged points

Wavelength – the distance between corresponding points on two adjacent disturbances

---

HT **Active transport** – the movement of substances against a concentration gradient

Auxins – a plant hormone that affects the growth and development of the plant

Conditioned reflex – a specific reflex response produced when a certain stimulus is detected

Negative feedback – when a signal from a receptor instructs an effector to reverse an action

Index

A
Acids 67
Active site 8
Active transport 7
Alkali metals 17–18
Alkalis 67
Amplitude 79
Analogue 84–85
Anion 20
Antagonistic effectors 5
Anti-diuretic hormone (ADH) 12
A_r (Relative atomic mass) 44, 71
Atmosphere 39, 40
Atoms 14
Attraction 49
Auxins 37, 38
Axon 59

B
Balanced equations 16, 44
Bases 67
Biosphere 39, 43–44
Body temperature 9
Brain 62–65

C
Callus 36
Carbon cycle 40
Catalysts 76–77
Cation 20
Cells 31
Central Nervous System 57, 58
Cerebral cortex 63–64
Chemical synthesis 69–70
Chemicals 66
Chromosomes 32, 33, 34
Clones 36
Collision theory 77
Collisions 29
Conditioned reflexes 61
Current–potential difference graphs 52
Currents 50–52

D
Darwin, Charles 38
Denaturing 7, 8
Diffraction 80, 81
Diffusion 6
Digital 84–85
Distance–time graphs 24, 25
DNA 31, 34, 35, 43

E
Effectors 58
Electric circuits 49–54
Electrolysis 46, 47
Electromagnetic induction 54
Electromagnetic spectrum 82
Electron configuration 14–15
Elements 13
Embryonic stem cells 35
Energy 30, 56
Enzymes 7
    pH 7
    Temperature 8

F
Feral children 63
Fertilisation 33
Forces 26–30
    Counter Force 28
    Driving Force 28

Frequency 79, 82
Friction 27

G
Generators 54
Glucose 43
Glycine 43
Gravitational potential energy (GPE) 30
Gravity 26
Groups 13

H
Hazard symbols 17, 18, 19
Heat stroke 9
Homeostasis 4–12
    Artificial 5
Hydrosphere 39, 42
Hypothalamus 10, 12
Hypothermia 4, 10

I
Incident ray 80
Interference
    Constructive 81
    Destructive 81
Instantaneous speed 24
Ionic bonding 21
Ionic compounds 21, 22, 42, 69
Ions 20, 21

K
Kidneys 10–11
Kinetic energy (KE) 29, 30

L
Light dependent resistor (LDR) 52
Life cycle analysis 46
Lithosphere 39, 42–43
Lock and key model 8
Longitudinal waves 78

M
Mass of product 72
Mass of reactant 72
Meiosis 32, 33
Memory 64–65
Meristems 36
    Apical 36
    Lateral 36
Messenger RNA 34
Minerals 45
Mitosis 32, 33
Modulation 84
Momentum 28
M_r (Relative formula mass) 71
MRI scanning 64

N
Negative feedback 5, 12
Neurons 58–59
    Motor 58
    Sensory 58
Neutralisation 68
Nitrogen cycle 40

O
Organelles 31
Osmosis 6, 7
Oxidation 45

P
Pavlov's dog experiment 61

Periodic Table 13, 96
Periods 13
Peripheral nervous system 57, 58
pH scale 67
Phloem 37
Photons 82
Phototropism 37, 38a
Potential difference 50, 51, 52
Power 55
Properties of metals 48

Q
Quartz 42

R
Rates of reaction 74
Reaction 27
Reactivity 45
Receptors 58
Reduction 45
Reflection 80, 81
Reflex actions 60
Refraction 80, 81
Relative atomic mass, A_r 44, 71
Relative formula mass, M_r 71
Repulsion 49
Resistors 51
Resultant force 27
Retina 58
Ribosomes 31, 34

S
Salts 42
Serotonin 65
Spectroscopy 14
Speed 23–26
Static electricity 49
Stem cells 35
Stimuli 57
Synapses 59, 62

T
Therapeutic cloning 35
Thermistor 52
Thyroid gland 58
Titration 73–74
Total internal reflection 81
Transformers 55
Transverse waves 78

U
Urine concentration 11, 12

V
Vasoconstriction 10
Vasodilation 10
Velocity 23
Velocity–time graphs 26
Visible light 82
Voltage 50, 51, 52

W
Water 42
Water balance 10
Wavelength 79
Waves 78–85
Work done 30

X
Xylem 37

Z
Zygote 33, 35

Acknowledgements

Author Information

Dr Dorothy Warren, is a member of the Royal Society of Chemistry, a former science teacher, and a Secondary Science Consultant with the Quality & Improvement Service for North Yorkshire County Council. Having been involved in the pilot scheme for Twenty First Century Science, she has an excellent understanding of the new specifications, which she is helping to implement in local schools.

Dr Eliot Attridge is a full member of the Institute of Biology, a chartered biologist CBiol, and an experienced Head of Science. He works closely with the exam board as an Assistant Examiner for Twenty First Century Science and was involved in writing the scheme of work for the new GCSE. His school, having been involved in the pilot, is now implementing the new GCSE.

Nathan Goodman has an in-depth understanding of the new science specifications, thanks to his roles as Secondary Science Strategy Consultant for North East Lincolnshire LEA and Regional Coordinator at the Institute of Physics for the physics teacher network. As an Assistant Headteacher, Nathan is involved in improving the teaching and learning of science at his current school.

Every effort has been made to contact the holders of copyright material, but if any have been inadvertently overlooked, the publisher will be pleased to make the necessary arrangements at the first opportunity.

The authors and publisher would like to thank everyone who contributed images to this book:

IFC	©iStockphoto.com / Andrei Tchernov
p.8	©iStockphoto.com / Linda Bucklin
p.26	©iStockphoto.com / Matthew Cole
p.33	©iStockphoto.com / Linda Bucklin
p.43	©iStockphoto.com / Monika Wisniewska
p.61	©iStockphoto.com / Dawn Hudson
p.61	©iStockphoto.com / D. Bird
p.64	©2004 Drs. Gary Glover and Lara Foland, Stanford University, Function BIRN
p.66	©iStockphoto.com / Luis Carlos Torres
p.75	©iStockphoto.com / Paul I. Jsendoorn
p.78	©iStockphoto.com / Peter Finnie
p.78	©iStockphoto.com / Brandon Laufenberg
p.78	©iStockphoto.com / Sittichet Sahunalu
p.83	©iStockphoto.com / Miroslaw Pieprzyk
p.92	©iStockphoto.com / Frank Tschakert

ISBN: 1-978-1-905129-69-0

Published by Lonsdale, a division of Huveaux Plc.

Project Editor: Charlotte Christensen

Editor: Rebecca Skinner

Cover and concept design: Sarah Duxbury

Designer: Ian Wrigley

Artwork: HL Studios

Notes